SERIES

Your expert guide to

MGB &
MGB GT

problems and how to fix them

Roger Williams

VELOCE PUBLISHING
THE PUBLISHER OF FINE AUTOMOTIVE BOOKS

Veloce *SpeedPro* books -

 ISBN 1 903706 76 9

 ISBN 1 874105 76 6

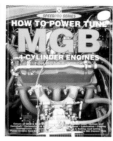 ISBN 1 903706 77 7

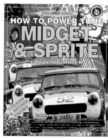 ISBN 1 903706 78 5

 ISBN 1 903706 78 8

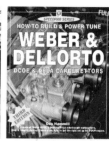 ISBN 1 903706 75 0

 ISBN 1 901295 62 1

 ISBN 1 874105 70 7

 ISBN 1 903706 60 2

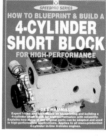 ISBN 1 874105 85 5

 ISBN 1 874105 88 X

 ISBN 1 901295 26 5

 ISBN 1 901295 07 9

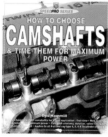 ISBN 1 901295 19 2

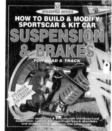 ISBN 1 903706 73 4

 ISBN 1 874105 60 X

 ISBN 1 901295 76 1

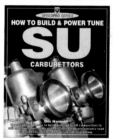 ISBN 1 903706 74 2

 ISBN 1 901295 80 X

 ISBN 1 901295 63 X

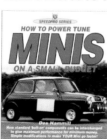 ISBN 1 903706 07 6

 ISBN 1 903706 09 2

 ISBN 1 903706 17 3

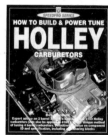 ISBN 1 903706 61 0

 ISBN 1 903706 80 7

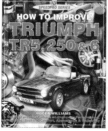 ISBN 1 903706 68 8

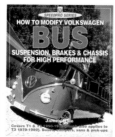 ISBN 1 903706 14 9

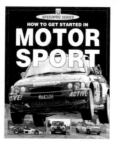 ISBN 1 903706 70 X

- more on the way!

3

Contents

Foreword

The MGB is an icon of British motoring history and examples are found in almost all corners of the world. A wealth of experience and technical knowledge exists within the main MG clubs, and MG specialists abound to service the needs of thousands of owners.

However, the cars are now quite old and more and more age-related problems are cropping up. In addition, a new generation of MGB owner has been brought up on electronic engine management systems, hydraulic tappets

and sealed-for-life components. The MGB may be a very familiar sight, but it comes from a bygone era as far as working parts are concerned.

Roger's book answers the requirement for a single publication that covers the vast majority of faults and problems owners of MGBs are likely to encounter. It's an easy reference that enables the MGB owner to evaluate and rectify problems with his car as and when they occur. It should make the identification of faults easier and

make it easier for verification so that correct parts are sourced to deal with the problem.

In decades past owners were quite familiar with the MGB's standard of engineering, as it was common to all cars produced in the 1950s, 1960s and even the 1970s. This book should re-acquaint owners with that lost general knowledge, and raise it to higher levels.

Roger Parker, MGOC

Introduction, about the author & acknowledgements

INTRODUCTION

Crossing the Alps from Italy into France in my Roadster, a modern, UK registered car followed me into one of the first service stations in southern France. "You're a long way from home," said he, very cheerfully, to which I replied "No further than you." Undeterred he went on to explain that he had an Austin Healey but would never consider bringing it abroad, never mind so far from home; I told him I thought he was missing out on the fun. We then went our separate ways.

This incident set me thinking and subsequently spurred me into action: consequently, this is the third book I've written to help would-be and existing owners enjoy their MGBs to the maximum and to keep costs within bounds. This latest tome is intended to help the average owner identify, verify and resolve the typical problems which are known to be common to the MGB, as well as those which are likely to occur with a car of advanced years. Where practical I've included get-you-home suggestions to be used in the event of a breakdown.

Many of my diagnoses are based on human senses. I've given particularly emphasis to "funny noises" - which I hope will give confidence to every owner, even those with little mechanical knowledge, to explore their car in more depth than they otherwise might and to use the car confidently, perhaps even as a daily driver - and why not?

Some owners may need help recognising the most fundamental problems, even those that are particularly prevalent in the MGB. So, if those of you who are more experienced feel some of the explanations are very basic, please bear with me: I'm trying to cover the wide span of mechanical experience found amongst MGB owners. Naturally, I hope that with this book at their side, many owners will expand their knowledge and experience - although I do urge caution when you're dealing with all matters mechanical. Almost any nut, bolt or component has the capability of causing serious consequences if not installed correctly. Not to put a damper on your enthusiasm but, in particular, elevated cars can fall on you if not properly supported, leaking fuel can catch fire if an inspection light or other potential source of ignition is allowed too close, brakes can fail if you have not correctly reassembled the hydraulics and, if you fail to isolate the battery before some work, an electrical short can destroy your pride and joy. So, take great care, **think about your personal safety at all times and take ALL necessary precautions**. If you get into a situation where you don't really know what to do next, **STOP**. Read the workshop manual (more in a minute) and don't be shy - ask someone with the right expertise for help; you can even 'phone your MG club's area secretary and/or your spares retailer or, perhaps, a local specialist. The MGOC (MG Owner's Club) has a technical helpline (which I used a great deal in researching this book) so, if you're a member and it's during the working day, call it. During the evening, try e-mailing or faxing. If you don't belong to a club, you can still get in touch and ask for a joining pack to be sent to you.

Please bear in mind that this is a reference book, not really intended to be read from cover to cover by any but the most dedicated enthusiast! In fact, if you do so you run the risk of becoming paranoid! While the best workshop manual is of limited use if you don't know what's wrong, this is no substitute for a workshop manual but rather augments such manuals and includes information that I doubt will be found in most. So, if you want to find out how to carry out any particular operation, the workshop manual appropriate to your car is what you need - manuals are available from the MGOC.

About the author

Roger Wiliams was born in Cardiff in 1940, but brought up in Guildford where he attended Guildford Royal Grammar School.

Aircraft were Roger's first love and he joined the de Havilland Aircraft Company in 1957 as a production engineering apprentice. He very quickly added motor cars to his list of prime interests and, during the next six years, not only completed his apprenticeship and studies, and then started on a career in the manufacturing engineering industry as production engineer, but also built two Ford-based 'specials.' Works managerial and directorial posts followed and these responsibilities, together with family commitments, reduced his motoring involvement to driving out of the company car park as quickly as possible!

Roger's business interest changed to company doctoring, which he enjoyed for some ten years, specialising in turning around ailing engineering businesses. In 1986 he started his own consultancy business, which specialised in helping improve client profitability by interim management or consultancy assignments, and renewed his motoring interests.

Roger's spare time is devoted to motor cars and writing. He has owned numerous MGBs, all of which he rebuilt over a period of some seven years, and still has two of his favourites - the V8 powered variants. He has two MGB books in print. More recently he has become involved with the Triumph marque too and has restored a TR6 and, most recently, a Stag.

Roger is a Fellow of the Institution of Mechanical Engineers and a Fellow of the Institution of Production (now Manufacturing) Engineers. He and his wife, who have two married daughters, have recently retired to France.

Acknowledgements

This book would never have been written without the help of a great many people who provided encouragement, information, photographs and diagrams. The list is too extensive to mention everyone but I hope all will accept my grateful thanks, and in particular a small number of absolutely crucial contributors without whom there really would have been no book. The MG Owners Club (MGOC) provided help in many invaluable ways: its Technical Officer, Roger Parker, read the manuscript and made many helpful suggestions, and Richard Ladds was an invaluable source of photographic material: the book has over 400 pictures, of which the MGOC kindly provided more than half. Roger Parker also wrote the Foreword. Matthew Bradshaw (Robinson Motors, Sandwich, Kent), Kurt Schley (USA), Mike Standring (Germany), Philip Chapman (France) and Terry Tearne also provided a deal of invaluable help, information and support. I am particularly grateful to you all.

Roger Williams

Using this book

As stated in the author's introduction, the primary purpose of this book is to guide MGB owners (or would-be owners) in the identification and rectification of the problems that are most usual with MGB sports cars.

There have been many versions of the MGB over the years, ranging from the earliest three-bearing engined cars fitted with three-synchromesh gearboxes, to the later chrome bumper models with five-bearing engines and four-synchro gearboxes, through to the rubber bumper models - of which there were basically two. Then there were the cars with automatic gearboxes (transmissions), which I've largely omitted due to their rarity and being mindful of the very specialised nature of automatic gearbox fault diagnosis and repair. Also, there are the open 'Roadster' variants and their closed 'GT' counterparts.

This book addresses the problems of all of the foregoing 4-cylinder 1800cc models, although some entries will not apply to every variant and you'll need to select those that apply to your particular car. All of the components/service prices are approximately those prevailing in the UK at the time of writing. These prices will be subject to normal market forces and will, of course, tend to rise with economic inflation.

It's possible, of course, that the goods and services mentioned will become unavailable or altered with the passage of time. Dimensions given in the illustrations are in millimetres, unless otherwise stated. Line illustrations are not to scale. Note that references to right side and left side are always from the point of view of standing behind the car looking forward.

Warning! - During work of any type on your car, personal safety must always be your prime consideration. You must not undertake any of the work described in this book unless you have sufficient experience, aptitude and a good enough workshop and equipment to ensure your personal safety at ALL times.

Important! - The author, editors, publisher and retailer cannot accept any responsibility for personal injury, mechanical damage or financial loss, which results from errors in, or omissions from, the information given in this book. If this disclaimer is not acceptable to you, please immediately return the pristine book and receipt to your retailer who will refund the purchase price.

Replacement parts

It's vital that you order replacement parts relevant to your actual car rather than its registered year of manufacture or chassis number. All the cars covered have enjoyed long lives and most will have had secondhand (possibly reconditioned, but still used) parts fitted, not all of which will exactly match the original specification of the car. For example, a late (18V) engine may have been fitted in an early car and, whilst less likely, it's entirely possible that an early engine could have been fitted into a late car. *18*

During *28* years of production the car changed substantially, and it would be easier to list those parts that didn't change than those that did! Clearly the year, model and chassis number of your car are important factors in identifying precisely what spares you need, but be aware that, at an earlier date, availability or expediency may have changed the basis on which you should be ordering spare parts.

Chapter 1
Engine will not start from cold

You may be wondering just where to start in what is a fairly extensive list of causes for why your car has decided not to start. In an effort to help you focus upon the reasons most applicable to your situation I have split this chapter into three basic sub-sections -

• **Engine cranks with, or close to, its normal vigour: 1-1**
• **Engine cranks, but slowly: 1-2**
• **Engine will not crank: 1-3**

I hope these very basic diagnoses will help you get going again as quickly as possible, though you need to appreciate that there may be more than one reason why your car won't start.

ENGINE CRANKS AT OR CLOSE TO ITS NORMAL VIGOUR

Consider whether the car has been reluctant to start first thing in the morning for some time, which may mean you need to check for one set of potential faults; whether it has been progressively harder to start as the colder weather advances; or whether the car has generally been starting easily until this occassion.

Engine has been reluctant to start for some time

1-1-1 This symptom suggests that the general tune of the engine is slowly deteriorating and that, at the very least the ignition, and possibly the carburation, need servicing. However, consider first whether the engine is turning over as briskly as it did. If not, check the fan/drivebelt tension and the battery and its connections. If the battery is at the correct acid level and there's no corrosion on the terminals, check the engine earth (ground) connection to the chassis. The braided "loop" or "earth strap" is required to ensure that the electrical return from the starter motor has an easy path to earth past the rubber engine and gearbox mountings. The strap's position can vary depending upon the year the car was manufactured, but chrome bumper cars were earthed across the left side engine mounting and later cars between the gearbox and body. Rust creeps into the interface between strap and body and creates a barrier. You need to thoroughly clean the contact areas of the strap, lightly cover in petroleum jelly/Vaseline, fit new washers and tighten securely.

If the car has not been serviced recently it would be sensible to carry out a full service. At the very least change the engine oil and filter, the fuel filter (if fitted), sparkplugs and contact breaker points, and clean the inside and outside of the distributor cap and ensure the central contact is in good order.

With the distributor cap off, check that the rotor arm is clean in the centre and at its periphery, and that the cap's four internal contacts are not worn, pitted or damaged. Check that the vacuum

1-1-1 (Picture 1) Unfortunately, but unavoidably, there are numerous connections within the ignition circuits that can result in a no-start situation. A frequently overlooked but important distributor of the high tension spark is the rotor arm, shown here. The centre terminal (arrowed) must make good contact with the carbon brush in the centre of the distributor cap (see picture 3). This is an early Lucas 25D model distributor which was superseded by the introduction of the rubber bumper cars with...

advance diaphragm is working by sucking on the (manifold end) of the thin tube, watching for the distributor's baseplate to move and hold in place for as long as you hold the vacuum (suck), before refitting the distributor cap.

We will look at the following points in much more detail as the book progresses, but the integrity of the high tension (HT) leads (wires) and connections are crucial to good starting so check them thoroughly. Are the HT connections corroded in the coil, the distributor cap or at the sparkplugs? Are the insulators and push terminals at the sparkplugs in good order? If the HT leads haven't been renewed for years, this might be a good time to replace them with a good quality set. Are the low tension electrical wires and terminals in good order and securely clipped to their mating part, particularly both sides of the coil and the distributor? A very light smear of petroleum jelly (Vaseline) on the terminals may assist conductivity.

1-1-1 (Picture 2) ...the Lucas 45D model, seen here. You can test the integrity of the vacuum advance diaphragm by attaching a pipe to the end of the diaphragm(arrowed). For those who don't recognise the vacuum advance diaphragm, Picture 1 is from a very early MGB and would be connected to the inlet manifold by a metal capilliary tube. If you need to replace the diaphragm you can fit a later one which may also necessitate your fitting the later plastic capilliary/vacuum connecting pipe.

Turning now to fuel related matters, check that the air cleaners are reasonably clean. A blocked air filter will increase the richness of the mixture as the engine gasps for air! Is the fuel filter in need of replacement? Only the later cars had a fuel filter fitted as standard, but it's a very good idea to fit one and many an early car now has this benefit. However, if one is fitted it

1-1-1 (Picture 3) The all-important carbon brush (arrowed) passes the coil's stream of high tension sparks through the cap to the rotor arm for directing (or distributing) to the relevant sparkplug.

will need replacing from time to time to ensure an uninterrupted supply of fuel.

Is the choke mechanism operating properly on both carburettors? In cold conditions the richness of the fuel/air mixture should be increased by using the choke. As soon as the engine starts the choke mechanism must move freely enough to allow the choke knob to be pushed in.

Does either of the carburettors leak fuel, even from the overflows, suggesting worn or stuck floats? Is there wear on the ends of either throttle spindle (which will allow air into the carburettor and dilute the fuel/air mixture)? Are **both** carbs getting a regular supply of fuel?

It goes without saying that you need to correct the faults as you find them. However, somewhere along this trail you'll probably find one, possibly several, weaknesses which are just enough to delay starting. If you don't I suggest you ask a garage or mobile tuning shop to check the engine and associated systems with an electronic fault-finder/tuning aid. This will find any low compression cylinders and spot sub-standard components like a faulty coil and HT leads, while simultaneously checking timing and carburettor settings.

Engine suddenly reluctant to start

1-1-2 Turning now to cars that usually start well but are suddenly causing grief, particularly at the onset of colder weather. My first concern would be the condition of the battery. The engine may still crank with only slightly reduced vigour, but if the battery is in less than peak condition there may be little voltage left to adequately

generate the essential sparks. Mind you, all of the checks in 1-1-1 are applicable and it would do no harm to run through them.

Colder weather does two things. It thickens the engine (and gearbox) oil, which makes the engine more difficult to turn over, consequently consuming more power from the battery and reducing the voltage available to the ignition system. A later car with a (built-in) ballast resistor definitely helps starting in these conditions since the ignition system only needs 6 volts to fully operate it. The colder weather also makes the fuel more difficult to vapourise in the carburettor and, if the engine is worn and compression a little on the low side, more difficult to ignite in the cylinders.

There are things we can do to help, starting with a battery check. Are the 6 battery cells topped up to just - but only just - above the level of the plates? Ah! You have a "maintenance-free," sealed-for-life battery, do you? Well, nevertheless, check the fluid level in each cell, because if the battery is of some age and/or has endured some hot weather during the summer, it can still allow the de-ionised water to evaporate. The acid then fails to cover the plates and performance deteriorates.

Are the battery terminals **really** clean, especially the mating faces (which should be lightly smeared with petroleum jelly/Vaseline before reassembly)? Is/are the battery or batteries of some age? Chrome bumper cars had two 6 volt batteries whereas later cars were updated with one 12 volt battery.

Is/are the battery/batteries weeping at the terminal posts, allowing a white deposit to accumulate? If so, this may be an early sign that a new battery is called for. The best test is an 'under load' check that any good battery specialist can carry out for you for a very nominal (usually free) cost. It really is of little value to run a voltmeter across the unloaded terminals as, almost inevitably, all that will tell you is that you're getting around 12 volts from the battery. However, it's the voltage that the battery provides when turning over the engine that really counts and specialists have a pair of tongs which short the terminals to simulate a load while simultaneously measuring the voltage. Of course, if your battery is not providing 12 volts when unloaded, it does need to be replaced!

A thinner grade of engine oil will reduce the drag on the starter, and the grade or viscosity of the oil that you use to refill the sump should depend on the severity of winter in your area. In the UK a 10W40 oil should be adequate for winter use in most 1800cc MGBs, and will help the cold starting in particular. The "10W" part of the specification tells you that the oil, when cold, has a viscosity of 10; which is pretty thin! Incidentally, the second part of the specification ("40") tells you that its additives will thicken that particular oil to a 40 viscosity when hot. You'll have to experiment, but it's possible that dipping the clutch to the floor when cranking the engine in cold weather will reduce drag from the gearbox oil. This gain is always offset to a degree by the drag from the clutch, and, overall, the technique may make little difference. It's worth a try, though.

1-1-3 Failure to start on a not-particularly-cold day has come as a rather unpleasant surprise. Don't despair, as the problem may be quite small, and is, more often than not, the consequence of over-enthusiastic use of the choke. This "floods" the engine with so much fuel that it can't be vapourised and ignited. The condition is usually accompanied by a smell of fuel. This diagnosis is suggested on the assumption that the engine was initially turning over briskly, that you did pull the choke knob out and that you have not flattened the battery. If either or both the first two assumptions are incorrect you'll need to skip this solution.

The first thing to do with a flooded car is to leave it for a while before attempting to start the engine again,

1-1-3 (Picture 2) To check that the choke is fully off look at the levers (arrowed), one on each carburettor, to ensure that the choke stop *is* closed against the body of the carburettor.

dashboard and, if you are in any doubt about whether or not the mechanism is working properly at the carburettors, take a moment to check that the choke is indeed fully off on both carburettors. Return springs can break and/or choke cables can become stiff, and what seems to you like a fully off choke at the dashboard may not be.

Okay, so the choke really **is** off. Push the accelerator (gas) pedal to the floor and hold it there while you crank the engine. There may be a short delay while the cranking clears the remaining excess fuel from the inlet manifold and cylinders, but there should be signs of life fairly quickly thereafter. A little choke and less accelerator/gas pedal may then be required to get the car to fully fire up shortly after that. If this is not the case, consider some of the other faults explored later in this chapter.

1-1-3 (Picture 1) The choke mechanism on the majority of MGBs is manually activated via a knob on the dashboard (fascia). Some readers may not know what happens at the other end of the cable and how they can check that the choke mechanism really is off when it should be. This is a shot of the SU HS4 carburettor (the HIF4 has a slightly different arrangement shown later) where the further up the lever (arrowed) travels, the richer the fuel mixture will be. This lever must be pulled down by a return spring when the choke knob is pushed home/off.

On really cold mornings the ease with which the fuel vaporises can be improved by warming the inlet manifold. Take care not to spill water over other parts of the engine - the electrics in particular - but a kettle full of almost boiling water, poured slowly over the aluminium inlet manifold will warm it, which, in turn, warms the incoming fuel/air mixture and helps the fuel to vaporise/ignite. If, however, you have to resort to such measures before the ambient temperature drops below freezing, there is something else wrong with the engine and/or associated systems.

however much of a hurry you are in. The longer you can leave the car the better but, at the very least, leave it for 5 minutes and preferably 15. This allows the surplus fuel to evaporate. If you have flattened the battery, you could use this enforced delay to find a set of jump leads and organise a donor car. (Note my advice, explained in more detail elsewhere, not to run the donor car's engine when jump starting.)

So, either via the MG's own battery or jump leads/jumper cables, try starting again. Push the choke right in at the

Engine cranks normally and fires, but will not run

1-1-4 This is usually the consequence of damp high tension (HT) ignition components. However, it makes sense to check that there's fuel in the tank and that the engine is not under- or over-choked.

Over-choking/flooding the engine are covered in 1-1-3, whilst under-choking has an obvious remedy!

The solution to this particular problem is usually to dry the high tension ignition components, and the distributor cap in particular. The inside of the cap is even more important than the exterior as, though less likely to be soaked by heavy rain, it is prone to condensation when a hot car is left to stand overnight. Obviously, this occurs more when the car is left outside overnight, but can still happen when the car is garaged. A car

1-1-4 A silicone spray product which has many uses but which is ideal for removing moisture from the *outside* of the high tension ignition components.

which has stood in damp conditions for some time also has a tendency to gather moisture.

If the car still does not start after thoroughly cleaning/drying all high tension ignition components (coil, HT leads (wires), distributor cap, rotor arm and sparkplugs), there could be fuel supply restrictions (described elsewhere). Before exploring fuel supply problems, however, apply a silicone spray (*e.g.* WD40) or similar water dispersant to the outside of the distributor cap and to the high tension leads and coil.

Engine cranks normally but does not fire

1-1-5 Provided that the car has been used until fairly recently, and not subjected to a major repair (*e.g.* a replacement engine fitted) or a long lay-up, chances are there is a fault within the fuel or ignition systems. We'll explore the slightly more exceptional circumstances in a due course, but, given the unfortunate record that the MGB's SU fuel pump has, one of the first checks is to establish whether the fuel pump is working.

Establish that there is sufficient fuel in the tank. Also take a look at the fuel filter if

you have one. Does it look part-filled (they rarely fill completely), and do the contents look reasonably clean? Then look and smell for fuel leaks (sometimes there's a smell of fuel because the car has been over-choked, in which case refer to 1-1-3. **Warning!** - If there is a fuel leak, take care not to do anything that could ignite the fuel. The carburettor bowls are the most vulnerable places for leaks, but it's worthwhile casting an eye right round the whole fuel system. Bear in mind that a stuck valve within one of the carburettor bowls should be ejecting the excess fuel under the car via an overflow pipe - which it is why it's a good idea to keep fuel smells in mind. Do you have a pool of liquid under the engine? If so turn to chapter 11.

Now spray the intake to the air filter(s) with an "easy-start" aerosol and try the starter once again. The choke knob should initially be pushed completely in, with the accelerator about halfway to the floor. There are doubtless other excellent

1-1-5 An example of the highly volatile aerosol sprays that can be squirted into the air intake in order to help the engine start in very cold weather, when the plugs have fouled, or to confirm fuel supply problems.

highly volatile 'easy-start,' sprays that combust far easier than standard fuel, but I am familiar with Bradex, which should start any car that cranks and has a functioning ignition system. If the car starts, runs for a few seconds and then stops, chances are that the fuel system is the basic cause of your problems. If, even with Bradex properly applied, the car fails to start, I would suggest that the ignition system is faulty: see 1-1-7.

1-1-6 Still not starting? If you think there's any chance that the plugs are fouled with oil (*i.e.* the engine tends to burn oil), then you should remove the sparkplugs for inspection.

General wear may have reduced engine compression to the extent that it cannot raise the temperature within the combustion chambers sufficiently to allow the fuel to ignite, fouling the plugs with oil when trying to start.

In order to ensure that the leads are put back on the correct plugs, it's a good idea to dot each lead with 1, 2, 3 or 4 blobs of typewriter correction fluid or nail varnish before pulling the leads from the sparkplugs. Then either heat the whole set of plugs in an oven, or apply a flame from a cigarette lighter to each electrode individually. Obviously, you put the plugs and leads back in the engine once comfortable that the plug electrodes are clean, although I would spend an extra five minutes checking that the gaps are correct before refitting the plugs.

Rather than risk trying to start what is obviously a difficult engine with choke, I would first try without choke but with a dose of the 'easy-start' aerosol spray mentioned in 1-1-5.

1-1-7 Still nothing at all? Well, it could be an ignition fault, but, bearing in mind how often the SU pump causes grief, it's time to check out the fuel pump by listening for its "tick." True, a fuel pump stops rapidly ticking once the carburettor bowls are full, but even after the first rush of rapid ticking (say, once per second for a few seconds), it will usually tick three or four times per minute, even when the engine is not running.

The first step is to switch on the ignition (but don't operate the starter), move towards the back of the car and listen for the pump to tick. If you've not heard it tick even once after, say, half a minute, it's almost certain the problem has been identified, so switch off the ignition for a moment. However, if the pump continues to tick with some rapidity (say, once every five seconds), switch off

1-1-7 This is the fuel pump situated in the front of the boot (trunk) in rubber bumper cars. It's usually covered by a metal 'top hat' which screws into the holes each side of the pump. A chrome bumper car's pump is less accessible at the bottom of the front of the right rear wheelarch.

straight away, particularly if you can also smell fuel, and search again for a fuel leak or a stuck valve in a carburettor!

You may have simply run out of fuel, or parked the car on a slope, slopping what fuel you have in the tank away from the right-side collection point. There could be a perforated fuel pipe, which, on the carburettor side of the pump will be obvious as there will be fuel all over the road!

However, the pipe that feeds the pump from the tank is made of steel and runs round the rear wheelarch where, over the years, it will have come into contact with a lot of water and possibly corroded, allowing air to enter the feed pipe. The result will be a rapidly ticking pump but no, or possibly very little, fuel: see chapter 11 to remedy stuck valves or any other fuel leakage problem.

One of the most frequent problems on an MGB is that a faulty SU fuel pump fails to pump fuel. The verification/short-term remedy is to locate the fuel pump and give it a bash with the ignition turned on, which will usually get it going again, but only for a short time. We'll look into the numerous, more permanent, solutions open to you in chapter 5, but your first priority must be to definitely establish that it is the pump at fault and to get the car going.

The pump will be found (chrome bumpered cars) at the bottom of the right side rear wheelarch, in which case no preparation is required. If, however, you have a rubber bumper car, you'll find the pump pointing backwards through the front vertical panel of the boot. In the case

of a rubber bumper GT you'll need to lift the rear deck and remove a black cover to get at the pump. You'll need to give the pump a bit of a thump, so check that you have something suitable with which to 'unstick' it. A substantial screwdriver and hammer is ideal, but a screwdriver and heavy stone (if you were out in the wilds somewhere) or tommy-bar and a heavy spanner will also do.

The fuel pump of a chrome bumpered car is more likely to be at fault but is luckily easier to get at! Anyway, the initial test and get-you-going step is to switch on the ignition (but don't try to start the car on the starter) and, with the aforementioned tools, tap the metal body of the pump moderately hard. **Caution!** - Take great care not to hit the plastic cap that forms the top inch or so of the pump, because you'll surely break it. This is easier said than done with rubber bumper cars, but you must aim your blow via the screwdriver or tommy-bar at the metal body of the pump. If the pump starts ticking rapidly you've remedied the problem temporarily. Wait for the ticking to slow and then try to start the car: it should start.

1-1-8 It's just possible that the pump will not spring into life when tapped, in which case switch off the ignition and check that the pump is receiving power and is adequately earthed (grounded). A test meter is the ideal way to do this but if you are caught in the supermarket car park or worse, you may need to improvise and use an electric bulb from the car or from your spares box. The festoon bulb fitted into the boot light is probably the nearest and fortunately also the easiest to get at and use for this purpose. Sadly, not every Roadster has a boot light, so you may have to find a bulb from the courtesy lamp or elsewhere in the car.

Prepare for the test by pulling the white wire carefully off the spade terminal on the top of the pump. With the ignition on, offer one end of the bulb to earth (ground) and touch the other end with the white cable's spade terminal. If the bulb lights the electrical feed to the pump is okay. Switch off the ignition. Check that both terminals on the pump and feed wire are not corroded; clean them if they are and reconnect the white wire to the pump. Try the ignition on routine again; if it fails to make the pump run inspect the earth terminal on the side of the fuel pump.

A male spade terminal will be found about halfway down the body of the pump and this should be cleaned, along with the

spade terminal on the end of the black earth wire (which, incidentally runs through the car's electrical harness to the boot lock catch). If the earth terminal or wire look dirty and/or corroded, clean them and try the ignition on test again.

Still no ticking? It's time to put your test bulb to use again. Disconnect both white (power feed) and black (earth) leads from the pump and turn the ignition on. Hold the black wire to one end of the test bulb and the white wire to the other end of the bulb: it doesn't matter which wire goes to which end. The bulb should light and failure to do so means a faulty earth return that must be made good before the pump will run. On a get-you-home basis this can be done by running a length of wire from the earth terminal on the pump to a suitable earthing point. No need to worry about insulating the wire from contact with the body either! However, if the bulb does light this confirms that the fuel pump is at fault: see chapter 5 and order a new pump (but only after you have read 5-7). Oh, and call for a tow truck...

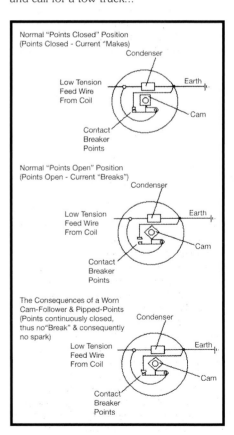

D1 How the distributor's contact breaker points work.

1-1-9 By now, if the engine has not started, you will have narrowed the fault to the ignition system. Consequently, it's time to check out the usual ignition problems and their solutions.

The vast majority of MGBs were made with traditional contact breaker-triggered ignition (see diagram D1, a schematic of the low tension side of the distributor). From 1975 Californian MGBs were fitted with electronic ignition, extended to all US MGBs the next year. Furthermore, since electronic ignition improves the reliability and increases the strength of the spark, your 'B may have been modified retrospectively. Read the following - and all ignition-related comment - with this in mind as some of it is not applicable to electronic ignition systems. If the problem seems to be with the electronics there is little you can do except await a replacement - unless you have had the foresight to carry an old contact breaker distributor base (as recommended in my conclusion) in the car.

One test not previously mentioned that applies to whatever ignition system you have is to remove an ignition HT lead from a sparkplug and fit a spare sparkplug

1-1-9 (Picture 2) The B's distributor could hardly be in a more inconvenient place. Provided you note the position of the vacuum diaphragm (usually pointing upwards) and rotor arm and replace the distributor body and arm in the same place, you should not interfere significantly with the timing if you remove the distributor. However, do *NOT* release the adjustment clamp (arrowed) if trying to retain the timing. The clamp also has two less obvious bolts that allow you to bring the distributor *AND* clamp to the bench, thus safeguarding the timing.

to it. Don't hold the high tension lead or the plug but ensure the body of the plug is earthed on the engine (not the alternator or distributor). Get a helper to crank the engine via the ignition key while you watch for the presence and vigour of a spark across the sparkplug gap. Ideally, you're hoping for a bright regular (perhaps once every two or three seconds) spark.

If that is what you get, switch off and

1-1-9 (Picture 3) The distributor is *MUCH* easier to work on off the car - but note that this one was taken off the engine without its clamp ... a bad idea.

1-1-9 (Picture 4) There are numerous low tension electrical connections and wires, and each must do its respective job if the car is to start and run reliably. This is the side terminal from a Lucas 25D distributor that should take the low tension current from the "CB" or "-" terminal (negative earth/ground cars) of the coil to the contact breaker points. The problem, as you may have spotted, is that the insulation has completely crumbled away, shorting the low tension ignition circuit to earth. This is just one example of the sort of fault that you need to look out for on a 25-35 year old car, particularly one that may not have had the service attention it requires. This problem is enough to prevent the car starting or to stop it during a run.

take a close look at your four regular sparkplugs for they would seem to be the problem. If they have not been changed for years this is definitely the time to fit a new, correctly selected and gapped set. If the sparkplugs were fairly recently fitted, check their appearance in the area of the electrodes. Black, oily and wet suggests a worn engine is contaminating the plugs, with oil preventing them from firing properly. Wet suggests that too much fuel is reaching the cylinders, possibly due to over-choking/flooding in which case it may help to leave the plugs out of the car for 10 to 15 minutes to allow the excess fuel to evaporate. Plugs contaminated with oil are rather more difficult to fully recover, but you could try drying the gaps with a clean rag and then holding them over a cigarette lighter. In both cases of contamination (*i.e.* fuel and oil), it's essential that the old plugs are correctly re-gapped before replacing in the engine.

If the spark you observe at the test plug is non-existent, weak or intermittent, carry out the checks described (if not already done) in 1-1-1. Re-try the test plug to see if there's any improvement.

If all is well with the high tension side of the ignition system, it's time to focus on the low tension side. The MGB's

1-1-9 (Picture 1) The value of a good set of sparkplugs cannot be over-emphasised in situations where the car is proving difficult to start. Conventional plugs should be replaced every 12,000 miles, but it's important that the correct grade of plug is fitted, so only use a plug specifically recommended for the MGB. Furthermore, the gap must be correct, if you want the car to start and run well. If maintenance poses a problem for you you'll be interested in a new development - multi-electrode plugs. The conventional type is shown left, one of the four-electrode alternatives on the right. As yet, I've not proved to my satisfaction that the new plugs will outlast without maintenance conventional plugs by a factor of four, but I'm working on it!

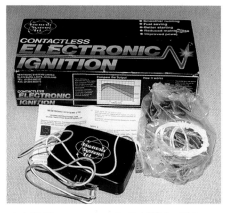

1-1-9 (Picture 5) These are the vital low tension components within a Lucas 25D distributor, including the side terminal wire that has full insulation (arrowed)! Be equally meticulous about the insulation and the interconnection of all the low tension components within the distributor, noting that 80 per cent of car breakdowns are related to electrical faults: I'd guess that in the case of the MGB, half of these relate to components in this photograph!

1-1-9 (Picture 7) The arrow indicates the contact breaker points on a 45D distributor, note the absence of any nuts to retain the points set - much better!

1-1-10 Many readers in the USA will have cars originally fitted with Lucas "Opus" electronic/breakerless ignition. This Lucas system does not have the best reliability reputation, so you may be interested in this aftermarket electronic ignition kit. I've been using these "Newtronic" (once known as "Piranha") kits on my MGBs for a number of years and believe electronic ignition is the way to go, preferably before you have a breakdown. You could always carry something like this as a spare!

distributor is located in a very inaccessible place and it's helpful to note the position of the rotor arm and remove the distributor by undoing the two bolts that fix the clamp to the block (i.e. leave the clamp fixed to the distributor). This will make checking and replacing the components mounted within the distributor much easier.

Dirty, pitted or incorrectly gapped contact breaker points can cause your current starting problems, too, and should be your next check. If the points have been in place for some time, in this

1-1-9 (Picture 6) Shows the two 'top hat'-shaped insulators as they should be placed above and below the contact breaker spring on the 25D distributor: it's *vital* that the contact breaker spring does not touch the post or the securing nut.

situation it really makes sense to replace them, taking care to gap the new points correctly. For the small cost involved, a new condenser could also be fitted as a matter of course at this juncture. Try the test plug again and, if still unsuccessful, a replacement coil starts to become a possibility, although several wiring checks could be required and these are detailed in the next chapter.

1-1-10 If you've been experiencing contact breaker ignition problems, some additional information may be helpful.

Contact breaker points on a conventional MGB ignition system need to be changed every 6000 miles. What you may not know is that these replacements start to deteriorate immediately they are put to use. Not only do the contact points start to burn, but the plastic cam that opens the points starts to wear. You can modernise your car's ignition system with one of several electronic systems which do not require contact breakers.

I desribed these modernised ignition systems in some detail in the Veloce SpeedPro Series publication *How to Improve your MGB, MGC & MGB V8*. This is one upgrade that I believe every MGB should incorporate and, in that context, mention that there are two types of breakerless electronic ignition systems. The magnetic (sometimes called the "Hall-Effect") and the infra-red/optical. Both offer greater reliability and better performance, whilst eliminating the need to change the contact breaker points since there are no moving or touching parts! There's a choice of manufacturer, too, Newtronic and Lumenition. The instructions supplied by both for their systems have been written with home installation in mind, and minimum by way

of tooling is required in order to complete the job.

I make but one suggestion for those planning to do the job themselves: fitting will be easier if the distributor is removed by unscrewing the two screws that secure the baseplate to the block. Naturally, your favourite MGB garage will be able to fit and/or supply and fit a system for you.

1-1-11 This suggestion need only concern those with an anti-run-on valve fitted to the car. If you want to know more about anti-run-on valves, see chapter 6, but the advantage that these valves provide when the engine is switched off could, very occasionally, work against you.

If the electrical feed to the valve fails the valve will remain open while you're trying to start the car; air could be induced into the inlet manifold and the resultant overly lean mixture could prevent the car from starting. Get a helper to switch the ignition on and off while you have an ear close to the valve. With each turn of the ignition switch you should hear the valve close (for ignition on) and open (for ignition off). If you don't hear anything try a test bulb on the electrical feed to the valve, or assume the worst and move into get-you-home mode by removing the vacuum pipe to the manifold at the valve and closing it off with a bolt and tape.

US cars with Stromberg carburettor

1-1-12 Owners of US cars that are proving difficult to start and are fitted with a Stromberg carburettor should check out 15-3-2.

ENGINE CRANKS, BUT SLOWLY

1-2-1 If the engine turns over, but too slowly to start, we need to look beyond the fuel and ignition systems for the cause. Although the engine is not actually cranking, the same underlying problems probably apply when the starter motor is whirring, but not fast enough to 'throw' the gear on the motor's pinion into engagement with the flywheel (so the engine doesn't crank). There again you can turn the key and nothing, but nothing, seems to happen. Most frequently these three faults all result from a "flat" (discharged) battery.

The short term solution is a pushstart or a set of jump leads to get the car going. Connecting a set of jump leads to the rear-mounted battery or batteries of an MGB can be a frustrating task, so if there's battery power (enough to light the ignition/oil pressure warning lights) I'd recommend a push or "bump" start. If you've a little more time you can, of course, recharge the battery using a trickle charger.

Before trying to get the car started, check that the alternator/dynamo drive or fanbelt is in place and adequately tight. If using jump leads from a donor vehicle, ensure the engine is stopped and ignition is off on the donor car, and that the vehicles are not touching in any other way; *e.g.* an open door, which could result in damage to the donor car's alternator.

If bump-starting your manual (stick shift) car, a downhill slope, even a very slight one, is essential. I will describe the technique to use in a moment, but note that the MGB is built solidly, a fact reflected in its weight. It's not possible to push- or bump-start a car with an automatic gearbox (transmission).

Warning! - Whether bumping or pushing, if your car has a steering lock don't forget to put the ignition key in and turn it one position; you would not be the first to have the car roll gently off the road as the result of a locked steering column! Set the choke as you would normally for a cold start: if you're not that familiar with the car, try about halfway out. Turn on the ignition and check that there's an ignition light, even a dim one. Once the car's speed is around walking pace, dip the clutch, put

the car in third gear and let the clutch out fairly smartly. All being well the car will fire, at which point swiftly dip the clutch and, using a combination of choke adjustment and the accelerator (gas pedal), keep the engine running.

There is a third way of getting a car going provided it has a little power in the battery - the tow start, for which is needed a towrope and a willing helper to give your car the necessary momentum. In my view there are more things to concentrate upon and more potentially to go wrong with a tow start, and would therefore recommend you resort to towing only if jump or push-starting are out of the question.

The tow start technique is very similar to bumping or pushing the car to get it going - except that it's the tow car which provides the momentum. Take great care to fix the towrope to a solid part of the tow car. The MGB should have a towing eye fixed to the front bumper iron which is the safe attachment point. Pre-arrange two signals with the tow car: "stop slowly please, it's going," might be a quick headlight flash, whilst headlights on could mean "stop as soon as possible." Keep the towrope as taut as possible when slowing and, whatever else you do, do not run over the towrope! If you are used to brake servo assistance, be aware of the probability that the servo will not offer any assistance when the engine is not running. Nor, for that matter, will it have much time to evacuate the reservoir once the engine starts before you'll need to apply the brakes.

You should establish the reason for the flat battery. Loose fanbelts probably cause the majority of flat batteries, with infrequent use of the car and insufficient output from the generator close behind. Radios with station-retaining memory and car security systems can consume minute quantities of power, which is not a problem if the car is used frequently. However, a couple of weeks' inactivity can be enough to run down even a reasonable battery.

The usual cause of a sudden and unexpected flat battery is a light or lights left on. It could be a door, bootlid (trunk lid), rear hatch or glovebox that's not shut properly, thus leaving the courtesy light on.

As discussed earlier, it's possible that the battery and/or earth (ground) terminals have worked loose, or have become corroded. The same cleaning and petroleum jelly (Vaseline) solutions apply

and, if carried out thoroughly, will prevent a re-occurrence for many years.

A couple of 'dodges' that may help you improve the contact between (particularly worn or corroded) battery posts and the terminals on the live and/or earth (ground) wires may also help. During cleaning you'll almost certainly need to use sand or emery paper on the mating surfaces of the terminals and posts: unfortunately, this reduces their size and decreases their secure clamping capabilities. You can file a sliver of metal (usually brass) off the bottom of the clamping terminal to move it down the (tapered) battery post and/or slip a couple of short lengths of solder between post and clamp/terminal to aid conductivity in the short term. Obviously if you find yourself having to use either of these dodges/bodges then you really need to replace the clamping terminal at the earliest opportunity.

1-2-2 If you're convinced the battery is well charged but the engine will not turn over with any enthusiasm, you need to look for reasons why that power is not reaching the starter motor.

Most car owners will have made sure that the contacts/clamps on the battery posts are clean (and, hopefully, smeared with petroleum jelly/Vaseline), but there are two earth (ground) straps that are easily overlooked. The first one is

1-2-2 (Picture 1) The earth (ground) connection from the battery to the chassis may be short but it offers several opportunities for persistent or one-off starting difficulties due to electrical resistance. The ring terminal becomes corroded, the cable at either end cracks (as arrowed here) or the clamp that attaches to the battery post tires and/or corrodes. This one doesn't look wonderful, but there's no point trying to improve the connections at either end with a useless piece of central cable as we see here. Time for a replacement.

reasonably easily seen and connects the battery to the chassis. Doubtless you will have taken care of the battery post connection but the other end of this quite short earth wire can become so corroded that it stops the electrical circuit from being properly made. The cleanliness of the ring terminal and chassis should be your first check, after which try the starter again.

There's a second earth (ground) strap that many owners will not have seen, although, in this context, it's equally important as it carries the earth return from the starter motor to the battery, too. So if the starter is still reluctant, look for the second earth lead that either loops across the left side engine mounting on early cars, or from gearbox to chassis rail on later 'Bs. In either position they have been known to break, come loose at one end or simply corrode.

There are many instances when it is important to use only genuine replacement parts, but this does not apply to either of the earth straps. Obviously, a genuine MGB replacement is ideal, but if either

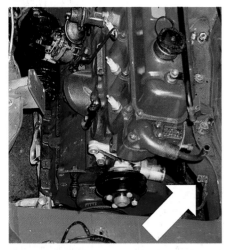

1-2-2 (Picture 2) The earth (ground) strap loops across the rubber engine mounting and can be seen in the bottom right corner of this picture. Note how it is attached to the left engine mounting, even though this engine is partway through being removed from the car. When the engine's in place, the strap *must* be securely attached to the engine and chassis, bridging the flexible mounting which would otherwise act as an electrical insulator. (This is an unusual method of removing engine and gearbox since it can only be used if the front crossmember has been removed: however, no engine hoist is required).

1-2-2 (Picture 3) This is the location of the earth (ground) strap on later cars.

strap is broken or frayed, reducing conductivity, and you're in a hurry, you can quite happily use a replacement from your nearest car parts supplier. Length is relatively unimportant, although it's better to be slightly too long. Always fit something that is thicker than the original for this will improve conductivity and, consequently, current to the starter motor.

If the connections to the starter are all in tip-top condition, but the starter motor still won't crank the engine with any vigour, it's time to start thinking about a replacement starter motor.

If necessary you can start the car by pushing, jump leads or towing: see 1-2-1.

ENGINE WILL NOT CRANK

Starter motor does not activate
1-3-1 Early cars with 3-synchromesh gearboxes. For further identification the models we are discussing here had a separate starter solenoid with heavy-duty cable connections easily accessible in the footwell above the starter. Furthermore, these models do not employ a starter relay.

The electrical system operates the starter on these early cars via a white/red wire straight from the ignition switch to a starter solenoid. It's the actuation of this solenoid that actually brings about the connection between the heavy-duty cable (wire) from the battery and the equally heavy-duty cable that runs down to the starter motor.

The first thing to check out is whether the two heavy-duty connections to the solenoid are clean and tight, and whether the white/red connection to the solenoid is in good order. These starter systems have the distinct advantage that you can actually trigger starter motor operation from under the bonnet, with or without the ignition switched on.

For the moment, let's leave the ignition switched off while we check the solenoid and starter by pressing the solenoid's central, rubber-covered button. The starter should engage and turn the engine (**Warning!** - keep hands and clothing away from moving components); if it does crank the engine you have an immediate get-you-home option in that, with the ignition turned on, you should be able to start the engine by the operating the solenoid manually.

If manual operation of the solenoid doesn't cause the engine to crank, it's the starter motor that's in need of attention.

Should your car have an aftermarket solenoid without a pushbutton you can do the same test by using a battery jump lead to connect the battery terminal to the terminal that connects to the starter motor. Make the final connection in a speedy, positive and forceful manner.

In a situation where the starter does work, you may feel you have also checked out the solenoid. In fact, the manual operation of the solenoid does not prove that the solenoid is functioning properly, and you may still need a replacement.

Test the solenoid by using your test lead and multimeter to check for incoming power through the white/red cable from the ignition switch. Connect one end of the test lead to the terminal on the solenoid, the other to a convenient earth (ground), and turn the ignition key to start. The test bulb should light for as long as you hold the key at start, which will indicate a replacement solenoid is needed. If the test bulb fails to illuminate, look carefully at the white/red cable for chaffing or breakage, then turn attention to the ignition switch.

Disconnect the battery and remove the ignition switch from the dashboard/fascia. Check that the terminals are all properly in place. paying, of course, particular attention to the white/red one. If all is well, connect your test lead/multimeter to the white/red terminal of the ignition switch and earth the other end, reconnect the battery for a moment and try the ignition switch at start. If the test light fails to light it means that a replacement switch is required. If it lights but the starter stays mute, there must be a break in the white/red wire between the switch and the solenoid. Don't forget to disconnect the battery when you refit the ignition switch.

1-3-2 Assuming that the engine's failure to crank is a sudden and unexpected problem and not the consequence of the car standing unused for years (during which time it is possible for the engine, usually the pistons in the bore, to seize/freeze).

Check that the battery is as well charged as you think it is. You can turn the lights on on a standard MGB without having the ignition on, so turn the lighting switch to "head" and take a look at the brightness of both headlamps. Needless to say, they should be bright - almost bright enough to drive by. If this is the case then the battery should be capable of starting the car.

The following will not be relevant to early MGBs with 3-synchro gearboxes. From the introduction of the 4-synchro gearbox with its associated wider gearbox tunnel, the MGB was fitted with an electrical relay to activate the starter. Initially it was a rectangular aluminium can with two mounting ears, later changed to a black tubular case with one ear. If you have either sort it will be found on the right side inner wing (fender) at the rear of the engine compartment, and it should "click" when you turn the ignition switch to start.

At this point the relay is feeding a mid-range current to the starter motor solenoid that is mounted atop the starter motor. In this scenario, we know we have sufficient electrical power in the battery and so, with the ignition key turned to start (as far clockwise as it will go), you should hear a click from this relay as it "makes." No click suggests either a faulty ignition switch - possible but frankly very unlikely - or a faulty relay, the much more likely cause. Check the four wires to the relay and their terminals are clean/sound/pushed right home and try again. If you can get someone to help by turning the key for you, you can actually feel the relay operating if background noise prevents you hearing it. If you cannot hear or feel the relay operate, a replacement may well be necessary to get you started in the normal way. It's worth checking that the black earth lead from the primary circuit of the relay is earthing/grounding properly. Pull the black wire off the relay and clean its connection before replacing it.

If the relay still fails to 'click' you can, of course, run various tests with a multimeter or your test lead/light bulb (described in chapter 19) to check that power is getting through from the ignition switch when the key is fully turned to start. It is also possible for the relay to click but still not transmit power to the secondary circuit, though this is relatively infrequent.

Once fairly sure that the starter relay is at fault, your get-you-home solution is to turn the ignition key to on (but not to start) and apply the normal amount of choke for a cold start (if applicable). From outside the car note which terminal is involved and remove the secondary circuit's brown wire from its (C1) terminal on the relay. Do so with care, it's live and will short if you allow it to touch anything. Remove the white/brown wire from its (C2) terminal on the relay (also making a mental note of which terminal it came from), and hold the two wires firmly together. There may be a few minor sparks for a split second but you are bypassing the relay and consequently the starter motor should start turning the engine and, hopefully, start the car, at which point separate the two wires and replace them on their respective terminals on the relay. (**Warning!** - keep hands and clothing away from moving components). This operation has not only got you going, but also confirmed it is the relay at fault and that a replacement is required.

Failure to turn the engine means you have either selected the wires incorrectly or that it is the starter motor, its solenoid or wiring which are at fault, in which case, separate the wires with some speed and consider 1-3-3.

1-3-3 It's possible that the starter motor or its solenoid have failed, but just before you get stuck into removing the starter, it's worth checking whether the various cables to the starter are connected properly.

Jack up the car and safely secure it so that you can get to the rear of the engine in reasonable comfort. The most obvious wire you will see is a thick cable running from the rear of the car (the battery, in fact) to a smaller cylinder coupled to the starter motor. **Warning!** - This is the main feed cable from the battery which is **always** live, unless disconnected from the battery! Does it look in good order and, more particularly, is it securely bolted to the starter solenoid? This terminal will also carry several brown cables in varying thicknesses which are used to distribute power to other systems. **Warning!** - If you have to use a spanner on this terminal nut, first disconnect the other end of the cable from the battery. You'll also note a (much slimmer) red/white wire coming down from the starter solenoid. This should be securely connected via a different spade terminal on the solenoid.

Depending upon the age of your MGB, you could also find a white/light-green wire connected to the solenoid that

provides power to the coil when cranking mid-seventies and later cars. This is unlikely to be causing your current problems, but it's worth noting its position (even making a sketch of the wiring connections) because, if the car will not start after this check, a service exchange starter motor seems inevitable.

Get-you-home methods are the bump, push or tow starts described in 1-2-1.

Starter motor whirs, but engine doesn't crank

1-3-4 If the starter motor is spinning with its usual vigour but not cranking the engine, you can be fairly sure that the problem lies either with the starter or the flywheel's ring gear.

Establish that the two bolts which secure the starter motor to the gearbox are tight - very tight. You might get a clue that something is amiss by looking down

1-3-3 As good as this flywheel ring gear (with which the starter motor pinion gear engages) looks, take my word for it that it only takes wear on 5 or 6 consecutive teeth for the starter motor to become quite ineffective. In this circumstance you can engage 4th gear and push the car forward a few yards in order to present the starter motor pinion with a different position on the flywheel. The starter will then be able to do its job.

1-3-4 (Picture 1) An "inertia"-type starter motor similar to those fitted to the early MGBs. Note the absence of a close-coupled solenoid.

on the starter motor to see if it moves, whilst a helper operates it. It should not move at all relative to the engine and/or bellhousing. If you do detect movement, disconnect the battery and tighten the motor's retaining bolts (one at the top of the motor, one beneath). Even if there's no obvious movement it's still worth checking the tightness of both bolts.

If the engine repeatedly fails to crank, whether hot or cold, I'd suspect that the ring gear around the periphery of the flywheel has become severly worn or has lost some teeth. As strange as it sounds, a four-cylinder engine usually comes to rest with the flywheel in the same position relative to the starter motor which means the starter always engages with the same teeth on the ring gear.

You can vary the flywheel's at-rest position by switching off the ignition and, as the engine is slowing, stalling it via the gearbox/clutch, thus presenting the starter

motor with a relatively unused sector of the flywheel's ring gear. If you try this a few times and find that the engine starts virtually every time an artificial stopping place has been forced on it, you can be pretty sure you are facing an engine-out repair and had better turn to the chapter on replacing the clutch to see what's involved. You are, incidentally, well advised to replace the clutch and flywheel in the interests of longevity.

If the reliability of starting does not improve after artificially positioning the flywheel a few times, you could be in for a pleasant surprise - or at least the easier repair outlined in 1-3-5.

Get-you-home methods are the bump, push or tow starts explored in 1-2-1.

1-3-5 There are two different types of starter motor on the MGB. The "inertia"

1-3-4 (Picture 2) The later "pre-engaged" starter motor looks quite different by virtue of the close-coupled solenoid that pushes the pinion gear forward to engage the flywheel a split second before the motor starts to turn.

motors were fitted only to 3-synchro gearboxed cars with the prefix "GHN3" or "GHD3" to their chassis number. These motors rely on the spinning of the motor to throw a sleeve forward to engage the pinion gear in the flywheel and then turn the flywheel.

If the starter motor spins rapidly, but quite ineffectively since it is unable to engage the flywheel, it could have a sticking pinion. A broken spring is one cause but a bent pinion and even dirt on the Bendix (a very coarse screw thread) can give the same effect.

Simultaneous with the introduction of the 4-synchro gearbox, the cars enjoyed the benefit of the "pre-engaged" starter motor. These units have a solenoid mounted atop the starter motor, and work by the solenoid pushing the pinion forward to engage the flywheel before, a split second later, spinning the motor and thus the flywheel.

These units are also susceptible to faulty, broken or sticking pre-engagement mechanisms, in which case the pinion is not pushed forward prior to the motor operating.

Whichever type of starter your MGB has, remove the it and take a look at the pinion assembly. While you have the starter motor off the car, particularly if you cannot see much wrong with the starter motor itself, use a mirror and flashlight to look at the flywheel ring gear inside the bellhousing. Assuming all looks well with the ring gear - and particularly if the starter is of some age - an exchange unit may be the best step. But you don't want to buy and fit a new starter only to find that it was the ring gear on the flywheel that was at fault.

Get-you-home methods are the bump, push or tow starts described in 1-2-1.

Chapter 2
Engine ran but stopped and will not restart

If you've broken down, or the car is playing up at a particularly inconvenient time, you may find it apt that breakdown services in the UK call these occasions COWS (Cut Out Won't Starts)!

Assuming there's no obvious reason why the engine stopped, the likely cause is an ignition or fuel problem. If there are other symptoms - such as mechanical noises or a jolt - turn to the relevant chapter. It's helpful to remember as much as you can about how the engine stopped, as that could give a clue to the fault. A sudden but complete cut-off without warning probably signifies that an ignition component has failed: look through suggestions prefixed 2-1. A spluttering, slow stop-start-stop pattern, ending in a complete stop suggests fuel starvation: read section 2-2.

Section 2-3 outlines faults related to overheating and low oil pressure, problems that are covered in more depth in later chapters.

Engine stops suddenly

2-1-1 Water will stop an engine: if you've driven through a large puddle or ford and the engine dies a few seconds later you've probably put two and two together. If your car's engine has been soaked the only solution is to dry it out - particularly the high tension components. However, if it's pouring with rain you may actually be better off just sitting still for five minutes as

2-1-2 The majority of high tension (HT) ignition components can be seen here, though the coil is not in view (mounted on the inner wing/fender just below the oil filter). If HT components have got wet, even damp, the engine is unlikely to run or will misfire. The five thick leads from coil to distributor and distributor to sparkplugs should be dried and sprayed with a water-dispersing agent such as WD40.

residual engine heat may be enough to dry the components without having to open the bonnet.

2-1-2 If water is not obviously the cause of the breakdown visually check the ignition-related electrics; if it's raining,

shield the engine as much as you can. You are looking firstly for water on the high tension parts of the ignition system (coil, HT leads, distributor cap and sparkplug connectors); thereafter for a loose or disconnected low tension wire (the thin one) between the coil and distributor. Flex one or two terminals on the ends of the wire to see that vibration has not fractured the copper current-carrying part of the wire, leaving just the plastic outer in place. Check carefully that the plastic outer/insulation has not cracked allowing the copper core to short onto an adjacent metal part. The wire that goes into the side of the distributor is particularly vulnerable as it gets very hot and the insulation becomes very brittle indeed. Check that all the low tension spade connectors are securely fixed to their terminals.

Turn your attention to the high tension wires (the fat ones) that run from the coil to distributor cap and then to the sparkplugs. If the engine died completely the most likely high tension wire to have caused this is the single one running from the coil to the centre of the distributor. Are the wire connectors pushed well into the terminal in the centre of the coil and the centre of the distributor? Vibration can loosen a poorly made HT wire connection. **2-1-3** Check whether the ignition warning light is on when the ignition is on. If it fails to light, try switching the lights on; if they

2-1-3 An ignition or a fuel problem? Hold a sparkplug against the engine to check that it sparks regularly and brightly when the engine is cranked: if so a fuel supply problem is indicated. Note that although these pliers are well insulated, some form of secondary insulation - particularly if the car has electronic ignition - is advisable.

don't work either it could be a battery/electrical supply fault: see chapter 17.

Assuming you have ignition and driving lights, switch off both and try the starter to check that the engine is turns over normally (if not, see chapter 6). Open the bonnet and pull off a plug lead from its sparkplug; connect a spare sparkplug (always a good idea to carry at least one spare). If you don't have a spare plug, remove a plug from the engine and then reconnect it to the plug lead. Lay the loose plug on a convenient piece of engine metal (to allow it to earth/ground) and have a helper operate the starter. Your job is to observe the spark across the plug gap: a strong, bright, regular spark suggests the problem is one of fuel starvation rather than an ignition problem, so jump straight to the suggestions prefaced 2-2 or see

2-1-4 (Picture 1) The condenser on the Lucas 45D distributor of a later car. If it quits, the engine stops.

chapter 5 for a more comprehensive investigation of fuel supply problems. No spark at all or a very weak one confirms an ignition fault: check out suggestion 2-1-4 and then turn to chapter 3 for additional information if necessary.

2-1-4 If you've not yet found the problem, it's quite likely that the condenser has short-circuited.

The condenser is a small, cylindrical, usually silver but sometimes gold-coloured, component that sits on the baseplate of the distributor. You won't see it until you remove the distributor cap.

If the condenser is faulty it means it has started "shorting;" carrying the low tension power straight to earth (ground), so denying the points the opportunity to switch the low tension current on and off. This, in turn, prevents the coil generating HT current which stops the engine - dead. The bad news is that a replacement condenser is usually the only solution to get you mobile again (although I've heard that the radio-suppressing condenser attached to some coils has got stranded cars home). Hopefully, you'll have the correct spare in your spares kit ... The good news is that many garages and most automotive parts suppliers will stock them, and they're a genuinely low cost item.

2-1-4 (Picture 2) Since the condenser is crucially important to the proper operation of a contact breaker ignition system, there's no alternative to fitting a replacement as your get-you-home solution. This is the 25D distributor from a chrome bumper car. Whilst the condenser is otherwise the same as that for a later car, the wire connector is different, so they're not interchangeable.

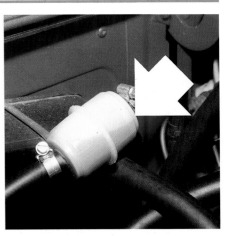

2-2-1 What does a fuel filter look like? Something like this, although this one is opaque, and many are made from clear plastic that enables you to see the fuel and any dirt rather better. You can see the fuel level (arrowed), but the filter never completely fills so don't worry if the level is as low as this, so long as the exit pipe feeding fuel to the carburettors is covered all's OK.

Engine splutters, runs badly before stopping

2-2-1 If the engine spluttered to a stop, or ran badly for a short while before expiring, it suggests a fuel supply problem.

Start by checking that there is fuel in the tank and then by listening for the fuel pump to tick with the ignition switched on but without the engine cranking. No tick, even after half a minute, almost certainly suggests an inoperable fuel pump.

There's a double-check and get-you-home trick all rolled into one: leave the ignition switched on and give the body (**Caution! - not** the plastic end cover) of the pump a tap. If the pump starts to tick vigorously you've found your problem and will be able to get home. You may have to give the pump another bash on the way, or you may get all the way home without further stoppages. You'll almost certainly assist this objective by driving for maximum fuel efficiency, as this will require less work from the pump. It may also help to let the pump cool down before trying to restart it a second time.

I once had to be towed from some road works with a completely inoperable fuel pump after a fairly long blast on a motorway. I parked the car and did my day's business and, upon my return, to my delight, the car started and ran 100 miles home with no further bother, but

2-2-2 Fuel pump woes are explored in detail in another chapter, but if your car has stopped because of a faulty fuel pump, it may help to know what, probably, is wrong with the darn thing. Within this deliberately sectioned pump take a look at the two sets of points, which are almost certainly what has brought your 'B to a standstill. They spark each time they open and consequently burn and pit to the point that they can no longer carry the requisite current to power the pump, whereupon the pump stops. This picture shows the blade points (on the right) removed for examination from their normal contact with the rocker points highlighted by the left arrow.

then I did stick to 50mph! If the fuel pump refuses to co-operate, try the roadside checks suggested in 1-1-6 or turn to chapter 5 for a much more comprehensive list of fuel pump remedies.
2-2-2 The fuel pump can be working and ticking vigorously, but if your earlier ignition review indicated a fuel problem you need to consider other reasons. Many are explored in chapter 3, but one quick check is worthwhile for those with a fuel filter.

Uncouple the fuel line (**Warning!** - be particularly careful not to spill fuel if the engine is still warm) from the engine side of the fuel filter and switch on the ignition. Have a cup, old bottle or similar receptacle to catch the fuel you hope will gush forth. If there's little or no fuel, switch off and remove the filter completely, replace the catch bottle and try again. If fuel now flows fit a replacement fuel filter to get you home, or use a piece of pipe to bridge the gap now left by the filter. Almost any replacement filter will do, provided you fit it so that the flow arrow points toward the carburettors and the flexible fuel lines clamp securely to the replacement filter.

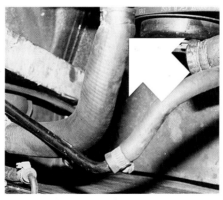

2-3-1 The radiator and relatively long water hoses on a rubber bumper 'B. Note the slight bulging (arrowed) due to age, the distance from rad to engine and the absence of a metal-bladed fan on the front of the water pump pulley. More than one MGB has crawled slowly home with a split hose wrapped with duct-tape - but regularly noting the condition of the hose should give you enough time to replace a cracking one.

Overheating, steam from engine/ hot smells

2-3-1 If the engine stoppage is accompanied by a hot/oily smell, sometimes quite a strong one, and/or steam or smoke, it's a classic case of overheating. If the car seemed reluctant to go - as if the handbrake was on - this would have been a warning of what was to come. If you are seeing, hearing or smelling signs of distress, stop as soon as you safely can, as the engine could be about to seize through overheating.

Warning! - an engine that has overheated to this extent gets very hot indeed, and should be treated with the greatest of respect in the interests of your safety. **Never** remove the water filler cap until the engine has completely cooled. I tried to slowly remove the pressure cap of an overheated engine once, and was very fortunate not to be severely scalded by the jet of water that shot out and hit the canopy of the fuel (gas) station I'd stopped at! You have been warned...

Check under the car for signs of a water leak. Better yet, at the first hint of overheating, check the temperature gauge - but remember that if the engine is short of water, once the level falls below the temperature sensor in the engine, the gauge may not actually show the full extent of the problem. Don't assume that

all is well just because the temperature gauge shows normal.

Check whether the ignition light is on with the engine running. If it is, there's every chance that the fanbelt (drivebelt) has broken. This means that the generator is not working which is why the ignition light is on. More importantly, the water pump will not be working either, hence the overheating.

If the fan/drivebelt is absolutely fine, and the ignition light is not on, the engine could still be overheating due to high ambient temperatures, a loss of water, low oil levels or a combination of these factors. The low water or oil level may not be your fault; a stone may have gone through the radiator, or an oil hose to the cooler may have chaffed through.

It always pays to carry a spare fan/ drivebelt, spare major water hoses and a small tin of radiator sealant. Hopefully, you'll have followed this advice and having caught the overheating before serious damage occurred, will now be able to correct the problems once things have cooled down.

If the engine has seized, all is not necessarily lost. You have very little to lose, so give the car an hour to cool down and then try the starter to see if the engine will crank. If it does, be sure to correct the causes of overheating with new hoses, radiator seal, or a new fan/drivebelt as appropriate, and to replenish all fluid levels before trying to run the engine for any length of time.

See chapter 13 for lots more information.

Engine failure preceeded by loud mechanical noises and/or low oil pressure

2-3-2 The likelihood of other engine or component failures stopping the car with little warning are remote. However, if you've been ignoring a low oil pressure warning gauge/light, or unusual mechanical noises, the possibility of big-end seizure or camshaft failure should be considered.

You'll know when these major failures occur as, not only will the car come to a very sudden stop, there will also be unmistakably painful (and expensive) mechanical noises.

Failures of this nature will necessitate an engine rebuild or even a new engine if a connecting rod has made a bid for freedom through the side of the cylinder block.

The only get-you-home method is a tow truck.

Chapter 3
Engine runs badly

If the engine has been performing reasonably well but suddenly, or possibly over the course of, say, 50 miles, loses performance and runs badly, but never quite cuts out, chances are the fault is ignition-related. Less likely are fuel supply-related problems, which are discussed in section 3-2.

3-1-1 Not only do the sparkplug HT leads need to be in tip-top condition for the car to run smoothly, but the connectors at each end need to be clean and secure. Here, we see number two plug lead with its insulated cover peeled back in order to ensure that the connection between the sparkplug bobbin (which needs to be screwed down tightly) and the HT lead connector is good. Note, incidentally, the correct route for the temperature gauge capillary tube.

Ignition system problems

3-1-1 Initially check that all four sparkplug HT lead (the fat wires) connectors are securely pushed onto their respective sparkplugs. This may sound obvious but it has happened to me and, in my case, I had checked the engine that afternoon before setting out on a 50 mile evening trip. I was completely taken by surprise after 49 miles to hear the engine go onto three cylinders. I popped the bonnet and found one HT lead connector loosely sitting atop its sparkplug - but only just. The solution to what seems like a catastrophe can be as simple as replacing a plug lead that, in this case, I must have carelessly knocked when checking fluid levels that afternoon.

3-1-2 Water, or even dampness, can be the death of an ignition system. If your system is good enough and dry enough to get your car started, it is rare that dampness will subsequently stop it, but it could cause "tracking" within the high tension electrics, particularly at the distributor cap. Once running, heat from the engine usually dries out any residual overnight dampness caused by condensation and/or fog and things improve. However **very** heavy rain or the splash from a deep puddle/ford can get up to the distributor and high tension leads, which are mounted fairly low down by modern standards on the right-side of the engine. The water/dampness can even

reach the coil. In these circumstances, provided the engine is warm, you're usually better not opening the bonnet, particularly if it is still raining. Leave the bonnet down in order to keep as much of the heat as possible within the engine compartment until things have dried out, when things should improve. If it is heavy

3-1-2 The coil is mounted on the right inner wing (fender) and, on most MGBs, points downward - although it's far easier if the top is uppermost when it comes to checking the terminals and fitting the HT lead. The temporary test light and wire (arrowed) will be removed before the car goes back on the road.

rain that you suspect, bear in mind that it needs to be pretty heavy to splash-up to the level of the electrics. Furthermore the event of water splashing up on to the ignition electrics it is more likely that the engine will missfire for a few seconds and then die completely. So if the missfire continues for a few minutes getting neither better nor worse, it probably is not caused by dampness/water, so read on.

3-1-3 If you're experiencing bad (and possibly worsening) engine performance, but the engine does at least keep going, the probability is that the condenser in the distributor is going "open-circuit." In other words it is as if there were no condenser, and the consequence of this type of fault is that the points burn very quickly and that the ignition circuits don't function as well as they were designed to - hence the poor engine performance. Typical

3-1-3 Changing the condenser and/or points beside the road is no fun, particularly if it's an operation you're unfamiliar with. Many would advocate removing the whole distributor, but I think the job is easier if you've followed my suggested list of spares and have a spare baseplate for the distributor, complete with a serviceable set of points and condenser; they don't have to be new. This baseplate is from the Lucas 25D distributor of an early/chrome bumper car; the 2BA retaining nut (arrowed) gives this fact away. Later cars had a Lucas 45D series distributor with a sliding spring mounting superseding the 2BA nut.

consequences are very slow acceleration, missfiring and a very curtailed rev-range. If you're experiencing any such symptoms, by far the best solution is to replace the condenser and contract breaker points as

a matter of course for the small sum they cost. The condenser is an item that takes up very little space, so always carry a spare. Unfortunately, there is no easy test to establish whether a condenser is faulty - hence my suggestion that you substitute a new one in any circumstances where the ignition system is giving cause for concern. Condensers can start off the day perfectly serviceable, but, usually when hot, start to become progressively less and less effective.

Lift the cap off the distributor and take a careful note of where things go around the distributor's points/condenser. I know you're broken down and are in a hurry to get going again, but if you're not familiar with ignition systems, it really is worth taking a couple of minutes to sketch the routing of the various wires and the order of assembly of the low tension wires and insulator. Note, for example, that you do **not** need to disturb the points unless they are burnt and need changing. Unscrew the crosshead screw that secures the condenser and the top 2BA nut on top of the pillar carefully (it is **very** easy to drop either, or both) and ease up the washer and then the usually white(ish) top hat-shaped insulator. Put both on one side out of harm's way and concentrate on the two ring terminals now left on the pillar. You may find that the condenser's terminal is on the top in which case it is a simple case of just removing the whole condenser and replacing it. If you happen to find the input wire's ring termination on top, lift that gently away for a second, remove the condenser and replace the terminals loosely on the pillar in any convenient order. The next step is one of the key details that must be done correctly. Put the top hat insulator back on the pillar such that it goes **through** the two wiring eyes and the pivot arm of the points and that these three components are insulated from the other low tension ignition components in the area. You should have the flat (wide) top of the insulator looking up at you, ready to accept the washer and 2BA nut - which you'll note can be screwed down but will be insulated from the two ring terminals and the point's pivot. Secure the condenser, put the cap back on the distributor and try the engine.

3-1-4 Even a correctly serviced car can experience problems. A degenerating condenser can burn or "pip" the points and cheap non-original equipment points sometimes have cam-followers made from soft material that wears prematurely. Both

3-1-4 (Picture 1) This picture shows the condenser (screwdriver points to it), the distributor cam (arrowed) and gives another general view of the Lucas 45D distributor...

reduce the ability of the points to open and close properly. Further, it's possible that the points securing screw was not quite pinched-up tight or even that the car was not properly serviced! Whatever the underlying reason, unless you have electronic ignition (fitted as standard to US MGBs from 1976 and retro-fitted to numerous UK cars of all years) the contact breaker points need to open and close as the distributor's cam rotates. If your car's points have virtually closed up, they will not be making and breaking the primary (low tension) ignition circuit as intended.

3-1-4 (Picture 2) ...whilst here we highlight the cam follower or "heel", which can prematurely wear if you fit a cheap contact breaker set and/or fail to lubricate the cam. Note the slot for points adjustment on the 45D.

To check, remove the cap from the top of the distributor. Be careful not to disturb any of the high tension lead connectors but push the cap/leads back out of the way. The cap cannot and need not move far as the sparkplug leads will prevent it, but you want to be able to see into the

3-1-4 (Picture 3) Contact breaker points being set with a feeler gauge.

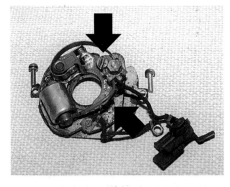

3-1-4 (Picture 4) Although the final picture in this set is very similar to an earlier one, it does illustrate how to adjust the CB points on the early 25D distributor. The actual points are on the opposite side of the baseplate, but if you *slightly* slacken the screw (arrowed) and put a medium to wide-bladed screwdriver in the slot indicated, you'll be able to adjust the points gap.

distributor. Remove the rotor arm by pulling it upward. Get someone to crank the engine while you observe that the points are definitely opening and closing. You may need to use a flashlight for the movement is really quite small. If it appears that the points are not opening and closing, you'll need to adjust them so that they are about 0.015in open when the heel of the cam follower is resting on one of the 'corners' of the cam. To get the cam into the correct position for checking the gap, pop the car into fourth gear and push it forward until any of the four cam lobes open the points to their maximum. For a roadside emergency the 0.015in gap does not have to be precise and something like the thickness of the cover of this book should put you in the ballpark.

3-1-5 With the cap off the distributor

check for another common ignition problem - a faulty rotor arm. They carry a fair belt of high tension current thousands of time a minute and need to be in good shape. Frankly, it is always prudent to carry a spare new rotor arm. If you have not got one available take a close look at the one you took off the car. You're looking for cracks, mechanical damage, corrosion or, most likely, tiny black "tracking" lines where the electrical charge has shorted to the distributor spindle. The cleanliness of whole arm is important, but the top centre of the arm where the black carbon contact in the cap touches and the brass end of the arm are the areas that need to be clean and undamaged. You can, of course, clean these areas with a fine piece of emery and replace the original arm, but frankly for what the arms cost you're better off fitting a new one if you're in a position to do so. The rotor arm has a small internal pip that fits into a slot in the distributor spindle, so you just need to make absolutely sure you have your arm orientated correctly and that you push it **right** home when replacing it. If rotor arm failure occurs while you're on the road, I promise you that you'll forever after carry a spare rotor arm with you!

3-1-6 I've talked of "tracking" on the rotor arm allowing the high tension spark to take a different route to that required

3-1-5 Two slightly different rotor arms, but both for use on MGBs. The internally moulded key is arrowed on what is, in fact, a new arm. The example on the right has had some use, judging from the dull appearance of the brass contact atop the arm. Can you see the (now discoloured) contact point for the cap's central carbon brush? It does not inspire confidence for good, high tension current distribution.

for a smooth and well-performing engine.

A dirty distributor cap can, and will, also cause tracking of the high tension current and is thus equally capable of causing a misfire as high tension current is mis-directed away from the sparkplugs. Look inside and outside the cap for thin black tracking lines and, if you have no alternative, clean the cap both inside and out. However the best solution is to replace it with a new cap - and certainly

3-1-6 The individual 'contacts' within the distributor cap (indicated here by screwdriver) are required to 'collect' the current from the end of the rotor arm as it whirls by. These contacts can only function effectively if clean, unpitted and undamaged, and provided that the spark is not enticed elsewhere by dampness or dirt within the cap, both of which cause tracking. You can see the central carbon contact very clearly.

for cars that are used to travel long distances away from home it is a very good idea to add a replacement distributor cap to your small but effective roadside repair kit.

3-1-7 A carbon "brush" sits in the top-centre of the inside of the distributor cap and this can also be the cause of poor performance if it is not making good contact with the rotor arm. It carries ALL the high tension current from the coil to the rotor arm from where it is directed to the correct individual sparkplug. Obviously, if you have a spare cap with you, then substituting it for the original cap takes this suggestion out of play. However if you're having to make do with a

3-1-7 A reminder of the importance of the central carbon brush making the best possible contact with the rotor arm.

roadside clean up of the original cap then it is worth **gently** pulling the brush a few millimetres from the cap to stretch the spring beneath the brush. The idea behind this suggestion is to ensure that the brush is indeed making good contact with the rotor arm. We covered the importance of cleaning the rotor arm earlier, but you'll appreciate the harder you make the path of the high tension current the less spark you get at the all important sparkplug gap. Hence the contact quality and cleanliness of carbon brush and rotor arm are very important to a good ignition system.

Note that if the carbon brush has disappeared completely, you can ball up some tinfoil to replace the brush: this will usually take you a few miles.

3-1-8 Owners of US cars (and others with similar electronic ignition systems)

3-2-1 (Picture 1) Fuel filters are often added as an accessory and can be sourced from a number of locations. This is a typical addition with the fuel flowing left to right through the filter and on to the carburettors.

need to be aware of the fact that the car can tickover/idle normally, but be hardly driveable. This is likely to be the consequence of one (of three) of the thin wires coupling the "Hall-effect" pick-up to the amplifier having broken after years of flexing. Most of the components for the earlier "Opus" distributors are now "NLA" (no longer available) and you'll need a retro-fit electronic/breakerless ignition system to return the car to normal vitality. Some parts, including the remote amplifier module, are available for the "Constant Energy" distributor fitted in 1980, but I think you, too, may be better served by fitting a modern aftermarket system - provided originality constraints permit.

Fuel supply problems

There are some fuel supply-related problems, usually starvation, that you need to consider if the ignition system checks so far described have not improved engine performance.

3-2-1 Are the fuel and air filters reasonably clean? If the car has just been serviced they should both be okay, but in this event I would take a moment to reassure myself that the fuel filter has been installed the correct way round. You'll see an arrow on the outside that should be pointing in the direction of the fuel pipe that leads to the carburettors. If it has been

3-2-1 (Picture 2) If the air filters look like this and the car will not run well, remove both and replace them with new ones as soon as possible. Furthermore, if they are contaminated with oil, also clean out the crankcase breather system before using the car with its new air filters.

3-2-2 There are three screws (arrowed) to remove to get to the float bowls. You may find the bowls part-full of dirt, or you may need to check, adjust or replace the needle valves that sit in the top cover of each fuel bowl. It's a very good idea to fit a new gasket each time you remove the cover but, at the very least, if carrying out a roadside get-you-going exercise, remove the cover with care so as not to damage the existing gasket.

installed the wrong way round, the filter could have collapsed and be causing fuel starvation. If the fuel filter has not been replaced in living memory then you may find removing them as a get-you-home expedient will transform the car's performance. Naturally, they should be replaced with new units at the very earliest opportunity.

Air filters can collapse internally due to contamination by oil from the crankcase breather. If this happens, remove the air filters as a way to get you home and replace them as soon as possible. You can also reduce the effectiveness of the crankcase breather by inserting a restrictor in the breather pipe to the crankcase. A 10mm diameter rod with, say, a 5mm hole through the centre might be a good starting point, adjust the hole size to find the right balance between too much and too little crankcase breathing.

3-2-2 Many MGBs left the factory without a fuel filter - in fact none of the early cars fitted with HS4 SU carburettors were fitted with such a device. If your car falls into this category, then you'd be wise to fit a fuel filter as soon as possible, particularly if the fuel tank is of some age in which case it will doubtless be providing a steady stream of rust particles to the carbs.

If there is a fuel filter fitted the following suggestion is unlikely to be of assistance and, consequently, later HIF SU carburettors are much less likely to require the attention that follows. By now those

3-2-3 Two of the three screws that have to be removed in order to lift the cover (dashpot) of an SU carb to reveal the piston inside. Take care not to damage - particularly drop - either the piston or cover.

without the protection of a filter will be ahead of me because, yes, the carburettor float bowls could well be half full of dirt and rust particles. Usually the front float chamber is marginally worse, so pull the overflow pipe off the top of the front carburettor, remove the three float-bowl retaining screws, lift the cover complete with incoming fuel line and float and surprise yourself by discovering a huge amount of debris. You need to clean the rubbish out, getting right into the lowest half of the bowl where the fuel is collected for the jets and, after reassembly, turn your attention to cleaning out the rear carburettor float bowl.

3-2-3 If yours is one of the earlier MGBs that does not have a fuel filter fitted and you've cleaned out the carburettor fuel bowls, if the car's still not running as you'd expect, there is another carburettor related solution to try.

This time we're looking at the carburettor needles/dampers with suspicion. The clearance between the bore of the external casing ("dashpot") and its internal piston is very small - by design. If the car has been standing over some months, corrosion can occur on either or both surfaces with the consequence that the piston sticks. This, in turn, means that

the needle that controls the volume of fuel fed to the engine is allowing excessive richness and the engine will run very roughly indeed. If the pistons in both carburettors get stuck "open" there is the possibility that the engine will hardly run at all, or it may "race" (i.e. tick over at a much higher than usual rpm).

Piston/needles stuck open due to corrosion would be very unlikely in an engine that has been used fairly regularly of late. However, one of your carburettor case's could have had a knock (creating a slight dent) or a small piece of dirt could have got into the piston/case: either problem could cause a piston to stick open with the same symptoms. We will look at the remedial work for the slightly dented case in the relevant chapter, but you can check for a sticking piston by removing the air cleaners and looking at the bases of the pistons in the carburettor bores - which with the engine at rest should have fallen to the bottom of their stroke(s). If either is stuck even partway above the bottom of their stroke you could have found your problem. It could be helpful to push the **piston** (best not touch the needle) upwards and let it fall. It should of course fall to the bottom: any tendency to stick needs sorting.

You need to remove the three screws that secure the casing ("dashpot") to the body of the carburettor and lift the casing vertically. Be very careful not to lift the piston/needle assembly up with the case and then to drop it! Lift the piston/needle and clean round the periphery of the piston. Very carefully and thoroughly clean the bore of the case and reassemble the carburettor, then try a test run You could be very pleasantly surprised.

3-2-4 You'll get the same symptoms as a sticking piston if one or both air cleaner bases have been fitted upside down. There's a central hole either side of the carburettor inlet or mouth that is used to fix the air cleaners to the carburettors. Above these holes is a second pair of

holes (of very similar size) that appear to have no purpose. You can see them very clearly in picture 3-2-3. In fact, these holes are very important as they provide a breather for the top of the damper piston. It's all too easy to fit the baseplate in such a way that the breather holes are closed off.

3-2-5 If your 'B always starts journies running well enough, but (usually on a long journies) then starts to give cause for concern, check that the fuel tank filler cap is venting. You'll appreciate that a tank full of fuel has little air within it, but as you pump the fuel from the tank the fuel you consume needs to be replaced by air via a small but steady supply. If you're travelling at a steady 75mph (in Germany of course) and your fuel consumption is about 25mpg, over the course of a couple of hours you'll have half-emptied the tank. The space left by the used fuel should, of course be filled by air vented into the tank via the filler cap. If the filler cap vent has become blocked the pump will have to work harder and harder as the fuel level falls and I've heard of fuel tanks actually collapsing inwards as the pump's suction removes fuel and creates a vacuum within the tank. You can check your cap is venting adequately by removing the cap immediately after a two-hour run. There should be little suction preventing you removing the cap but if the cap is reluctant to separate from the tank and only does so accompanied by a hiss of inrushing air, you need a new fuel filler cap.

3-2-6 Further information on badly-running cars can be found in chapter 15.

Poor drivability can be the result of a weak mixture and this is explored in 15-1-2 (SU carbs) and 15-3-4 (Stromberg carb).

Poor idle/tickover can be the result of incorrect mixture adjustments. If the car will hardly idle at all take a look at 15-3-1, whilst an uneven idle on US cars with emission control equipment could signal a faulty ERG valve: see 15-4-4.

Chapter 4
Engine reluctant to start when hot

This symptom is usually related to the over-supply of fuel.

Over-rich fuel mixture

4-1-1 Air cleaners (filters), if not changed at the prescribed intervals can cause a restriction in the airflow to the carburettors, which has the effect of enriching the fuel/air mixture. This doesn't matter when you're starting the

4-1-1 (Picture 1) Take off the air cleaner covers by removing the four longish bolts. Watch out for the long internal spacers and the rear captive nuts that, with HS4 carburettors, will release part of the choke mechanism.

4-1-1 (Picture 2) Fit a new air cleaner (filter) element into each canister, noting that, these days, they are usually available to special order via a Rover dealer, although every MG specialist will have them in stock.

car from cold, since you're probably richening the initial mixture by choke anyway, so the extra drag from a partly clogged air cleaner is not going to make a lot of difference. However, when hot starting you would not think of using any choke and neither would you want to

enrichen the mixture via an old and restrictive air cleaner.

Take a good look at the air cleaner elements and change them if they look well used, or if you cannot recall the last time they were changed. If they look OK, leave them off the car for a few days (unless you live in a dry, dusty climate) until you have established whether their absence makes a difference. If the car hot starts better without the filters then new filters are required.

Not an 1800cc MGB, but I've found the slim air filter I use on my 3500cc MGB must be changed every 5000 miles (although it looks quite serviceable) if I am to get first-time everytime hot starting.

4-2-1 Post-1975 US cars have the automatic-choke mechanism fitted to the right side of the Stromberg carburettor. While these devices do give their fair share of problems, there are a couple of simple checks/adjustments worth exploring before too much blame falls on the auto-choke.

First, feel to ensure that the water jacket, heat mass and plastic insulator ring are getting up to full water temperature. If the thermostat has failed, or there is a blockage in the water pipes, the auto-choke may not be presented with a representative temperature.

Second, there's a certain amount of leeway with the position of the choke water jacket, and it could be set too far clockwise - which would have the consequence of enriching the mixture too much. If you have hot starting difficulties, try undoing the three water jacket screws and turning the water jacket slightly anti-clockwise.

4-3-1 Still difficult to start your Stromberg carburetted 'B when hot? Extra fuel for cold starting is supplied by a supplementary needle/jet in the automatic-choke. It's therefore very difficult to observe at home whether or not the choke is operating inappropriately when the engine's hot. If you feel the choke's operation is questionable remove it for some important checks. You don't need to break into the water system, simply fold the water jacket back out of the way. With the auto-choke removed from the carburettor, clean the inside with carb cleaner and check that -
- the top port in the body is clear of obstruction
- the choke spring-loaded operating lever is free
- the throttle opening cam is secure on its shaft
- the base plug is secure

Careful re-assembly after the foregoing checks and repairs will resolve most problems. It's a good idea to lightly smear the (orange) gasket with grease before reassembly and use a thread-locking compound such as "Loctite" on the three slotted retaining screws to ensure that they stay really tight.

It'll probably be necessary to half-open the main throttle while offering the choke back to the carb body in order to sit the operating finger just past the vertical - at about 1 O'clock. The screws that secure the water jacket should not be tightened as aggressively as those holding the choke to the body of the carburettor. You'll find more information on the Stromberg carburettor in chapter 15.

4-4-1 All carburettors are designed to run cold, which is normally achieved by the flow of air through them and the cooling effect of vaporising fuel. However, carburettors are bound to get warm when not in use and sitting above a hot exhaust manifold. There's nothing you can do to prevent some warming of the carbs and, within reason, this is perfectly satisfactory.

MG took great care to ensure that carburettors are not heated excessively by fitting a heatshield, a number of gaskets and two thick insulation blocks, all intended to avoid fuel vaporisation as a consequence of the carbs getting too hot. These devices worked well in the days of leaded fuels but, today, we have unleaded fuels that vaporise at lower temperatures, making carburettor heat insulation even more important.

So, to get to the point, are all the gaskets, blocks and the (metal) heatshield properly in place? The metal heatshield should have an extra layer of insulation (originally asbestos I think) riveted to each end to give the float chambers extra protection. Are these insulators in place and in good condition?

4-5-1 Having got the insulation on your MGB at least up to original standard, if you're still not satisfied with the hot starting you could get an idea of whether or not heat is the problem by experimenting, as follows.

As soon as you stop the engine, open the bonnet and leave the car the length of time that usually results in starting difficulties; say, half an hour. Does that help? If so, you're clearly on the right track. If you note some improvement but are still not completely satisfied, try the same routine but this time lodge a knob or two of ice on each carb. Give the ice a few moments to melt and cool the carbs, and then try starting. If this improves matters it's clear you need to find a way of keeping the carburettors cool during the hot-standing period. More insulation is the answer: try the following either progressively or in one step -
- Cover the metal heat shield in aluminium foil, polished reflective side toward the engine
- Stick special self-adhesive insulating/reflective material on the float chambers
- Stick special self-adhesive insulating/reflective material on the metal heatshield
- Wrap the exhaust **manifold** (not the whole system!) in heat insulating tape; this could be the only step you need to take if your car has a tubular/fabricated exhaust manifold. These retro-fitted manifolds emit huge amounts of extra heat compared with original, cast iron manifolds, and this may be the sole reason for your hot starting problems. Tip: for mild steel manifolds, leave some space between turns to allow some heat to escape.

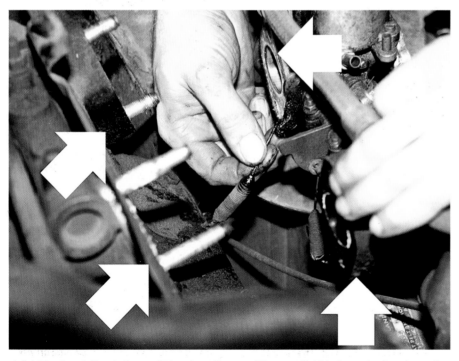

4-4-1 The insulation between SU carburettors and the manifold is important and may be more complex than you expect. Starting in the top left corner, these arrows highlight the rear carburettor insulating block, the metal heatshield, the front insulating block and the gasket that goes between the carburettor and the block. In addition, there should be another gasket between each block and the heatshield, and a further pair between the heatshield and the manifold!

4-6-1 The other potential consequence of heat within the engine bay is vaporisation of the fuel within the fuel line that feeds the carbs, causing reluctant hot starting and also slow cold starting. Check this out by disconnecting the fuel line at the front carburettor **a day after** a long run, place a collecting jar under the fuel line and have a helper turn on the ignition. **Warning! - Don't do this when the engine is hot as the tiniest fuel spill onto the hot exhaust manifold could be lethal.** If there's a delay in fuel getting though to the front carburettor the fuel is almost certainly vaporising in the fuel line. In this event, wrap the line with reflective insulating bandage. It's a good precaution with today's highly volatile fuels in any case.

4-7-1 The overflow tubes running from the top of the carburettors down the side of the engine are deceptively important and need to be free flowing (unblocked). They can get bunged up, usually at the bottom near the sump, and you should clear them both.

When the engine is turned off the temperature of the carburettors rises, the fuel in the float chambers expands and any excess needs to escape down the overflow pipes. If these are blocked the excess will be forced up the main jet and could flood the carburettor body and/or the inlet manifold, making the engine

4-6-1 The metal fuel line is routed alongside the gearbox (arrow A), up alongside the rear of the engine, and across the top front of the gearbox tunnel (arrow B) to the top of the left footwell. These are all warm, if not hot, areas that initially gave few problems, although MG did find it necessary to install a short heatshield just in front of the heater. Today, we use much more volatile fuels and the heat that the fuel picks up through this pipe run can cause vaporisation, particularly if your engine bay is at above average temperature. The braided hose (arrow C) has an inner rubber core and the outer braid, when shiny, has some reflective properties. So, again, it would appear that MG took some precautions against heat absorption. This entire fuel supply line needs to be kept as cool as possible. Luckily, today, we have some excellent insulating and/or reflective materials that will do the job.

4-7-1 (Picture 1) Both HS4 carburettors used on the chrome bumper cars have an overflow pipe running from the top of its float chamber (arrowed) down the side of the engine block...

4-7-1 (Picture 2) ...while the later HIF carb s also employ two overflow pipes. These eminate from the integral float chambers and run down the side of the block. Both types of carb have a twin pipe clip adjacent to the sump bolts to secure the bottom end of the overflow pipes.

very difficult to start until such time as the excess fuel evaporates. If you're not sure where they are, the accompanying pictures feature a pair of overflow pipes at the front and some rather special non-standard overflow pipes.

4-8-1 If you still have a problem you need to address the condition of your carburettors. They could simply be out of adjustment, but I'm more inclined to think that wear in the float pivots and/or the needle valves is causing too high a fuel level in either or both float chambers, thus feeding the engine with excess fuel.

This is not of too much consequence when starting a cold engine as extra fuel is required, but excess fuel will cause problems when trying to start a hot engine. Both float pivots and needle valve(s) are instrumental in controlling the supply of fuel to the carburettor(s) and, when worn, the needle valve at the top of each float chamber can leak, allowing the pressurised fuel in the fuel line to overfill the carburettors even after the engine is switched off. This can generate excess fuel not only in the float chamber but even within the carburettor body.

This situation is made even worse if float levels are set a bit high and/or wear in the float pivot allows the fuel level to rise above the ideal. The consequence of this excess fuel is that the plugs become wet and disinclined to spark until the

4-8-1 The needle valve and pivot that controls the float on the HS4 carburettor. This is an early adjustable type of float and, while its importance and function did not change, the design of the HIF carburettor float is quite different. You may find the additional detail in chapter 15 helpful.

cranking has dissipated the excess fuel, at which point the engine will eventually start.

Essential remedial work requires at least new needle valves in both carburettors. Do not miss the opportunity of replacing the float pivot pin(s) if either have excessive play, and possibly the float, too, because you might be surprised by how much these components can wear and how much play (lash) results.

4-9-1 Wear of carburettor jets and needles may be allowing too much fuel into the engine. If the jets and/or the needles are worn, excess fuel will be presented to the engine at all times. This is not likely to be a problem when starting the engine from cold, but could result in high hydro-carbons when the emissions are tested and/or excessive fuel consumption. Sooty sparkplugs could be a clue, although the colour of used sparkplugs has completely changed with the introduction of unleaded fuels. You can partly compensate by closing the jet(s) slightly, but this is really only a medium-

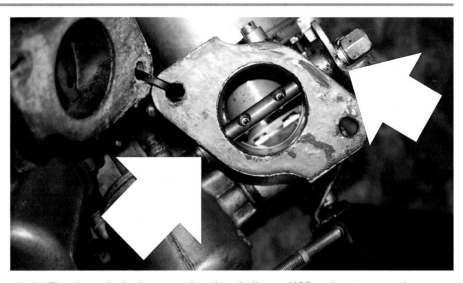

4-10-1 There's no doubt that worn throttle spindles on MGB carburettors are the cause of more misdiagnosis than perhaps any other single problem. Each carburettor has two points (arrowed) that are vulnerable to wear, which can be hard to fully determine unless you open the throttle disc. This picture is interesting in that the throttle disc has been removed (note the two countersunk recesses for the screw heads), to allow removal and replacement of this worn spindle.

4-9-1 As you see here, the fuel supply is controlled by a tapered needle moving in and out of a precisely calibrated jet. Wear in one or both components overfuels the engine.

term remedy and can only be done so many times before it becomes ineffective, and it's time for new needles at the very least.

However, if you only replace the needles in an SU carburettor you are really only doing half the job for there will probably be more wear in the jets than in the needles. So do a proper job and

replace both needles and jets in both carbs to fix this problem. The consequential fuel saving might pay for the parts!

Over-weak fuel mixture

4-10-1 Switching our thinking to the other fuel supply extreme; worn throttle spindles could be allowing excessive air to enter the engine resulting in a lean mixture. The test is to set the throttle partially open (to ensure the throttle butterfly (disc) is not restricting spindle movement) and wiggle both ends of both spindles; any movement up or down or in or out is bad news.

You'll find more information in chapter 15, but you can be sure that your car will run inconsistently if excessive air is drawn into the induction system at or downstream of the throttle butterflys.

Coil ballast resistor problems

4-11-1 If the car is still reluctant to hot start, my final suggestion is electrically-orientated and applies only to those late MGBs that were fitted with a ballast resistor within the electrical harness.

You can't see the ballast resistor, but a white/light-green wire at the coil will tell you that the car should be fitted with a **6 volt** coil and have a ballast

resistor operating during normal running: 12 volts is fed to the coil when cranking to aid starting. The (white/light-green) wire draws 12 volts direct from the starter solenoid when starting. This, in effect, bypasses the ballast resistor circuit to provide a boosted HT voltage from the 6 volt coil only while the starter motor is operating.

The engine may well start immediately when cold, even if this white/light-green 12 volt circuit is faulty, but with a hot engine, particularly if a worn carburettor is also providing a rather rich mixture, there may not be enough of a spark to start the engine. To check, set a small multimeter to its low voltage (say, 0-25 volts DC) scale. Hold the meter's positive lead on the "SW"/"+" terminal on the coil and the meter's black/earth lead to a good clean earth (ground). You should see 12 volts indicated when the starter is operating, and around 6 volts when the engine is running normally. 6 volts all the time suggests the direct feed wire from the starter is broken and 12 volts all the time tells you that you do not have a ballast resistor in circuit. Hopefully, in this situation, you'll have a 12 volt coil fitted!

Chapter 5
Fuel pump does not operate

The SU fuel pump has been fitted to the MGB in two locations and if, like most an MGB owners at some point, you're suffering fuel-pump difficulties you'll need to establish where yours is located. Up to the introduction of the Rubber Bumper MGBs, the pump was stuck low down at the bottom of the right-side wheel arch. Just right for collecting all the water, dirt and rubbish that was flying about from the adjacent rear wheel! It is amazing these pumps work as well as they do for so long. However, you hardly need me to tell you that, in fact, they do not work as reliably as we have grown to expect of the fuel-pumps in modern-day cars and, not to put too fine a point on it, they can become a pain. Mind you, this is not entirely due to their vulnerable location, for in about 1975, MG relocated the pump such that the end containing the electrical contacts poked backwards through the front panel of the boot/trunk. They would not have made that alteration without some reason, and I think it was to protect the pump's electrics. However, the move did not resolve all the SU pump's reliability problems (which are I think exacerbated by the contact-breaker-like operation of the original design), but that is why you're reading this chapter.

5-1-1 If the fuel pump has stopped working after a lay-up, while it is probably the points that are the problem, it's still worth checking that the relevant electrical

5-1-1 The points (arrowed) on an SU pump are clearly visible once the rubber sealing ring and plastic cover are removed.

connections are good before you remove the pump from the car.

Use a test lead/bulb to ensure that the main (white) electrical feed is delivering power to the pump when the ignition is switched on (see 1-1-8 if you want the details).

The electrical connection most prone to problems is the one midway down the pump body; a male spade terminal on the pump and a female Lucar connector on the end of the black earth (ground) wire that emerges from the harness. Chrome bumpered cars with the pump situated under the right wheelarch are the most vulnerable to corrosion of electrical terminals/connectors due to the pump's proximity to water, salt and general dirt. Dirty connections are always suspect, and should be cleaned, smeared with

petroleum jelly (Vaseline), reassembled, and checked for a good secure/tight fit male into female before the pump is tried again by turning on the ignition.

5-2-1 If the pump is staying completely mute after a lay-up chances are that the points have corroded during this period of inactivity. Infrequent use allows surface corrosion to build up on the contact breaker points situated under the black plastic cap. The result is that the

5-2-1 You don't have to remove the pump from the car in order to check that this earth terminal (arrowed) and the live connection - seen at the top right of the picture - are clean and secure. This is a fuel pump from a rubber bumper car - identified as such by the capped vent on the end of the plastic cover.

electrical current cannot flow, so the fuel pump becomes inoperative. The minimum cost remedy is to clean the points (see 5-6-1).

However, I am very sceptical about the reliability of SU fuel pumps that continue to use contact breaker points. My recommendation is that you skip down the page and study one of several upgrades described in 5-7-1.

5-3-1 So what if the fuel pump simply stopped and will not restart however hard it's tapped? Most of the time this problem is due to points wear because of age and/or extensive use. The

5-3-1 Shown off the car for clarity, is the live (negative earth/ground cars) terminal upon which the whole performance of your car depends. On rubber bumper cars this end of the pump is protected by a top hat-shaped guard at the front of the boot (trunk). Chrome bumper cars have this terminal right down by the right rear wheel, the perfect place to trap all the rubbish, water and salt that's thrown up from the road!

frustration and inconvenience is exacerbated by the fact that this wear can occur quite soon after cleaning the existing points, fitting a new set of points, or even just after a brand new pump has been installed.

In most cases you will be able to get home by tapping the pump's metal body with a spanner, hammer, wheel brace or some other weighty item. I don't recommend the method, but have heard of an owner getting his (RHD) MGB home by leaning out and bashing the pump from the driver's seat! I came close to meeting

my maker whilst laying alongside a 'B GT (bashing the fuel pump) on a sharp, left-hand bend on a cold wet winter's night when 32 tonnes of articulated truck brushed past me!

If the car will not run even for a short time after you've bashed the pump, it suggests that something else is wrong and that the power supply and earth (ground) checks explored in 1-1-8 are definitely worthwhile. Assuming that one of these checks reveals a lack of power at the pump, what do you do then?

Go to the right rear corner of the engine bay and look for the collection of wires that I call a 'crossroads.' You're looking for the white wires joined via bullet connectors within a tubular connector with black insulation. One of the white wires dips down under the floor of the car, eventually emerging at the fuel pump! A picture of this area will be found at 19-1 if you are in doubt.

MGBs were originally manufactured without a fuel pump circuit fuse, but it's possible that a previous owner thought it a good idea to fit a "line" fuse to the fuel pump feed wire. If this is the case, check that the fuse has not blown; if it has replace it with a new one, or if it is not blown but is corroded, clean the connecting faces, refit the fuse and try the ignition-on routine again.

It's more likely you'll find just the standard bullet connector rather than a line fuse, in which case, with the ignition off, pull the two wires from the connector tube. They're likely to be very reluctant to separate, but if one or both wires are a loose fit in the connector, you may have found another cause of the power supply problem.

Before you improve the connection, it's worth checking the power supply at the connector using your test lead, a multimeter or spare festoon bulb. This check needs to be made on the white wire which emerges from the main harness, not on the white wire which seems to be diving down into the depths of the rear of the engine bay. Find a clean earth (ground) spot on the bodywork (maybe a screw/bolt head) close to the area where all these wires converge. Have a helper turn on the ignition (but not operate the starter).The bullet connector should supply enough power to light the earthed bulb/testlight or register on the multimeter's dial. If power is reaching the connector, the pump problem is most likely lack of conductivity through the bullet connector.

This apparently simple bullet

connection can generate two types of conductivity fault. The more straightforward one is corrosion of the bullets and sleeve. Clean every contact face as meticulously as you can. If you do not have a piece of emery or sandpaper, a nail file will certainly help. If the bullets were a loose fit in the connector gently squeeze the tubular connector slightly, remembering it is likely to be 30 years old and fragile. Reassemble the connection with a light smear of petroleum jelly (Vaseline) to protect it in the future. (Of course, it's a good idea to renew the connector components at the earliest opportunity).

Try the pump again, if it runs, great! Otherwise, read on ...

Try one last bulb/multimeter test on the white wire feed at the pump. No power at the pump suggests that the white wire feeding it is broken somewhere along its length, and some get-you-home ingenuity is called for. If you've followed my advice and carry a piece of insulated electrical wire of almost any thickness and a reel of insulating tape, you could rig up a temporary electrical feed to the pump from any convenient live point. The power can come from anywhere, including the car's sidelight (parking light) circuit: using this method you could at least turn the fuel pump off without getting out of the car by turnig off the sidelights.

5-4-1 If the pump still refuses to go, or runs intermittently to little effect, it's time to get the pump off the car. **Warning!** - Before starting removal of the pump you

5-4-1 The fuel pump on chrome bumper cars needs the two breather pipes shown here. The top cap breather pipe (arrowed) was omitted from rubber bumper cars since the top vent was protected by the boot (trunk). Failure to use the airtight breather pipes applicable to your car and fuel pump will result in an ingress of water and termination of fuel supply...

need to take several precautions for your personal safety -

- Elevate and support the car safely.
- Wear fully enveloping goggles.
- Ensure ventilation is adequate. Elaborating on this last point, it's best to do this work outside if possible, and certainly nowhere near a pit where fumes can collect.
- Be sure that there's absolutely no chance of anyone smoking close to where you're working.
- Disconnect the battery.
- Do not use mains or car battery powered lead lights. Their bulbs can cause a fire or even an explosion if faulty or the bulb gets broken when in close proximity to fuel. A small, cool torch (flashlight) with a protected bulb is much safer.
- Note the relative positions of the in and out fuel pipes. A paper label stuck round the top pipe is never a bad idea.
- Minimise the content of the fuel tank before you start. Even then you could still find that the feed pipe from the tank to the pump will siphon fuel all over the ground! Be prepared for this by having a brake hose clamp (a pair of Mole/vise grips could serve in an emergency) to hand to close off the pipe by squeezing it.
- You should find at least one, possibly two, vent pipes if your car is chrome bumpered, probably made from windscreen (windshield) washer tubing, connected to the pump; both are more important than they look. Disconnect them with care and check that neither is holed (which can allow water into the pump), pinched or blocked. One will be connected to the cap and one to the body of the pump and, whilst precise location is unimportant, the ends must be open and exit into a dry location. The boot/trunk is favourite but often one is routed inside an adjacent chassis member.

5-5-1 With the fuel pump off the car, check that the inlet filter is not blocked. You'll get a clue to whether further stripping and cleaning is necessary by removing the wide/flat dome cover from the inlet chamber. If the chamber behind the cover is clean, the filter is probably clear and not in need of further attention. If, however, there's dirt in the inlet chamber, it will be necessary to clean the inlet gauze filter.

This can be done without upsetting the rocker mechanism or points by undoing the six screws that fasten the tubular body to the base casting (where the inlet and outlet pipes were connected before you removed the pump from the

5-5-1 You can check the cleanliness of the pump's inlet chamber (and get a very good idea of the inlet filter's condition) by removing the large cover. This can be done with the pump in place provided you are careful not to get dirt into the pump.

car). Take great care when actually separating the two parts since the main pump diaphragm is sandwiched between the two halves, and you must not damage it. If, as I expect it will be, it is stuck, separate it from the lower casting, leaving it stuck to the tubular body. There are a couple of screws to remove to allow access to the inlet and outlet valves - and the inlet filter gauze. If you find it hopelessly blocked with rubbish you'll have to clean and reassemble everything, and also establish why or when the pump was fed with dirty fuel. Corrective action could include removing and cleaning the existing tank, or even fitting a new one.

The separation midway down the pump has a second advantage in that you can also exercise the diaphragm and over-centre mechanism in the top (tubular) half of the pump by pushing up the centre of the diaphragm until it is moving as freely as the return spring permits, and the over-centre points mechanism at the top of the pump is working (clicking or ticking) every

5-6-1 (Picture 1) The six screws retaining the cylindrical solenoid to the main body have been removed and the two parts separated so as to leave the main diaphragm attached to the solenoid.

time you push the diaphragm upwards.

5-6-1 If the filter is perfectly serviceable, it's time to look at the points if you want to avoid a replacement pump. Replacing and adjusting the points is well documented elsewhere and does not bear repetition here. However, let us establish that **two** contacts are involved: mounted on the blade and on the rocker.

The blade can be seen arrowed in the accompanying photo and is removed for cleaning in about five seconds by loosening (not even removing) a single screw. You'll note two hardened contact points on the blade and, facing these, a

5-6-1 (Picture 2) The inlet chamber is nearest the bottom of the picture and the inlet filter gauze and cover are positioned on the left. The gauze is actually upside-down for clarity and will need to be replaced gauze-down in the base on reassembly. The outlet valve is on the right side of the picture.

5-6-1 (Picture 3) Although this pump was very clean indeed, I stripped the inlet (left) and outlet (right side) covers for the benefit of those who find the inside of their pump filled with rubbish. Note that there is a thin, fragile diaphragm (arrowed) beneath the outlet chamber cover that is intended to smooth the flow of fuel, and which is best left undisturbed if possible.

matching pair on the other half of the make/break contact system - the rocker. Although I do not propose to detail setting-up of the rocker/points, here are a few helpful tips -

• Read section 5-7 before starting!

• You could be saved frustration by replacing not only the points but the condenser, too. You may get a pump going again with new points alone, but, in my experience, chances are that when

5-6-1 (Picture 4) The condenser is arrowed, but the prime reason for the photo is to show the screw that has to be loosened to enable the blade half of the points to be removed. The condition, and in this case the true extent of the burning, of both blade and the more difficult-to-get-at rocker points, can now be assessed.

exercised - particularly if the exercise is vigorous and prolonged - it will stop again when it heats up. In this case, it could be the pump condenser that is causing the problem so, for the cost involved, I'd renew the condenser at the same time as the points - that is were I ever persuaded to do the job again!

• You will (or should) find that the plastic end cap is sealed to the body with both tape and a broad rubber band. You'll need to re-use the band so remove the tape carefully in order to preserve the band.

• Watch out for the tiny, rubber sealing washer sited inside the cap, on the threaded pillar. You will need to re-use it, but it is easily lost and important, particularly on chrome bumper cars.

• Many people try simply cleaning the points but, in my view, this is only a short-term, get-you-home proposition. The twin points on the blade are easily accessible and an oil stone will quickly smarten them up. However, the other pair of points are just as important and are virtually impossible to more than superficially clean in place. Consequently, if you're going to do the job properly, the whole contact set

5-6-1 (Picture 5) You need to virtually remove the rocker pedestal in order to gain access to the twin contact points mounted on the rocker part of the pump. If you are intent on retaining your SU pump then, having come this far, replace the rocker completely. This requires you peel the diaphragm from the base of the solenoid and unscrew it from the rocker via the central screw thread arrowed - but read 5-7 first...

5-7-1 (Picture 1) One of the modern alternatives to the original SU pump is this Facit "Silver-Top" electronic fuel pump. This is the pump I have installed in the right front corner of the spare wheel area in my 'B GT. Note that the fuel pipes must be the higher specification, non-porous type and "out" must be at the top. The pump *must* be installed vertically as shown.

needs to be removed, and if you are going to go to that trouble it would be better to fit a new pair of contacts - or would it? Read on ...

5-7-1 I have made numerous adverse comments about SU fuel pumps, and do not now use one, preferring instead a modern, electronically-operated replacement. My point (pun intended) is that the original SU design is dated, very dated. Even if both sets of points and the condenser are renewed, and beautifully set up, the pump's still an obsolete design serving a role that's vital to the reliability of the car.

If a clean up of the blade points gets you mobile for a few days, then great, but please appreciate that you really need to take long term remedial action if you're not to suffer the whole fuel pump nightmare again. If your car's at home in its garage I recommend you forget all about the existing contact points and condenser of your SU fuel pump, and instead take one of the three routes that we explore next.

Fuel pump upgrades

5-7-1 Option 1. Fit an alternative make and design of pump altogether. I've fitted a Silver-Top Facit electronic fuel pump to my 'Bs.

Specialists such as Demon Tweeks are able to offer several alternatives, but make sure to tell them what carburettors the pump will be feeding since it's important that the replacement pump provides no more than 3psi. More than that and the float chambers in the carburettors are likely to be prone to

5-7-1 (Picture 2) A fuel pressure regulator. It's adjustable and you might just be able to see the figures (arrowed) around the edge of the case. I use this universal fitting on my Triumph Stag to reduce the pressure generated by an overly vigorous fuel pump to something more acceptable to the Stromberg carburettors.

flooding. Excessive fuel pressure can be corrected by a fuel pressure regulator (see photograph), but this adds to the cost and it's better to buy a pump with the correct pressure output in the first place.

With very little modification the new pump can be completely sited in the corner of the boot (trunk) and, over the course of 8 or 10 years, will provide completely reliable fuel delivery. You'll need to cut two holes in the wall of the boot and route one suction pipe from the bottom of the pump to the fuel tank. The second (delivery) pipe goes from the top of the pump to the original fuel pipe that used to take fuel from the SU pump, under the floor of the car to the engine. You can use flexible rubber, non-porous fuel hose of the correct diameter, available from your local auto parts shop, or a little bit of plumbing with copper pipe may actually enable you to route the pipe more easily to meet with the original delivery pipe. The copper pipe solution is actually preferred from a safety point of view for reasons explained in a moment.

You can solder plumbing fittings to the new pipe off of the car to provide tight bends that will enable you to tuck the new pipe out of the way, and securely clip it to the underside of the car. You can easily marry the new pipe to the original with a couple of inches of fuel hose and some clips. **Warning! - Never** try soldering the original pipe or, indeed, any component that has been used to carry fuel. However, if the original (steel) pipe on your car looks corroded, this could be the opportunity to replace it.

Use an equivalent-sized copper pipe from either your local plumbing merchant or favourite MG spares retailer, and take the pipe right through from fuel filter to the new pump.

Warning! - Internally fitted pumps, or any fuel pipe connections within the car/boot, require some form of venting that is able to move fluids as well as vapours. A major fuel leak is a potential hazard but, in fact, the odd drip, or the vapour that escapes from a loose clip or through the very slightly porous nature of most exterior grade flexible fuel lines is, in some ways, at least as dangerous.

A little additional information about flexible fuel hoses is in order here. In the UK at least, flexible fuel hoses can be purchased in three quality standards. In ascending order of cost normal exterior and interior qualities can be bought from

most auto parts suppliers - the latter being of the higher, non-porous specification you need for an interior fuel pump installation. The third and best quality is specifically made for the interior fuel pipe runs applicable to competition cars, and is probably only available from motorsport-orientated specialists.

5-7-2 Fit a new, modern, electronically-activated SU pump. This is a completely new pump which looks the same as the original unit, and much of the body of the pump is actually identical, but the all-important triggering mechanism

5-7-2 (Picture 1) This is the modern 'electronicised' SU fuel pump with, you'll note, a significantly altered pedestal as compared to the original arrangement, as seen in Picture 2.

5-7-2 (Picture 2) The original contact breaker type of pedestal.

(originally the contact points) has been replaced by a solid-state electronic device.

The pump is made by Burlen Fuel Systems (UK Tel: 01722 412500) and is completely interchangeable with the original pump - even down to the familiar 'ticking' sound. The manufacturer assures me that the electronic controls of the new pump mean it will activate immediately, even after a long winter lay-up.

5-7-3 Replace the original contact points triggering mechanism with a new, electronically-activated module on the existing pump. The module is identical to that incorporated in the completely new pump I've just described, and offers a financial saving to those prepared to change the triggering mechanism on their existing pump.

I'd only consider this route if I had a fairly new SU pump that, like many I have owned, is giving aggravation very soon after purchase. The contact switching of the new top module is by a "Hall-effect" electronic switch and a solid-state timing device.

Understandably, Burlen points out that its warranty is limited to the cost of the module kit. The fitting and setting instructions supplied with the module kit are comprehensive and the tools required will be in almost every MGB enthusiast's tool kit. The appearance and sound of the modified pump is the same as the original - if you're worried about that sort of thing...

5-7-3 You can buy just the printed circuit board pedestal electronics to fit to your existing SU pump. I believe this option is only viable if you are unfortunate enough to have recently bought a new SU pump of original contact breaker specification, only to have it fail.

Chapter 6
Engine noises

Noises can let you know that all is not well, though are sometimes misleading when caused by tyres and/or the road surface, or something loose in the boot (trunk). I recall taking a Mercedes to the factory in Stuttgart for repair and, when collecting it, was told that the car had just been taken for a test drive around the factory circuit and the mechanic had heard a noise he was not comfortable with; would we take a seat whilst they investigated. Ten minutes later a beaming mechanic appeared, triumphantly bearing a lipstick which had been rolling around an otherwise empty glovebox!

There's no doubt that noises are important in detecting a fault before the car stops, early investigation diagnosing the problem and minimising damage. Most, but not all, engine noises continue when the car is stationary with the engine running. Be aware, however, that some engine noises will change in intensity, some may even disappear altogether, depending upon the load applied to the engine.

Squealing

6-1-1 If something in the engine area squeals occasionally, particularly when you first start up in the mornings, when the headlights are on or when you increase the engine revolutions, this suggests the fanbelt/drivebelt may be too slack or worn. A worn belt may be less obvious to spot

6-1-1 A loose or overly-tight fanbelt (drivebelt) is bad news, so is a worn one. The tension may be perfect, but if the belt is worn and sitting too low in the pulleys it can squeal and fail to drive water pump and generator properly. The adjustment points are arrowed.

than you may think for a worn belt thins down whereupon the narrow bottom of the belt sits on the base of the pulley groove. In this circumstance the sides of the belt are no longer driving on the sides of the pulleys as they should and the majority of the belt's driving capacity has been lost - yet the tension of the belt seems quite satisfactory. So start with a check to ensure the belt is NOT sitting too low in its pulley grooves, and be aware that this problem can also occur if the wrong fanbelt has been fitted. Then a quick check of the belt's tension with the engine stopped comes next - does the

belt's longest run move up/down by more than about 0.5in (12mm) from its "at rest" position? If so it is almost certainly the cause of the squealing and you need to increase the tension not only to remove the unpleasant noise but more importantly to eliminate the rapid fan/drivebelt wear that will be occurring every time the belt squeals. To increase the tension in the fanbelt you need to slacken (but not remove) the three bolts that hold the alternator or dynamo in place. This is most comfortably tackled when the engine is cold and you'll need **two** spanners to undo and retighten the bolts. Two mounting bolts are usually underneath the generator and are frustrating to get to. However these only need to be slightly loosened (possibly one turn, maybe two at the most), but the one bolt that passes through a slotted tensioning arm on top of the generator will need an additional half turn to allow it to slide up the slot. You may need a partner's help to pull the generator away from the engine while you check the tension on the fanbelt and nip the top **sliding** bolt up sufficiently tight to stop the generator from swinging back and releasing the tension. Check the fanbelt tension again and, if satisfied, tighten all three bolts: job done!

Grinding

6-2-1 The water pump's or generator's bearings could be making the sort of

6-2-1 The water pump and its pulley. This is a chrome bumper 'B, but the usual metal fan blades are missing because this car has been fitted with an electric cooling fan. You won't need to remove the alternator completely, but will need to be able to access and turn this pulley in order to assess the condition of the bearings in the water pump.

grinding noise that you could make by shaking a tin can full of gravel. This could, possibly, be the consequence of over-tensioning the fanbelt/drivebelt, wear and tear in the bearings or a leaking seal allowing water into the pump's bearings. Check that the belt is correctly tensioned as described in the previous section: too taut a fanbelt/drivebelt can damage the water pump/generator bearings. Free off the belt and try moving the water pump and generator pulleys about, up-down, in-out and also rotate them to feel for "grittyness". If movement or roughness is present in either, or you can see a dribble of water from the pump, remove the belt completely and run the engine for 15 to 30 seconds. If the noise has disappeared, you've shortlisted the water pump or generator bearings as the culprits. Try to recall whether you have been loosing coolant in recent days? "Yes" to water loss and/or gritty movement/play in the pulley

and you need to be planning to fit a replacement water pump. We will look at replacing the generator later but new water pumps are available as are service-exchange units, and consequently you should dismiss any thoughts you may have had of rebuilding your original water pump.

There were three types of water pump and you need establish whether you have the early, middle or late type. For the chrome-bumpered cars, where the radiator is mounted only just in front of the pump, it will be necessary to start by removing the radiator and you'll save yourself a little work if you remove the bottom hose at the water pump. Owners of post 1976 rubber-bumpered cars will not find removing the radiator necessary as it is mounted some distance further forward and access to the water pump is consequently good. Some US cars specification cars will need to have the air pump removed and all owners will need to remove the generator and fanbelt/drivebelt.

If your car has a mechanical fan (many MGBs are fitted with electric fans either as original equipment or as a retrofitted upgrade) this might be the best time to remove it and to take a close look at the four mounting rubbers used to secure the mechnaical fan. They perish and thereafter generate a (harmless)

6-3-1 The alternator installation. Note the top pivot points (arrowed) and the adjusting link - in this case, about halfway across its adjustment length. Slacken off these fastenings to allow the alternator to be spun and its bearings checked.

"tinkling" sound when the engine is running and are best renewed as a matter of course. **Caution!** - Do not overlook buying a new pair of locking tabs for the fan mounting bolts. The water pump will come away from the front of the engine after four bolts have been removed and the undoubtedly stuck gasket broken. You'll need a replacement water pump and gasket, and a new fanbelt is advisable too, as is some gasket sealer (e.g. Blue Hylomar) to use sparingly on both sides of the gasket during reassembly.

Screaming

6-3-1 Screaming noises usually signal a bearing is seizing. If you have an alternator (cars made after 1968) and the ignition light is on, then that will be where the problem lays. However, late cars with electric fans (1976 rubber-bumper cars) can generate a very similar sound when the front fan bearing seizes. You can tell from the driver's seat where the problem is and whether to drive home - for the fan will only shout when the car needs to cool down and can probably be driven home provided the engine is not overheating. If it's the alternator the noise will be pretty consistent and raise in intensity when you increase the revs: this problem is best fixed before you try to drive home.

Tinkling

6-4-1 As unlikely as this may sound, owners of chrome-bumpered cars generating a "tinkling" sound from the front of the engine will almost certainly find the four rubber fan mountings have perished. The noise is harmless, if irritating, and caused by the fan touching the four central tubular spacers as it revolves. You need to unbolt the fan, replace the four grommet-like rubber cushions around the fan's hub.

Tapping or rattling (from front of engine)

6-5-1 On the other hand tapping or rattling (but not "tinkling") at the front of the engine suggests a worn timing chain and/or sprockets. I personally would fix this problem as soon as I identified it, for worn timing gear means that the relationship between the camshaft and the crankshaft can never be consistent or held to the optimum for maximum engine performance. If the engine is otherwise sound, I would recommend getting the timing cover off and fitting a new chain and tensioner while simultaneously assessing the wear on the sprockets.

6-5-1 This section through the front of an MGB engine shows the timing chain, which does stretch and wear. The sprockets also wear, resulting in a loose chain and the noise described in the main text. You can also see the inside of the water pump in this picture.

Ticking (from cylinder block)

6-6-1 A centrally located rapid "ticking" noise at idle could be altogether more serious. It will be hard to pin down precisely, but if it appears to be fairly central and regular at about five to ten times per second you could have a broken piston ring or a worn piston/bore causing "piston-slap". You may hear better and even pin the location down more closely by using a screwdriver as a sort of stethoscope: place the blade against the engine block and your ear against the handle. Listen to the engine with your 'stethoscope' as it idles (**Warning!** - Keep your head and the screwdriver well away from all moving parts). The noise may well increase in rapidity as the engine speed increases slightly, but will then disappear as the engine rpm increases. This is not a problem you want to leave for too long before at least removing the cylinder head to inspect the piston crowns and bores. Unfortunately this may tell you very little for the broken ring, if there is one, may not be visible. However it could be the top ring on one piston, in which case you'll see it or it could be that it has already scored

the bore of the effected cylinder and you'll certainly see that. The removal of the head will enable you to assess the wear on the cylinder bores and/or any play between pistons and bores which may be the cause of the noise and be an important factor in deciding your remedial policy. A major step at the top of each bore and lots of piston movement tells you that there is significant bore wear present and that you're unlikely to get out of the current problem by just fitting new piston rings. On the other hand a small hardly noticeable step (which you may get a local garage or friend to measure for you), and no significant bore scoring, could mean that you only need new piston rings to get out of your immediate problem. If significant bore wear or scoring is present then a replacement engine via one of several routes seems unavoidable. Little bore wear, piston movement and no bore scoring gives you the option of removing the sump, releasing the big-ends,

6-6-1 Piston rings: the majority of MGB engines have 3 compression rings and one (wider) oil control ring lower down each piston.

removing the the pistons/conn-rods, fitting new piston rings with a step manufactured in the top ring, fitting new big-end bearing shells and reassembling. You then need a de-coke gasket set for the cylinder head

6-7-1 Adjusting valve number 4 tells us, using the rule of 9, that the very next valve (number 5) must be fully open. If you look closely, you can see that the rocker arm is depressed and the valve spring compressed.

and if the head has not been fitted with hardened inserts to allow the use of unleaded fuel, this could be the time to deal with that issue too. More on that subject in 6-7.

Rattling or ticking (from top of engine)

6-7-1 A constant and rapid rattle at the very top of the engine almost certainly signifies that the valve clearances ("tappets") need adjusting. The workshop manual will explain how this is achieved and the clearances required, so I'll confine my remarks to advice on the actual adjusting -

• It's best to do the adjustment with the engine cold, but do ensure the clearances you set are those for a cold engine.

• Use the "rule of 9" to find which valve clearance to adjust. The "rule of 9" works like this, let's say you wish to start at the front by adjusting the clearance between the first valve and its rocker (the very front "tappet" of eight). To adjust any tappet you **must** ensure the valve beneath it is fully closed. You can do this by ensuring that the rocker arm/valve (tappet) that adds up to 9 is fully open. So using the 9 rule, 9 minus 1 (the tappet we are about to adjust) equals 8 - in other words the 8th valve must be open to allow us to adjust the clearance of number one valve properly. Get the car on level ground, or on a slight downward slope, and switch-off the ignition. Pop it into third gear and get a partner to let the handbrake off and push the car forward until number eight valve has been pushed fully down by its rocker. Handbrake on, and adjust number one tappet. Handbrake off, roll the car slowly forward until number 7 valve is fully depressed and put the handbrake on. By the "rule of 9" we know that 9 minus 7 allows us to adjust number 2 tappet with confidence. Proceed with the "rule of 9" until all tappets have been adjusted.

• Ideally, refit the rocker cover with a new gasket, but I must admit I rarely bother with the new gasket unless the original one has cracked/broken.

Not forgetting to select neutral, try the engine. Don't panic if she still rattles a little bit on start-up, the real test is whether the engine rattles when hot. The rattle should at least have decreased. If the engine still rattles a little there is probably no real problem, for the MGB engine has a reputation for tappet noise. Indeed, you can buy a cast aluminium rocker cover that not only looks better than the original pressing but also reduces the almost inevitable tappet rattle. However if the engine rattles as badly as ever, you need to read on ...

6-8-1 A rattling or ticking noise that remains even with the tappets are correctly gapped and whether the car is static or on the road can signal worn cam followers

or a worn camshaft. Further diagnose this problem by placing a 0.010in feeler between each rocker and valve stem in turn with the rocker cover off and the engine idling. The ticking will stop with the feeler in place and restart when you withdraw it if your engine is suffering from these problems.

6-9-1 If the engine still has very noisy top end even after adjusting the tappets, the engine probably has a worn rocker shaft and/or worn rockers. As you may have guessed, it is not the valve contact faces of the rockers that have worn, but rather the rocker bores such that they are slopping about and thus rattling on the (probably also worn) shaft on which they pivot. This would not be an unusual problem by any means.

To check, remove the rocker cover, the four retaining nuts and remove the rocker shaft assembly complete. Each rocker should pivot on the shaft without restriction but there should be no obvious clearance between any rocker and its shaft. In this circumstance you should expect to find several if not all rockers can be moved up/down on the shaft signifying excessive clearance between rockers and shaft due to wear.

You can buy all of the rocker/shaft components individually, but if most of

6-10-1 An example of AWAs (Anti-wear additives) intended to reduce valve seat recession (VSR). The bottle is squeezed until the top measuring part (arrowed) is filled.

the rockers are worn the simplest and most cost-effective solution is to purchase a complete new assembly. There are two types of rocker pillar - with a central oil passage or an offset one: check which you require before ordering.

6-10-1 If tappet rattle returns or increases within a relatively short distance (say 3 or 4000 miles) of adjusting the valve clearances the engine could, in these days of lead-free fuels, be suffering from valve seat recession (VSR) and you need to be alert to this possibility. While this does not help those readers outside the UK, nevertheless many may be interested, even surprised to learn that leaded petrol is still available from certain retailers around the UK and that the list is growing all the time. The coverage is national and there should be at least one source in every reasonably sized town. If this interests you and is a potential solution to your VSR, take a look at <www.bayfordthrust.co.uk>. The first corrective step is to re-adjust the tappets and, I suggest, you make a note somewhere as to the recorded mileage. If you're fairly sure that the car's cylinder head has not been modified for the use

6-9-1 The rocker shaft and bearing (arrowed) that eventually wears. The shaft and this bearing work under the constant upward pressure of the valve springs, so some wear is inevitable over time. Not related, but also highlighted is a valve seat: these need to be harder in an engine using unleaded fuels (see 6-10-1).

of lead-free fuel, you should either switch to leaded fuel or, if this is not practical, select one particular additive and add the recommended dose to each tankful of lead-free fuel you buy. Unless you drive the car very hard, you should find the VSR (valve seat recession) is now minimal and your tappet adjustment interval extended to at least 12,000 miles. If you're not familiar with these additives a summary of the situation may help. No additive will protect the cylinder head or perform as well as leaded fuels. The additives (full name is Anti Wear Additives or AWAs) will be most effective in light to normal driving conditions. Sodium, phosphorous, potassium and manganese components form the basis of the majority of these additives that will, unless you drive fairly hard, add years to the life of your current cylinder head. **Caution!** - Use a reputable make and **always** stick to the same brand. **Never** mix any additive with leaded or lead replacement (known as "LRP" in the UK) - more in a moment - fuels. Numerous products have undergone tests at the Motor Industry Research Association (MIRA) and, at the time of writing, eight were declared as having met the pre-set valve seat recession criteria. No doubt additional successful products will come to the market but at the time of writing they were confined to -

Additives With Octane Boosters
(Treatment costs about 8 pence per Imperial gallon of fuel in UK)
- Millers VSP-Plus
- Castrol Valvemaster Plus
- Nitrox 4-Lead

Additives Without Octane Boosters
(Treatment costs about 3 to 4 pence per Imperial gallon of fuel in the UK)
- Red Line Lead Substitute
- Superblend Zero Lead 2000
- Castrol Valvemaster
- Nitrox 4-Star
- GTA Power Plus Formula 2000

There's no point buying the more expensive product with octane booster, but if your car needs the higher octane rating of Super Unleaded fuels (see fault 6-12-1: Anti-run-on valves), you may find a cost saving is possible by using standard unleaded 95 RON fuel with the octane boosting additive. Most makers claim that the octane booster increases ratings by 2 or 3 points which takes the resulting combination to (virtually) the octane rating of leaded fuel. Once you've started to use

a lead substitute product, regularly check tappet clearances and keep a record of any adjustments necessary until confident that VSR is minimal.

Lead replacement petrol (LRP) is also available in the UK, and this product took over most of the UK's "Four Star" (leaded fuel) pumps in autumn (fall) 1999. To the best of my knowledge, no fuel manufacturer has submitted a sample of their LRP fuel to MIRA for VSR tests.

6-11-1 If you drive your MGB with some vigour, and/or cover significant distances on motorways/interstates, the tappets will need frequent adjustment because VSR is, even with regular use of AWAs, continuing to happen under these driving conditions. It's unlikely that an MGB will run indefinitely on unleaded fuels without some modification, anyway, though this is usually necessary later rather than sooner and, in one or two cases, not at all.

It'll be necesssary to retard the timing immediately the change is made from

6-11-1 The cutter can be seen forming number 2 cylinder's exhaust valve recess, while, in the foreground, the result of number 1 machining can be seen.

6-11-2 In the foreground the insert has been machined flush with the combustion chamber, while the next insert is being machined to the profile of the exhaust valves.

leaded to unleaded fuel. The need for more frequent tappet adjustment is an irritation, but so what? Tappet adjustment takes but an hour from start to finish, and if you're covering only 5000 miles a year, an annual tappet adjustment will be all that's required.

You won't be causing irreparable damage to the engine, or running the risk of needing a new and very expensive cylinder head. When the head eventually needs modification, the valve seats that have been recessing due to the use of unleaded fuels will be machined out and replaced with hardened inserts.

This procrastination doesn't apply, however, if a cylinder head refurbishment or engine rebuild is required for other reasons, such as a de-coke or broken valve spring, or an engine rebuild, when it makes no sense to put an unmodified head back in place. Nothing less than an unleaded head conversion will do in this case.

Many automotive machine shops can create the cavity and insert a hardened valve seat insert at each exhaust valve position in the cylinder head. Have new OE valves or special 'unleaded' valves with hard chrome flashed stems fitted and phosphor bronze valve guides.

The moral of this story is: don't rush to spend your money; wait until it's necessary or the engine is dismantled for other reasons.

Popping and banging after ignition switched off (running-on)
6-12-1 The noise that an engine makes when "running-on" is very hard to describe: there will be a very distinct misfire accompanied by the most violent shuddering of the whole car. Running-on only occurs when the ignition is switched off, when, instead of gently stopping, the engine seems to go into convulsions. This usually continues for only a few seconds but occasionally it will be longer.

This problem never occurs with modern, fuel injected cars, because the injectors cease to operate once the ignition is off. Cars like MGBs have a reservoir of fuel in the carburettor float chambers, so air drawn through the carbs by the still-running engine will continue to carry fuel to the cylinders for quite some time. Probably longer than you can tolerate before you're forced to stall the engine via the transmission.

Fuel octane rating might be the cause of run-on. Alternatively, the cylinder head may be in need of a de-coke, or the

6-12-1 This anti-run-on valve is used in several applications. Here, we see its preferred vertical installation in a TR6. Fit the valve anywhere that allows you to route a vacuum pipe from the valve to the inlet manifold. The essential electrical supply should be controlled by the ignition switch.

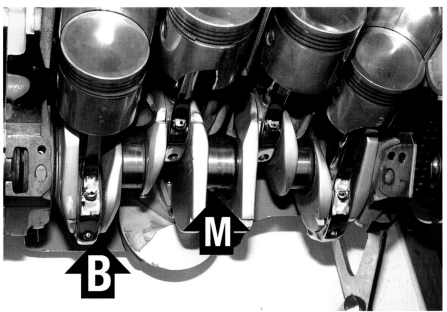

6-13-1 A later "5-bearing" MGB engine. Properly maintained with regular oil and filter changes, the crankshaft bearings will last for tens of thousands of miles. However, when they do show signs of wear, the main bearings (arrowed "M") and the big-ends (arrowed "B") need attention. In an engine that has covered many miles, it's rarely practical to simply replace these (shell) bearings; all of the bearing journals should be reground and replacement shell bearings - sized accordingly - fitted.

sparkplugs may be long overdue for replacement: both these problems can create carbon deposits that glow red hot igniting the mixture in the cylinders randomly.

If your 'B is running-on, switch to super unleaded fuel (usually 97 octane), or use an octane boosting AWA. If the sypmtoms persist, try fitting anti-run-on valves. These electro-magnetic valves close when the ignition is on and are ineffective in that mode. However, they are coupled into the inlet manifold and, as soon as the ignition is switched off the valve(s) automatically open and allow air into the inlet manifold. This dilutes the fuel/air mixture to the point where the engine has insufficient fuel to run. The accompanying photograph shows two anti-run-on valves which are available from Rover dealers, the MGOC and most MG specialists at about £35 each (the part number is ADU9535). They were fitted as standard to all MG Metro 1300s, as well as most other Metro models, should your local spares/parts department need a model to refer to. Initially try one valve, which will usually do the trick, but resort to two if necessary.

If the problem still persists, look for other reasons, such as compression ratio in excess of 9.5:1.

Owners of US cars (fitted with emission control equipment) should read 15-4-6.

Loud tapping (and low oil pressure)

6-13-1 A noise variously described as tapping, rattling, thumping, hammering

or knocking, and not dissimilar to the pinging sound caused by pre-ignition, probably signals worn connecting-rod "big-end" bearings. If the oil pressure is below 50psi at, or above 50mph, and you experience a very pronounced metallic rattle from the engine during acceleration you can be virtually certain that the crankshaft and all the main and big-end bearings require replacement - preferably before irreparable damage occurs: this problem needs immediate attention. This is a major 'engine-out' repair; consider buying an exchange-reconditioned engine from a reputable supplier.

6-13-2 Any knocking or thumping noise from within the engine is unlikely to be easily corrected and is best listened to via a screwdriver used as a 'stethoscope'(tip on the engine block, your ear against the handle): **Caution!** - keep your head, hair and clothing away from all moving parts. The usual noise from seriously worn big-end bearings is a regular heavy knocking occuring about five times per second on tickover. You obviously cannot use your 'stethoscope' to confirm this next point but, while driving, do you think the severity of the knocking reduces when the engine is

under load and increases while the engine is less heavily loaded? If so, it's very likely that a big end has "run" in one of the connecting-rods.

To get you home, remove the HT lead/wire from one sparkplug at a time until you find the one that reduces the knocking. Thereafter, leave that plug disconnected and proceed home or to the nearest garage very carefully. **Caution!** - If the bearing seizes on the crankshaft the engine may be ruined, particularly if the connecting rod breaks.

All is not necessarily lost if a bearing "runs" (starts to melt). I've recovered a big end *in situ*. You'll need to drop the sump and undo the cap from the offending connecting-rod. Push the piston up the bore a bit to give yourself room and take a look at the crankshaft journal. Initially it will probably look horrible, with a build-up of bearing-shell material which you'll need to carefully remove using a very narrow strip of medium emery cloth. If this idea frightens you, consider that you probably have very little to lose - a damaged crankshaft journal will have to be reground. Further, any material you remove will be the soft deposit from the bearing shell rather than the hard crankshaft surface - so emery away until you either have the whole journal scrupulously clean or can see it is hopelessly scored and irrecoverable - in which case start thinking about a replacement engine or a major rebuild.

Assuming you have been lucky and the surface of the journal looks smooth, you now need to check it for ovality using a micrometer. If it's oval by much more than "one thou" (1 thousanth of an inch) you're probably looking at a short-term solution and should consider this next step in that context. You may decide that although the journal cleaned up OK the life of the repair is such that a replacement engine makes more sense. If, however, the car is used infrequently, rarely hammered and is your second car, then I suggest you buy a set of replacement shells of the correct size and fit one pair to this big end (in fact, you might as well do the rest at the same time). The backs of the shells you've removed should carry the size and part number - take them with you to your auto-parts supplier. Do change the oil filter and clean the sump out before bolting everything back together and refill the sump with best quality oil. The engine may go for thousands of miles thereafter - mine did...

Rumble from deep in engine (and low oil pressure)

6-14-1 A constant rumbling sound, possibly getting worse when the engine is under load, suggests the main bearings supporting the crankshaft are worn. Early MGB engines (up to October 1964) had only three, but from about halfway through the chrome-bumper production run, and thereafter, five main bearings were introduced to advantage.

6-14-1 (Picture 1) The usual remedy for an engine with worn bearings is to remove it from the car to allow crankshaft removal. Note that it is not necessary to strip all the ancillaries from the engine before lifting it out...

6-14-1 (Picture 2) ...although it's probably best to withdraw the gearbox simultaneously with the engine. The oil pressure relief valve position is arrowed.

6-14-1 (Picture 3) Take this opportunity to repair/replace components that are now easily accessible. For example, a new clutch would be a good idea.

In all probability the oil pressure will be low if the mains are seriously worn. The rotating nature of the crankshaft in its main bearings means that generally all the main bearings are going to be roughly equally worn and you'll be prudent to be considering a replacement engine unless you act quickly. The benefit of early remedial action is that your car's current engine can almost certainly be reconditioned. The danger of procrastination is that the oil pressure will drop to the point where damage occurs throughout the engine because of inadequate lubrication.

Rattle during deceleration

6-15-1 A rattle only noticeable when decelerating is caused by worn or loose gudgeon pins (aka: piston pins/wrist pins) - the pins that connect the connecting-rod to the piston. The only practical repair is to fit new pistons and you can do this without removing the engine, provided the cylinder bores are not unduly worn.

6-15-1 The gudgeon (piston) pin passes through the piston (arrowed "1"), through the little-end (small-end) bearing in the connecting-rod and through the opposite side of the piston. Note, too, the sectioned main bearing shell (arrowed "2").

Whistling or wheezing

6-16-1 Whistling or wheezing noises need to be investigated quickly because the noise could be the consequence of a blown head gasket. Check whether there is oil in the coolant and/or vice-versa, and consider whether the car's been losing either fluid. Less serious, and more probable, is that you're hearing air being drawn into a partial vacuum area (eg: the brake servo hose or inlet manifold); a vacuum hose may have split, the carburettor or manifold gasket could be leaking, or air can even be drawn in through worn carburettor butterfly spindle/bush. A leak in the servo system could reduce your braking capability, while any of the other problems will introduce a lean mixture to the engine, raising temperatures and possibly burning valves.

If you suspect the hose leading to the servo, for the cost involved, replace it (note that they do, eventually, become, for want of a better word, porous). Certainly any surface cracks need to be taken seriously and the pipe replaced if you enjoy the assistance that the servo gives you when braking!

Leaking carburettoror inlet manifold gaskets may not have quite the same safety connotations, but for the reasons already stated are best identified and resolved. With the engine set to a fast tickover (say about 900/1000rpm), spray an aerosol of carburettor cleaner onto each point where you think a leak could be occurring. Do not spray over too large an area but use a progressive, focused method - listening for a change in engine note as you spray each individual area. No change in engine note suggests no leak but a slight drop (accompanied incidentally by a slightly darker exhaust for a second or two) will identify the joint to strip down and repair.

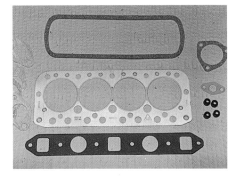

6-16-1 Don't forget that appropriate gaskets are required on reassembly if the cylinder head is removed. This is a typical "top-end" gasket set, you'll need the MGB equivalent of this. The manifold gasket is at the bottom of the picture.

6-16-2 Whistling or wheezing noises confined to idle/tickover or when decelerating but that disappear when accelerating is caused by an induction vacuum leak. With the engine running at idle/tickover speed, spray carburettor cleaner on each joint (one at a time) in the induction system - *e.g.* the carburettors/spacers, spacers/heatshield, heatshield/manifold, manifold/cylinder head. Any air induction will be identified by a change the idle speed when the cleaner finds the weak spot. **Caution!** - Don't spray carb cleaner onto a Stromberg diaphragm - it'll destroy it!

6-17-1 In America it's called "pinging," which I think is more appropriate than "pinking," which is what the particular noise is called in the UK. Both terms are intended to describe the innocuous sounding pinging noise (a light metallic rattle) that the engine can make during acceleration and when the fuel/air mixture is igniting prematurely ("pre-ignition") in the combustion chambers.

You need to give this noise your serious attention because, in extreme cases, pre-ignition will be eroding small pieces of aluminium from the pistons with eventual dire consequences.

Over-advanced timing is often the cause of pre-ignition so, without delay, if you notice pre-ignition noises (particularly if you've recently done anything that could have affected ignition timing), check the timing or, better yet, get it checked by a professional. The static advance will vary depending on the engine, compression ratio, fuel and distributor, so I cannot give you a definite figure, but if the setting in use is more than 10-11 degrees BTDC then something is amiss.

Carbon build-up in the combustion chambers, on the piston crowns and on old sparkplugs is probably the next most frequent reason for pre-ignition. A "de-coke" (removal of carbon from combustion chambers and piston crowns) may be necessary or, perhaps, just new sparkplugs. Before removing the cylinder head, checkout these other possibilities -

• The carburettor is worn or badly set-up. Check the throttle spindles in particular for serious wear.

• The distributor is worn. Check for excessive spindle movement, the vacuum diaphragm, that the mechanical advance is not seized and that the return springs are not stretched or loose.

6-17-1 With the distributor on or off the car, strip it to this point to check that the spindle (arrow "1") has little or no sideways play, the vacuum diaphragm (arrow "2") responds to sucking, the advance weights (arrow "3") move freely, the return springs (arrow "4") are not floppy and thus in need of replacement.

Popping or loud bangs from exhaust

6-18-1 Exhaust popping/backfiring on over-run is caused by incomplete combustion: check ignition timing/ignition system/mixture controls. The popping will be exacerbated by a hole or badly-fitting pipe within the exhaust system or, in the USA, a faulty gulp valve.

6-19-1 You may hear a strange noise from a cracked heatshield. However, this immaculate 'B has a new one fitted.

Sizzling noise

6-19-1 A sizzling noise from twin carburettor cars that's only present at medium to higher rpm (whether the car's static or in motion) is most likely caused by a cracked carburettor heatshield. If your car's is indeed cracked, weld repair the original or replace it with a new component.

Jingling or thumping from beneath car

6-20-1 Jingling noises are usually the result of loose exhaust system clamps, a thumping sound the consequence of interference between the exhaust system

6-20-1 You're probably familiar with exhaust clamps, but have you thought of fitting them with the tails of the U-bolt pointing upward? Ground clearance will be improved by this simple trick.

and the underside of the car. These noises may only occur at a particular range of engine rpm, but will be in evident whether the car is in motion or at rest.

Loud exhaust noises from beneath car or engine compartment

6-21-1 Assuming your MGB's exhaust system is not holed by corrosion, and bearing in mind that, today, most systems comprise up to four pieces, exhaust "blows" are most likely to occur at the joints between the sections. Sometimes

6-21-1 You may have noted the liberal use of an exhaust sealer in picture 6-20-1. This will ensure you only have to do the job once.

components are not fully mated, leaving a small hole each side where the slots in one of the male pipe joints has not been completely covered. Overtightened clamps can distort pipe joints and cause leakage too.

It makes assembly slightly messier, but will probably save future problems if you smear exhaust assembly paste around each joint before putting the pieces together. A leaking joint can be rectified by the same treatment, although it will be necessary to disassemble it before applying the paste to ensure a proper seal . Exhaust clamps do ease off around 200-300 miles after installation and need to be checked and, if necessary, retightened.

6-21-2 The twin sealing rings that seal the joints between the exhaust pipes and the standard cast iron exhaust manifold can leak, especially if old. They can be removed (with difficulty), and should be renewed whenever you separate their joints or if a leak is occuring. At the same time clean around the recessed seats in the manifold with medium sand or emery paper to present the new seals with smooth seats to minimise the possibility of leaks. The new sealing rings have one metal and one textured face, but I've never met anyone who knows which way they are supposed to be fitted. I've always fitted the metal face to the exhaust pipe (i.e. the fibre to the manifold), but also used a smear of paste on the mating faces for insurance.

The joint between pipe and manifold is difficult to get at and needs to be tightened evenly and fully if you're to enjoy leak-free longevity. You **must** use six **brass** nuts on the manifold studs (new ones are a good idea in order to avoid the

6-21-2 These metal/fibre rings seal the exhaust manifold to the exhaust pipes. They should be renewed each time the joints are disturbed along with a set of six brass nuts. Caution! - don't fit steel nuts, you'll never get them off.

frustration of finally tightening the last one only to have it strip!) If the thread on any of the manifold studs is looking less than pristine, the stud is best renewed.

6-21-3 There were two types of cast exhaust manifolds - those with thick and those with thin flanges. In itself this is of little consequence, but if you have an early car with a thick flange the inlet manifold will have a correspondingly thick flange. So, say your exhaust manifold studs are stripped, or broken and you spot a good secondhand exhaust manifold at an autojumble, you do need to ensure that the flange thickness is the same as the old one. Get it wrong and the nuts/washers that hold both inlet and exhaust manifolds in place will not lay flat against the flanges and clamp them to the head properly. Furthermore, if you have a late car with a thin flange and try to fit a thick flanged manifold in its place, you'll find the studs are too short too. Incidentally, you can get your favourite spares specialist to re-stud your exhaust manifold if the six bottom studs are past it.

Chapter 7
Engine oil pressure low, filter upgrade & oil loss

Oil pressure reading low

An MGB engine in good condition will have 60-70psi of oil pressure while cruising with about 3500rpm showing on the tachometer (rev-counter). This pressure drops dramatically when the engine is idling, but is not a matter of concern provided the it swiftly rebuilds to at least 50psi as the engine revs increase. An oil pressure reading of below 50psi at, say, 3000rpm, should cause concern about the general condition of the engine - if the reading is accurate.

If the oil pressure suddenly reads lower the problem requires immediate investigation.

7-1-1 The oil pressure gauge could be faulty, telling you that you have a major problem when you don't.

Some US cars have both an oil pressure gauge and a warning light. In most circumstances this duplication is of little value, but should the oil pressure gauge reading suddenly drop to a low or even zero reading, or the warning light illuminate, a useful means of cross checking is immediately available. If the gauge and light warn of low oil pressure, stop immediately and investigate.

Two types of oil pressure gauge have been used in the MGB. All the chrome bumper and early rubber bumper cars had oil pressure and water temperature gauges combined within one instrument (both parts of the gauge operated mechanically).

7-1-1 (Picture 1) A oil-pressure/water temperature gauge. The top half of the gauge is devoted to oil pressure: this engine looks in excellent shape, although has yet to warm up, so the pressure may drop slightly. These oil pressure gauges can be susceptible to the capillary pipe in the engine bay corroding/fracturing.

From the introduction of the rubber bumper cars the water temperature gauge (see chapter 18) and oil pressure gauge became separate units - the oil pressure gauge still being operated mechanically. The oil pressure gauge is actuated by the oil pressure in a pipe that runs up to the instrument panel from just behind the distributor. This pipe couples at the top of the footwell into a steel capillary tube that runs up to the rear of the gauge where its connection is sealed by a tiny leather sealing washer. If any part of this pipeline should break or become uncoupled, an oil leak will develop at that point and the gauge will give a low reading, or register zero if the leak is severe.

You must correct this fault before continuing your journey to avoid engine damage due to a lack of oil. If the capillary pipe has cracked your get-you-home solution will be to cut the line at the crack, fold the end (engine side of the pipe) over and clinch it as tight as you can with a pair of pliers or Mole (vise) grips.

7-1-1 (Picture 2) The vulnerable steel capillary pipe that runs from the junction of the flexible pipe to the oil pressure gauge. It rusts and sometimes is not clipped securely to the top of the footwell, so vibrates, wears and breaks. Here, you may just see the arrowed stub of the rusted and broken capillary pipe.

7-2-1 There are several points at which the oil pipes to and from the oil cooler can leak, causing a drop in oil level and/or pressure. Where they pass through the radiator diaphragm is the most vulnerable spot. The grommets are hard to fit, so often the pipe is left to rub against the sharp edge of the diaphragm. Take a good look at these pipes when next you check the coolant level in the radiator.

7-2-1 For cars without a dual oil pressure-gauge and light for cross checking, you have to assume the worst if the oil pressure gauge reading suddenly falls with the engine running. Switch off the engine immediately.

Wait for five minutes or so - longer if you can - and look under the engine, particularly under the oil cooler and hoses leading from the engine to the cooler. If you see any oil leaks investigate further; it could be that an oil cooler pipe has chafed through or the oil cooler has sprung a leak. If this is the case your get-you-home method will be to remove the good pipe from the oil cooler (**Caution!** - with great care as it is very easy to damage/destroy the oil cooler) and reconnect it to the engine, bypassing the cooler and damaged hose.

7-3-1 Check the oil level on the dipstick and, if below the "low" mark, top up the oil level in the sump (oil pan) before starting the engine again.

7-3-1 The oil level dipstick, seen here in the sentre of the shot, is known to all. Less well known is the oil pressure gauge take-off point, which is nicely shown here. The flexible part of the capillary line is also in view in the bottom left of the picture. This engine is most of the way out of the car, being removed from the underside of the chassis.

7-4-1 If the oil level was correct and you found no signs of an oil leak, think about when the engine oil and filter were last changed. If the oil or filter have not been changed in accordance with the car's recommended service intervals, or an incorrect filter has been fitted, loss of pressure could be due to a blocked oilway, bypass valve or oil pick-up (in the sump/oil pan).

In this situation start by changing the oil and filter which, in the majority of cases, will improve the pressure. **Caution!** - Don't run the engine for too long if the pressure does not rise above 50psi almost immediately. In this event, remove the sump, which - fortunately - can be done with the engine in the car. Check and clean the mesh on the pick-up and, for a cost of around £30, fit a new oil pump after cleaning as much of the revealed oilways as you can access when the old pump is removed.

7-5-1 If the oil pressure has been low for some time, but you're fairly certain that the engine is not seriously worn, consider the oil pressure relief valve. I once fitted a reconditioned engine to my MGB GT and was very upset to find the oil pressure hardly exceeded 50psi. I called the reconditioner and established that they rarely fitted a new oil pump or pressure relief valve (there's a lesson here). However, instead of trying the easy solution first, I dropped the sump and replaced the pump - to no benefit whatsoever! At much less cost, I then replaced the pressure relief valve by unscrewing the dome-shaped cap from the left rear of the engine's crankcase (just in front of the backplate) - with a resulting increase in pressure to 70psi!

7-5-2 If the oil pressure reading seems to pulsate, the problem could be caused by a weak pressure relief valve spring or worn seating. The solution is to replace the spring and cone as explained

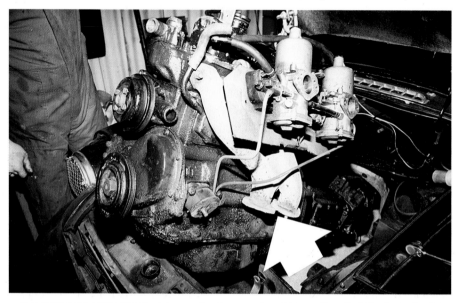

7-5-2 The pressure relief spring and valve aare here, beneath a slightly domed nut.

in 7-5-1. You'll see the location of the pressure relief valve arrowed in the accompanying picture.

7-6-1 If the oil pressure has been low for some time it's most likely because of general engine wear, hopefully after long and faithful service. Low oil pressure at tickover (idle) in a high mileage engine is not a cause for concern provided that the pressure increases to at least 50psi as engine revs increase.

There's little you can do to compensate for worn mains or big-end bearings. You can try fitting a new oil pump, pressure relief valve and rocker assembly, all of which are reasonably easily reached, and refilling the sump with a thicker grade of oil to perhaps extend the life of a tired engine for a while. The real solution, however, is refurbishment at least of the bottom end, or fit an exchange "short" engine.

Oil loss (without exhaust smoke)

7-7-1 There are several non-critical points at which an MGB engine will leak oil and, of course, low oil level can induce low oil pressure. You do not need to set too high a standard, particularly for the early 3-Bearing engines.

The front seal within the timing chain cover is a popular spot and should cause you to check that the crankcase vent/breathing arrangement is open and working.

Beneath the exhaust manifold there are two oblong cam follower covers sealed against the crankcase by a rubber gasket. Unfortunately, the area gets hotter than most other engine parts and the gaskets perish quickly and leak oil.

Oil dripping from the bellhousing drain hole is most probably from the engine; the rear crankshaft seal, to be specific. The three-bearing engines originally fitted up until the late 1960s had only a "scroll" arrangement designed to 'screw' escaping oil back into the crankcase. It performed poorly, as do all such designs, regardless of engine manufacturer, and was replaced by the much more effective rubber "lip" seal in five-bearing engines. When regrinding the bearing journals, the scroll can be ground off the rear of the earlier crankshaft and the much more effective lip seal fitted, but the crankshaft has to be removed from the engine to do this.

Oil filter upgrade

7-8-1 The early paper/felt element oil filter arrangement used on the first hanging

design (superseded in 1968) and second (upright) design of oil filter arrangement are best upgraded. Whilst the former designs represented the latest technology in the 1960s, they're prone to leaks and are certainly unavoidably messy when it comes to changing oil filters.

With the introduction of the 18V series of engines these filters were superseded by two disposable canister designs where the modern canister filter is screwed onto an aluminium filter housing. This housing was, in turn, mounted to the original fixing point cast into the side of the block and, once fitted, the housing did not move for the life of the engine.

The first filter had a very accessible upright disposable canister arrangement mounted on housing number "12H3273." The disposable filter stands up alongside the distributor and is very easy to get at for oil changes. However, it does little to reduce the messiness of oil changes as the oil escapes as the filter is undone. More importantly, the inverted attitude of the canister allows oil to escape to the sump (oil pan) while the engine is at rest, so each time the engine is restarted there's a few moments' delay before oil pressure is built up.

The final hanging disposable canister filter arrangement is the best and utilises housing number "12H4405." You should

7-7-1 Typical crankshafts. One with the original "scroll" seal (bottom) and one modified ready for a split "lip" seal (top). These are actually Triumph crankshafts from the same era as the MGB's and using the same ineffective rear scroll oil retention arrangement. Later five-bearing MGB cranks require no such modification.

7-8-1 (Picture 1) Very early MGB engines were fitted with a felt filter contained in this filter case. Note the oil cooler take-off at the top of the filter case, and how the crankcase was cast and machined to accept the oil filter at this point. While not the worst of filter arrangements, this design did make changing filters a messy business and, from the "18GD" engine, it was superseded by that shown in photo 7-8-1 (Picture 2).

7-8-1 (Picture 2) The penultimate oil filter arrangement for the MGB engine. Very accessible indeed; you could do worse than upgrade to this type of filter and fixing. However, the final design with this type of canister filter pointing downwards was unquestionably the best of the lot, even though it is less easily reached than this one.

have little difficulty getting hold of a second-hand final oil filter mounting housing, so make this upgrade when you next change the engine oil. You may find that the later canister filters are more readily available and cheaper too.

Oil consumption high (with exhaust smoke)

7-9-1 High oil consumption after changing to a synthetic oil. It's unwise to run an engine on normal mineral oils for tens of thousands of miles and then switch to a synthetic oil, particularly one that is high in cleaning additives (as most are).

I use carefully chosen synthetic oils suited to basic engines in all my classic cars, and believe in their benefits.

However, the individual engines were only introduced to synthetic oil after a major engine rebuild and after about 9000 miles 'running/breaking-in;' in other words, after the high spots within the engine had been smoothed off but before the engine had had an opportunity to severely "coke-up."

If your car's engine has become nicely coked on mineral oils and you introduce it to a synthetic oil high in scouring and cleaning additives, all of the carbon coated seals between pistons, rings and bores will be cleaned away, and the inside of the engine will be scoured clean. The result will be that the engine starts to consume oil excessively and puff out blue smoke - and possibly lots of it - from the exhaust. In most cases you'll have done

little permanent damage, but drain the sump and switch back to a good mineral oil as quickly as possible.

The scouring action of some synthetic oils is very effective, and can occasionally release debris, blocking oilways and causing permanent damage to severely "coked" engines.

7-9-2 High oil consumption that is not caused by leakage is almost always due to general engine wear. Worn cylinder bores, piston rings and pistons are the main reason why the engine uses more oil, and can usually be determined by dark exhaust smoke (particularly under hard acceleration), and excessive back pressure in the crankcase. The excessive back pressure can chuff oil fumes out of the crankcase breather or oil filler. A cylinder pressure test will give a clue to the effectiveness of the pistons, rings and bores.

Worn valve stems and guides also cause oil consumption to increase. This problem can occur separately from the worn bore/rings syndrome or simultaneously.

Usually the only remedy is to have the worn part of the engine refurbished; a fully reconditioned warranted engine fitted by a reputable supplier such as the MGOC is the best option. There could be two exceptions. One, if you're fairly sure that it's the valves/guides which are worn (and you'd be surprised just how much they can increase oil consumption), it would be quite in order to refurbish the cylinder head. Don't just fit new valves, do the job properly and have new guides fitted, along with new valves, of course. If you've not already done so, this is clearly the moment to go for an exchange "unleaded" head (to allow the use of unleaded fuel) as described in chapter 6. Two, US cars fitted with a Stromberg carburettor and a crankcase PCV control valve: see 15-4-3.

Chapter 8
Clutch problems

Not every clutch problem requires the engine to be removed but, unfortunately, replacement of the actual clutch cover, friction plate and thrust bearing certainly will. In the majority of other cars you gain accesses the clutch by putting the car on a hoist and dropping the gearbox. Sadly, it's not quite so easy with the MGB in that you have to take the engine out of the car - and it's a heavy "lump" even with many of its ancillaries stripped off. There are those who prefer taking engine and gearbox out in one piece because marrying the engine to an *in situ* gearbox can be a bit of a nightmare. Getting the two bolted together on the garage floor does, therefore have advantages but you've then got a **really** heavy lump of metal to lift to at least 3 feet off the ground. **Warning!** - This task takes care and thought and the right lifting equipment: **never** try lifting an engine using anything other than a proper engine hoist and it really is worth the trouble to buy, make or ask your local scrapyard for a pair of the substantial L-shaped lifting brackets that BMC fitted to the vast majority of its engines ... but not to the MGB!

I don't propose to give a detailed description of removing the engine (a workshop manual will tell you how) other that to say you **must** start by disconnecting the battery. If you have not removed your car's engine before, spend a while looking at its installation: some

forethought will save you a great deal of effort if you can find ways to leave some ancillaries in situ while disconnecting others as one major assembly. A few examples may help - remove the radiator and water pipes as one assembly. Many take the oil filter assembly off the block complete with cooler pipes and tie the lot back out of the way. Of the ancillaries, the starter motor certainly needs removing as does the distributor cap/HT leads. Personally, I always remove the whole distributor to guard against accidental damage, but most would not consider this necessary. For a clutch replacement most would remove the air filters but leave the carburettors and manifolds *in situ* and treat the alternator in the same way.

If you feel that removing the engine yourself for the first time is daunting, either subcontract the job to your nearest MG specialist or seek the help and guidance of someone from your local MG group.

In most area groups there is usually someone with experience who is prepared to point out the "must does" and shortcuts.

Squealing
8-1-1 A squeal that only occurs when the clutch pedal is depressed and which can be even more pronounced when the engine is cold, usually signals a worn, dry

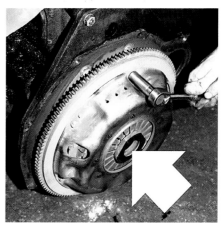

8-1-1 (Picture 2) ...is located deep in the flywheel and will only be accessible with the clutch pressure plate off the flywheel. You can see the very end of the gearbox first-motion (input) shaft that runs in the spigot bush in picture 8-5-1.

8-1-1 (Picture 1) The sintered spigot bush...

or damaged spigot bush in the flywheel.

The gearbox's first-motion shaft sits in the bush and the shaft and bush usually revolve together - until the clutch pedal is depressed when the first-motion shaft should slow, then the noise starts. Although very irritating, spigot bush noise signals nothing too serious, although you'll want to fix it next time the engine and gearbox have to be parted for some other reason.

Replacement is of the bush is covered in the next section but, nevertheless, it's worth mentioning that the bush needs to be soaked in engine oil for 24 hours prior to fitting to prevent it drying out in service. Furthermore, the gearbox is best offered up as straight as possible to the rear of the engine (often easier said than done!) in order to prevent damage to the spigot bush. Many prefer to marry gearbox to engine on the garage floor - and this is certainly one of the reasons why.

Since the spigot is in a blind hole removal requires a little knowhow. Pack the hollow centre of the installed bush with grease and the push a close-fitting dowel, bar or clutch alignment tool into the centre of the bush. If you now hit the other end of the dowel/bar with a hammer, the hydraulic pressure created should force the old bush out of its recess.

Difficult gearchanging/clutch drag

8-2-1 If gearchanging is becoming progressively more difficult, or the engine seems to drive the car when the clutch is disengaged, you could have what is called "clutch-drag". This is where the mechanism that releases the clutch friction disc is failing. First and reverse gears usually become particularly hard to engage, sometimes even grating. It can also be hard to disengage any gear, but especially first and reverse.

There can be internal gearbox faults that make changing gear difficult, but usually the problem's caused by a worn component within the clutch assembly and/or its operating mechanism. I'm sure you'll agree it makes sense to eliminate potential external (hydraulic) problems before removing the engine to fit a new clutch.

Start by checking the fluid level in the clutch master cyclinder reservoir and if it is well above the bottom of the reservoir (as it should be), it may be worth bleeding the hydraulic system, replacing the old fluid as you do so.

8-2-1 (Picture 1) This is one component that can contribute to clutch-drag - the master cylinder. In this case a rubber-bumper car unit with close-coupled brake servo. Chrome-bumper cars have the same clutch master cylinder sitting in a slightly different pedal box.

Hydraulically speaking, there are three components that can be the reason behind inadequate clutch plate separation: the master cylinder, the flexible hose and the slave cylinder. You should start by checking each for fluid leaks and correcting any that you find. When you get down to the slave cylinder area at the bottom of the gearbox's bellhousing, not only check for leaks but also that the bleed nipple is clear and that the flexible hose is not cracked, kinked, pinched or collapsed. If you're in doubt about the health of the

8-2-1 (Picture 2) The flexible hydraulic line (arrowed) which can collapse internally with age and the clutch slave cylinder (which can tire and cause clutch drag). Furthermore...

flexible hose, drain the system of fluid, replace the hose (not a nice job, but preferable to taking the engine out), and remove clean and inspect the slave cylinder. I would, at the very least, fit new seals to the slave cylinder, even if the originals look OK. However, if in doubt, fit a complete replacement slave cylinder and bleed the system using all new fluid.

8-2-1 (Picture 3) ...the clevis pin and arm in the slave cylinder can wear. The hole (arrowed) is slightly oval and will cause loss of movement.

8-3-1 In the absence of an obvious hydraulic problem, in pre-1978 cars there are external (to the gearbox) a group of mechanical components that can, and do, wear which now need to be checked. These components are all located in one place revealed by your removing the pedal box cover.

A few words about removing this cover are appropriate because it can prove

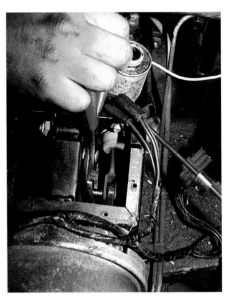

8-3-1 (Picture 1) A worn clevis fork can also cause lost movement in the clutch actuation system. Here, we are withdrawing the pin to check for fork wear...

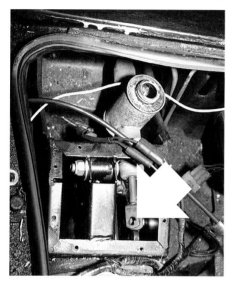

8-3-1 (Picture 2) ...and here is a worn fork. The clevis pin should also be renewed but the problem is that the top hole in the clutch pedal is also likely to have worn and, strictly speaking, should be bushed (the easiest solution) or welded and redrilled to the correct size.

very difficult unless it has been removed fairly recently, or you have a remarkable MGB. The plate is retained around its base by four crosshead screws, most of which are likely to be rusted in place. You should try penetrating oil, but one in particular is very difficult to access: I resort to drilling the heads off at least the two screws that are nearest to the inner wing/fender without much delay. Unfortunately, the news gets worse, for these screws are well down out of reach of a normal drill and I've had to make up a special 5mm drill bit brazed into the end of a length of 10mm rod! The top and sides of the cover are sealed using double-sided rubber strip and once you know this they separate easily using a couple of screwdrivers.

You can now see the three components which need inspection: the cross hole in the top of clutch pedal, the clutch master cylinder's fork and the clevis pin that goes through these parts. If each of these three components is worn by say 1mm then collectively you'll be loosing 1/8in (3mm) at the top of the clutch travel. This is multiplied several fold by the time the movement reaches the clutch plate so it is important to remove as much play (lash) as possible: you should certainly repair or replace the pedal and clevis pin. The fork/clevis on the end of the master

cylinder may be a little more problematic for, although you can get hold of and fit new master cylinder pushrods (which incorporate the fork/clevis), this may be a waste of time if you're going to have to fit a complete new master cylinder. I therefore suggest you leave any wear in the fork/clevis for the time being and reassemble the mechanism to see whether you have virtually cured your problem. If the improvement is indeed dramatic perhaps you should get hold of a new master cylinder pushrod as soon as practicable to eliminate any remaining play.

8-4-1 Assuming you're still not getting the separation needed to eliminate clutch-drag, your next consideration should be the clutch master cylinder itself. You may be influenced by the fact that the gearchange is much improved by your efforts to date but not yet back to how it should be because there's still some play as the result of wear in the master cylinder's fork. It could be worth fitting a new master cylinder in order to remove the remaining play, however, you may care to go for a test run to see if the difficulty of changing gear gets worse/returns when you hold down the clutch pedal for a few moments before putting her into gear. This is best done on the open road or in a car park. It should make little difference to a properly performing hydraulic system - the car should go into gear reasonably easily however long you've had the clutch pedal depressed.

Not so with your car? Try this while stopped somewhere away from other traffic. Depress the clutch and put the car into first gear. Keep the clutch pedal

8-4-1 (Picture 1) If the master cylinder is failing to maintain hydraulic pressure repair kits are available, but my advice is fit a new cylinder. Access to the rear of the master cylinder is through the rectangular opening behind the master cylinder.

8-4-1 (Picture 2) From inside the cockpit remove the hydraulic banjo bolt...

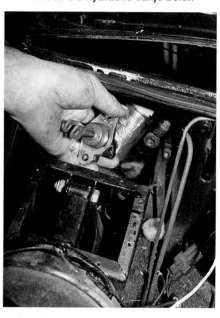

8-4-1 (Picture 3) ...only then is it practical to remove/replace the master cylinder. Note the banjo hanging down just to the right of this new cylinder. This is the rubber bumper master cylinder, but the procedure is just the same for chrome bumper cars.

depressed and wait for up to a minute to see if the clutch engages itself, even with your foot hard down on the clutch pedal. If it does, it means that the clutch master cylinder is bleeding fluid past its internal seal, allowing a reduction in pressure in the hydraulic system and the clutch to engage. Replace at least the seals within the master cylinder using a repair kit. Note that replacement seals only work well some fifty per cent of the time, so you may be better of replacing the master cylinder with a new one, particularly if significant play remains within the cylinder fork/clevis.

8-5-1 If all is not still to your satisfaction, hydraulically and thus externally we have exhausted the possible solutions and need to start thinking about

8-5-1 Unusually, the MGB clutch thrust bearing (arrowed) is made from carbon. Richard Ladds, of MGOC, is pointing to the front of the gearbox input shaft that runs in the spigot bearing. Note the two 'ears' on the carbon thrust carrier? They're clipped in place on the clutch release arm and need a fairly unrestricted pivot to allow the bearing and carrier to move forward squarely to the shaft.

a problem within the bellhousing. The MGB can be more susceptible to internal clutch problems than the majority of cars, at least if the owner habitually holds the clutch pedal down when the car is stationary, say at traffic lights. A roller-type thrust bearing actuates the vast majority of modern clutches and although these do wear and can fail, they rarely wear **down** in the same way as a well used MGB carbon thrust bearing does. The MGB's design incorporates not a roller but a graphite/carbon-faced thrust bearing within the gearbox's bellhousing. This adds another consideration to the usual clutch separation problems since, as I've intimated, the thickness of the bearing reduces with extensive use, with the consequence that there is less material available to separate the clutch plates. In normal use, it must be said that MG got it about right and usually the friction plate is pretty worn by the time that the graphite thrust bearing is worn out. However, although hard to diagnose in isolation, if everything else is in top order yet the clutch is still dragging, a worn graphite thrust bearing becomes the only remaining suspect and it should be replaced. As you will have gathered from the preamble to this chapter, any faulty internal clutch component requires that the engine be removed and, consequently, you should replace the whole three-piece clutch set and take the opportunity to check the

other internal components as explained in the next section.

Clutch slip

8-6-1 If the engine is not always driving the car along consistently, suspect a slipping clutch.

The usual initial symptoms of a slipping clutch are a change in engine note and a corresponding increase in rpm when you accelerate, climb a hill or go round a sharp bend. We need to be sure that these symptoms are only occurring when the overdrive is **not** in use, because there's also a clutch within the overdrive unit which can also slip and exhibit similar symptoms.

Definitely establish whether the symptoms occur **only** when overdrive is engaged (in which case you need to turn to chapter 9), or whether they can be induced by, say, accelerating hard regardless of whether or not overdrive is engaged. In the latter case, read on.

A slipping clutch is often accompanied by a smell like overheated brakes, whereas a slipping overdrive clutch won't smell at all.

If the symptoms of a slipping clutch are present, the clutch friction plate has either worn or become contaminated with oil, and can no longer carry the power from engine to transmission; it will have to be replaced. Don't make the mistake of thinking that the problem will get better, in fact it will get worse until drive is lost completely and the flywheel face may become damaged.

Clutch replacement tips

8-7-1 With the engine out of the car the full extent of the clutch problems should become clear. Regardless of what you find, do fit a full new three-piece clutch set: friction plate, cover plate and carbon thrust ring/bearing: to do otherwise is a false economy.

With the clutch cover removed, check that the friction plate had been installed the right way round. In spite of being stamped "flywheel-side," they do get installed the wrong way round and it would, in one sense, be reassuring to know if this was the reason why the clutch failed.

Check the friction plate for wear. Is the lining worn down to the rivets and, if so, has this resulted in the surface of the flywheel being grooved or crazed? Is the friction plate contaminated with oil and, if so, where did the it come from? If the surface of the flywheel is not perfectly flat

8-7-1 (Picture 1) After you've soaked the spigot bearing and replaced it in the flywheel, fit the friction plate to a clutch alignment tool and push the tool into the new spigot bearing (to keep the friction plate aligned with the spigot bearing, something you'll be *very* grateful for when marrying gearbox to engine!) Then the pressure plate goes on its three dowels arrowed here.

8-7-1 (Picture 2) Tighten the pressure plate bolts *progressively*. Note the engine lifting bracket referred to at the beginning of this chapter.

and free of oil and grease, take this opportunity to fix whatever the problems are in order to provide the clutch friction plate with an appropriate driving surface. A grooved and/or crazed flywheel surface would be the problem I would most expect to find and necessitates marking the position of and removing the flywheel.

Take this opportunity to check other

8-7-1 (Picture 3) Offer gearbox to engine *squarely* so as not to damage the spigot bearing.

8-7-1 (Picture 5) This picture is just a reminder to ensure that the cylinder (hanging loose here) and its flexible hose are in perfect order. There's no better time to replace either or both than when the engine bay is empty.

areas, starting with the inside of the bellhousing. Is it coated in oil? Although much less likely, if oil contaminated the clutch friction plate, it's important to discover how before reassembling the clutch. A leak from either the rear engine seal or front gearbox seal are the most probable causes.

Take a look at the teeth around the circumference of the flywheel. These are where the starter motor engages and, if worn in one position, the best solution will be to order a service exchange flywheel from your preferred spares retailer. However, if the starter ring gear is perfectly satisfactory (as it often is) but the face of the flywheel is grooved, find a small local machine shop which can reface it; the life of the new clutch will be multiplied several times over if the flywheel surface is good. Your local MG club will probably be able to tell your where to get the refacing done.

While a workshop manual will cover the detail, reassembly of the clutch should be done carefully to ensure longevity. Start by replacing the sintered bronze spigot bush in the crankshaft (paragraph 8-1-1) as a matter of routine. If you're refitting your original flywheel, whether refaced or not, ensure that the positional mark you made just prior to removing the flywheel is rotated through 180 degrees. The flywheel always stops in the same position on a four-cylinder engine, and this rotation

should ensure the starter engages on a different sector of the ring gear in the future.

Thoroughly clean the gearbox first-motion shaft splines, faces of the flywheel and cover plate to remove **all** oil, grease or preservatives. I use thinners but an aerosol brake cleaner will do the same job.

Be absolutely sure that the side of the pressure plate marked "flywheel-side" is facing the flywheel, and use new spring washers under the heads of the cover plate bolts.

A tool (mandrel) to centre the friction plate while you progressively tighten the cover plate is essential. It can be a borrowed front first-motion shaft from an old gearbox, or most auto parts shops sell universal/adjustable centring tools for modest cost. Keep the centring tool square with the cover plate as you **progressively** tighten the cover bolts.

The carbon thrust release bearing clips in place with two spring clips, after which check that the forward and rocking movements of the bearing are smooth and unhindered. At the same time it's

8-7-1 (Picture 4) Access to the bellhousing bolts is so much easier on the garage floor. Don't forget the cable clip mounting for the gearbox harness, nor to test that the overdrive and reverse light switches still work well before you think about installing the engine.

important to check that the clutch fork/ lever is in good order; it has been known to break but worn pivot bearings are quite common and, since this would reduce clutch travel and effectiveness, are best replaced now if there is even the slightest doubt about their integrity.

Take a moment to check two things: the clutch slave cylinder and the flexible hose leading to it: there will never be a better time. I've found cylinders so full of sand and grit (not only behind the boot, but inside too) it's amazing they worked at all. If the cylinder is full of rubbish clean it out or, better yet, strip it and fit a repair kit comprising a new internal seal and boot.

The other important, but usually overlooked, component in the hydraulic chain is the flexible hose that connects to the rear of the slave cylinder. It will last for years, but is never checked in the way that brake hoses are scrutinised and replaced, so the one fitted to your 'B could be as old as the car ... If so, it really is worth replacing as it can break up internally and close up, particularly when bent through the 90, or so, degree angle necessary for installation. It is easily changed when the engine is out of the car but access is very restricted once the engine is reinstalled.

Chapter 9
Transmission problems

Most MGBs were fitted with a four-speed manual gearbox, many of which had overdrive on 3rd and 4th gears, giving, in effect, six forward gears. A relatively small number of cars were fitted with a Borg Warner 35 series automatic gearbox.

Automatic gearbox (transmission) problems are best dealt with by auto gearbox specialists, so I've not covered them here. Instead, I have included a section on how to convert an automatic gearbox car to manual with overdrive, which I judge to be of more interest to the majority of auto-box owners.

Within this chapter I'll outline the various types of manual gearbox used and describe how to upgrade four-speed manual transmission to MOD (manual with overdrive).

The original MGB gearbox was the "3-synchromesh" type fitted up until autumn (fall) 1967. These gearboxes were offered with the option of a Laycock "D-type" overdrive.

With the introduction of the Mark II MGB (designated GHN4 and GHD4), the "4-synchromesh" gearbox appeared, along with a wider transmission tunnel. As an aside, whilst its possible - with a lot of work - to fit a 4-synchro gearbox into an early MGB with a narrow transmission tunnel, it's not really worthwhile.

The 4-synchro boxes were also offered with the optional extra of a Laycock overdrive unit; this time the

"LH-type." The 4-synchro overdrive units were slightly altered internally with the introduction of the rubber bumper cars, demonstrated by the fact that the chrome bumper cars require a different speedometer drive pinion than the later cars. So, if swapping another 4-synchro

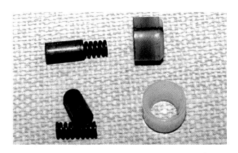

9-1-1 The brass plunger and its part-recessed spring are fiddly to get in place and, consequently, have been known to be left out when assembling the gearlever (through the transmission tunnel) to the gearbox. The result of this omission can be an annoying rattle. The other component you see in two views in this shot is the nylon bush that cushions the bottom ball on the gearlever from the remote control extension. If this has been omitted or, more likely, slipped out of place upon assembly you'll have lots of play in the gearlever and a very indirect gear selection.

gearbox for the original, establish that the alternative came from the correct donor to avoid some very strange speedometer readings. Incidentally, I should also mention that is not just a question of swapping the plastic speedometer drive pinion to match your car, the internal drive gear is different too (don't ask me why!). You can stay with the later car's speedo drive gearing and have your speedometer recalibrated to compensate.

For those with a non-overdrive manual gearbox who are thinking of fitting overdrive, you should be aware that the back of a non-overdrive gearbox will not accept an overdrive unit. More later ...

This chapter is split into three main sections as follows -
- Gearbox faults: section 9-1
- Overdrive faults: section 9-2
- Upgrading: section 9-3

GEARBOX (TRANSMISSION) FAULTS

Rattle, swishing or zizzing noises from gearlever/gearstick
9-1-1 Noises from the gearlever itself are not unknown and need not signal gearbox problems. An irritating rattle at almost any speed probably signifies the anti-rattle spring/brass contact was not installed when last the gearlever was fitted. Withdraw the gaiter and three special shouldered screws that should be fitted

with special double-coiled spring washers. If the washers are missing or broken, it's worth buying three and fitting them under the heads of the shouldered bolts and trying the car because it's just possible this has fixed the rattle! If not, next time remove the gearlever and look for the small hole drilled in the side of the "ball" - it should have a internal coil spring capped by a brass cap fitted most way into the hole in order to provide anti-rattle pressure on the gearlever's housing. It is a bit of a fiddle to fit, and yours wouldnot be the first car where a previous owner hadn't bothered to refit it. Grease the ball, insert the anti-rattle spring/cap in the hole and refit the gearlever.

A swishing noise from the gearlever, most noticeable when the car is idling/ticking over, is very common and nothing to worry about. You can try injecting silicone sealer into the bottom of the screw thread in the plastic gearknob before screwing it on to the lever, or fitting a non-original wooden/leather knob if the noise irritates you to that extent.

Ticking noise while reversing
9-1-2 A ticking noise while reversing is fairly common. The rapidity of the ticking increases with the speed of the car. This noise is caused by chipped teeth on either/both the reverse gear or laygear, usually caused by selecting reverse when the car is still moving forward or when the clutch is not fully disengaged. There is no simple fix: a partial gearbox strip and rebuild is required - although you can lessen the cost by removing/replacing the 'box yourself or fitting a secondhand or reconditioned gearbox. If your 'box does not have overdrive, you might make a virtue out of necessity by taking the opportunity to fit a

9-1-2 The inside of an MGB 4-synchromesh gearbox. I include it to give you a good idea as to what is inside the 'box & to steer you away from any notion of a DIY restoration job.

secondhand overdrive gearbox. Don't forget to budget for a new clutch (definitely worthwhile almost regardless of the condition of the existing unit) while you have the engine and gearbox apart.

Whining noise ("gear whine")
9-1-3 The MGB's gearbox may not be an engineering masterpiece, but it should not normally be terribly noisy. As mentioned elsewhere the "straight cut" first gear in a 3-synchro box is inevitably noisy, however if your 'box seems to be making excessive noise in all gears - but is otherwise performing reasonably well - a check on the oil level is definitely worthwhile. The 3-synchro boxes are not too difficult to access, but the dipstick on the original 4-synchro boxes is very hard to get to and, consequently, sometimes gets forgotten. 0I cannot get the gearbox rubber cover's position changed for you to make it more accessible, but you can simplify future oil level checks if you loop and twist a piece of stiff wire around the top of the dipstick once you've removed it. MG actually resolved the dipstick access problem when introducing the rubber-bumper cars by deleting it! Instead they provided a filler/

9-1-3 (Picture 1) This dip-stick is difficult to access since you need to remove a large rubber bung (2"approximately!) from the top of the gearbox tunnel & reach down to grip the loop at the top of the dip-stick. This non-original piece of floppy string might help, but I advocate using wire so it stands up towards the top of the gearbox tunnel!

level side plug on the main gearbox case - which you get at from underneath the car.

Contrary to most owners' experience with other cars, MGB gearboxes, whether overdrive or non-overdrive, use **engine oil** for lubrication. None of the 1800cc-engined car's gearboxes use gear oil, although EP (extreme pressure gear) oil is specified for the MGB GT V8 gearbox (its internal parts are changed to cope with this thicker lubricant). So, fill your 1800cc MGB 'box with engine oil. Since the MGB gearbox was designed, there have

9-1-3 (Picture 2) Later gearboxes have this combined filler/level plug. This may require you to lay on the floor but it is actually a more satisfactory arrangement.

been significant advances in lubricant technology and various additives and synthetic oils have become available, these are well advertised and, in appropriate circumstances, do a wonderful job. These special lubricants may quieten or smooth-out your manual gearbox operation without any complications or side effects, but be aware that they could adversely effect synchro operation if they are too slippery. **Caution!** - take great care when contemplating putting any additive or synthetic oil into your **overdrive** gearbox - you could be killing the car with well-intentioned but ill-advised kindness because they can prevent the overdrive's clutch linings from gripping (you could find yourself reading paragraph 9-16 before you know it...).

Most gearbox or overdrive problems arise because the service schedule has been overlooked. A gearbox oil change with simultaneous attention to **both** overdrive filters (as described elsewhere in this chapter) at the prescribed 24month/24,000 mile intervals will do more good than any additive or synthetic oil for an MGB's overdrive gearbox.

9-1-4 If the oil level is satisfactory, excessive noise in a particular gear can be caused by worn gear teeth. Note, however, that pre-1968 3-synchro gearboxes have a straight cut, non-synchromesh first gear - so this one is always noisy.

Excessive noise in **all** gears with the correct oil levels is likely to be the result of worn bearings within the gearbox. There's not much you can do in the short term, I'm afraid, but we'll return to this subject shortly.

Difficult or noisy gearchanging

9-1-5 If the synchromesh on your otherwise reasonable gearbox seems slow or ineffective, you might have the wrong grade of oil in the gearbox. The MGB gearbox is designed to run with **engine oil**, but the MGB box is often refilled with EP80 or EP90 by mistake. Sometimes the use of thicker oil is deliberate since it reduces the noise from the gearbox somewhat! Take a critical look at the oil on the dipstick if your gearbox has one, but the only way to be really sure the gearbox has the correct oil is to drain it and refill it with the correct grade of fresh oil. Inspect the drained oil closely: a **slight** brassy look is normal however brass fragments signal broken synchro rings or bushes. If the oil is very grey in colour, or there are grey coloured steel chips present, or the oil has become a thick grey sludge, a bearing, shaft or a gear is disintegrating. All save the slightly brassy look, signal your gearbox needs a major overhaul.

9-1-6 If it's still difficult to select a gear or gears after you've corrected the oil grade and level, the probability is that gearbox wear is the problem (assuming you've looked at the malfunctioning clutch symptoms and solutions in chapter 8).

For the vast majority of readers there is only one solution to a worn gearbox - a service exchange unit from a reputable retailer and removal of the engine complete with gearbox seems the next step.

There is still one remote possibility

9-1-6 (Picture 1) Before you completely condemn your 'box do make sure that it is not the clutch master cylinder or...

9-1-6 (Picture 2) ...its slave cylinder at fault. You & your wallet would feel very upset if you fitted a reconditioned gearbox & new clutch, only to find it was still difficult to engage a gear.

which is worth investigating if the appearance of the gearbox oil was not too bad, but the gear changing continued to be stiff and unpleasant. After you've removed the gearbox, and just before you start 'phoning around to get the best deals, check that the remote gearchange extension is securely fastened to the top of the gearbox: if it turns out to be loose, it could be the cause of your difficult gearchanging (unfortunately, you now face the dilemma of whether to replace the original box or go ahead with fitting a service-exchange one?)

9-1-7 Before you order the service-exchange unit be sure to check that the overdrive unit currently installed in the

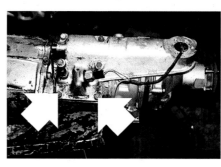

9-1-6 (Picture 3) The "remote" gearbox extension. The arrowed fastenings need to secure the extension completely to the main case. Although missing from this shot, the gearlever slots in the right/top of the extension & operates the gear selectors through a series of rods that run up inside the extension. If this extension were to come loose, the gear selection process would suffer. This shot is a 4-synchro 'box with an LH overdrive unit. The switch we can see is the overdrive inhibitor switch.

car is correct. In my introduction to this chapter I mentioned that with 30 year old cars there is the ever-present possibility that an earlier owner has fitted a secondhand replacement that may work admirably, but which does not match the original specification of the car. This happens very frequently with engines and, albeit with less frequency, with gearboxes and overdrive units too. You maybe quite unconcerned about originality, but nevertheless you'll want your speedometer to show the correct road speed. You may even want to take the opportunity to upgrade your non-overdrive gearbox to one that incorporates overdrive. You'll not be able to easily fit the wider 4-synchro gearbox into the narrow tunnel of a 3-synchro car, but it's possible that someone has fitted a 3-synchro box into a later car designed for a 4-synchro gearbox. So this is the moment to assess these details.

Check on the colour of the speedo-drive gearwheel. The first gear ratios varied from chrome to rubber bumper and the colour of the speedometer drive pinion will help identify the gearbox. If in doubt look for the identification plate on the overdrive unit to tell you whether it's a D-type or an LH-type.

Don't forget to take a close look at the surface of the flywheel, to order a new full three-piece clutch set and new spigot "Oilite" bearing too: all well before you

9-1-7 (Picture 1) Is your overdrive the correct one for your car? Laycock's clear labelling makes this decision easier, as you see here in outline &...

come to fit the replacement gearbox.

Finally, check the integrity of the rubber parts of the gearbox mountings - they're usually saturated with oil and disintegrating: don't miss this opportunity to put this situation to rights.

9-1-7 (Picture 2) ...in close-up. As the label tells us, this is an LH type.

OVERDRIVE FAULTS

Does not work at all

9-2-1 If you think the overdrive on your car has never worked, be aware that many MGBs were fitted with an overdrive switch but no overdrive unit behind the gearbox! So, before you decide that the overdrive unit is not working, crawl under the car to check that one is actually fitted.

The rear part of a gearbox intended for use with an overdrive is quite different from the non-overdrive gearbox. On the overdrive-type gearbox unit, about six inches of the front of the rear flange has a flat base with one square and one rectangular plate. It looks like, indeed it is, a second part to the gearbox. Additionally, cars made after 1968 (with a wider transmission tunnel) also have a 3/4 inch hex plug in evidence.

The non-overdrive gearbox does have a second part to its case, but this tapers over about 18 inches to the rear flange. A photograph of each type, as viewed from below, is included to aid those who are uncertain what an overdrive unit looks like.

9-2-1 You may have all the control switches but if your gearbox is not coupled to an overdrive unit, overdrive will never engage! This is how the rear of a NON-overdrive gearbox looks. Take a peek at yours.

Slow to engage, will not engage

9-2-2 Fairly frequently the overdrive becomes very slow to kick-in, and may not engage at all. This can be because the oil level is low in the gearbox (the overdrive and gearbox share the same oil). I have heard it said that some owners leave topping up the gearbox until the overdrive protests - at which point they know that the oil level does need attention. Not a good idea at all ...

9-2-3 If the overdrive is always slow to engage, and has been that way for some time, then the problem is probably a worn hydraulic pump within the overdrive unit.

This problem is common to both types of overdrive. The pump is driven by a camshaft that is in turn driven by the rear shaft at the tail of the overdrive unit. The O-rings wear and since you can get to them without removing the gearbox/overdrive it may well be worthwhile replacing the O-rings yourself or getting your nearest transmission specialist to do the work for you. If you do decide to replace the O-rings yourself, read a workshop manual very carefully, watch out for the non-return ball and be sure to clean the filters (see 9-2-4) at the same time. Frequently, this work will fix the overdrive.

9-2-4 A surprisingly frequent reason that the overdrive fails to engage is because of blocked internal filter(s). The locations of the two filters in the LH-type are detailed in the workshop manual. It is the pressure filter hidden behind the largest of the plugs that is usually missed out during maintenance, although it is the more important of the two.

Whilst the bottom of the overdrive unit is open, clean all the parts - the solenoid, piston, ball, housing and oil pressure relief valve. Withdraw the pump,

9-2-3 The rear cover has been removed from this LH overdrive to enable this shot to be taken to show the all important pump (you will not need to do this to get at your pump!). Also missing from view is the central drive-shaft incorporating the pump's drive cam.

feeling for its smooth movement, clean it meticulously and check it's moving in and out smoothly; they do stick and this reduces the oil pressure, which stops the overdrive from working.

9-2-5 Oil and filters all in order but the overdrive will still not engage? Applicable to the D-type units only, but there is a vacuum protection switch fitted to prevent owners of the earlier cars

9-2-4 (Picture 1) This is the LH units sump. It needs to be removed to get at the filters.

9-2-4 (Picture 2) The sump will come away with the gauze sump filter leaving...

9-2-4 (Picture 3) ...the various plugs on view which allow access to the filter & pump. You need a twin pronged spanner to undo each plug. The pressure filter should come away with the largest (end) plug without difficulty, but take particular care when considering inspection of the pump & removal of the (central) plug - these two "loose" components are easily dropped as you remove the plug. A small spring & ball-bearing form a non-return valve on the end of the piston & these are easily lost if care is not taken when removing them.

engaging overdrive while accelerating hard. This switch can become blocked, stick or its electrical contacts can become dirty. The (two) wires to and from the switch can become fatigued and/or their terminations corroded. Consequently, the switch may fail to close when intended, thereby telling the overdrive control circuits not to operate. Take a look and check/correct all these details, confirming your diagnosis if necessary by temporally connecting the two wires together for a brief test - thus bypassing the switch. If all then goes well with the switch bypassed, you need a replacement vacuum switch.

Intermittent operation

9-2-6 An intermittent overdrive may signal low oil levels (see 9-2-2) or an electrical problem. The inhibitor switch is the cause

of most electrical problems within the overdrive circuits.

With the overdrive engaged, wait for it to drop out and try moving the gearlever without changing gear. If, say, holding it backwards or to the right re-engages overdrive, but overdrive then drops back out when you let the gearlever take up its normal position, there's a good chance the inhibitor switch shims need adjusting.

The inhibitor switch should 'make' (close, and complete the circuit) when the car is in third or fourth gear, and remain open (break the circuit) to inhibit the overdrive from engaging when in first or second gear. A cam on the appropriate selector pushes the switch plunger in when third/fourth gears are engaged.

In the case of a faulty overdrive, start by inserting the probe of a test light or multimeter into the bullet connector adjacent to the solenoid; it should be live and the bulb illuminate/meter show battery voltage when you position the gearlever

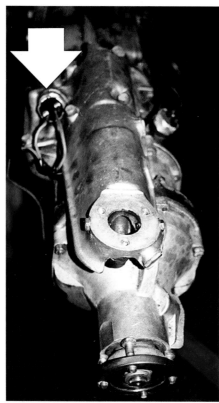

9-2-6 (Picture 1) The remote gear-change extension houses the overdrive inhibitor switch (arrowed) on its left side. The switch just visible on the right is the reverse-light switch.

9-2-6 (Picture 2) The overdrive inhibitor switch viewed from the businesses/ actuating end (left side) & from the end you are probably more used to seeing - the electrical connection end. The fibre washer/shims are obvious & may need to be added to or reduced in order to get the ball-like plunger on the end to operate the internal contacts properly.

and the overdrive switch to engage overdrive (with ignition on).

If the light fails to illuminate it will be necessary to get to the inhibitor switch atop the gearbox... which is the most inaccessible of components. For access, drop the rear gearbox crossmember several inches and, along with it, the rear of the gearbox. Remove the oval chrome trim from around the gearknob and, if your car has a central console, remove that, too. Check the inhibitor switch for continuity; adjust the number of large shim washers, or replace the switch, as necessary.

Suddenly stops working

9-2-7 Don't despair, particularly if the overdrive control switch is on the top of the gearknob. All chrome bumper cars have the switch fitted to the dashboard/ fascia and this rarely suffers anything worse than dirty contacts which a dose of switch cleaner usually fixes. Rubber bumper cars (the ones in question) however have the switch fitted to the top of the gearknob; others use the left stalk on the steering column to operate the overdrive.

I consider it a safety advantage to have the switch on a steering column stalk and it has certainly proved a more reliable place to fit the switch because the constant flexing of the wires to switches mounted on the gearlever fractures them from time to time. The wires always break at the base of the gearlever, but can be accessed without removing the gearlever. You'll need to remove the trim oval ring and gaiter - whereupon the two wires that control the overdrive will be obvious. The yellow (some cars have yellow/red) wire takes power to the switch while the other

9-2-7 (Picture 1) Cars with the overdrive control switch on top of the gear-knob can experience problems. This is not with the gear-knob switch itself but...

9-2-7 (Picture 2) ...with the wires at the base of the gearlever eventually breaking with fatigue.

one (usually yellow/purple) will carry power to the solenoid when the switch is "on". The break could be in the copper conductor within one or both wires and consequently may not be obvious at first sight. Continuity tests should reveal which wire is broken, although I'd replace both. Provide the biggest loop of new wire that the space permits in an effort to stop a fresh fatigue fracture occurring too quickly.

9-2-8 The next most frequent overdrive problem is nothing to do with the overdrive, but rather with its electrical protection and control circuits, and is applicable to both types of overdrive.

Using the wiring diagram applicable to your car/overdrive unit, progressively check and test the circuit from one end or the other. Do not test points in the circuit randomly as this will confuse you and extend the time it takes to isolate and resolve the problem. You're looking for a broken or disconnected wire or terminal, or an electrical component (switch, relay, inhibitor or solenoid) that has become

defective. Since the solenoid is rarely at fault, start checking at the front of the circuit and work back towards the overdrive unit until you find a lack of electrical continuity.

The 12V test lead/bulb shown in chapter 19 is the only tool necessary. Securely fix one crocodile clip to a sound earth (ground) and then create the situation where the overdrive should work; *i.e.* ignition on and an appropriate gear engaged. If there's a vacuum switch in your system you'll need to bypass it if the engine is not running. If you do the the checks without the engine running, and since they may take some time, it's a very good idea to pull the battery side terminal off of the coil in order to protect the ignition system.

Check for continuity at the end of the first part of the circuit, the power supply. If the test bulb lights, all is well; move on to test the continuity of the overdrive relay primary circuit. If that's okay, what about the relay's secondary circuit? Eventually you'll find a point at which the test lamp fails to light and will then know where the problem lays. Nine times out of ten, though, it's the inhibitor switch (see 9-2-6) that's at fault.

Engine revs drop to idle speed on over-run

9-2-9 If the engine revs drop back to idle (tickover) speed on overrun when overdrive is engaged the clutch within the overdrive unit is probably worn. This requires specialised attention beyond the scope of this book and will necessitate removing the overdrive unit from the back of the gearbox.

Contrary to general opinion, the overdrive unit can be removed from the gearbox by just lowering the back of the gearbox: a much better solution than removing the engine and gearbox.

Won't disengage

9-2-10 Caution! - If overdrive fails to disengage try not to drive the car forward more than is essential, and never engage reverse gear. Reversing the car with overdrive engaged will severely damage the overdrive unit, and could make a tow-truck a necessity.

The inhibitor switch should ensure overdrive disengages when first, second or reverse gear is engaged, but, if you're suspicious that overdrive is not disengaging when you ask it to, put the car into first gear (never test in reverse) and determine if it feels as though you are

asking the car to move off in second gear. If so, check that the overdrive switch - either on the dashboard (fascia), on the top of the gearlever or on the left column stalk (depending upon the year your car

9-2-9 The (conical) clutch within the overdrive unit is arrowed in this cross-section. The picture is taken with overdrive "out". To engage overdrive, the clutch return springs are compressed by two hydraulic pistons (we can see one) which pull the clutch lining into contact with the fixed outer clutch ring. That effectively brakes the inner part of the unit & directs the drive via "planet" wheels within the assembly. If the clutch lining is worn, or incorrect lubrication has reduced its frictional qualities, the clutch will slip & overdrive will become intermittent, rapidly getting to the point of not operating at all.

was manufactured) - is definitely set to "out" (overdrive disengaged position).

Try driving the car at a steady speed in top (4th) gear and determine whether the engine rpm is what you would expect in this gear. If you would expect 3000rpm at 50mph in top without overdrive engaged, are you getting instead the rpm you would expect when overdrive is engaged, say, 2500 at 50mph? Try a few on and off flicks of the switch, feeling for a response from the overdrive whilst keeping an eye on the tachometer, which should show an increase in rpm each time you take overdrive "out." If you establish that overdrive is operating when 3rd or 4th gears are engaged, check whether it stays in when first or second gears are used.

If overdrive disengages when first or second gears are selected, you don't need to worry about damaging the overdrive unit when it becomes essential to reverse. The problem is probably in or around the overdrive control switch, which is much the easiest component to get to.

You'll notice a big step in the gearing when changing from second to third, which probably signals that the control switch is stuck in the "in" position, or that the wires or terminals at the rear of the switch are touching. If this is the case, repeatedly operate the switch at the roadside to try to free it; if this fails to improve the situation, try removing and insulating the wires at the rear of the switch to see whether it improves matters.

If overdrive remains engaged in **all** gears, there's very little you can do at the roadside. Pulling the white electrical feed wire(s) from the fuse box will take out ignition feeds to fuel pump and other such vital circuits, and so is of no help whatsoever. Very early cars had a direct power feed from the ignition switch.

The only practical way of isolating the overdrive circuit is to break the circuit at the output side of the overdrive control switch. It's unlikely that this disengage the overdrive, but if it does you can drive and reverse normally and will know that you have a switch problem somewhere in the overdrive circuit to resolve before reconnecting the wires.

Caution! - If disconnection fails to disengage the overdrive, be absolutely sure to avoid engaging reverse gear. If you forget you get the briefest of warnings - the back of the car will lift as if the handbrake is on as you take off. Failure to immediately disengage reverse will break the unidirectional gearing within the overdrive unit.

Once you get the car home, jack it up and support it safely in order to make various checks whilst a helper operates the controls. Check that the inhibitor switches are operating - not a pleasant task with the gearbox *in situ*, as described in 9-2-6.

If all seems well with the electrical controls, is the solenoid stuck in the engaged position? You might be able to hear (even feel) the solenoid operating, or not operating, as the case may be. Switch on the ignition and put the car in 4th gear; have a helper switch overdrive in and out via the overdrive switch. If the solenoid fails to respond, closer investigation is called for as it would seem to be stuck. The mechanism on the early 3-synchro gearbox with the D-type overdrive is

reasonably easily reached via a side cover and three small screws. With the cover removed, have your helper repeat the in/out cycle whilst you watch for the mechanism to work. If it doesn't it means that the solenoid requires adjustment, unsticking or - rarely - replacement: clean the filter at the same time.

The solenoid in the later LH overdrive fitted to 4-synchro gearboxes is less visible since it's within the overdrive unit, hidden under a square cover secured by four screws. Immediately adjacent to the cover is the sump - which is the large rectangular item secured by six bolts. The gasket to the cover sandwiches a filter gauze that filters all oil as it returns to the sump before being pumped back through the system. Once the cover is removed you will be able to check the solenoid. Note that there are two filters, the more important of which is the pressure filter hidden under a plug within the base of the unit. It will be revealed once the sump is removed; refer to the workshop manual before going too far.

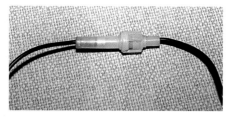

9-2-11 (Picture 1) Always fit a line fuse to an overdrive circuit.

9-2-11 (Picture 2) The usually reliable solenoid - this is the LH one. The D type is slightly different, but still reliable. Care is needed when removing the solenoid as it is very easy to lose the parts refered to in the main text.

Overdrive tips
9-2-11 To reduce the jolt on the whole of the transmission, partially depress the clutch pedal as overdrive engages or disengages.

If overdrive is fitted to your car or you plan to fit it, always add a line fuse to the circuit to protect the wiring.

Remember that rarely does the solenoid need replacing, just cleaning and/or freeing.

GEARBOX (TRANSMISSION) UPGRADES
Adding an overdrive unit
9-3-1 Adding an overdrive to a non-overdrive car is a really worthwhile upgrade which will improve fuel economy, reduce noise levels and allow more relaxed driving.

Next time the non-overdrive gearbox has to be removed, give serious consideration to replacing it with an overdrive unit. Though, unfortunately, an overdrive unit cannot simply be bolted to the rear of the existing gearbox since the non-overdrive gearbox tailshaft (output shaft) is too long, and does not contain the appropriate oil pump drive cam. The tailshaft can be modified, but at horrendous expense. Scan the club magazines "spares for sale" columns and buy a complete gearbox and overdrive assembly, then have it professionally overhauled.

You should get some idea of the wiring and fitting work by reading the workshop manual, and sections 9-2-10 and 9-3-1 of this book. In addition to the gearbox and overdrive unit, you need only a longer speedo cable and small wiring sub-harness for the top of the gearbox. You may buy these with your gearbox/overdrive, but both items are available new.

Converting auto-transmission to manual transmission
9-3-2 The auto to MOD (manual with overdrive) conversion is popular because it reduces noise levels at speed and improves fuel economy. The higher ratio of the 'fifth' (overdrive 4th) gear provided by a MOD 'box is a huge improvement and, coupled with the increased mechanical efficiency of a manual gearbox, will certainly reduce fuel consumption.

Buy the cheapest second-hand MOD gearbox you can find, along with a wiring sub-harness, flywheel, clutch pedal (or the complete manual pedal box assembly, for simplicity), and speedo cable from the same source. Make sure the gearbox is in good enough shape to be reconditioned, and includes the necessary clutch release mechanism, gearlever and inhibitor switches; that the flywheel matches the gearbox and has no ring gear teeth missing, and that the speedo cable seems usable. Have the gearbox and overdrive reconditioned (for a cost of around £500.

The rear axle ratio was sometimes higher on automatic cars. The 3.7:1 'automatic' axle ratio was introduced at car number 158231, so only a very few early autos had the 3.9:1 crownwheel and pinion. Consequently, it will probably be necessary to swap the rear axle in order to get the full better acceleration offered via MOD transmission. Whichever model you own, it will also be necessary to pull the engine and gearbox out of the car to effect this conversion.

The first thing to do after removing the engine with its old auto-box is to fit the clutch flexible hose to the bracket mounted on the right side chassis rail. Fit a new clutch slave cylinder to the hose. Fit a new (copper) clutch hydraulic pipe to the top of the flexible hose and shape it to run under and around the steering column. Connect two red/white wires together with a bullet connector: this circuit prevented the car starting with the auto-box in gear, and links ignition system and starter motor.

Buy a new three-piece clutch, a new manual gearbox-type spigot bearing for the end of the crankshaft, and a set of flywheel/crank fixing bolts, since all are different between auto and manual cars. Remove the auto gearbox, drive plate and flywheel, bolt on the 'new' flywheel followed by the clutch assembly and manual gearbox.

Don't forget to measure the correct volume of engine oil and fill the gearbox before connecting the engine/gearbox to the car. If you do forget, you can still do it without removing the gearbox, but it's much easier with the gearbox on the ground.

Be aware that an electrical fault in the reverse (back-up) light or overdrive circuits will be hard to access and could necessitate removing the engine/gearbox again. It's most important that you fit the inhibitor and reverse-light switches together with the associated electrical sub-harness carefully and that you test the electric connections **before** installing the engine/gearbox in the car. Consequently,

you'll need to temporarily fit the gearlever.

The manual gearbox mountings will be the same as the auto's, but replace all the rubber components that will have become contaminated with oil over many years before finally installing the engine/gearbox unit back in the car, and fixing the gearbox rear crossmember and propshaft.

The reverse light wires will fit the original auto-box bullet connections, but there will be a yellow/red overdrive wire to incorporate into the car's electrical system. This is best done using a solenoid and, whilst not mandatory, it's a good idea to protect the overdrive electrical system using a line fuse. If this worries you, tape up the yellow/red wire (from the gearbox sub-harness) temporarily and ask an auto-electrician to carry out this small operation for you. You'll be able to use the car in the intervening period.

Provide an appropriate overdrive control switch for your MGB which should be fitted to the dashboard/fascia, gearlever top or left side stalk on the steering column. Save the electrician time by bringing the two associated wires forward through the bulkhead (firewall). One should be coloured yellow (and will marry with the yellow/red wire via a bullet connector); the other is coloured white,

which will be needed to provide the power for the overdrive circuit when the ignition is switched on. This is where the relay should be inserted before the wire is indirectly coupled to the white ignition circuit.

Finally, there is the speedo, clutch pedal and hydraulics to attend to. The auto-box speedo cable will be too short and should be replaced with the one acquired earlier.

The existing brake pedal will be too wide, but it's possible to alter the base and fit a narrower rubber, or you can acquire a second-hand replacement pedal. In either case drop the existing brake pedal and top pivot bolt, re-arrange the spacers/washers and fit both brake and clutch pedal on the same pivot in the same pedal box.

Fit a new clutch master cylinder and banjo hydraulic fitting, along with the essential copper washers. Mount them without fully tightening everything and couple the top end of the clutch's hydraulic pipe to the rear of the master cylinder. Remove the large square 'grommet' in the bulkhead to allow access to tighten everything.

The final step is to bleed the clutch hydraulic system. Hard work, but it **will** transform your car.

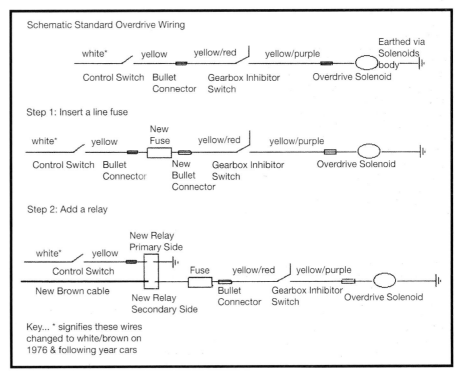

D9 Improving the overdrive's electrical controls.

Chapter 10
Front suspension, steering, wheels & tyres

The MGB's front suspension is a pretty rugged, well proven set up that was also used by several earlier MGs. Nevertheless, components do wear and create symptoms, which we'll explore in a moment. However, the wear and longevity of the front suspension, particularly the components within the swivel pins, can be dramatically effected by the regularity and intervals with which they are, or are not, serviced. For maximum longevity, be sure to grease the six front suspension nipples every 3000 miles or 3 months (whichever comes first) - twice as frequently as MG recommended - if you wish to avoid a number of the following faults.

Rattle, clunk or thump when you drive over a bump

10-1-1 A rattle, clunk or thump from one, or both sides, of the front of the car when you drive over a bump initially indicates a check of both front shock absorbers. The front shock absorbers are of a lever arm-type and, consequently, very different in appearance to the majority of tubular telescopic units fitted to cars of a more recent design. The MGB's shock absorbers actually serve two purposes: firstly to dampen the front suspension movements, secondly they also act as the top "wishbones" of the car's front suspension. Check that neither unit is leaking copious amounts of fluid: the telltale will be a trail of oil from one of the pivot points. No oil

trail and you need to clean around the screw cap and top up with shock-absorber hydraulic fluid (**not** engine oil!) since a lack of fluid could be causing the noise. Note that even if only one shock absorber is leaking, you need to fit a **pair** of service exchange units and top them up with shock absorber oil.

New shock absorbers are also

10-1-1 (Picture 1) The front shock absorbers are well proven design used by several MG models before the MGB. However, they can leak hydraulic oil from the pivot seals (one of two is arrowed), while loose mountings and various suspension rubber stops and bushes can also cause front suspension problems.

available, but I must say that if you're about to spend the sort of cash needed for new lever arm shock-absorbers you're

10-1-2 (Picture 2) There is provision for refilling a shock absorber with hydraulic oil via the filler plug. If a shock absorber is leaking, this should be the first step, until such time as you can effect a more permanent repair.

probably better off buying a decent conversion to telescopic shock absorbers as described in *How to Improve MGB, MGC and MGB V8* (another Veloce publication by the same author). In fact, the original lever arm shock absorbers are prone to losing their fluid and consequently their damping function. "Reconditioning" often involves little more than replacing the seals and giving the units a quick blast with a spray gun. Unfortunately, the result can often be that the replacement "shocks" remain oiltight for only slightly longer than the time it takes you to return the original units! An exaggeration of course, but intended to draw your attention to the importance of getting a warranty on the serviced units you're buying. Furthermore, it may not pay to buy the cheapest exchange shocks and it will do no harm to ask your supplier whether spindle wear has also been rectified?

10-2-1 If you still hear a clunk when you drive over a bump having ensured the fluid level in both shocks is to the top, then take a look at the four shock absorber mounting bolts on each side of the car. At least two of these mounting bolts are hard to get at, and you would not be the first owner to find they had not been tightened properly after a change of shock absorbers. Your workshop manual will tell you the required torque bor these bolts - although you chances of getting a torque

10-2-1 A persistent "clunk" can be the consequence of the shock absorber mounting (four) bolts loosening - the two inside ones (arrowed) are particularly hard to get at and are hard to tighten properly when replacing the shock absorbers. Yours may not have had the requisite attention from a previous owner.

wrench to the inner bolts is about nil! Nevertheless, you need to find a way of tightening the inaccessible bolts, purchasing a special curved C-spanner if necessary. If the shock absorber mounting bolts are all really tight, then take a look at the top conical rubber bump stops. They can harden with age and break or even fall off, but the remedy is simple - replace suspect bump stops with new items.

10-3-1 A clunk when you drive over a bump from one or both sides of the front suspension can also signal that one or even several suspension components are wearing. I would be particularly suspicious about this if you get a not dissimilar noise when you take your foot off the pedal after braking.

10-3-1 (Picture 1) There are several places where the front suspension and steering mechanisms of an MGB can wear, particularly if not frequently greased. The top thrust ring is not in view here, but its location is arrowed. Any play needs to be taken up by shim washers and/or a replacement bearing ring.

The front upward/downward movement of the suspension coupled to the swivelling requirements of the steering are achieved via a "kingpin" that joins the top wishbone to the bottom wishbone and provides a tubular vertical link on which the stub axle can pivot. Within this assembly the weight of the front of the car rests on a pair of substantial phosphor-bronze thrust washers and shims. In time, the thrust washers wear under the weight of the car and the turning of the stub-axle and some vertical play/lash is introduced

10-3-1 (Picture 2) The replacement ring/thrust washer looks like this. A selection of plain steel shim washers may also be required, but you MUST be sure to fit a new Nyloc nut at the top of the kingpin.

(one potential source of your rattle or clunk).

You can check one side at a time by jacking up the car safely using each front spring pan in turn and then, using a tyre lever for example, try lifting the road wheel vertically. There should be no perceptible vertical movement of the stub axle on the king pin and anything above a few thousandths of an inch is likely to generate a noise when you drive over a bump. You can correct this fault by removing the top trunnion and increasing the shimming by the amount of play that you have noted so that there is no vertical movement of stub axle on kingpin (the stub axle must not bind, or stiff steering will become a problem!) While you have the top of the front suspension stripped to attend to excessive stub axle movement, I'd strongly recommend you renew the top (barrel-like) trunnion bushes on both sides of the car. Also take the opportunity to check very carefully the additional faults, listed in the following text, that can also cause the same rattle/clunkin noise from the front suspension. You may find you have more than one fault.

10-4-1 A common problem that causes a clunk/rattle/knock from the front suspension is wear in one, or both, of the bottom wishbone pivots - known as the bottom trunnions. This, too, can be heard when you release the brake pedal after braking and can take two forms. Either the bronze cross bush within the bottom of the king pin becomes worn over many years of satisfactory service, or the cross bolt that passes through the two pressed bottom wishbones seizes in the bronze bush (due to inadequate lubrication), causing the bolt to act as a suspension component. In due course the now twisting bolt elongates the holes in the pressed wishbones thus accelerating the wear (and therefore play and rattling/clunking noises).

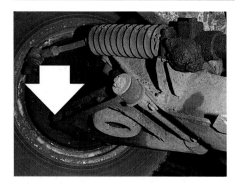

10-4-1 (Picture 1) The bottom outer wishbone pivot is one of the usual wear points on an MGB's front suspension. It's located here, just inboard of the dustshield.

10-4-1 (Picture 2) Support the car carefully and safely and remove the cross bolt as directed by a workshop manual. Usually the bolt is seized into the bottom trunnion, in which case...

10-4-1 (Picture 3) ...one or both wishbones will be worn, like this...

10-4-1 (Picture 4) ...or the bolt has seized in a wishbone, like this.

10-4-1 (Picture 5) Alternatively, this bronze bush will be worn. Replace and repaint everything whilst the bottom trunnion is stripped, which means...

10-4-1 (Picture 6) ...a new kingpin assembly (arrowed), bottom bolt, grease seals, and, if appropriate...

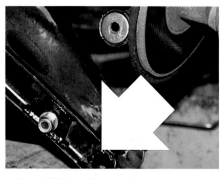

10-4-1 (Picture 7) ...repaired wishbones. Note the welded repair to this wishbone that has now been married to the spring pan.

10-4-1 (Picture 8) Assemble the rubber grease seals each side of the new bottom trunnion and...

10-4-1 (Picture 9) ...bring the bottom wishbones up until you can slot the new bottom trunnion bolt through the whole assembly.

10-4-1 (Picture 10) Tighten the castellated nut, and don't forget the split pin.

In either case, there's no alternative but to strip the front suspension the side in question - although I would strongly recommend that both sides of the front suspension are dealt with simultaneously. The important detail that you must check, and which will not be mentioned in a workshop manual, is whether there is any ovality in any of the wishbone holes: such ovality must be repaired before reassembly.

10-5-1 If the wheel/stub axle assembly has an unacceptable amount of play when rocked from the top and bottom, the most likely explanation is wear in the stub axle/kingpin assembly we see in photograph 10-4-6.

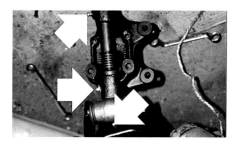

10-5-1 (Picture 1) Many a front suspension repair could be avoided if only the car had been greased every 6000 miles, as recommended by BL. I recommend more frequent attention from a grease gun, in the case of the front suspension, at these three nipples each side of the car.

You're unlikely to detect all but the most extreme cases at home, and this is the sort of unpleasant surprise you can get when the car undergoes its annual MoT test (or the equivalent roadworthiness test in your country). The wear is detectable if you watch the kingpin/stub axle joint while a helper carries out the test for play.

The easiest solution to both fault 10-4-1 and 10-5-1 is to fit service exchange kingpin/stub axle/bottom trunnion assembles and I'd strongly recommend you fit them to both sides of the car at the same time.

The main cause of kingpin wear is inadequate lubrication so, although the service exchange assemblies are not terribly expensive, delay the next front suspension stripdown by liberal and frequent greasing of the three grease nipples each side.

When ordering replacement reconditioned stub axle assembles check whether your intended supplier will be despatching the parts pre-assembled and

10-5-1 (Picture 2) To emphasise the point, I make no apologies for drawing you pictures! Here...

10-5-1 (Picture 3) ...here, and...

re-shimmed ready to bolt to the car, and whether new bottom seals, bushes and bottom trunnion bolts are included in the price? You'll need new top trunnion (barrel-shaped) bushes, so order those, too, and read paragraph 10-6-1.

10-5-1 (Picture 4) ...here. Do it today!

Upgrading suspension bushes
10-6-1 Because they are strengthened with a metal insert, the standard rubber top trunnion bushes give reasonable service, but if you have to replace them

10-6-1 (Picture 1) The top trunnion bushes are at the top of the kingpin, as shown by the arrow.

consider polyurethane replacements. Your spares supplier can tell you what is available, but I prefer 'Superflex' because they seem to offer the right balance between hardness and the inevitable increase in road noise that non-rubber suspension bushes cause.

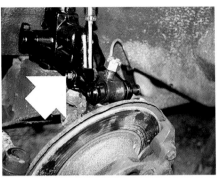

10-6-1 (Picture 5) It will be necessary to open the arms of each shock absorber by loosening the arrowed nut shown in this shot, and driving a wedge between the arms.

10-6-2 (Picture 1) The four per side standard inner bottom wishbone bushes often look less serviceable than they really are...

10-6-1 (Picture 2) Although the most resilient, the top trunnion bushes can begin to look pretty tatty and could be the reason for an MoT failure.

10-6-1 (Picture 3) Support the car as per the workshop manual, remove the split pin, undo the castellated nut and drive out the top bolt.

10-6-1 (Picture 6) Use lots of copper-based grease during reassembly with the new half-bushes, pop them in place each side of the top trunnion and bring the trunnion up into place. Put the top bolt through the assembly and properly tighten everything.

10-6-2 (Picture 2) ...but you may be well advised to attend to them whilst fixing another front suspension problem. Here, the bottom trunnion had to be repaired, so we took the opportunity to replace the inside bushes, too.

10-6-1 (Picture 4) A new special top bolt is a very good idea, and fix in your mind which way to slot it through the arms of the shock absorber. The flat (arrowed) will eventually need to sit up against the stop cast into one shock arm.

10-6-2 Upgrade the weak bottom inner wishbone bushes at the first opportunity. The standard bushes come as four per side rubber cone-like weaklings that need to be upgraded. Sooner or later your car will fail its MoT (or equivalent)

because the edges of the bushes are curling out of the wishbones but, long before that, you could feel the car wandering or having a vagueness about the steering. As you've already read there could be other causes too, but collapsing inner wishbone bushes could be a contributory cause and will recur if you fit original-type replacements. You have a choice of two upgrades. At the very least fit (two per side) the metal/rubber bonded V8 variant. They don't increase road noise and give the front suspension longevity coupled to added rigidity. Polyurethane replacements are also available and frankly, were I rebuilding my car's front suspension tomorrow, I'd be hard pressed to know which upgrade to choose.

A couple of tips may encourage you -

You can leave the hydraulic lines connected, but you're best to avoid stretching the flexible brake hoses. Undo the caliper(s) and place them on a box as far out of your way as possible. MGB V8-type bushes will have to be pressed into the inner ends of the wishbones in your vice/vise. This means that the wishbones will need to be removed from the car. Read a workshop manual and use a **trolley jack** to get the front spring(s)

10-6-2 (Picture 3) Remove all the old bushes from the bore of the wishbone inner pivot, regardless of whether or not you are planning to fit V8 bonded rubber or polyurethane replacements.

10-6-2 (Picture 4) We chose to fit two per side, V8 bonded rubber bushes, seen here getting a little lubrication to help them into place. Note the metal inner and outer sleeves with a bonded rubber core between each: much stronger than the originals.

10-6-2 (Picture 5) They can take a bit of getting into the wishbone. Here, the vice/vise is being used to squeeze the bush into the wishbone, while the box spanner acts as clearance to allow the bush to come through the other side just a little.

out and back in place. Use a socket to squeeze the outer metal tube into the wishbone - it will consequently need to be slightly smaller than the hole in the wishbone collar. As you near the end of the operation, you'll need to back the vice jaws away and insert a large washer, or another larger socket, in order to give the bush space to centralise in the wishbone's collar. **Caution!** - Do not exert any pressure on the rubber when pressing the bush home - you'll damage it.

10-6-2 (Picture 6) Back together with a nice large washer and castellated nut and split pin. I've had V8 bushes in both my MGBs for 10 and 12 years respectively and can confirm that they improve steering and road-holding.

Polyurethane bushes are slightly easier to fit. You'll still need to remove the coil spring and much of the front suspension, but you should not need to use a vice since a smear of Copperslip, or a squirt of washing-up liquid and pressure from a G-clamp/cramp should accomplish the task without moving the wishbones away from the car.

Stiff or unusually heavy steering
10-7-1 If the steering appears stiff or particularly heavy, the kingpins could just need greasing. However, if greasing fails to improve the situation the kingpins may be seized/frozen beyond recall - in which case the service-exchange solution mentioned in 10-5-1 will need to be employed. See also 10-10-1.

Front wheel wobble, vibration
10-8-1 One cause of front wheel wobble or vibration is worn, sloppy kingpins, in which case the solution described in 10-5-1 needs to be implemented.

10-8-2 If the front wheel bearings are worn, there's no alternative but to replace both bearings on the side in question, and replace them quickly. The task is not too

10-8-2 (Picture 1) For the full story study a workshop manual, but replacing wheel bearings requires removal of the dust cover from the hub, shown here. This is a bolted wheel hub with its dust cover popped off with a screwdriver. Unfortunately, it's rather more difficult with a wire-wheeled hub; make up a short arm with an eye at the end (as seen in Picture 8), to allow you to bolt it to the dust cover within the hub.

10-8-2 (Picture 2) From either hub you should have (left to right) the castellated nut, large tanged washer, outer thrust bearing and several inter-bearing shims.

10-8-2 (Picture 3) Withdraw the hub/disc/rotor leaving the stub axle shown here. Incidentally, this is your opportunity to refurbish the dust cover.

10-8-2 (Picture 4) Put the disc/rotor in the vice/vise, noting that this is also an excellent opportunity to replace the disc.

difficult, although getting the outer rings from the hub requires thought and care, but the job will be explained in a workshop manual.

It's been known for MoT testers to mistake the 0.002-0.004 inch endfloat (lash) designed into the MGB front wheel bearings for unacceptable wear. By modern standards the sort of roadwheel movement one gets in an MGB is very unusual indeed and leads inexperienced

10-8-2 (Picture 5) From the OUTSIDE of the hub you need to knock the INSIDE bearing's outer ring from the hub. You'll find there are a couple of little recesses hidden under all the old grease to allow this operation - but be sure to tap opposite sides of the ring in turn so that it comes out square. Then from the INSIDE of the hub tap out the OUTSIDE ring.

testers to the conclusion that the wheel bearings are shot. More than one MGB has had a shim removed from each front hub so that it shows no play/float at the hub (**Warning!** - dangerous for a long journey), only to have it replaced immediately after the MoT... The better alternative is to keep a photocopy of the appropriate page from the workshop manual in the glovebox to show to the tester.

10-8-3 A squeal from one front wheel is possibly caused by a small stone caught between disc and dustshield, but it could also be a wheel bearing that's either seized or about to seize. Stop as quickly as possible and investigate. If it's a bearing your get-you-home (provided it is a very short journey) solution is to back off the outer bearing, get some grease in there, tighten the bearing as far as possible and drive very slowly home. Replace both bearings in that hub as outlined above before you take the car out again.

10-8-2 (Picture 6) Whatever you do, make sure the internal spacer (arrowed) is in place before you start. I put my new outer rings in the refrigerator overnight in order to help them go into the hub easily. Tap the new rings in place with a piece of hardwood (to make sure you do not chip the bearing surfaces) while the rings are still cold. Again, it's vital that you alternate side-to-side so that each ring goes in square.

10-8-2 (Picture 7) Finally, replace the inner ring; tap it in square as shown here.

10-8-2 (Picture 8) Removing the dust covers from a bolted wheel hub is rarely a problem. Getting the cover out of a wire-wheeled hub requires something like this screwed to the end of the cover before you can pull the cover out.

Steering vague/car wanders

10-9-1 If the steering seems vague or the car wanders, particularly at speed, check the front shock absorbers. This is more difficult than it sounds with an MGB for, unless they are completely shot, the usual test of pushing each front wing/fender down in turn will tell you very little.

The only satisfactory test is to remove the top trunnion and move the shock absorber arm through its full arc, which should be hard work if it is working properly. A lack of resistance confirms the shocker is faulty. An ineffective shock absorber should initially be topped up with shock absorber oil (**not** engine oil). If the oil starts to run out from the pivot points or the shock absorber remains ineffective, it should be replaced. The unit on the opposite side **must** also be replaced at the same time.

A shock absorber that is showing signs of leaking (fault 10-1-1) is suspect, and if your car is suffering from such leaks and indirect steering, replacement shock absorbers are called for; top quality service exchange units are very good value for money.

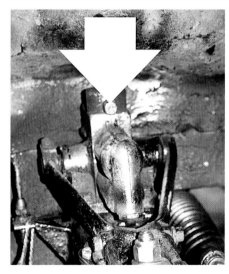

10-9-1 The area surrounding the top up plug should be cleaned so that dirt does not enter the shock absorber when the plug is removed. A length of windscreen washer tubing will help direct oil accurately into the top of the shock before you securely replace the screw.

10-10-1 If the steering continues to feel vague and possibly stiff, but the shock absorbers are in good order, have the front tracking professionally checked and the toe-in correctly set. While the

10-10-1 The car's front tracking may be at fault which could be caused by replacement of one or several worn parts, or by knocking the kerb with a front wheel. If you're getting this sort of uneven tyre wear, or the steering feels strange, get the tracking checked.

mechanic is there he should automatically check that the balljoints on the outer end of the steering mechanism are not worn. In the UK these balljoints are subject to close scrutiny at the annual MoT test.

10-11-1 If the problem still persists, the steering rack is the next consideration. It could be worn due to a lack of internal lubricant, which could eventually make it stiff and adversely affect the directness and positive feel of the steering.

Carefully check around both

10-11-1 (Picture 1) The annual roadworthiness test may reveal a split gaiter/boot (arrowed "1"), or you may notice an oil leak and become concerned that a split gaiter will allow dirt to enter and prematurely wear the steering rack. The MoT test may reveal that a steering ball joint (arrowed "2") is worn. In either case it will be necessary to remove the balljoints, thus upsetting the tracking.

10-11-1 (Picture 2) You'll need to clean the trackrod treads to make the following jobs easier...

gaiters/boots (the rubber bellows at each end of the rack) for cracks or holes from which oil may have leaked. If necessary, change the gaiters. Although not necessary to remove the steering rack, the ball joints at each end of the rack must be removed in order to slip the new gaiters onto the end of the rack - which, unfortunately, will upset the tracking (more on this shortly).

After changing the gaiters top up the

10-11-1 (Picture 3)...and almost certainly will need a ball joint splitter to...

10-11-1 (Picture 4) ...separate the tapered shoulder on the balljoint from the track control arm.

10-11-1 (Picture 5) Count the number of turns off the trackrod for each ball joint, and the number back on again, although it's still best to get the tracking checked afterward.

rack with the recommended oil. This is most easily achieved by jacking the car so that it is tilted sideways, and releasing the clamp that secures the gaitor to the track rod (usually a plastic tie), and syringing in the oil. Refasten the open end of the gaiter to achieve an oil-tight seal.

Provided you measured the centres

10-11-1 (Picture 6) Once the inner end of the gaiter is secured to the rack with the clip supplied in most gaiter kits...

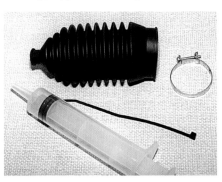

10-11-1 (Picture 7) ...a syringe will be necessary to inject the (thickish) EP90 oil into the rack through the small end of the gaiter. You may or may not get a cable tie-type clip in your kit...

10-11-1 (Picture 8) ...but one will be necessary to seal the small end of the gaiter to the trackrod.

of the ball joints and replicated that after fitting the new gaiters, the resultant wheel tracking should not be too inaccurate. Try the car for a few days and, if there's an improvement, get it professionally tracked. If no improvement, it's time to consider the rack itself.

Excessive play/lash at steering wheel

10-12-1 Play in the steering can also cause the car to wander, with the almost inevitable over-correction making the problem worse. This play is the result of wear within either the steering rack or the universal joint (UJ) within the steering column. You should be able to feel the play/lash at the steering wheel when the car is stationary, and also notice, when in motion, that turning the wheel slightly has little or no effect on direction.

Check the universal joint by having a helper turn the steering wheel from side-to-side whilst you watch the UJ for (tiny) flexing movements. They may be small

10-12-1 You may find the differences between the larger chrome bumper universal joint (nearest the camera) and a rubber bumper steering rack interesting.

and seem insignificant, but remember that wear in the UJ is multiplied several fold by the time the rim of the steering wheel is reached. Feel for movement in the UJ, (**Warning!** - you need to be sure your partner does not turn the steering wheel too far or too quickly thus trapping your hand!) If the UJ is worn it's easily replaced, although you'll have to drop the rack forwards for a few minutes by removing it from the front crossmember.

If the UJ is not showing even the smallest sign of play, then the play must be in the rack. On the off-chance that the rack is not securely fastened to the front crossmember, check the four rack mounting bolts. If tight, there's a wear problem within the rack: buy a service exchange rack.

10-13-1 Service exchange steering racks are readily available at reasonable cost, and come pre-filled with the correct grade of oil and new gaiters. Order a new pair of ball joints and lock nuts with your rack; you'll need a balljoint splitter to separate each ball joint from its steering arm.

After changing the rack and getting the ball joints as near the same distance apart as on the original rack, have the car professionally re-tracked at the earliest opportunity.

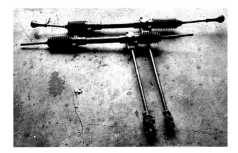

10-13-1 A pair of service exchange steering racks. The top one with the longer shaft and ball joints is the rubber bumper version, which, incidentally was also used on the factory V8 models.

Steering shake or vibration

10-14-1 Steering shake when driving at some speed, usually above 50 mph, should prompt you to check the tightness of all eight front wheelnuts or, if the car has wire wheels, the two front hexagonal or eared spinners.

However, the usual cause of steering shake is unbalanced wheels. Cars with wire wheels are particularly prone due to the difficulty of getting wire wheels balanced properly. Every tyre factor you call will tell you that they can balance wire wheels perfectly. Some may even believe that to be the case. However, the fact of the matter is that few non-specialists have the requisite adapters for wire wheels and still fewer can actually carry out the balancing operation properly. Often the wire wheels themselves are far more difficult to balance as the result of their construction, another reason you should find your nearest wire wheel specialist and have them balance your "wires".

Bolted "Rostyle" wheels are also prone to vibration when oversize tyres are fitted. A nice balance can usually be achieved by your local tyre retailer provided the wheel is "true" (i.e. not buckled or with a rim distortion), the centre-holes are not worn and the oversize tyre is not too wide for the 5J (5 inch) rim width. More and more MGBs are sporting alloy wheels that are not only lighter but

also correspondingly easier to balance, even with oversize tyres in place. There are some very attractive alloy wheels about too, however, be aware of one disadvantage - in due course they can corrode around the rims with the consequence of a permanent slow loss of pressure until such time as you get the tyres off their rims and get an alloy wheel specialist to refinish the inner rims.

10-14-1 You'll be familiar with the wheel nuts shown here, but I wonder if you were aware that they are available made from stainless steel? These cost more than the chromed originals, but don't rust. Note the attractive stainless steel rim embellisher.

Rapid and/or uneven tyre wear

10-15-1 Rapid or uneven tyre wear is often caused by incorrect tracking/toe-in of the front wheels, and should be checked and adjusted as discussed in 10-10-1. Extremely out-of-balance wheels (which will be accompanied by violent wheel shake as per 10-14-1) could also cause uneven tyre wear. Uneven tyre wear can be the result of over or under tyre inflation.

10-16-1 A gentle thump thump/wop wop sound that increases with road speed is likely to be a flat spot on one or more of the tyres. You might also get a feedback through the steering wheel if one or both front tyres are badly effected.

Check each wheel by jacking each corner of the car in turn and spinning the wheel while holding the palm of your hand held lightly against the tread: you'll feel any flat spots. If flatspots are the result of vigorous braking (in which case the reduction in tread may be noticeable), there's little choice but to replace the tyre. However, if the flat is the result of a winter lay-up, it's probably worth persevering as often these flat spots disappear with a little road mileage.

It's possible to reduce the flat spots by over-inflating the tyre(s) on a hot day. Park the car in the sun and/or take it for a gentle, cautious drive (**Warning!** - Over-inflated tyres will not provide good grip). Don't forget to correct the tyre pressure immediately afterward. Prevention being better than cure, during lay-up periods jack the car just enough to take the weight off of the tyres.

Clunk from front of car when brakes applied

10-17-1 If you hear a clunk from the front of the car when you brake, it could be caused by a number of front suspension faults (see 10-1 to 10-5) or even a loose brakepad. However, if you have a wire-

10-17-1 (Picture 1) If you can move the tangs on the brake pads up and down, replace at least the pair of spring clips above and below the tangs. Note the very small amount of clearance between the tangs and the ends of the clips and that it is (just) possible to get the clips in the wrong way round - giving the tangs too much room to move.

10-17-1 (Picture 2) The wire wheels fitted to this type of hub can cause a clunk from the front of the car when you brake.

wheeled car and have checked and resolved all suspension wear problems but it still "clunks", then the chances are you have worn splines and/or wheel hubs. Unfortunately, the only real solution is to replace both wheels and hubs.

Tyres deflate (wire wheel cars)

10-18-1 If you have a wire-wheeled MGB and a tyre that regularly deflates, you could have a straightforward puncture of the inner tube or you may have a puncture caused by exposed spoke ends. Not every newish MGB owner appreciates this, but you **must** have an inner tube inside a tyre that is fitted to a wire wheel. The second important detail to note is that the spoke ends ranged around the inside of the wheel rim **must** have a rubber protective strip covering them completely to protect the inner tube.

10-18-1 No, not the inside of a wire wheel rim but another sometimes related problem - loose spokes. These creak, particularly when braking, and here, not untypically, look very unsightly.

Converting to wire wheels

10-19-1 If you have a car with bolted steel wheels you should be alert to the potential problems associated with converting from steel or alloy/bolted wheels to wire wheels. Full kits are available to effect this change and, although they're expensive, I think they may well be the safest solution.

At the front of the car the change is relatively simple in that the bolted hubs that carry the wheel bearings need to be removed from the stub axles. **Warning!** - The new splined hub is "handed" - which is to say you **must** fit the left side splined hub to the left side of the car. Further, while assembling the new splined hubs to the stub axles you need to ensure that the requisite bearing clearances are adhered to (adjustment is via shims). The wire wheel then pushes onto the spined hub

and the spinner is fitted to retain it.

At the rear of the car it is a different story for the width of the bolted wheel-type rear axle is actually 1.5in (about 37mm) wider than that of a true original wire wheel-type axle. MG's reasoning was very sound although this fact is inconvenient to would-be converters! The wire wheels are wider at the spline - as the briefest of looks will confirm. Therefore, if the wire wheels were fitted to an axle intended for bolted wheels, they would extend outwards too far. Solution, reduce the width of the axle for wire wheel cars. So, if you have a car with bolted wheels and plan to change to "wires", then you do need the specially designed and manufactured rear hubs for this, rather than original equipment hubs.

Clicking noise that varies with road speed

10-20-1 On cars with Rostyle wheels this noise is caused by one or more of the small central caps being loose. For the time it takes, remove all four, spread the fingers that hold each cap to the wheel, tap each cap back in place (gently with a light hammer and a protective piece of wood), and try moving each before taking the car for a - hopefully - quiet run.

10-20-1 The Rostyle wheel, with the central, potentially noisy, cap arrowed.

Anti-roll bar bushes

10-21-1 The effectiveness of the anti-roll bar will be reduced if the rubber bonded bushes (top and/or bottom) degenerate and allow some movement. To bring road-holding back to the original standard, fit a new bush within the end of the

anti-roll bar and a new link to the bottom wishbone. To upgrade the anti-roll bar, fit polyurethane bushes; they transmit more suspension movement to the anti-roll bar and improve road-holding at the expense of increased road noise.

10-21-1 (Picture 1) The anti-roll bar with, nearest the camera, the end bush. The pivot bushes, located under the main frame rails, need to be in good shape too if the anti-roll bar is to work efficiently.

10-21-1 (Picture 2) The link between the suspension wishbone and the anti-roll bar needs to be able to translate the full wishbone movement to the roll bar, too. Note there are two lengths of link: one each for rubber bumper and chrome bumper models.

Chapter 11
Fuel smells

There are three main sources of leaking fuel - assuming you have not run over a rock or kerb and damaged the underside of the car. **Warning!** - The first step is the same whenever a fuel leak is suspected - stop, switch off the ignition and take a look as quickly as you possibly can. **Never go looking for fuel leaks with a naked light or hot bulb such as is fitted to most inspection lamps**. Always use a cold light, such as a flashlight.

Fuel smell at front of car
11-1-1 If the worst of the fuel smell is coming from the front of the car, the probability is that a carburettor is overflowing and if your car is an early one with HS4 carburettors (identified by their

11-1-1 The float with its pivot (arrowed) as used on early HS4 carburettors. The needle valve can be seen just to the left of the pivot. Later HS4 carburettors and all replacement floats use a one-piece plastic moulding, and the metal/adjustable arm is replaced by a non-adjustable, integrated plastic moulding. The lay of the float arm and its contact with the needle valve are all-important to fuel supply control which has a significant effect on fuel level and the smooth running of the engine. A worn/faulty needle valve or a damaged float can cause overflow of fuel from the carburettor.

separate float chambers alongside the main body of the carburettor) you should check carefully around the top of both float bowls. The later HIF carburettors had an integral float chamber and need to be checked at the side of each body. Look at the left side on the front carburettor and at the right side on rear carb (when looking from the left side of the car). In theory, the overflow pipe leading away from each carburettor should carry all excess fuel safely out of harm's way, but the outlets of these pipes often get blocked, leaving the fuel no choice but to escape via the joint between the float chamber and its top/cover.

There is a remote possibility that one of the floats could have sprung a leak and

is sitting lower than it should in the float chamber and therefore allowing too much fuel to enter. However, the normal cause of overflowing float chambers is worn float pivots and/or a stuck needle valve in one or both carburettors exacerbated by a blocked overflow pipe or pipes. As a roadside repair, the first step is to note which fuel pipe connects to which fitting on the float-chamber top/cover and then to remove it from the offending carburettor. Check that the float itself does not contain any fuel and whether the float pivot is badly worn. In either case, the only get-you-home repair is to bend the float's arm such that it makes earlier contact with the needle valve in the top cover. You'll of course need to effect a much more professional repair when you get home.

If all seems reasonably in order with the float and pivot, your problem must stem from the needle valve. It could be worn, or it could have a tiny piece of dirt lodged in it causing it to stick open. You don't need to remove the valve from the cover as part of a roadside fix, although you may find it necessary to remove both the fuel supply pipe and the overflow pipe to allow you to blow into the fuel supply opening. You can check that the needle valve is operating correctly by opening and closing it with your finger while blowing into the fuel inlet pipe. Once satisfied it is working satisfactorily, refit it and re-examine it for wear upon your return home, when you should also fit a new gasket to the top of float chamber and unblock the overflow pipes.

11-2-1 You now need to get down to check that the excess fuel is not being ejected from the overflow pipes at sump level. You'll almost certainly see a puddle of fuel under the left centre of the sump - which is good news in the sense that the overflows are not blocked!

However, the bad news is that it has now become much harder to tell which carburettor is causing you grief. You might be able to run the end of a finger over the overflow pipe ends to see which is wet with fuel. More likely you'll have to switch the ignition on (and therefore the fuel pump) in order to establish whether it is the front or the rear overflow pipe that is ejecting fuel. Once you know which carburettor to attack, the subsequent remedial work is as outlined in 11-1-1.

11-2-1 The HS carbs (shown here) have their overflow pipes exiting at the rear of the float bowl (arrowed), but are likely to show signs of fuel leakage around the edge of the bowl top if the overflow pipe is blocked.

11-3-1 If you do have carburettor needle valve problems subsequent to the repairs described in 11-1-1 and 11-2-1, you should take a close look at your car's fuel filtering arrangements. None of the early MGBs were fitted with a fuel filter, although many have subsequently had one retrofitted. However, over the years dirt gets into the fuel tank and, as we will see later in this chapter, the tank actually rusts from the inside. Collectively, therefore, there can be a fair amount of grit laying on the bottom of most MGB fuel tanks. A certain amount will be sucked up with the fuel and with nothing to

11-3-1 When dirt gets into the carburettor it initially has to get past the needle valve that controls the fuel level. Any that gets stuck under the needle valve has the potential to cause fuel level problems. You can get an idea of how much dirt there is in the fuel system by looking down into the float chamber. In an ideal world there should be none. The small 'dam' is there to protect the fuel jet from the worst of an accumulation of dirt. Eliminate dirt from the carbs by thorough cleaning and by fitting an effective fuel filter.

remove it *en route* most will collect in the carburettor float chambers, inevitably some will lodge in the needle valves causing you fuel level problems from time to time.

If you don't already have one, you should consider fitting a fuel filter into the fuel line around about the heater area. For those with a fuel filter already in place but still experiencing fuel level problems, it would be as well to buy a new one and to make sure it is fitted with the fuel flow directional arrow pointing towards the carburettors.

11-3-2 An SU HS-type carburettor may leak from the bottom of each float chamber where a small rubber ring, or gland, is located on the tail of the pipe that leads to the jet. You can see this gland in photograph 15-1-5. The gland should seal the joint, particularly when compressed by the tapered brass plug on the end of the jet, but has been known to weep and generate a strong fuel smell, particularly noticeable when the garage door is first opened.

The best get-you-home remedy is to tighten the hexagonal tapered plug a little. Not too much, or you run the risk of stripping the thread. If that fails to work then a new gland - backed up by a small steel washer - will do the trick. The washer is deceptively important as it prevents the plug from twisting the gland, yet it's often overlooked.

11-3-2 A source of fuel leaks is the rubber gland in the bottom of the float chamber. Unscrew the brass nut and fit a new gland and small steel washer to the end of the flexible jet tube before offering the assembly back to the float chamber. Always double-check the replacement for leaks.

Fuel smells from beneath the car
11-4-1 Not all fuel leaks will come from the carburettors and we need to check the next most likely source - the flexible fuel lines. Note that these may be in place throughout the car and that, consequently, you need to be aware that the leak could be from any part of the fuel line leading to the carburettors including the interconnecting flexible fuel lines between them.

Obviously, any mechanical chaffing or vibration will eventually bring about a leak from the rubber hoses that connect the various parts of the fuel system, however not everyone is aware that most of the original rubber fuel hoses are in fact incompatible with unleaded fuel... Consequently, what seems like a perfectly sound flexible fuel hose from the outside maybe being eaten away from the inside by the unleaded fuel you're now using. In due course a fuel leak will occur and it's best that you're alert to this possibility until you change the hoses for unleaded-compatible ones.

Try not to make the same mistake as I did in that I had filled the tank with unleaded fuel a few days earlier and went to the garage only to find an unmistakable

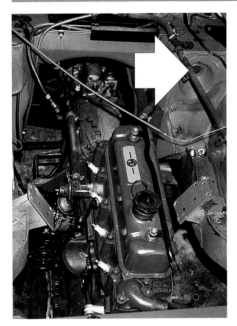

11-4-1 These are not the only flexible fuel lines in an MGB, but note that many old rubber materials are not compatible with the unleaded fuels of today.

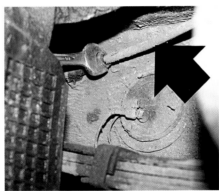

11-5-1 Originally made from steel and located to collect all the spray that's going, this fuel pipe runs forward from the fuel tank. On chrome bumper cars it runs over the top of the rear axle to the fuel pump located at the bottom of the right rear wheelarch, so corrodes quickly. Rubber bumper cars are marginally better as the pipe does not run round the inside of the wheelarch. Both can corrode, however, causing fuel leakage.

and very strong smell of fuel. What would have happened were I smoking at the time I dread to think. However - you have already guessed I had a fuel leak from a perished hose joining two metal fuel pipes together. There was petrol/gasoline all over the floor and a steady dripping from the hose in question. I hastily assembled a couple of fuel cans and symphoned what was left from the tank and thence into another car. I replaced the offending hose and forgot about that problem ... a month later the whole scenario, including the full tank, happened all over again! There was a second flexible connecting pipe I was unaware of that had now perished too. If I had taken the trouble, I could easily have changed that one as well while the tank was empty first time around. So, once one hose goes the rest will probably follow quickly: change the lot in one go!

11-5-1 If you have the original steel fuel pipes still in place in your car look too for dampness, sometimes even wetness from a fuel leak from a apparently "solid" metal pipe. Impossible I hear you say! Not so, in that there are actually two ways that a supposedly "solid" steel pipe can leak. Firstly the pipe is actually made from flat steel strip that is formed into a tube and (automatically) welded down the length of its seam. The pipe remains perfectly

serviceable and entirely satisfactory for many years but a seam-welded steel pipe in otherwise good condition can corrode at this welded seam and, after many years become porous. This leads to dampness from weeping fuel and just as pungent a smell of fuel as a full-blown leak. The second way these "solid" pipes can leak is straightforward corrosion. There are one or two spots that are particularly vulnerable and corrosion will eventually hole the original steel pipes that make up the majority of the system, so be assured leaks are possible from anywhere on any of the steel fuel pipes.

The steel fuel pipes around the right side rear wheel are most at risk of corrosion, with the pipe that runs from the fuel tank (being behind the rear wheel) the most vulnerable of all. In chrome-bumpered cars this pipe not only runs alongside the fuel tank, but around the wheel arch on its way to the fuel pump - thus increasing its exposure to water, salt and grit and, consequently, its susceptibility to corrosion. Out of interest, any corrosion that allows fuel to leak from this particular pipe also allows air into the very pipe that the pump is using to suck fuel from the tank. Consequently, the fuel pump may be unable to suck more than air and while it will tick furiously there will be little fuel at the carburettors to show for it. So, if you were ever at all suspicious as

to the integrity of the fuel pipe you would do well to replace the pipe with a copper replacement before the car grinds to a halt.

Provided you can buy a metre of genuine fuel compatible rubber hose, it's possible to cut the steel pipe each side of the corrosion, slip the flexible hose over the ends and fasten both with a pair of jubilee clips. **Warning!** - I don't recommend you delay too long before making a permanent repair.

Fuel smell at rear of car
11-6-1 The fuel tank can leak and also generate the telltale fuel odour from the sender aperture. This can be the result of the six fixing screws (early cars with the 10 Imperial gallon tanks secured by two metal straps) or locking/sealing rings (later cars) having been miss-assembled, although if you have not touched this area of the tank in recent months, this is unlikely.

In both cases the seal behind the sender is made of rubber and if you switched to unleaded fuels some months ago, it's possible that the sealing ring is of some age (possibly original, and therefore at least 20 years old!) and is not compatible with unleaded fuels.

11-6-1 (Picture 1) Here is the sender unit aperture, located on the right side of the tank on an early car. Later cars had the fuel supply line incorporated into the sender unit. Clearly, this has not been leaking. However, the seal...

You can see the tank sender assembly by lying behind the rear right side wheel and should be able to spot whether it looks damp. If the car has been through a puddle recently seeing a fuel weep may be a bit more difficult but you could run your finger round the mud and check whether it has a fuel smell. If so, you'll have to decide how bad the leak is and act accordingly.

11-6-1 (Picture 2) …looks like this (arrowed) and is pictured along with the new sender unit and clamp ring that post-GHN3 cars used.

Try tightening the six bolts (early cars) or tapping clockwise one of the tangs on the outer locking ring if yours is a later example. However, I would not do either of these things in a roadside situation as you could make the leak much worse as you upset a sealing ring already almost disintegrating from attack by incompatible fuel!

Siphon fuel into a (proper) fuel can until the level of fuel in the tank is below the sender aperture. There should be several gallons left in the tank to get you home or to a place where you can address the problem in safety and reasonable comfort. For the record, in case you're wondering, the early tanks hold 10 Imperial gallons as do the later US cars. However the UK cars from late 1967 enjoyed an extra couple of gallons capacity.

To fix the problem properly the first order of business is to drop the fuel level in the tank low enough to allow you to remove the sender unit without having fuel escape all over the floor. You can always lift the right side of the car using a trolley jack and secure the car safely with an axle stand. This will not only make access to the sender unit easier, but also tip your fuel towards the left of the car - away from the hole you're about to open in the right side of your fuel tank. **Warning!** - For safety's sake, disconnect the earth/ground wire at the battery terminal. Treat the sender unit wires and their connections very carefully; its likely they've been there for years and have become rusted and very fragile. Indeed, if you've become uncertain about the accuracy of your fuel

gauge of late, this might be the moment to replace the sender unit completely along with the connections to it. There are several different types of sender, but all are still available and for what they cost, a new replacement is really not a bad idea. So take a look before you start removing the old unit from the tank and if yours is really rusted, order a new one.

In any event you'll need to order a new rubber seal but also, in the case of later cars, a new locking ring. The removal method for the early six bolt sender unit is obvious, but the later cars locking method may warrant a moment's explanation. The tank has three oval equally spaced lobes welded to it, while the locking ring has three cut-outs which you need to line up with the lobes by knocking the locking ring round anti-clockwise - whereupon the locking ring should pull off. Rust will be your main problem, and I strongly recommend you spray the whole assembly with WD40 or Duck-oil at least a couple of days before trying to knock any one of the three tangs round with a hammer and punch. You only need to move the locking-ring about one-third of a turn to get the cut-outs and the lobes to align, but it'll be difficult.

Clean everything and start reassembly by putting the new rubber seal either onto its studs (early cars) or into the "hole" in the side of the tank. The sender goes in next with, in the case of the early cars, the nuts last. In the case of the later cars you'll need to take care to get a small orientation cut-out in the correct place and to double check that the sender has gone in truly flush with the seal. Mind you, you'll find out whether you got the sender positioned correctly when the **new** locking ring goes into place. I think it a good idea to lightly smear petroleum jelly/Vaseline on the face of the locking ring that will interface with the sender for easier movement and long term rust prevention.

The penultimate step is to drive a tang on the locking ring clockwise by about a third of its diameter. You should note the cam-like action of the locking ring on the tank tightens the sender onto the seal for a fuel tight joint - provided you drive the locking round as far as is practicable. Pop the sender feed and earth/ground wires onto the sender (again a smear of petroleum jelly on the contacts is a really good idea) and try the joint first for leaks before switching on the ignition and checking the fuel gauge.

11-7-1 A particularly strong smell of fuel from the back of the car, after filling

11-7-1 The vulnerable front edge is arrowed but note that the top front half of this - not untypical - tank is in a pretty awful state, and doubtless was leaking fumes. It's not difficult to believe that the front half of this tank was depositing large quantities of rusted metal into the fuel system.

the tank and/or when the car is pointing downhill, could also indicate a leak from the tank. The MGB fuel tank is vulnerable to corrosion along the very front/top. A line about 1in (25mm) wide across the tank's width can be damp with leaking fuel and, in severe cases, if the tank is full and the car pointed downhill, you can actually see a line of fuel leaking onto the ground under the front of the fuel tank.

Assuming your tank has not yet got to the line-of-leaking-fuel stage, take a look at the **top** of the front of the tank, almost under the floor of the boot/trunk. If the car has been through a puddle recently, spotting a fuel weep may be more difficult, but you can run your finger along the top of the tank to see if there is a fuel smell. Take a look at the front of the tank; is it vertically streaked, has any underseal gone soft, is there a strong smell of fuel, is the tarmac melting under the front edge of the tank? If you have a full fuel tank and park the car nose-down on a hill, it's often possible to see the fuel dripping.

If this is your problem then you have no option but to replace the fuel tank.

11-8-1 You may have to replace the fuel tank because of external corrosion, as described in 11-7-1. It may be, however, that you are fed-up with internal rust particles constantly choking the fuel filters or carburettors.

Rust gathers at the bottom of the tank as the result of condensation and a certain amount of water in the fuel. The

11-8-1 (Picture 1) A stainless steel MGB fuel tank will eliminate the possibility of internal and external corrosion. It can still collect lots of dirt - and even water - when being filled.

water always sits on the bottom of the tank, with the resultant inevitable corrosion in a mild-steel tank. Some replacement MGB tanks (there are three types) are available in stainless steel - which is more expensive but will not corrode.

In the case of an early car where the tank is held in place with a pair of (metal) mounting straps, look very critically at those you are about to remove and, if in any doubt, order a new pair, along with a pair of the rubber packing strips.

When fitting a new tank to a later

11-8-1 (Picture 2) Be careful when removing the sender unit wires; the earth/ground tag in the centre of this one has disappeared, making a new sender necessary.

11-8-1 (Picture 3) If you're hoping to re-use the existing sender unit you may think again when you try to knock the tanged retaining ring round to unlock it.

11-8-1 (Picture 4) The sender unit revealed - it helps if your are unconcerned about damaging the tank and the ring when you remove it.

car buy a 'fitting kit,' which will provide all of the tank to boot/trunk floor fastenings you need, including several captive nuts.

Finally you will need a new foam floor seal.

A few tips may help. If your new tank is made from mild steel, as soon as it arrives, paint it with several generous coats of enamel paint, stick the rubber anti-vibration strips in place and apply several coats of wax preservative. Be particularly generous with paint and preservative along the top front of the tank.

Warning! - For safety's sake, disconnect the earth/ground wire at the battery terminal before starting work. The tank should be emptied of as much fuel as possible and the car safely jacked to a practical working height. A fuel tank

11-8-1 (Picture 5) Reassemble everything you can on the workbench. Here, we see the new sender going in after the rubber seal. Richard Ladds of the MGOC is obligingly pointing out one of three locking tangs on the tank. The locking ring drops over this and then locks under it when knocked (gently) round by about 100 degrees.

11-8-1 (Picture 6) There are a few captive nuts to tap on - and you really must get these in place before you offer the tank up to the car...

containing several gallons of fuel will weigh more than you might imagine, and can be difficult to handle at arm's length under the boot of the car. A pair of trolley jacks and at least two hefty lengths of wood will help drop the old tank and lift the new into place.

11-8-1 (Picture 7) ...as you can see here. Richard is fitting a nut onto a bolt that has been pushed down...

11-8-1 (Picture 8) ...from the boot/trunk floor. A new sponge sealing ring has to be pre-fitted round the tank filler tube before the tank is lifted up under the boot floor.

Once the old tank is on the floor, drag it out of the way and take an inspection light to the underside of the

11-8-1 (Picture 8) Last but not least, refit the filler tube.

boot floor. Clean the area with a wire brush, spray the floor generously with wax preservative, let that 'flash-off' and spray it again. Fit the new sender unit to the new tank and use the jacks to lift and hold it up against the boot floor.

Before offering the washer/washer/bolt combinations through the boot floor to secure the tank, place a heavy-duty steel washer under the head of the bolts and a fibre sealing washer under the steel washers. Once all of the bolts are 'started,' tighten them progressively, refit the sender wires and fuel line and fill the tank with **clean** fuel.

11-9-1 If the unions on the fuel pump are weeping, it won't take much to generate that unmistakable smell: a tiny weep from just one of the four faces of the banjo connections to the pump will do it.

This can happen more often than you might think, largely because copper washers are fitted instead of the correct fibre washers. Chances are, if either of the banjo unions is leaking, you'll find that one, possibly two, copper washers have been fitted in error. Before you start to investigate, buy four fibre washers, one for each side of each banjo: I bet you'll use them...

Fuel smell after something has struck underside of car

11-10-1 Damaged fuel lines can leak fuel, though are the least likely reason for fuel leakage. The damage is usually caused by

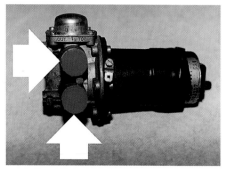

11-9-1 These two fuel inlet/outlet connections are often fitted with copper washers and can weep fuel. Fit fibre washers each side of each banjo to avoid this problem. "Out: Top" tells you which way to mount the pump and the correct pipe connections.

flying stones or traffic-calming humps, but can also occurred when maintaining the car.

From the pump forward, the fuel line runs under the floor of the passenger compartment. **Warning!** - It **must** be clipped safely to the inside of the 'chassis' box section that runs fore and aft beneth the floor of the car. At the central crossmember it has to loop down and over the member while protected by a rubber shield and flat metal clamp. Thereafter it progresses upwards into the gearbox tunnel, eventually emerging into the engine compartment.

Careless jacking could crush the line and if you've driven over a kerb, stone or bank you may have ruptured the fuel line. The immediate action is obvious of course - switch-off the ignition and therefore the fuel pump in an effort to minimise fuel spillage.

Prevention is always better than cure: ensure the fuel line on your car is routed correctly and clipped securely. It's possible to install copper fuel lines instead of the original steel lines: an excellent long-term investment provided they're installed properly and safely.

Chapter 12

Propshaft, rear axle, rear suspension & rear wheels

It can be difficult to pinpoint where noises - particularly from the back of the car - are coming from. I once changed a rear axle as I was sure that a most unpleasant mechanical transmission noise was coming from the back of the car. The noise continued afterwards and I eventually traced it to a worn front universal joint (UJ) ...

Some noises can have serious consequences, so unusual sounds from the rear of the car should be taken seriously.

The MGB was fitted with two types of rear axle: early Roadsters had what was called a "banjo" rear axle which you can identify by checking to see if the front nose of the differential is bolted to the main axle casing. Banjo axle and component parts are quite different to that on later Roadster and all GT "Tube"-axled cars introduced around April 1967. A sub-contractor named Salisbury manufactured tube axles, and they are often referred to by this name, too.

Clunk from rear of car when starting off or changing gear (wire wheels or "knock-on" alloys)

12-1-1 Most MGBs with wire wheels will make a 'clunking' noise from the rear axle area when starting off and/or changing speed. The same can be said of cars with "knock-on" alloy wheels; i.e. those with a splined drive. Except in extreme cases this poses little immediate danger so, once you have established that it's the rear splined hubs that are the source of the clocking, you can relax to some extent.

The following is not relevant to bolted-on wheels, regardless of style. If you do not have wire wheels on your car and yet can regularly hear a clonk, you should skip this section and refer to 12-2-1 for possible reasons and solutions.

To understand what's causing the clunk on wire wheel cars we need to appreciate that the splined hub engages with the wheel via a large number of male splines (rather like a very fine-toothed gear wheel): the inner part of the wheel hub

12-1-1 (Picture 2) ...like this. Wear in either wheel or hub spline can result in a bit of a 'clunk' when you start off but wear in both will generate an awful thump.

has the equivalent female splines. When both male and female splines are new they mesh very closely indeed, with very little play/lash. In fact, a good wheel can be surprisingly hard to fit to a good splined hub. However the splines on both male and female parts of the assembly are, as I mentioned a line or two ago, fairly fine and wear with use.

Unquestionably, this wear is accelerated by repeated hard use when, the hub's male spline is twisted violently in the female/wheel's spline on fast take-offs. Equally, repeated emergency braking

12-1-1 (Picture 1) The wire wheel has a series of splines, almost like small gear teeth, that fit over a similar arrangement on the hub...

stops will also take their toll on the splines. After many thousands of miles play/lash builds up and you'll feel this free movement if you rock each wheel on its hub next time you're changing a rear wheel for any reason.

Make sure the handbrake is on to eliminate all hub movement and carry out your test before you fully tighten the spinner that holds the wheel on the spline to feel the full extent of the play.

The clunk noise that you're hearing is the take-up of the play in the splines when you accelerate and brake. The greater the play, the more obvious the clunk.

"That's okay," I hear you saying, "I'll just tighten the spinner up a bit more than usual." Sadly the solution is not as easy as that although, certainly, a tight spinner is a very good idea in any event. However the torque of the engine, particularly in low gear in one direction and the inertia of the car in the other direction will totally override any frictional resistance you can apply to the wheel/hub by tightening the spinner, however tight!

You may be tempted to think that, now you know what and where the problem is, you can ignore it. In the vast majority of cases this is true. However, be aware that the wear on both splines actually accelerates dramatically as the freeplay increases. In extreme cases both male and female splines become as sharp as razors as wear removes material and you could see up to 2 inches (50mm) rotational movement of the tyre! Wear to this extent is most easily seen on the hub's splines, and if yours have become very much reduced in size and very sharp, then it is time for remedial action.

The solution is not simply to buy a new set of wire wheels, however. This will reduce by half the play between wheel and hub but, unless the hubs are in good shape (unlikely), there will still be too much play between hub and wheel, and the whole play/movement/wear cycle will start again on both hub and (now new) wheels, dramatically foreshortening the life of the new wheels.

The proper solution to worn hubs and wheels is to renew both. That way, play will be virtually eliminated and both hubs and wheels will give the long life their manufactures intended.

Clunk from rear of car when starting off or changing gear (bolt-on wheels)

12-2-1 A 'clunk' from the rear of a car with bolted wheels could be caused by

something as simple as loose wheel nuts. You wouldn't be the first to forget to fully tighten them after maintenance work. However, they've also been known to simply work loose, to the extent that wheels actually part company with the car!

Contributory to this and movement of a steel wheel, even with tight wheel nuts, is the not-uncommon practice of over-tightening the nuts. The garages I use now complete final nut tightening with a torque-wrench but, for many years, most would tighten the nuts with an air gun. If the gun's torque is set too high, tightening can spread the steel and open up the bolt holes to a point where the wheel can become loose and even pull off over the wheel nuts! It's definitely worth checking by jacking each corner of the car and rocking each wheel with, at the back, the handbrake on (if you do find this fault, check the front wheels too). If the wheels are worn or damaged, the only solution is new wheels as soon as possible.

Clunk from rear of car on take off

12-3-1 With bolted wheel and wire-wheel cars alike, a clocking noise - particularly when starting off - could signify a loose hub on its halfshaft.

12-3-1 (Picture 1) The nut that holds the hub to the halfshaft is easy to see and check for torque on bolted-wheel cars as seen here. It's just as vital that it's tight on wire-wheel cars but...

The hub is secured on the halfshaft by a single large (1 1/8in AF) slotted nut. On a bolted/Rostyle wheeled car this is in full view once the wheel has been removed, but it's much more difficult to see when the car is fitted with wire-wheeled splined hubs. It's still there, but way down inside the hub and infinitely more difficult to see.

These nuts should be prevented from

12-3-1 (Picture 2) ...it's located down inside the hub and is much less obvious and far harder to get at. Take a look at the workshop manual, or get your local MG specialist to check it if you're still getting 'clunking' noises. This is an MGC rear axle, but the halfshaft nut is identical.

coming undone by a split pin, which is easily accessed in the case of a bolted wheel hub but can only be got to on wire-wheel hubs via a cross/access hole in the splined hubs. If your hubs are both really securely fixed to the halfshaft, and the nuts are tight to the extent that there's no movement whatsoever, all is well.

However, some owners clearly think that the presence of a substantial split pin means that the nut does not have to be tight - wrong! **Warning!** - The nut **must** be tightened to the specified torque, **plus** whatever additional force is necessary to reach alignment of the splitpin holes in order to hold the hub securely onto the tapered end of the Salisbury axle halfshaft: don't forget to replace the splitpin.

If your car's hubs are loose, remove the split pin and check the nuts are tightened to the correct torque figure.

12-4-1 While in the vicinity of the rear hubs, take a moment to assess each rear hub bearing, which do wear and can cause a rear-end 'clonking' noise. Hub bearing condition is vital to the safety of the car, and this is one of the many checks in the UK's annual MoT test. Readers may have seen the rear of their car being raised slightly and a bar used under each rear tyre to check for rear wheel play, which would signify wear in a rear hub bearing.

It's not so easy to carry out this check at home. A good idea of severe wear can be acquired by shaking each rear wheel in

12-4-1 (Picture 1) There are two reasons to think that a rear hub bearing is wearing; the play/lash described in the main text and this - oil leaks from the stud holes or down the rear of the backplate.

12-4-1 (Picture 2) To give you some idea of what is involved in getting to the oil seal and bearing, loosen the hub retaining nut and remove it...

12-4-1 (Picture 3) ...A decent hub puller will be required to remove the hub from the halfshaft...

turn once an axle stand has taken the weight off the ground. Anything more than the slightest movement means that further investigation is called for.

An oil leak from a rear hub will also indicate wear. Whilst a leaking hub oil seal does not necessarily mean that the bearing needs replacement, it should arouse suspicion. There are several other reasons why a hub oil seal may leak, as discussed elsewhere, but it will have to be replaced, which will enable you to assess the condition of the substantial ball bearing located at each end of the rear axle. A hub bearing can be worn without the oil seal leaking, particularly if the oil level in the rear axle is lower than it should be.

12-4-1 (Picture 4) ...to get at the four (one of which is arrowed) bolts that retain the backplate and the bearing/oil seal housing.

Clunk on take off, ringing/ whirring noise when underway and, possibly, vibration too

12-5-1 The next most frequent source of rear-end noise is the propshaft/driveshaft, or - more specifically - the universal joints at each end of the propshaft. Whether it's the front or rear UJ that's worn, the resultant 'clunk' is often accompanied by a ringing sound that seems to emanate from the back of the car.

In the early stages of wear the noise will be most in evidence upon starting off - when a single clunk will be heard. As the wear becomes more advanced, an unusual ringing/whirring noise will become evident, which will not change pitch as you change gear but which will vary with road speed. An unpleasant vibration could also accompany the noise. What has happened here is that the tiny roller bearing within one of the UJs is starting to, or has already, broken up, allowing several millimetres of play/lash

12-5-1 (Picture 1) If there's play/lash in either UJ, before removing the sliding spline from the front end of the propshaft/ driveshaft, record the orientation of the flanges at each end of the shaft; it's important they're reassembled correctly. There will be four circlips to remove like this for each UJ.

12-5-1 (Picture 2) Tapping the yoke of the u/j, as shown here, should eject each of the four bearing cups in turn, whereupon the central spider should come away easily.

and throwing the propshaft out of balance.

The play will normally be easily detected by driving the rear of the car onto ramps (or elevating the rear via a safe pair of axle stands), putting the car in gear and setting the handbrake on. Underneath the car hold the drive pinion at the front of the back axle with one hand and first twist then shake the propshaft with the other. There should be no movement within the rear UJ; move forward and check the UJ and sliding spline at the front. If either UJ (or the sliding spline) move, this is the source of the noise and/or vibration. If all's well, grease the UJ (if it has grease nipples) and/or the sliding spline (which certainly should have a grease nipple). 12-6-1 gives some repair tips.

12-5-1 (Picture 3) Take the four bearing cups off the new spider and ensure the needles are all nicely disposed and, if the bearings are not lubricated, add plenty of clean grease to each cup. Put the spider into the UJ yokes and push the two opposite cups into place from the outside. The vice/vise shown here will help get the cups about 90 per cent into place, but you'll probably find that a carefully selected socket will be invaluable to help press each cup fully home. Whatever you do, don't press a cup in beyond its circlip groove. Get the circlips in place for the first pair of cups before starting to fit the second pair of cups into the other yoke.

12-6-1 'Clunking' noises accompanied by vibration can also mean a loose coupling between the propshaft and the rear axle drive flange: check this whilst under the car looking at the rear UJ.

If you need to rectify a faulty UJ you have choices but, undoubtedly, the easiest and quickest is to buy and fit a complete used propshaft. Measure the overall length of yours (*in situ*) and be aware that there were several slightly different lengths. Be careful to inspect the UJs (and sliding spline) of any prospective purchase thoroughly, and avoid anything that on one-hand flops about or is seized solid.

You may prefer to fit new UJs, but you'll need to do this carefully and in accordance with a workshop manual. If you do go down this route do be sure things are completely clean and that no dirt can get into the new UJ while you're fitting it to the propshaft.

Another tip is that, occasionally, the UJs' manufacturing tolerances are such that getting the second circlip in place proves very difficult. In this circumstance you need to acquire a thinner circlip.

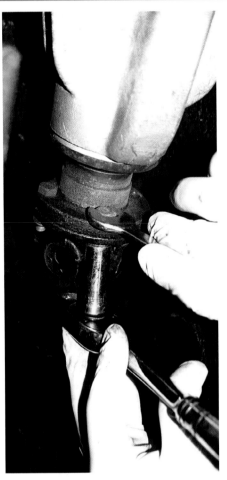

12-6-1 (Picture 1) A loose UJ can generate some uncomfortable rear-end noises. Check both UJs.

12-6-1 (Picture 2) The two inside yokes should be aligned, as shown here. Check a replacement propshaft or your own after any repairs have been carried out.

Given a choice, always buy UJs with grease nipples, even if they cost more than the "sealed for life" alternative.

Finally, when repairing the front UJ

there is a temptation to separate the rather unwieldy rear of the propshaft at the sliding joint. **Caution!** - If you decide to separate the joint, do mark both sides so that you reassemble them in exactly the same relationship: failure to do so will induce a pulsing in the drive and/or an unpleasant vibration since the orientation of the UJs at each end of the shaft is important - and not a lot a folk know that!

Rattling or clunking from rear when underway

12-7-1 A rattle and/or 'clunking' sound when driving along, even over reasonably smooth roads, can signal a loose, malfunctioning or faulty component in

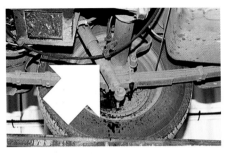

12-7-1 (Picture 1) This is the preferred - but non-standard - telescopic rear shock absorber...

12-7-1 (Picture 2) ...but, if your car has either of these links, then it has the original lever arm shock absorbers. The longer one is from a rubber bumper car.

one of the shock absorbers. The noise will likely be even more pronounced when you drive over a bump and could vary slightly depending upon whether you have telescopic or conventional lever arm "shocks" fitted.

You can assess which type of rear shock absorber is fitted to your car by removing one rear wheel. Telescopics are a straight tube that runs upwards from just below and behind the rear axle to a mounting point on the bodyframe some 12in (300mm) above the rear axle.

The original lever arm shocks are bulbous in appearance, are mounted on the inner wing about 12in (300mm) above the rear axle and have an almost horizontal (lever) arm that points forward and is coupled to a separate link that drops down to a plate fixed to the bottom of the leaf spring.

12-7-2 If the noise sounds like 'cluck,' regardless of the type of shock absorbers fitted to your car, the first check each side is that the two through bolts that secure the shock absorber to the frame/inner-wing are secure. You'll need to get the wheel(s) off since the head of the bolt is on the inside of the frame rail and will need to be held very securely with a spanner/wrench while you torque the outer nuts up. Check that there is a spring washer in place under the nut(s) and if missing take a few extra minutes to remove the loose nut(s) and position a large plain and a new spring washer under the nut.

12-7-2 (Picture 1) This shot also includes the bottom of a lever arm shock, but the picture's prime purpose is to show the location of the top two shock absorber retaining bolts.

12-7-2 (Picture 2) The bolts are quite long and must be really tight. These are used whichever type of shock absorber is fitted.

12-7-3 A rapid rattle is likely to mean faulty telescopic shock absorbers. The rattle can vary from a twice per second

12-7-3 (Picture 1) The tubular telescopic shock absorber is a very worthwhile upgrade to consider if/when conventional lever arm units require replacement. telescopic units will initially cost more to buy and fit than recon. originals, but will give better roadholding and have a longer maintenance-free life. These are Spax adjustable gas units, as fitted to both my MGBs.

tattoo whilst driving over a flat piece of road, to a more laidback rattle that - strangely - occurs only when the suspension is working hard. Some telescopic units are adjustable via a small screw in the bottom of the unit, and it's worth turning that a couple of times in the "harder" (usually clockwise) direction to see if it makes any difference. If neither the rattle nor the ride change, then a **pair** of replacement shocks are required.

Another likely cause of a rattling noise is that the top or bottom rubber mounting bushes have become displaced (usually the result of inadequately large washers each side when the shocks were installed), or have simply worn. In either case the bushes should be replaced and flanked by large, heavy-duty washers.

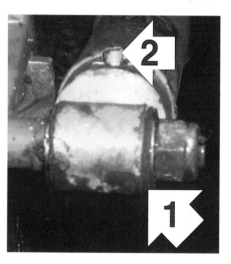

12-7-3 (Picture 2) The steel washers (arrowed "1") that retain the rubber bushes need to be bigger in diameter than the bushes by at least 5mm, to avoid the rubber bushes spreading. The second arrow highlights the adjustment screw on a Spax unit.

12-7-4 A 'clunking'/rattle from cars fitted with lever arm "shocks" can emanate from three sources -

Start by inspecting the tubular rubber bush at the bottom of each link. These have to work pretty hard and eventually perish with the result that the central metal mounting "bolt" comes into contact with the tubular external end of the linkage and a rattle develops. Not, initially, a very noticeable one, but one that can increase as the perished rubber deteriorates further. The usual first sign of trouble is the no longer parallel alignment of the central

12-7-4 (Picture 1) Although we saw these a couple of pictures ago, the focus here is the bonded rubber tubular tops & spherical bases. This shot shows how the link couples the bottom bracket, bolted beneath the rear leaf spring, with the shock absorber arm. The rubber bushes eventually tire, as we can see here, allowing the metal components to touch & rattle.

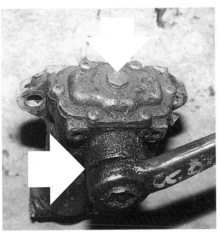

12-7-4 (Picture 2) This picture focuses on the Armstrong lever-arm rear shock absorber itself, as originally fitted to all MGBs. It is best replaced by a pair of telescopic shocks, however the picture is helpful to those who still have them fitted to their cars. One arrow draws your attention to the filler plug in the top of the shock. If the level of hydraulic oil within the body falls due to a leak at the (arrowed) pivot, not only will you get a rattle, but you will reduce the effectiveness of the shock!

12-8-1 (Picture 1) The extensive rubber pads above and below the axle can compress and leave these four nuts slacker than they should be.

12-8-1 (Picture 2) This is the front eye rubber bush for a rear spring. It serves a dual purpose in mounting the spring and carrying all the drive, braking and cornering forces. Note the location of this axle stand, under the front spring hanger just forward of the eyebolt: the best location for safely elevating the body to work on the rear suspension.

mounting and tubular end to the link.

The second check is at the top end of the link - where it attaches to shock's lever arm. Is that also in good shape? If the integrity of either end of the link is doubtful, you'll have to replace the link by removing the rear shock and axle plate to the bench as one assembly. Whether the link looks OK or not, it's prudent to also take a look at the shock absorber itself. You're looking for signs of an oil leak.

If you had a rear end rattle and are not yet sure that you've found the cause, remove the body access plug, clean the plug and its surrounding area and unscrew the fluid level filler plug on the top of each shock absorber. If the level is low, whether you can see signs of an oil leak or not, top it up with the correct hydraulic oil. If that temporally fixes the rattle but it returns a short while later, check for oil leaks again and, if present, fit service-exchange shock absorbers on **both** sides of the car. Service-exchange shock absorbers are not expensive and it's important that the car is balanced by your fitting replacements to both sides simultaneously. You can, of course, take this as an opportunity to fit

telescopic units, which will improve the handling of the car - a topic well covered in *How to Improve MGB, MGC and MGB V8* (also from Veloce Publishing and by the same author).

Dull thud from rear when a wheel hits a bump

12-8-1 An occasional dull thud when travelling over a bump, pothole or poor road surface warrants you checking that the U-bolts that hold the rear axle to the rear springs are tight. To be fair, once initially tightened and then retightened to the correct torque around 500 miles later, these rarely give cause for concern never mind any form of suspension noise. However, it's possible that you or a previous owner has fitted new rear springs but forgotten to subsequently retighten the U-bolts after the rubber cushions each side of the rear springs have settled. The required torque setting will be found in a workshop manual.

If all's well with the U-bolts, take a look at the front spring eye bolts that not only secure the front of the springs to the chassis, but also locate the rear axle. It's very unusual for there to be any problem

with the rubber bush at the front of the spring if the spring is in reasonable shape and not over 30 years old!

However, if your car's rear springs are of some age, possibly sagging and almost certainly very rusty, take look at the rubber eye bushes because it's possible

12-8-1 (Picture 3) It looks as if this central tube has separated from its bonded rubber bush, and certainly needs replacing. Since the spring also looks well used, this is clearly a case for a new pair of rear springs.

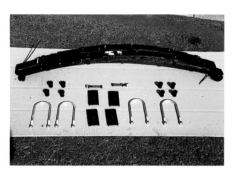

12-8-1 (Picture 4) Order a complete kit, as shown here. Safely support both car and axle, and change one spring at a time.

12-8-1 (Picture 5) In addition to the front eye fastening, remove the two U-bolts...

12-8-1 (Picture 6) ...and the rear shackle, seen here with the sideplate removed.

12-8-1 (Picture 7) Use lots of copper-based grease at every stage of reassembly, and remember that the springs are heavy; get help to offer up each replacement.

they've perished and are neither locating the rear axle as you would wish nor providing the cushioned spring movement important to reasonably silent rear suspension. If an eye bush has perished you'll need to replace **both** rear springs. The springs come with new bushes in place and will transform the drivability of your car if the old springs were "past it".

I must tell you that removing a pair of rusted rear springs from an MGB is high on my list of hated jobs and one you may be very wise to subcontract to your

12-8-1 (Picture 8) You may need to compress the spring to lengthen it sufficiently to get the shackle into place (before fitting the plate)...

12-8-1 (Picture 9) ...and to drop the axle to marry it to the spring...

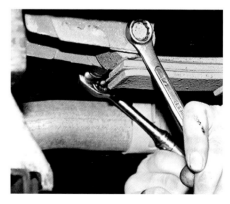

12-8-1 (Picture 10) ...Finally, tighten the eye bolt with the car's weight on the axle.

nearest MG specialist. Why? The bolts that pass through the two eye bushes at the front of the springs are always rusted solid into the rubber bushes, are very difficult to get at and almost inevitably have to ground off (with an angle grinder) or cut through with a thin blade (a junior hacksaw).

Clacking noise from rear on acceleration or decceleration

12-9-1 Post-1977 cars had a rear anti-roll bar which has been known to work loose and 'clack' between acceleration and deceleration. Check the bolts that fasten the bar to the bodywork and tighten if necessary.

Clunking and whining/wowing noise from rear axle

A back axle, even a properly maintained one, can generate a severe 'clunk' when starting off. If there's a lot of whine, too, consider your next move in conjunction with 12-10-3. If the axle is acceptably quiet, the most likely reason for the noise is worn halfshaft splines and/or worn differential gears.

12-10-1 Major repairs to the differential are outside the scope of this book, but many owners could attempt to at least check and even replace worn halfshaft splines. They reside inside the centre of the axle, but can be accessed from each rear hub. The workshop manual will give you the detail, but I'll briefly explain what is involved.

12-10-1 Getting the mesh and backlash correct in the crownwheel and pinion we see here is vital, and it's this detail that requires a professional's help. The halfshaft (arrowed "1") can be removed to reveal its inner splines as explained in the main text. I've also identified (via arrow 2) the front oil seal. This is the later Salisbury axle.

Disconnect the battery and fit solid axle stands (jack stands) under the axle. With the backplate and four securing bolts removed, refit the hub and an old brake drum and knock it outwards from the axle, taking the halfshaft with it. You will need at least a couple of feet (625mm) of clearance each side of the axle to withdraw each halfshaft.

With the halfshafts withdrawn, examine the splines and, if worn, buy a pair of second-hand shafts with good splines. However, the wire-wheeled axle is shorter than the bolted-wheel axle, so you will need the appropriate length of halfshaft for your particular axle. There are also two types of axle (Banjo and Salisbury), so you'll also need the correct type of shaft. Not all variations are readily available second-hand so you may find, for the most cost-effective repair, that you'll have to reassemble the axle for the time being, having ascertained that it is the internal halfshaft splines that are worn and causing the noise.

Keep an eye open for good second-hand halfshafts of the right specification and do the repair once all replacement parts available. This is also a good time to fit new hub bearing and oil seals with long-term reliability in mind.

12-10-2 If the halfshaft splines are not worn then the "clunk" is almost certainly the result of worn crownwheel and pinion gears or, more likely if your axle is not whining, worn pinion thrust washers.

Before you start rectification work, one of the new thrust washer repair kits (available from most MG specialists & certainly from the MGOC) should be ordered. Don't re-install the halfshafts, but do drain the axle of oil (if you chose not to do so earlier).Scrupulously clean the area to ensure no dirt whatsoever enters the differential and remove the backplate from the differential.

Before getting into the main task, it's a good idea to check that the crownwheel and pinion are in good order, so look closely to ensure they have smooth polished teeth and that there are no missing teeth,wear marks, chips or cracks. If you are unsure about any detail of the CW&P, get an expert up to check for you - but most non-whining axles will in fact be in useable order & should allow you to proceed to the main task which necessitates removing the (two) thrust washers along with their planet gears. To help identification, the two gears that are aligned with the halfshafts are called

"sun gears" - the planet gears we are interested in mesh with the sun gears to form a box-like gear train within the differential carrier.

The two thrust washers sit on a common shaft and are sandwiched between each of the two planet gears and the differential carrier. The common shaft is retained by a roll-pin that passes through the diff carrier and the shaft, the next and probably the most difficult task is to remove that roll-pin...

Turn the diff until the roll-pin holding the through-shaft is in view and using a **correctly-sized** pin punch drift the roll-pin out towards the front of the car. **Caution!** - Do not use a nail or other poor quality drift - it really is worth stopping to buy the correct tool if you don't have it already. You only need to partly drift the pin out forwards & you **must** keep checking that the exiting pin has not moved so far forward as to touch the axle casing (thus preventing the diff carrier from rotating). Once you've pushed sufficient of the pin out, rotate the differential carrier such that the protruding part of the pin now points backwards, and pull the pin towards the rear of the car until it is completely out of the diff carrier.

Now you can use a pin punch or nail to help draw the shaft up out of the diff carrier, thus releasing the planet gears.

If you now rotate the diff carrier the two planet wheels will both start to exit the gear-train, one forward, one backwards along with their respective thrust washers.

The two sun gears have fibre washers behind them & these both need to be replaced (one at a time) before you reassemble the planet gears (each with a new thrust washer) within the diff carrier. The diff will need to be rotated in the opposite direction to disassembly and the planet gears presented as they were removed - *i.e.* one from the front, the other from the back.

After some fiddling you'll be able to press the planet-gear cross shaft through the carrier, both planet gears and their thrust washers and secure the shaft with a **new** roll-pin drifted in from the back of the car.

A new gasket is needed on the differential cover. The halfshafts/hubs should be refitted and the correct grade of oil used to fill the axle. This might be a good time to fit a pair of new hub bearings and you certainly should take the opportunity to replace the hub lip seals.

If the axle whines or there is still a significant "clunk" when starting/stopping you either need to get your nearest MGB specialist to attend to the crownwheel and pinion for you or consider swapping the axle for another used axle or to buy a service-exchange replacement.

12-10-3 Axle 'clunks' and/or whining/wowing, can be caused by various internal differential problems outside the scope of the average motor mechanic, never mind an amateur enthusiast.

12-10-3 Useless if the wear within the axle is too advanced, but for axles with early wear/noise, this additive may help.

A clunk between acceleration and deceleration at any speed is probably signalling worn differential and pinion shims. Whining or wowing noises at higher speeds in any circumstances (*i.e.* acceleration, deceleration or coasting) is likely to be caused by faulty backlash or a loose pinion in the differential assembly which, in turn, can be the consequence of worn bearings.

Any or all of these faults really require the skills and experience of a specialist. Your best contribution in this instance is to remove the axle from the

car, withdraw the halfshafts, backplates and hubs, and let said specialist sort the problem.

However, before you take that final step, I have one suggestion that may reduce the whine from the rear axle, provided wear is not too advanced.

Forte (UK telephone number 02476 474069) sells a "Diff and Gear Treatment" additive that not only reduced noise levels in my car's rear axle, but (the maker tells me), reduces gear friction, lowering operating temperatures whilst protecting against corrosion, contamination and sludge, and extending the operating life of the differential.

Rubbing noise from rear wheels
12-11-1 Rear tyres/tires touching the bodywork? Owners of MGBs fitted with wider tyres are likely to find that the outside of the tyre just kisses the left side rear wing when the car goes over a bump. However, this remedy is really intended for cars with standard width tyres which are experiencing tyre-rubbing problems.

If the outside of the standard width tyres of your wire-wheeled car keep fouling the inside of the rear wing, chances are you have a bolted wheel axle fitted with wire wheels. The opposite fault occurs with a bolted wheel car with a wire wheel axle, when the inside of the tyre keeps brushing the inner wheelarch.

Oil leaks from rear axle
12-12-1 The oil level within any mechanical component is important to quiet operation and longevity. The engine is very accessible, and even has a dipstick with which to check the oil level.

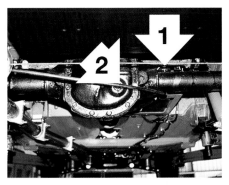

12-12-1 (Picture 1) Relevant in a few minutes; arrow 1 points to the breather. The oil level/filler plug (arrowed "2") is rather more obvious on the backplate of the rear axle and...

Unfortunately, the same cannot be said of the rear axle which becomes noisier and noisier for want of oil. It's worth getting the MoT testing station or your local garage to check the oil level at least annually - more frequently if the axle leaks. Clearly, it makes sense not to overfill a rear axle, but this is easy to do accidentally. If the rear axle is filled to the level plug with the back end of the car elevated to aid accessibility, chances are it will be overfilled. It could then appear that the axle is leaking when it is simply over-lubricated.

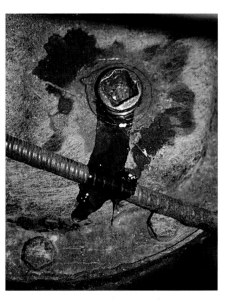

12-12-1 (Picture 2) ...requires a square socket to remove. I always use the square drive on my 1/2 inch socket set.

12-12-2 Oil leaking from the rear axle warrants closer examination if the rear backplate is damp or covered with oil. The top of the MGB differential backplate has a 'shelf' that collects dirt and water and holds it in contact with the pressed plate. Result - it rusts, but worse, if you don't spot that it's severely corroded it eventually allows rust and dirt into the differential and oil to leak out. A periodic check (when you top-up the axle) is prudent and, since prevention is better than cure, a rub-down and generous coat of "Hammerite" is even more worthwhile.

12-12-3 A blocked axle breather, shown in photograph 12-12-1 (Picture 1), can cause oil leaks from any of the three rear axle oil seals. The breather allows air within the axle to escape as it warms up and expands, each time the axle is used. If the breather becomes blocked, the expanding air cannot escape and pressure builds up within the axle.

This extra pressure - particularly if there's any significant wear in the oil seals - forces oil and not air from the axle until the axle cools and/or escaping oil relieves the pressure. The oil breather on the top of the rear axle is not easy to get at but, if oil is escaping from a rear axle oil seal, the breather should be your first stop.

Take great care not to drop dirt into the axle while checking that the breather is clear. The whole affair can be unscrewed at the axle and cleaned out away from the car, or you can 'pop' the top off the vertical tube and sort the blockage out *in situ*. I think the former is actually the best method, although, if your car has the later plastic breather, chances are it will be brittle and could disintegrate if unscrewed carelessly. They are available to buy and not expensive, so it's not a disaster if this does happen, unless you let bits of it fall into the axle tube.

12-12-4 Oil leaks can also be caused by one of the two hub seals we touched on in the previous suggestion being worn, or the pinion oil seal which we will get to shortly. If either of the hub seals is worn, there's no alternative but to replace the leaking seal.

Access to the hub seals is described in 12-10-1, and they can be changed at home. In my experience, a worn/leaking oil seal is usually associated with a worn bearing, so change both seal and associated hub bearing - or at least take a very close look at the bearing before reassembly. You don't need to break into the hydraulic brake circuit to do this; pass a light piece of rope across the back of the car to hang the backplates from, avoiding strain on the hydraulic pipework.

12-12-5 The hub oil seal does not actually run on the halfshaft but on a ground cone that sits on the halfshaft and is held in place by the hub. The cone provides an excellent running surface to ensure minimal wear to the oil seal lip and longevity. Surprisingly, the steel cone wears, albeit after hundreds of hours of use, but eventually the plastic lip on

the oil seal actually wears a grove in the metal cone.

The consequence of this is that even a new hub oil seal has nowhere for the lip to seal, so many a rear axle with a brand new oil seal very quickly starts leaking again. Very disheartening, but this problem can be avoided if the running surface of the cone is carefully examined before the new seal is fitted. If the cone is worn, replace that, too.

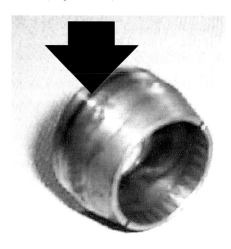

12-12-5 This polished seal lip is fine, but the oil seal lip can wear a groove in this surface which destroys the ability of the seal to do its job.

12-12-6 Replacement of a leaking pinion oil seal in the early Roadster Banjo axles can be done at home, provided the pinion nut can be removed. Torque pre-loading has to be applied to the pinion of a Salisbury axle on reassembly, so this is a job best left to those with the experience and necessary equipment.

The Banjo pinion oil seal can be replaced with the axle in the car, but hire a heavy-duty box spanner set since the normal half-inch square drive may not be up to this job. You'll most likely need a tubular extension to the tommy bar, too, and I draw your attention to the special pinion locking arm in photograph

12-12-6 (Picture 2): you may need something similar.

Elevate the car on a stout pair of ramps, apply the handbrake very securely and drain the axle of oil. Undo the pinion nut, tap off the drive pinion and remove the dust cover and (gently) lever the oil seal out, noting the direction that the lip faces. Tap the replacement seal in squarely and replace cover, pinion, spring washer and nut. Torque the nut to the specified figure.

12-12-6 (Picture 1) This is the case of an early Banjo axle as fitted to Roadsters. Note, for identification only, that the nosepiece - including the whole differential - can be unbolted from this axle type.

12-12-6 (Picture 2) This is the sort of aid you'll find essential to restrain the differential pinion whilst you attend to the retaining nut. The four fastening studs are for attaching to the pinion. There appears to be a slight 'set' in the arm, which demonstrates the force often required to move the retaining nut.

Chapter 13
Overheating & water loss

An overheating engine can be caused by many things and we will explore them all, with one exception - insufficient oil - as I take it for granted that you have not allowed the oil level to drop and then wonder why the car is overheating.

Warning! - There are two common and important aspects of an overheated engine, regardless of the cause, that you must remember at all times: personal injury and/or damage to the engine could be the consequence of removing the pressure cap from the system before the engine has been allowed to cool; adding cold water to an overheated engine is very likely to cause terminal damage. It's not the temperature of the radiator that's important when adding water to an overheated engine, but the residual temperature of the block. The water system may seem to be cool at the radiator, but the block has a far greater mass which will retain heat far longer than the radiator. Adding water can create a geyser of pressured water and steam as the relatively cold water hits the hot block.

Don't forget to refill the system with coolant and, where appropriate, anti-freeze, once the problem is resolved.

13-1 TEMPERATURE GAUGE READS HIGHER THAN USUAL

The general characteristic of the car is to run hot but not, of course, to expel coolant from the radiator pressure relief system. 'Normal' readings of post-1976 cars tend to be slightly above the mid-way position on the temperature gauge, while unleaded engines will run slightly hotter still. Therefore your gauge will read a little on the hot side of normal without there being anything wrong.

13-1-1 If you have installed a new engine, or even new pistons in an original cylinder block, expect the coolant temperature to run a little above what you have previously got used to seeing on the gauge, probably around halfway between "N" and "H." Any higher than that and you should stop and investigate straight away.

The new engine needs time to "run-in;" a euphenism for the 500 miles or so it takes to knock off the worst of the (minute) lumps from the rebored cylinders and bed the piston rings into the bores and pistons. You should never use synthetic oils at this time but do try to keep engine revs between 2500 and 3000rpm as much as possible, partly to allow things to bed-in, but also to ensure you do not overheat the engine.

At the end of this initial 500 mile period change the engine oil and filter, after which, for the next 1000 miles the engine should be run at between 2000 and 3500rpm as much as possible, provided the temperature gauge is not reading much above "N." If it is, return

to your engine supplier to discuss the situation; it may be of no consequence, or an adjustment - timing and/or carburation - may be required.

13-1-1 With an 82 degree thermostat in place, the gauge should register "N" most of the time, once the engine has warmed up.

13-1-2 If your engine is well-used and well past any possibility of overheating due to running-in, consider whether the overheating happens most times you take the car out but is not usually severe enough to boil the coolant. (I am presuming that the ignition warning light is not on, or the fanbelt loose.) Timing that is too advanced, or carburettors that are set too lean, can individually or collectively cause the engine to run too hot and, in extreme cases, actually cause permanent engine damage. Both can be checked at home but a visit to your local tuner is the best way of getting these possibilities checked out.

13-1-2 You'll need a timing light similar to this to check the timing accurately enough to make a difference to overheating problems. Note that this light has power cables as well as the timing strobe cable running to it - which will give a worthwhile light. Timing lights not fitted with power amplification give a weak light, often not discernible in some daylight conditions.

13-1-3 Check that the fan is installed and operating as it should. MGBs were originally fitted with two types of fan. Chrome bumper cars had a mechanical/metal fan blade fitted to the front of the water pump when they left the factory, but a great many have been retrofitted with an electric 'blower' fan at the front of the radiator. It's not unknown for the original mechanical/metal fan to be fitted backwards after a water pump or engine replacement repair ...

Warning! - Don't put your hands near the rotating fan, but satisfy yourself that the fan on your overheating car is pulling air backwards through the radiator. Open the bonnet and have a helper run the engine at about 2000rpm. At the front of the car feel if there's airflow forward from the engine bay through the radiator towards the front grille. If air is blowing forward, then the fan needs reversing. A confirmation/second check is to feel whether there's a good strong backward airflow by, say, the distributor. If you're starting to wonder about the fan's orientation, stop the engine, note its

13-1-3 (Picture 1) Early MGBs had a metal fan, while...

13-1-3 (Picture 2) ...rubber bumper cars enjoyed the benefits of an electric one. In fact, US rubber bumper cars and all factory produced MGB GTV8 cars were fitted with two, as seen here.

direction of rotation as it comes to a stop and check that the leading edge of the fan is nearest the radiator, thus pulling air backwards through the radiator. If it has been assembled incorrectly reverse it using four new rubber mounting grommets and two new locking tabs as you do so.

Turning to electric fans, be they original or retrofitted, the most usual problem in an MGB is a lack of exercise. Positioned at the front of the car, they collect all the weather and dirt that's going, getting none of the warming benefits of

sitting behind the radiator.

There could be electrical problems, including a blown fuse caused by a reluctant fan motor, which is discussed in Chapter 19.

But, exploring overheating problems, check that the fan is free to rotate. With the ignition/engine off, flip the fan blade with a finger or screwdriver. It should spin easily and freely but, if not, remove the front grille and lubricate the shaft bearing (behind the fan blade) until the fan spins freely. If the fan is seized solid or does not respond to front bearing lubrication, replace the unit (although you could try stripping the motor on the basis that there's little to lose). As a preventative measure, fit an override switch and make a point, particularly during the winter, of operating the fan motor for about five minutes once a week.

13-1-4 If the car has been running hotter for a while, check the possible external causes first. Are the brakes binding, which will make the engine work harder and generate more heat? Does the car pull to one side when braking? Does it seem very sluggish? When you de-clutch does it coast to a stop rather quicker than you would expect? Have you noticed that any particular wheel or hub seems hotter than the others? Do either of the front discs glow after you have used the car? Can you smell hot brakes' Do you hear an unusual squeal when braking? Do you believe that fuel consumption is higher than usual? These are all symptoms of binding brakes (see chapter 16).

13-1-4 (Picture 1) A binding front caliper could cause overheating of both car and brake disc/rotor, but...

13-1-4 (Picture 2) ...it does not have to be a front brake that's binding. Possibly the handbrake cable or a backplate lever is seized.

13-1-5 If the brakes are definitely okay, when the engine is cold take a look under the pressure cap situated atop the radiator or on a separate header tank. Does the coolant surface have oil on it? Can you smell exhaust gases in the water?

What you are checking for are the early signs of a leaking cylinder head gasket. Should you see an oil film or get a whiff of exhaust, have the cylinder compressions individually checked and take advice on whether the head needs to come off the engine block.

If all's well consider the age of the pressure cap on top of the radiator/header tank. There were three types of cap, allowing 7, 10 and 13psi pressure within the coolant system. Often the caps are used for years and years and the seal and the spring tire to the point that the system is not pressurised to the correct figure. Or the wrong pressure cap is fitted. In each case the coolant will boil earlier than it should and may escape, particularly

13-1-5 The three types of pressure cap are very alike and can be seen above the respective thermostats. All pressure caps have their pressure rating stamped on the top.

from the early systems that were not fitted with a header tank. If your B's pressure cap looks tired, fit a new one of the correct pressure for your model.

If a leaking head gasket is diagnosed, consider fitting an exchange "unleaded" cylinder head.

13-1-6 If the car is still overheating, but not usually enough to boil the coolant, and you have checked that the ignition light is not glowing (meaning that the fan/drivebelt is turning the generator and water pump), the airflow through the radiator may be partially blocked by external debris.

13-1-6 This MGB radiator has seen better days. In good condition, the B's radiator has good capacity, but if external blockages build up they'll restrict the flow of air through the radiator.

As originally fitted, the radiator on an 1800cc MGB has a generous cooling capacity and, certainly in moderate climates like in the UK's, will rarely cause a problem. The overheating may not be severe on cool days but you may see the gauge needle climb to (and stay) halfway between "N" and "H" on warmer days - and this should really be your signal to carry out some preventative maintenance.

Step one is to be absolutely sure that the exterior of the radiator is unrestricted. As I said, the capacity of the MGB radiator is such that a couple of badges or an extra (small) plaque on the front grille should make little difference to it's cooling ability. Ensure the radiator fins are not restricted. The front of the radiator is out of sight and it's easy to miss a gradual build-up of leaves, feathers, flies, moths and road grit. Use a garden hosepipe from the engine side of the radiator to jet-wash any build-up from the front of the radiator. Cover the ignition electrics with an old towel to keep them dry.

13-1-7 Check, and maybe replace, the thermostat on the top of the cylinder

head. This is an unnecessary step if you know for a fact that the thermostat is fairly new, what temperature it opens at and that it has been fitted correctly. In this event move straight to 13-1-8.

If you plan to remove the thermostat housing, pre-purchase a new gasket for it. There is a choice of opening temperatures - 72, 82 and 88 degrees centigrade - when buying a new thermostat. 82 degree thermostats are usual and, if properly fitted, will result in a gauge reading of "N." (You'll appreciate that if an 88 degree unit had been fitted previously, the temperature gauge needle would have sat a little under halfway between "N" and "H," and this could be the reason for the apparant 'overheating.') As an aside, the reason for fitting an 88 degree thermostat is to increase the effectiveness of the MGB's rather weak heater. The engine will run more efficiently at the higher temperature, too.

If the thermostat has been in place for some time it will be pretty dirty. It's okay to clean it but, before trying to unseat it, check that the bulb of the thermostat is fitted downwards into the cylinder head. If it's been fitted incorrectly (sensing bulb up) this will almost certainly be the cause of the overheating, and it's just possible that you'll simply need to reverse it, bulb down towards the upcoming hot water from the engine. Take a close look at the old one to see whether you can spot "82" or "88" stamped on the flat flange, although I recommend you fit a new "82" thermostat in almost every situation where the car is mostly put to summer use. Photograph 13-1-5 shows a selection of thermostats.

13-1-8 If the overheating continues but is still not severe enough to boil the coolant, you probably have a partially blocked cooling system. Even in cooler climates, once the capacity of the radiator is reduced by an internal blockage, overheating will be the result.

Mild overheating is usually the consequence of a combination of sludge in the cooling system and a build-up of scale on the inside of the cooling tubes. The sludge slowly gathers in the bottom radiator tank and restricts the flow of water through the cooling tubes, while the scale on the inside face of the cooling tubes actually slows the transfer of heat from the water to the cooling tubes. Often you can actually locate blocked areas by running your hands over the radiator and feeling for cooler areas.

This problem can be tackled with

the radiator in place, but cover the ignition electrics to keep them dry. This internal cleaning task will take a little time because it needs to be done in three stages. Back-flush the radiator by completely removing the main top and bottom hoses at their radiator stubs and inserting a hosepipe into the **bottom** of the radiator with the water pressure turned up as high as it will go. You may need a piece of rag to help close the hole around the hose. The idea is to reverse the normal flow of coolant (which is normally top to bottom) and flush as much of the accumulated sludge from the bottom of the rad and as many of the cooling tubes as you can. If a cooling tube is completely blocked it's unlikely this treatment will be effective, but partly blocked tubes will be cleared if you persevere.

Initially, dark, discoloured coolant will come out of the top outlet, but this will gradually clear. If you can't get the coolant to flow freely from the top outlet, go straight to 13-1-9 as you need a replacement radiator.

Once the back flushing of the radiator is complete, step two will be to run water from the hosepipe through the engine's water passages (**Caution!** - the engine **must** be cold). You'll first need to remove the thermostat to allow the flushing water free passage and, if you've not already done so, check the points made in 13-1-7.

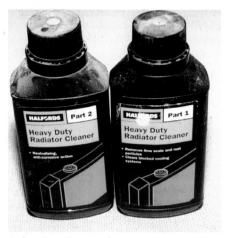

13-1-8 There are many brands of two-part radiator cleaner, but these tend to be more aggressive than mild single-flush chemicals and are recommended when alternative flushing routines have failed. Note that "Part 2" is a neutralising agent; important if you don't want to end up with a leaking radiator...

The normal coolant flow though an engine is bottom to top (as it heats the water rises) so reverse that by putting the hose into the top - the hole vacated by the thermostat - and passing a stream of clean water through the block. It is not likely to make a material difference but you may as well open the heater valve and get as much water to flush through the heater as possible. The water should exit with some speed though the water pump's bottom outlet and you should keep up the treatment until the water is flowing clean. I would then reverse the flow by putting the hose in the water pump's outlet - you may be surprised how much brown stuff comes out the thermostat opening.

The third stage is to treat the system with a chemical cleaner/descaler. There are numerous proprietary treatments available at most auto accessory shops. Some of the more aggressive, and therefore better, treatments require a two-part process with the cleaner having to be followed by a neutralising chemical. You'll be required to run the engine as part of both processes - be sure to do so **without** the thermostat (though you'll have to replace the housing) and when flushing mid process and refilling with neutraliser, be careful to use hot water in order to avoid the risk of cracking the cylinder block.

If you follow the cleaner/descaler manufacturer's directions faithfully you'll remove some of the scale coating the cooling tubes and passageways to advantage. I say "some" because, if a tube is completely blocked with either silt or scale, its passage is unavailable to either coolant or cleaning chemicals.

After the flushing and cleaning/ descaling its time to reassemble everything with I suggest new top and bottom hoses and new hose wormdrive clips. Don't forget to refill the cooling system with the heater valve **open**. I would suggest you don't yet use antifreeze or other inhibitors - at least until you're sure you have resolved your problem. **Caution!** - inhibitor/ antifreeze should be added as soon as these investigations are completed.

13-1-9 Still overheating? There are still other possible causes and the next most likely solution involves replacing the radiator. It's probable that the radiator core is so full of sludge or scale that it cannot do its job of passing the heat from the coolant to the atmosphere.

Probably the cheapest way to solve the problem is to remove the existing radiator and take it to your local radiator

13-1-9 Prior to 1973 all MGBs had a 'solid' front valance. During 1973 these ventilated panels were introduced, offering increased airflow to the radiator and engine via two rectangular slats.

specialist (there's one in most towns) and have them re-core it. You can also buy service exchange units from most of the MG spares specialists, or you can still buy a brand new radiator. The last two methods involve packing/postage costs and delays, so I recommend the local man. Be sure to flush through the engine, as explained in 13-1-8 when you fit the new radiator, and new top and bottom hoses and hose clips are a good idea.

The airflow to the radiator of an early chrome bumper cars with a solid front valance can be increased by fitting the later front valance with its extra cooling holes (picture 13-1-9).

13-1-10 If you're still worried about apparant overheating, and yours is a rubber bumper car, then I think it time to check the temperature gauge.

The MGB was fitted with two types of temperature gauge. The majority of cars had a dual oil pressure/water temperature gauge. Both halves of the gauge are operated mechanically and while the oil pressure half works very reliably it has to be said that the temperature sensing side is prone to failure. "Ah!" I hear you mutter. Don't get too excited because it's most unlikely that the gauge is reading higher than the true temperature of the coolant! Why?

In these dual gauges the temperature is registered by a bulb full of alcohol that expands as the temperature increases. The unreliability of these temperature gauges is always caused by incorrect installation resulting in the pipe from the alcohol filled bulb to the gauge fracturing. This allows the alcohol to escape (you will smell the alcohol for a few days when this is occurring) and the gauge progressively reads lower and lower - not, you'll note

13-1-10 Although not on an 1800cc MGB, this photo illustrates the correct way to install the capillary tube for a dual gauge MGB. As the pipe seems too long for the car (the excess length is intended to act as a flexible joint between a vibrating engine and static body), it sometimes gets routed round the side of the engine bay and then straight to the front of the engine. The correct way is to clip it to the side of the rocker cover, coil as much as possible into the 2-3in diameter loops you see here, before fastening it to the top of the footwell. It adds a touch of class - as well as providing a little added support - if one of the heater water pipes is threaded through the coil. With the capillary installed this way, the engine can jump about as much as it likes since the coil takes up the vibration.

higher. So, if you have a dual gauge and it reads high, then the car's almost certainly running hotter than intended.

I will get onto the rubber-bumper single (i.e. not dual) electric gauges in a second, but first let me add a tip for those with the dual/mechanical gauges in so far as the installation of the tube leading from the sensing bulb to the gauge is concerned. I would estimate that over 50% of these have been fitted incorrectly in that there **must** be a **coil** of tube between where the tube leaves the engine and where it is fastened to the body. This coil is to allow the tubing carrying the alcohol to flex without cracking. Too rigid (i.e. no coil) a route from engine to body will result in tube fatigue, cracking, a loss of alcohol and ultimately no temperature readings.

So, what's different about the post 1976 rubber-bumper's (and one or two earlier non UK specification cars) single instrument temperature gauge? It is electrically driven and while it will read lower than the coolant temperature for most faults (which we will explore in

chapter 18), there are two circumstances when it could erroneously show "H" (hot) when in fact nothing is wrong at all. Firstly, if a short to earth occurred in the electrical wire anywhere along its route from sensor at the front of the engine to the gauge, the gauge will read "H". Secondly, if the sensor shorted to earth, again the gauge would go straight to "H".

So if your electrical gauge is showing a tendency towards "H" but is not actually reading hard up against the "H" then you're probably seeing a true representation of the coolant temperature. If the gauge reads hard up "H" then it could be the sensor or wiring that is at fault. In this eventuality the gauge needle will go straight to "H" as soon as you switch on the ignition: this immediately tells you that the gauge is faulty, not the engine overheating.

Still not quite sure about the electrical-type gauge? Start with a visual examination of the Lucar connection to the sensor, the wire leading to the harness and indeed the harness itself to ensure that nothing that is visible has chaffed. Assuming all's well, then it's worth fitting a replacement sensor and cleaning the terminals and connectors. If you've still not sure whether the engine is overheating or the gauge is misreading your last resort is to have a mobile tuning/repair van call to measure (with a temperature-sensing "gun") the actual temperature of the cylinder block, regardless of the gauge's reading.

13-1-11 If all the foregoing has failed to remedy true overheating then I can only suggest one final possibility - the cylinder block's cooling passages are still blocked with silt and that means it will be necessary for you to remove as many of the core plugs/Welch plugs as you can get at to pressure wash the cooling passages. Removing core plugs is not too bad a task with the engine in the car, but you'll certainly need to get most of the ancillaries off both sides of the engine to do it. Fitting (new) core plugs is not so easy with the engine *in situ*, but is achievable. Clean each core plug's seating carefully and run a small bead of sealant round both seat and plug before hammering the replacements into the block.

13-2 TEMPERATURE GAUGE SUDDENLY READS "H" (HOT)

13-2-1 If you note a sudden increase in coolant temperature and the ignition warning light comes on, stop as quickly

as is safe. The car probably has a broken or very loose fanbelt/drivebelt. Consequently, the alternator and the water pump are not being driven and the coolant is not being pumped around the engine - which will be the cause of the glowing red ignition light and, sooner or later, any overheating you may have noticed. Caught early enough, that is before the coolant boils and losses occur, the roadside remedy is as easy as fitting the new fanbelt/drivebelt (that I hope you have in your spares kit) as detailed in 6-1-1.

13-2-2 If you note a sudden increase in coolant temperature, even if the ignition warning light does not come on, stop as quickly as is safe because the car could have lost coolant for a number of reasons.

In the context of falling coolant levels it is important to remember that the temperature gauge is not as reliable an indicator of an overheating engine as you might think, and it is as well that you understand why. When the engine cooling system is full and operating normally the sensor for the gauge is comfortably submerged in coolant and, provided it is working properly, will give a reasonably true reflection of the coolant temperature. As the coolant temperature starts to increase (for whatever reason, though for this illustration we'll presume a leak has started in the radiator), the gauge **will** reflect the initial increase in temperature. However, should you fail to see the initial higher reading on the gauge and the coolant loss continues to the point that the gauge's sensor is no longer surrounded by coolant, from that point the accuracy of the gauge will be very suspect. Most likely it will fall from its peak reading and

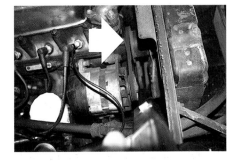

13-2-1 The arrow highlights the water pump which obviously stops circulating water if the fanbelt should break, or become so worn that it slips on the crankshaft pulley at the bottom of the engine.

consequently can be falsely comforting, for with only air (or steam) to work with, the sensor can tell you that the temperature of your coolant is only just above normal when the truth of your situation is far more serious.

I was taught always to drive with my eyes circling from the road ahead to the mirror to the road ahead to the instruments. Obviously if you follow this sort of routine you'll swiftly spot the initial increase in the gauge's reading and be on your guard when it drops back. However, if you're in the habit of only looking at the gauges when you think you have a problem, you could be fooled by the reading presented and should bear these comments in mind when you go to investigate.

13-2-3 So, we've come to a standstill due to an overheating engine - what to do now? Open the bonnet by all means, but **Caution!** - **don't** take the pressure-cap off the system until the engine cools down and **don't** refill with cold water for the reasons explained earlier.

It is possible that you neglected to get all the air out of the cooling system when recently filling it with inhibitor/antifreeze, flushing the system through or carrying out

13-2-3 Take a careful look at the hoses and the numerous clip joints; it takes only one undetected leak to significantly reduce the water level over the course of a few days.

a change of radiator. In this event you'll not see a leak, but it's prudent not to take anything for granted. Take a look round for obvious leaks and check that hose clips are tight. If this is the first time you've driven any distance since carrying out cooling system maintenance, the likelihood is that the system was not completely filled or that a hose clip was not fully tightened. Always open the heater valve when refilling any coolant system and then run the car long enough to ensure the thermostat opens. Let things cool right down and then re-check the water level before assuming all is well.

If no cooling system maintenance/repair has been carried out recently, the first thing to try and establish is whether the coolant level has actually dropped and whether there is visible coolant leakage. Radiators, particularly old ones, can "out of the blue" spring a leak from a cooling tube and while this is not to be welcomed, it is one of the faults that can usually be temporarily fixed in a roadside repair.

You may have heard stories about breaking the white of an egg into the radiator to seal such a leak, and while this does work, there are today much more effective radiator sealers available from almost every garage and auto accessory shop. These sealers all tend to be referred to as "RadWeld", even though there are several different brand names and all will solve your problem on a get-you-home basis. A quick check of the hose clips and hoses is definitely a good idea.

A tired pressure-cap, dribbling water pump or leaking hose joint can bleed small quantities of coolant but, over a few weeks, the cumulative loss will bring you to a halt if you have failed to notice the loss and take corrective action.

13-2-4 A sudden increase in coolant temperature, often to the extent that the engine coolant boils, can be due to a sticking thermostat. The thermostat has stuck in the closed position if it's causing overheating, but I must tell you that I don't know why this occurs from time to time.

When removed from the car the offending thermostat usually looks perfectly serviceable but the only solution is to replace it. If you're in a roadside situation you can, as soon as things are cool enough, remove the 'stat completely as a get-you-home expedient, but don't be tempted to permanently leave it out.

13-2-5 Overheating, even in extremely cold conditions? The concentration of antifreeze you use in the cooling system is more important than

purely preventing the coolant freezing. Drivers with inadequate (or no) antifreeze in the cooling system can find the engine initially warms-up normally but unbeknown to them the (very) cold air passing through the radiator can turn the contents of the radiator to frozen mush if the antifreeze concentration is inadequate. Once the engine has warmed up, the thermostat will open and the engine will try to circulate coolant through the radiator for cooling - however if the coolant in the radiator is an icy mush it will not pass sufficient water through the radiator to cool the engine. Result, the apparent contradiction of a car pulled up on the side of the road overheating on the very coldest of days!

The get-you-home solution is to patiently wait for the engine heat to thaw the mush in the radiator to the point that water will circulate, top the coolant up if necessary and blank the front grille off with an old newspaper or piece of card. Once home, add sufficient antifreeze to cope with the clearly arctic conditions you and your car are currently enjoying.

13-3 COOLANT IS BEING LOST

13-3-1 If you have to top-up the coolant with unnatural frequency but cannot see any lost coolant, you clearly have a leak, but the question is - from where?

A worn water pump gland or seal has fooled me for several weeks since it only leaked when the pressure in the system was increased by running the engine. However, at this time because the engine was hot, a slight weep quickly evaporated. Over longer periods most external coolant leaks become visible from the tell-tale streaks of dried antifreeze.

However, if you still cannot see anything after a week or two you can get a pressure tester which increases the pressure in the system and measures the speed of its decay. This not only helps you establish that there is a problem but, since you're carrying out the test with the system cold, you can feel in places you would otherwise be unable to get to - and the bottom of the water pump might be a good starting point! Your sense of smell may be the best way of establishing whether the heater matrix is leaking, but an extended pressure test may generate a drip or two from the plenum chamber's drain located above the gearbox. Whilst you're down there groping above the gearbox, do clean out the strangely-shaped drain tube.

13-3-2 It's not always easy, but when examining the engine for water loss, don't overlook the core plugs/Welch plugs along the side of the block. These plugs are made from pressed steel and they permanently have one face in water, so they can rust through. Core plugs usually weep at first but, if you fail to spot a weeping one, it will quickly get worse. RadSeal or its like is the temporary get-

13-3-3 (Picture 1) To get at the heater matrix first remove the heater from its bulkhead/firewall location.

13-3-3 (Picture 2) The effort needed to get this matrix out has been worthwhile as it has clearly been leaking for some time. A replacement is called for, so take the opportunity to upgrade to a larger capacity one available from the MGOC.

you-home expedient: **all new** core plugs the long term solution.

13-3-3 Coolant can be lost from a perished heater hose or even the heater matrix. If the former, you would get a coolant leak from the offending hose, but a leak from the matrix would not be seen - though you might smell antifreeze in the car. The get-you-home solution is to re-arrange the good heater hose so that the heater is bypassed until a more permanent repair can be done. Don't forget to top-up the system after re-arranging the hoses.

If this temporary re-routing puts a stop to coolant losses you can be sure that a faulty hose or the heater matrix has been leaking. Fit a new hose first and, if you start to lose coolant again, it has to be the matrix. A pain to replace, but considering an upgrade at the same time may make it a little less painful.

13-3-4 Continual water loss can be the result of a "blown" cylinder head gasket. You may see an unnatural volume of vapour/steam being emitted from the exhaust - which is a classical warning sign. Even if the exhaust looks normal, once you start to suspect the integrity of the head gasket you should check whether the oil in the sump is turning "milky" or emulsifying. It will have a very grey colour, and if you note any symptoms of contaminated oil you should not drive the car until the cylinder head gasket has been replaced and the oil and oil filter have been changed. **Caution!** - Do not leave coolant contaminated oil in an engine, even an unused one.

13-3-5 The possibility of a cracked cylinder head seems like very bad news, but there is worse - a cracked block. I actually bought my first MGB with a cracked block, which - I have no doubt now - was why it was for sale. The crack, even when I found it (it took me two 'head-off' attempts), was amazingly small to account for so much water usage.

Whether it's a crack in the cylinder head or in the block, a replacement is

required. Cracks in heads and blocks can be repaired, but the availability of MGB spares is such that a repair is not cost-effective. Cylinder heads and blocks are interchangeable between Roadsters and GTs, and you can even use a block and/or cylinder head from an 1800cc Marina or Ital, though this shouldn't be necessary.

13-4-1 If your late (rubber-bumper) MGB causes you grief with leaks from the plastic filler plug on the top of the thermostat housing, rest assured you're not alone ... That does not help much, but rather than struggle to get a plastic replacement plug to start into its thread (I find the thread form is dreadful) what about a metal replacement? Standard on Triumph Stags, a direct replacement in brass fits perfectly. The part number is ARA 2404.

13-4-1 (Picture 1) The usual plastic screwed filler plug but...

13-4-1 (Picture 2) ...a brass one is better, even if it costs a bit more. Have a spare O-ring-like rubber seal in your spares box: they cost pence. If you try to refit the old one, you could find it has stretched and is bulging out all over the place.

Chapter 14
The heater doesn't work very well

The MGB heater has always been a weakness in the car's design. Upgrades are available and are covered in another Veloce publication *How to Improve Your MGB, MGC & MGB V8.*

One trap that many new owners of MGBs fall into when filling the radiator is to forget to open the heater control valve to "hot" and thus trapping air in the heater matrix and/or in the pipes feeding coolant to the heater. The resultant airlock will usually clear when the heater control is eventually switched to "hot" but, simultaneously, this lowers the cooling system's water level and could still prevent the heater from giving of its best while conceivably overheating the engine too!

14-1-1 When an under-performing heater is on the engine cooling fan should not normally be running. If you have an early car with a metal fan fixed to the water pump there's not too much you can do about this, certainly not in the short-term. However, owners of cars with an original or retrofitted electric cooling fan should check that it's not running.

An electric fan override switch can be left on by mistake, or the fan auto-switch can stick on. The solution to the first problem is easy, although you may care to think about fitting a fan-on warning light. The latter fault is slightly more of a problem to fix in the long-term for clearly a replacement thermostatically controlled switch is required. As a temporary fix,

14-1-1 (Picture 1) The metal cooling fan that you can do very little about, since it runs all the time whether needed or not. You could replace this fan with an aftermarket electric one, or blank off some of the radiator as shown in picture 14-2-1. The thermostat housing is arrowed.

14-1-1 (Picture 2) An aftermarket electric fan and...

14-1-1 (Picture 3) ...its adjustable thermostatic control.

14-1-1 (Picture 4) These are the twin original equipment (OE) fans fitted to some cars.

provided the temperature gauge is working, disconnect the fan anywhere along its circuit or remove the (probably a line-type) fuse. MGB electric fans have a push-together connection adjacent to the fan motor but you'll have to remove the grille to get at it, so removing the line fuse is your first choice.

14-2-1 The first step for any under performing heater is to try to establish whether there is actually something wrong within the heater. So, although not apparently relevant, we need to ensure that the engine and cooling system is coming up to its intended operating temperature - about 82 degrees centigrade.

First check is whether the temperature gauge needle reads "N" (normal)? If it does sit on, or roundabout, "N", move on to 14-3-1. If the gauge regularly reads between "C" (cold) and "N" carry on with the checks in this section.

With the engine cold, start by

14-2-1 Elegant? No! Effective? Yes! The beauty of this type of radiator blanking is that you can get to it very quickly if needs be. I've been known to hop out in a traffic jam to remove blanking like this. A newspaper directly in front of the radiator, as described in the main text, is less noticeable.

removing the thermostat from its housing and checking that it is closed - as it should be when taken from a cold engine. If the engine is not getting hot enough the problem is not going to be a thermostat that is stuck closed (that will cause overheating), but it could be a thermostat that is stuck open. However, it could have closed as you were removing it so we are as well to test it by attaching a piece of string to the rim and suspending it into a pan of cold water on your cooking stove. You should find it starts to open at the water nears boiling and, if you remove it from the hot water, it should close up again. If it fails to close completely, fit a new 82 degree unit.

Still a poor performance from the heater? Since we're sure the thermostat is working, we must presume that the heater is under-performing and the accuracy of the temperature gauge is doubtful (see chapter 18 for the latter) because we can be pretty sure the engine coolant is achieving the correct heat.

If you live in a very cold climate you can accelerate the warming-up process by blanking-off part of the radiator to incoming air. This will not only be beneficial to the engine, but also bring the heater into operation much earlier than it might otherwise. If you feel blanking-off the rad would be a good idea, then start with a strip of newspaper running down the full length of the rad and covering about 25% of its width. If that speeds the warm-up but you still feel it takes too long, increase the width covered to half the rad. I would be surprised if you ever needed to go further than 50%, but in very cold climatic conditions it is possible and I've run with about 70% blanked off in sub-zero conditions! **Caution!** - Don't forget you've blanked off the radiator when the weather improves. Note that blanking off part of the radiator is not such a good idea if the effectiveness of the temperature gauge is in doubt.

14-3-1 So the coolant temperature is correct and the temperature gauge is telling you so, yet the heater is hardly working.

The heat-control is the upper of the two knobs on the dashboard/fascia and, via a Bowden cable operates the valve on the cylinder head. There are several problems with this arrangement - often the arm atop the valve seizes and the either the Bowden cable/control knob becomes locked or the cable separates from the valve's arm. It is also not unknown for the Bowden cable to seize

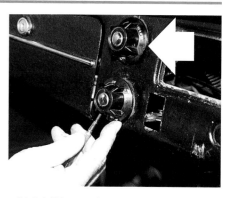

14-3-1 (Picture 1) This is the dashboard control that, on all but post-1976 RHD cars, controls the bowden cable which, in turn, controls the heater valve...

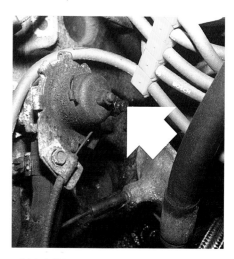

14-3-1 (Picture 2) ...bolted to the side of the cylinder head. The bowden cable actuated arm mentioned in the main text is arrowed. If there's any doubt whether it's the cable or the valve that is restricting heater performance, separate the inner cable from the valve arm (at the arrow) and the outer cable from the valve body at 7 o'clock.

14-3-1 (Picture 3) These cables are rarely lubricated, even over a 30 year period: not surprisingly they stiffen or even seize/freeze.

for the want of lubrication. So, you need to have a partner operate the dashpanel knob while you watch for the reaction, if any, at the heater control valve. If the movement is minimal you may find it helpful to disconnect the cable at the valve end and work the dashpanel knob and the arm atop the valve independently until you discover what is causing your restricted movement. Try running a little oil up the Bowden cable while you have it disconnected and distribute it through the cable by continued operation of the knob for a couple of minutes. Usually, it's the valve's arm that is most reluctant to move through the full extent of its intended arc (about 90 degrees) - and you'll need to lubricate it with copper-based grease and work it until it does. Reconnect the Bowden cable and check you're still getting the valve arm's to travel a full arc via the dashboard knob. If all is now well, great! If not, feel the temperature of the two flexible pipes leading to and from the heater: if they're cool, read on ...

14-4-1 We know the engine coolant temperature is hot enough to provide some heat and that the lever on the top of the heater valve is opening. The next step is to check the piping from the engine to the heater is fitted correctly, that it is not restricted and that the heater matrix is allowing coolant to pass.

Starting with the pipe connections, check that the top-left inlet on the heater is piped to the heater control valve mounted on the cylinder head. The bottom-right side pipe should run forward to the water pump. If they're not connected in this manner you'll need to follow that pattern

14-4-1 (Picture 1) This is how MG designed the top heater pipe to be fitted - the top hose takes return water to the bottom radiator hose via the pipe that runs over the top of the rocker cover.

14-4-1 (Picture 2) Back-flushing the heater matrix with a domestic hose. Not much water coming out of the other end yet, which could mean the matrix is completely blocked.

when reconnecting them shortly. However, for the moment, remove the top-left pipe from the heater (hopefully, going to the control valve) completely.

Next, remove the bottom-right pipe from the heater outlet and observe the flow of water from the bottom outlet - it should initially be a steady and fairly swift flow for a few seconds, whereupon it will slow to a drip once the matrix empties. If it is never more than a dribble you can be fairly sure you have a blocked heater matrix and you should also take a look at both pipes. You'll probably find one, possibly both, choked with sludge, in which case try and clear as much of the blockage as you can and reconnect the bottom one to a domestic hosepipe in an effort to blast as much of the rubbish out of the other pipe as possible. You could be lucky and start to see a stream of dirty water coming out of the top outlet. In this event, keep going until the water is flowing clear and free then fit a new pair of flexible hoses (connected in the manner described above) and try the heater again, making certain you travel far enough to open the thermostat and get hot water circulating round the heater.

14-5-1 Still chilly? In that case feel the two (new) flexible pipes leading to and from the heater - they should be hot. If they are indeed hot, but you're not feeling the benefit of that heat in the cockpit, you need to ensure air is getting though the intake and that the chromed grille at the back of the bonnet is not blocked.

When you turn the fan on there should be some obvious air movement. If the fan is not working take a look at

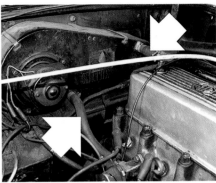

14-5-1 (Picture 1) Here, both heater pipes are arrowed for clarity. Feel both to establish temperature.

14-5-1 (Picture 2) The cables underneath the bulkhead make it an awkward job, but if the heater matrix is blocked or badly restricted, you have little choice but to remove the heater assembly and...

14-5-1 (Picture 3) ...remove the five retaining clips so that the front comes off - complete with motor.

chapter 19 to resolve that issue but, generally, airflow is not normally the cause of these sorts of heating problems.

Time to consider the heater matrix - which would appear to have a number

14-5-1 (Picture 4) The matrix then just lifts out; if yours looks like this, replace it. You can still buy original replacements but it's better to upgrade to a new high-capacity matrix.

14-5-1 (Picture 5) Before you put the repaired assembly back in the car, give a moment's thought to the fan. It may work as well as an original ever did, but you can upgrade the fan, too, and this might be the moment. The best/biggest upgraded fan impellers require you modify the front cover of the heater - this is your chance!

of its tubes silted up and, although water is passing through the matrix, there are insufficient heat-transfer tubes working to materially warm the air transferring to the cockpit. Sorry, because it's a very frustrating job, but you'll probably need to replace the matrix, which means removing the heater assembly. You could try flushing the whole system through with the descaling chemicals mentioned in 13-1-8 before finally making up your mind. If you decide upon a new matrix, investigate upgrading to a larger one.

14-6-1 If, on the other hand, you have had water from your hosepipe flowing freely through the matrix and fitted a pair of new flexible hoses to the heater matrix but find, after your test run that the new hoses are not getting hot, we need to consider the heater control valve that is mounted on the cylinder head.

Start by removing it. Given the circumstances, there's a very high likelihood that it is blocked or that the control lever is seized in the closed position. If the lever is working well (unlikely) check whether there is a blockage inside the water passages at one or both ends, or right through! Have a poke around to see if you can establish whether it seems like a local blockage or whether you think the valve is completely blocked. In the first case it is possibly worth dropping the valve into kettle descaler overnight, rinsing it very thoroughly so that all of the descaler is gone and then blowing though it, firstly to see if it is open and secondly to establish that it closes when you move the lever accordingly.

Frankly, you're most likely going to end up replacing the valve with a new unit

but, before you actually order the replacement original-type valve, do take a look at chapter 10 of my earlier book *How to Improve the MGB, MGC and MGB V8* (also from Veloce) where alternative and better heater valves are explored.

Before you refit the cleared original or a new valve, do take a look inside the water passage within the cylinder head. Clear any blockage trying to ensure the rubbish comes out of the head not into it and be sure to fit a new gasket between the valve base and the head.

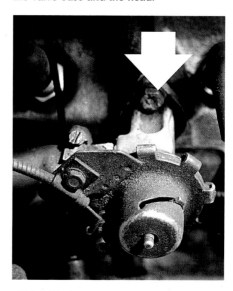

14-6-1 The heater control valve may have to come off the head if hot water is not flowing through the pipes leading to and from the heater. This is one of the retaining bolts; the other is below the valve.

Chapter 15
Carburettors & correct fuel/air mix

The correctness of the fuel/air mixture delivered to the engine by the carburettors is very important to the long term well-being of the engine, as well as the short term performance that you enjoy. An inadequate proportion of fuel is described as a "lean" mixture while too great a proportion of fuel is described as a "rich" mixture. Slight variations from the ideal 14.5 parts fuel to 1 of air (14.5:1) are normal and to be expected, particularly as engines and carburettors wear. However, extreme variations are potentially damaging to the engine and, consequently, need to be addressed with some urgency.

An engine fed with an excessively lean mixture will suffer piston and/or valve damage due to overheating. An excessively rich mixture is not only a source of environmental pollution and unecessary expense but "bore wash" will very quickly damage pistons, rings and cylinder bores while eventually the excessive fuel will dilute the lubricating oil and thus cause more extensive engine damage.

The task of giving good advice here is made less than straightforward by the variety of twin SU carburettors fitted to the MGB and, later, by the added complication of emission controls. Furthermore, from 1975 our friends in the USA enjoyed a unique single carburettor installation - a Stromberg CD175-5T fitted with emission control equipment. In view of this variety of carburettor specifications and the fact that standard adjustments are covered in the available workshop manuals, I'll limit my advice to exploring

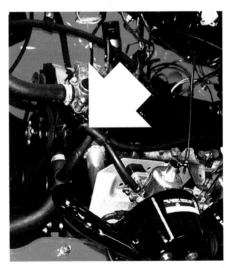

15-1-1 (Picture 1) This MGB is fitted with SU HIF4 carburettors, so was probably made after January 1972. Cars built after August 1975 will be subject to UK annual exhaust emissions testing. This seems an excellent opportunity to highlight the pipe that removes emissions from the engine on all MGBs.

the symptoms of general carburettor maladies and describing the appropriate fixes. I'll also address some symptoms that emanate from emission control system faults.

This chapter is divided into four sections -
- Common fault symptoms/problems
- SU HIF specifics
- Stromberg CD175-5T specifics
- Emissions control equipment specifics

A workshop manual should help you to translate my recommended solution into the remedial action for your system.

We'll start with what I perceive to be by far the most frequent problem - the symptoms that signal a rich mixture.

Warning! - Always take every appropriate precaution to prevent the risk of fuel fires when dealing with carburettors and other fuel system components.

15-1 COMMON FAULT SYMPTOMS/PROBLEMS

The car has failed an emissions test

15-1-1 The car has failed the emissions test. In the UK all MGBs registered after August 1st 1975 have to undergo a gas test for CO (carbon monoxide) and HC (hydrocarbon) emissions at tickover. The

15-1-1 (Picture 2) A possible solution to unacceptable exhaust emissions - fuel additive.

acceptable limits for cars of the MGB era are 4.5 per cent and 1200ppm respectively, although vehicles registered after the MGB era will have to meet more stringent standards. Of course, regulation regarding acceptable emissions vary around the world.

High hydrocarbon readings are the result of an incomplete combustion process within the cylinders. Even today, carburettor technology dictates that combustion can never be absolutely complete - which is why the much more efficient EFI (Electronic Fuel Injection) is found on modern cars.

Hydrocarbon emissions are particularly difficult to minimise during cold start-ups and at tickover/idle (at which speed the emission test is done). If your car fails the test it's because fuel droplets which fail to burn are being vented to atmosphere in the exhaust gases.

Cars never fail an emissions test by running too lean; the test is designed to protect the environment against the consequences of an over-rich mixture. In fact, a large number of UK and US based MGBs won't need to be tested for emissions, which is probably just as well since the SU carburettor is not generally known for its good hydrocarbon emission characteristics.

There are a few things you can do to help your MGB's readings:
• Set the tickover speed to 1000rpm to help both CO and HC.
• Lean the mixture by adjusting the jet position to improve CO emissions. This is accomplished by screwing **out** the adjusting screw in the front of the body of the HIF4 carburettor. While not normally applicable in the UK, for the record, you'll need to screw the adjusting nut **up**, towards the body, of the earlier HS4 carburettor.
• Ensure otherwise rarely used cars are used extensively for a week or two before the emissions test. Under-used engines suffer from sticky piston rings that lead to poor HC readings.
• Check the condition of the valves via a cylinder compression test. Leaking valves (it only takes one) will lower compression ratios, reducing that cylinder's ability to fully combust each charge and thereby increasing HC emissions. Furthermore, if it's an exhaust valve, you could be losing some unburnt charge to the exhaust system, too.
• Make absolutely sure the ignition-related adjustments are at optimum - check tappets, plugs, points, distributor cap, high tension leads, indeed anything that could reduce combustion quality.
• Change the engine oil just before the test. Cars that have run rich for some time (or been over-choked while starting) will have a sump full of oil contaminated by fuel. The longer the oil has remained unchanged, the more hydrocarbons the oil can contribute to the emissions via the sump breather.
• The higher the combustion temperature the more likely the engine is to burn the fuel/air mixture effectively. A very small improvement in HC emissions might therefore be achieved by fitting a higher-rated water temperature thermostat.
• Excessive CO and HC exhaust emission levels can be caused by general engine wear and, in this case, there's only one effective solution - rebuild the engine.

However, before you start to think too seriously along those lines remember that you will get many of the same symptoms from a build-up of lacquer, gum, varnish and carbon deposits within the engine. It's worth first trying an additive in the fuel or sump in an effort to clear the worst of this contamination. Forte (UK tel. number 02476 474069) make two: one to add to the fuel that cleans the pre- and upper cylinder areas (carburettor jets, valve guides and piston rings), and one used in the sump that improves oil control ring cleanliness and thus reduces CO levels emitted via the crankcase breathing system.

Excessive fuel consumption/ erratic running/high emissions
15-1-2 Fuel consumption seems excessive. Contemporary road tests credit the MGB with around 25mpg (Imperial gallons) for mixed (i.e. town and long distance) driving. Time, mileage, wear, fuel and conditions are unlikely to have improved what we should regard as the absolute ideal. What we use our car for, how we drive it and traffic conditions all affect fuel consumption; optimising the condition of ignition components and timing, maintaining the engine, and frequency of use can be instrumental in improving fuel economy. But the condition of the carburettors probably has the greatest single affect on fuel consumption and the condition of the throttle spindles that has

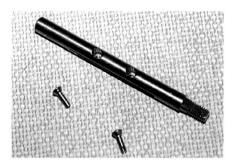

15-1-2 Replacement throttle spindles are easily obtained for any of the carburettors mentioned in this chapter, and most will come with a pair of special throttle butterfly/disc screws. A new spindle will remove the wear and resulting leaks if just the spindle is worn, but if the body of the carburettor has also worn, a replacement, standard-sized spindle will help but not completely remedy the problem. Reconditioned body/spindle assemblies are available for the worst of conditions.

the greatest single affect on carburettor setting accuracy.

The very first check to carry out on any carburettor is to establish whether throttle spindle wear has reached an unacceptable level. You may need to disconnect the various return springs to get a true evaluation. The test is simple - do the throttle spindles move about within their housings. The smallest, almost indiscernible, movement is possibly acceptable, but if you can see a gap opening and closing you should refurbish the carburettors or fit service-exchange units.

Some wear is to be expected, but you'll be unable to adjust the carburettor to compensate once the "play" becomes 0.005in or greater. Carburettor cleaner sprayed (both sides) where the shaft exits the body will tell you what you don't want to hear. If the tickover changes for a moment, the shafts and/or carburettor bodies have unacceptable wear, and therefore air induction, and need rectification. Throttle spindle wear totally destroys not only the efficiency of the carburettors, but also your control of the mixture.

You may conclude that throttle spindle wear is bound to let in more air than the carburettor really wants and that, consequently, the resulting mixture will be leaner. This would be true except that as the spindles have gradually worn, the mixture has been progressively richened to compensate and enable the car to run properly - until the time comes when it is not possible to continue to effect a reasonable fuel/air balance in all operating conditions. So carburettors with worn throttle spindles can actually increase fuel consumption and adversely effect emissions, and the root cause of the problem needs to be resolved by fitting service-exchange bodies or replacing the throttle spindles.

15-1-3 Poor fuel economy, erratic running and high emissions can also signal wear in the needles and jets. You'll appreciate that the SU and Stromberg carburettors control the volume of fuel delivered to the engine by the vacuum lifting each carburettor's piston which in turn lifts a tapered needle out of the main fuel jet. Consequently, the higher the vacuum, the greater the clearance between needle and jet and the larger the flow of fuel to the thirsty engine. I should add that the needle taper is **very** carefully graded and tuned to the engine's quite different fuel requirements at differing

15-1-3 The needle and jet used in the HS4 SU carburettor. The HIF SU uses a similar principle with slightly different jet. In each carburettor the relationship between needle and jet is crucial. The top needle/jet is how they should sit relative to each other during most hard driving conditions which generate a medium/high vacuum. The needle is roughly half withdrawn from the jet; both needle and jet will wear. The relationship between the lower needle and jet probably never occurs in practice since the needle is so far into the jet that fuel cannot pass between the pair, so there shouldn't be any wear on the needle at this point.

speeds and throttle settings.

In short, the needle is a high precision method of metering the fuel available to the engine and you'll consequently appreciate that any wear on the needle will effect its fuel metering accuracy. Consider therefore that wear on the needle only occurs by rubbing against the jet - but that the jet correspondingly wears, thus roughly doubling the fuel metering error. However, while wear in the jet confuses the metering right up the vacuum range, the vast majority of needle wear takes place where the needle is most frequently positioned - the mid to top part of the needle. In fact sometimes you can actually see a ridge in the needle! So, if your engine is over-rich on low revs, including idle emissions, but seems starved of fuel at mid to high revolutions, the chances are very high that the carburettors have needle and jet wear and that that **both** items need replacing. If you have a Stromberg, chances are that a replacement needle will make an amazing difference.

15-1-4 Bad drivability, poor fuel economy, erratic running and high emissions can also signal that one or both carburettor pistons are sticking. It is vital that the SU pistons move smoothly up and

15-1-4 As you can see from this shot, clearance between the outside of the piston and the inside of the bore of the dashpot top is minimal. Corrosion, dirt or mechanical damage will restrict the piston's free movement and could even stop movement completely, resulting in some strange operational characteristics.

down within their housings and this is very easy to check with the air filters removed and the engine switched off. Simply feel for the smooth upward movement of each piston and watch for its consistent return to the bottom of its stroke. Dirt or corrosion can adversely effect piston operation to the serious detriment of the carburettor's performance. A piston that fails to return to the bottom of its stroke will definitely adversely effect fuel consumption and, indeed, emissions.

Remove the three top cover (dashpot) securing screws and correct any obvious contamination by the gentlest means possible. If there's nothing too obvious, or you've tried the car after what you thought was an adequate cleaning of piston and bores only to find no improvement, remove the covers again. This time look for signs of (slight) interference between piston and bore. It may only be a small single high spot, but it could be enough to slow or even hold the piston's movement resulting in some very strange performance characteristics!

You need to polish the bore at the point where the piston binds, but it must be done with great care with **very** fine emery paper or with metal polish. Remove only just enough material local to the high spot, remembering this needs a slow "do a bit and try it" approach.

Carburettors difficult to balance

15-1-5 If you're having difficulty balancing the carburettors, or in trying to get the front pair of sparkplugs to look the same as the rear pair, the needle valves that control the level of fuel in the float chambers could be sticking.

Look for drops (or a stream) of fuel from the overflow pipes down by the sump and/or you may get a clue by a smell of fuel. Do you have a filter fitted in the fuel line to the carbs and, if so, has it been replaced in recent history? If you do not have a fuel filter in line, first clean the two carburettor float chambers of the inevitable dirt that will have collected. Check that the fuel cut-off (needle) valves in the float chamber tops are opening and closing fully when they should, and fit an in-line fuel filter.

If the needle valves are not working to your complete satisfaction, or you have been experiencing flooding, consider not only replacing your needle valve/seat assembly but upgrading them via the use of 'Grose Jet' valves. They're not original but are much more effective and reliable.

Whichever replacement you're considering, use a small spanner to unscrew the brass seat from top of the float chamber and inspect the tip of the valve. You'll almost certainly see that it's no longer cone-shaped but has a ridge

15-1-5 The separate float chamber of the HS4 carburettor makes for easy access and maintenance as this exploded view shows. The float is obvious but note the tiny needle valve (arrowed) that closes, thus stopping the intake of fuel once the float is lifted high enough in the chamber.

worn into the cone which prevents the now non-conical valve from sealing properly. Age and mileage can vary the depth of the ridge from car to car, but any ridging requires that you replace **both** parts of the valve in **both** carburettors.

Whether you fit original needle valves and seats or Grose Jets, you'll then need to check that the fuel levels within the float chambers are not only set at a sensible level but also more or less equal in each carburettor. With the piston/needle assemblies removed and aided by a battery powered torch/flashlight look down into the **jets** for the fuel level. You almost certainly will need to ruffle the surface of the fuel by blowing gently. The fuel level should be approximately 4 to 6mm (just less than a quarter inch) below the top of the jet. If it varies significantly from this average then you certainly need to give the floats, float pivots (you will be amazed how they can wear) and the needle valves themselves remedial attention until the fuel levels are correct and apparently equal carb to carb.

It doesn't happen often, but it's not unknown for the float within the float chamber to leak and partially fill with fuel. Consequently, a punctured float will not ride so high on the fuel in the float chamber with the result that it will appear that the needle valve is faulty because the fuel level is too high. If there's any fuel in the float, replace the float. If you're suspicious but cannot see or hear any fuel, it's worth immersing the float in warm water (rather as you would a bicycle inner tube) to check for a leak. If there is one present you'll see the odd bubble of air escaping as the air within the float warms up and expands.

15-1-6 You can get all the symptoms of sticking needle valves purely as the result of an incorrectly set float within one float chamber. With twin carburettors we go to a lot of trouble (or we will do, shortly) to match the airflow, needle, jet throttle openings, etc, in order to balance the carburettors - but it's all wasted if the fuel level in one carburettor varies from that within its partner.

The float and needle valve setting within each float chamber control the fuel level - and these need to be adjusted until the fuel levels are more or less the same. Can't see the fuel level? Start the car, let it run for a few seconds and switch-off. Take the tops off both carburettors and remove the pistons/needle assemblies and peer down into the jets. You may need to blow gently to ruffle the surface of the fuel

15-1-6 (Picture 1) This float is in the position it would adopt if the float chamber were empty of fuel. The needle valve in the top (arrowed) is open and fuel will flow into the float chamber once the fuel pump pressurises the system.

15-1-6 (Picture 2) Here, the float is in a more realistic operating position with the needle valve closed. Consider, however, the effect on fuel levels if the float arm was bent and the needle valve not yet closed...

but it should be about 4 to 6mm (just less than a quarter inch) below the top of each jet. Adjust one or both floats until the fuel levels are identical but within the 4 to 6mm tolerance.

Idle/tickover speed is inconsistent

15-1-7 This can be a typical symptom of carburettors with worn throttle spindles. However, whatever the cause, the effect is that often a previous owner has set the

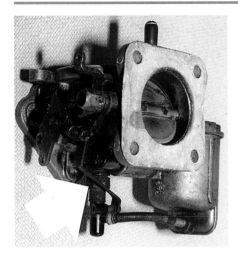

15-1-7 (Picture 1) This is the jet position when the choke is fully off; note the absence of a gap at the arrowed point. However...

15-1-7 (Picture 2) ...if the choke is incorrectly set the jet will withdraw; not to this extent, of course, but it only needs to be a fraction out in one carburettor to upset things generally and idle consistency in particular.

idle/tickover too fast in an effort to stop the engine from constantly stalling.

The jet/choke linkage position is the first thing to check: there should be a small clearance between the fast idle adjusting screw and the fast idle cam. If you have twin carbs are they set more or less identically?

If all is well but you're still experiencing difficulty in achieving a consistent idle, check the induction system for unintentional air induction. Start with a close visual examination of the carburettors and inlet manifold. Don't forget the servo valve and/or vacuum piping if fitted. If nothing is obviously wrong the next step is to start the engine. Set it at a fast idle/tickover and spray the various joints and spindles with an aerosol carburettor cleaner (Moss part number MRD1023). This is best done with a tubular plastic nozzle on the aerosol button, and with a partner watching the exhaust for a changed (usually darker) emission while you're at the sharp end listening for a slight change in engine tone. A systematic approach is usually helpful and I would start with the manifold to head joint and spray test each possible source of a leak progressively nearer the carburettor spindles. **Caution!** - Don't accidentally spray carburettor cleaner into Zenith-Stromberg (usually just known as Stromberg) carburettors as the carburettor cleaner will quickly render the diaphragms useless. Chances are that your vacuum leak test will reveal at least one worn throttle spindle.

Idle/tickover is erratic/sparkplug deposits different colours/poor fuel economy

15-1-8 This combination of symptoms suggests your twin carburettors are out of balance - which is another way of saying that the fuel/air mixture provided by one carburettor is different from that provided by the other one. Frankly, the most satisfactory solution is to get a professional to balance the carburettors using professional gas analysing equipment.

For those feel they must try for themselves first, remove the air cleaners, loosen the inter-carburettor throttle linkages and set the tickover/idle at about 800 to 900rpm. Using a small screwdriver

15-1-8 (Picture 1) The piston lift button is situated on the outside of each carburettor.

or the carburettor's in-built piston lift button, raise one piston about 3 or 4mm (0.15in). The engine will respond in one of three ways -

• An immediate increase in engine revs will signal that the carburettor is adjusted to give too rich a mixture. Expect the increase to be about 50 to 100rpm, so, although a helper watching the tachometer could be useful, the clearest sign will be a change in engine note. Lean the HIF by slowly unscrewing the mixture adjustment screw or, in the case of HS4s, close the main hexagon by one flat and try again. Strombergs are adjusted via their needles as explained below.

• A reduction in engine revs signals that that carb is currently supplying too weak a mixture and that the adjustment hexagon should be lowered by one flat and the test repeated.

• A slight change in engine rpm (a momentary hesitation) quickly followed by a return to the previous rpm. indicates that that particular carburettor's mixture is correct.

Before actually starting to adjust the carburettors, double-check the adjustments you plan to make by letting things cool down and checking the appearance of the sparkplugs.

If the plugs served by a carburettor you are intending to lean look as if they have in an over-rich environment (black, sooty deposits), it probably confirms you are going about things correctly. If the plugs already show signs of a lean mixture (white, flakey deposits), think again. That said, the colour of sparkplug deposits is by no means as conclusive as it used to be;

15-1-8 (Picture 2) Listen for the hiss as air is sucked through each carburettor inlet - a piece of tube positioned in the same place within each carb will tell you if the noises are the same. Adjust the throttle butterfly positions until airflow of both carbs is identical.

different fuels generate different colour deposits, as you may have noticed if you've looked at your exhaust tailpipe recently. It used to be simple: a whitish exhaust pipe was what you were looking for with leaded fuels; a sooty one told you the mixture was too rich. Today, a sooty black exhaust is quite satisfactory if you're using straightforward 95 RON unleaded fuels, and you can expect a different colour again if you were to change to super (97 RON) unleaded. Hence my earlier recommendation that the job be done professionally, although adjusting SU carburettors is actually relatively straightforward, as special tools are not necessary.

If your 'B has a Zenith-Stromberg carburettor, buy or borrow a special tool that passes down through the top of the carburettor, enabling the mixture to be adjusted. The tool also prevents the piston from turning (which would damage the diaphragm) and, via a hexagon key, adjusts the mixture.

Adjust the throttle settings to provide equal airflow through each carb's venturi. You can buy a proprietary balancing tool but, if you've got a good ear, quite satisfactory results can be achieved by using a 12in length of 0.25in bore rubber or plastic tube as a stethoscope. Listen for the hiss of passing air at the inlet to each carburettor and adjust the throttle butterflies to achieve an identical sound in each, indicating equal airflow through each carburettor.

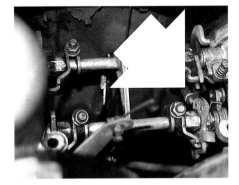

15-1-9 The jet/choke linkage can be affected by incorrect adjustment of several mechanical linkages, but probably the first thing to do is ensure that the throttle 'fast-idle' screw has a small clearance when the choke is closed, while also checking that this mechanism is hard up against the 'off' stop every time your helper pushes in the choke.

Engine oil smells of fuel/over-rich fuel supply

15-1-9 If you smell fuel in the engine lubricating oil you probably have a very rich mixture, for at least some of the time you are using the car, and are washing the bores with fuel. Is the car showing signs of an over-rich mixture - high fuel consumption, smoke from the exhaust, etc? Use the suggestions already outlined to correct the situation as quickly as possible. Once the basic problem has been resolved, don't forget to change the engine oil.

15-1-10 If you smell fuel in the engine lubricating oil check that the air filters/cleaners are not clogged. By today's standards original MGB air filters are inefficient, and must be maintained in top condition. As they are used the holes in the paper filter material become clogged - perhaps not noticeably so to you, but the engine will have to work progressively harder to draw air through the filters, and the fuel/air mixture will get richer.

Were the MGB being designed today a quite different filter medium would be

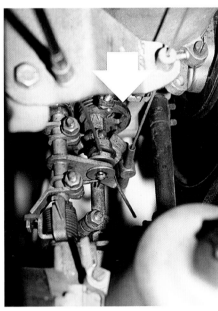

15-1-10 The HIF carburettor choke mechanism is quite different to its HS predecessor (picture 15-1-7). The rotary valve is arrowed here but you will see the choke cable (just to the right of the highlighted mechanism) still coming up from below the carburettor. However, note the flat plate now used to secure the choke cable's inner.

used, increasing servicing intervals and improving the flow of air to the carburettors. This topic is covered - along with numerous others - within the pages of *How to Improve the MGB, MGC & MGB V8* (also by Veloce), although every MGB retailer - including the MGOC - will be able to supply a set of K&N air filters for your car. **Caution!** - Be aware that the airflow through these filters will be so much improved that you should also fit richer needles to the carburettors to avoid the likelihood of running with a lean mixture.

15-1-11 The choke/enriching control is badly adjusted, the cable kinked or broken or the knob left partly pulled out.

The correct adjustment of the "choke" or fuel enrichment mechanism of any carburettor is of great importance. For those unfamiliar with the HS4 SU method of actuation, the jet is drawn down when

15-1-11 (Picture 1) These are the standard MGB air filter canisters, which may be original but are better replaced with the less restrictive, freer flowing...

15-1-11 (Picture 2) ..."K&N" filters, which are easier to maintain but which require a change of carburettor needles in order to prevent excessive fuel mix weakness.

the choke is applied thereby increasing the clearance between needle (which is unaffected by the choke's position) and jet and increasing the fuel flow to the engine.

The later SU HIF and Stromberg carburettor have different choke/enrichening arrangements and you should move forward a few paragraphs to explore the relevant section for your car's carburettor. One detail remains common to all twin carburettor chokes: before any choke adjustment can be made accurately, the carburettors must be synchronised and balanced as per 15-1-8. There needs to be a definite clearance between the choke operated cam and the throttle mechanism and, although obvious, for maximum effect the choke needs to open both carburettors simultaneously.

To adjust the chokes first undo the two 2BA fastenings from the choke control bar that connects the two carburettors. A workshop manual will give the correct settings and clearances for your particular carburettor.

If you feel the car is actually running well, consider your use of the manual choke. Is it out for too long, could it be partly closed earlier, is the mechanism closing properly and are all the return springs doing their intended jobs?

Although not an MGB case history, and peculiar in that this V8 Triumph car had twin choke cables operated by a single knob (one cable ran to each carburettor), I nevertheless mention it as an example of the damage that bore-wash can do. The owner spent some £1500 on a reconditioned engine and very carefully ran it in. The engine settled down nicely and he was delighted with it for about 18 months - when it started to use a lot of oil. He returned to the garage who had supplied and fitted the replacement engine to complain and was obviously upset to discover that one of the twin choke cables had broken leaving one carburettor permanently over fuelled. Bore wash had ruined half of the engine's cylinder bores and pistons and necessitated a further rebuild. As if all that was not bad enough, the thinned oil had also resulted in some crankshaft damage resulting in a further full engine rebuild being required along with the associated cost. If the oil smells 'fuely' it really is worth investigating.

Backfiring/spitting back through the carburettors

15-1-12A Backfiring or spitting back signals a lean mixture; check for air leaks in the induction manifold/carburettors and associated pipework.

This symptom can also be caused by ignition timing errors, but before investigating that side of the engine management, use the spray technique described in 15-1-7 to check for air leaks if you cannot see a problem.

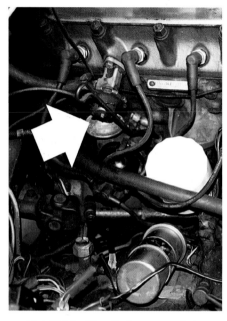

15-1-12A Ignition timing can only be checked at home using a stroboscopic timing light. Don't forget to temporally disconnect the vacuum tube to the vacuum advance diaphragm (arrowed). Caution! - mind the fan; I've ruined a number of timing lights by letting the fan hit them.

Engine won't run properly without some choke

15-1-12B If the car runs appallingly and/or will not run even when warm without the choke then clearly the mixture is too lean. There are a number of potential causes but I'd start by checking the smooth

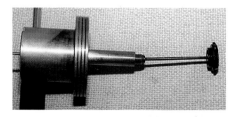

15-1-12B The piston, shown here with its damper has to be spotless, as does the bore it runs in.

operation of the carburettor pistons - for if dirt or corrosion prevent a piston lifting then the engine is bound to be under-fuelled by that carburettor, see 15-1-4.

15-1-12C If the driveability is poor and/or the engine runs hot, then the carburettor adjustment may be set to provide too weak a mixture. Although relatively unusual, be alert to the possibility that if the symptoms are extremely bad this condition can be brought about simply by the needle in one carburettor working loose and dropping into its jet - thereby closing off all fuel supply from that one carburettor.

It's more usual that one, or both, carburettors are out of adjustment and it might be an idea to start by taking a look at all four sparkplugs. Any that are glazed/white or have the central electrode burnt or central insulation cracked will signify overheating and, consequently, an over-lean mixture requiring urgent correction. Any plugs that exhibit these symptoms but are also speckled with tiny spots of aluminium are to be treated even more seriously. If all four are speckled with aluminium you have what is called "pre-ignition", possibly the result of incorrect timing, or the wrong sparkplugs and, though the carburation may be contributing, it is unlikely to be the primary cause. More likely you'll find one pair of sparkplugs (i.e. those serving number 1 and 2 cylinders, or the pair serving 3 and 4 cylinders) indicating that one carburettor is out of adjustment.

15-2 SU HIF SPECIFICS

The Horizontal Integral Float (HIF) SU carburettor was fitted from 1972 to 1974 to cars destined for USA and to rubber

15-2 (Picture 1) The HIF SU carburettor which, although more complicated than its predecessor, is only slightly more efficient and much more difficult to set up.

15-2 (Picture 2) The different choke arrangement on the HIF SU carburettor.

bumper UK cars. It was the result of a major development programme and the consequence of ever-tightening emissions legislation, and incorporated the float chamber within the lower half of each carburettor body. The same needle/jet fuel metering approach was used but the jet was mounted on a bi-metal strip, which raised the jet very slightly as fuel temperature increased, slightly leaning the mixture and reducing hydrocarbon emissions.

This design was also intended to improve the emulsification of the mixture under light throttle openings - again, with the objective of reducing emissions.

If you have an HIF carburettor on your car you will note that the throttle disc now sports an additional spring-loaded, anti run-on valve, and that the enriching

'choke' is now a more effective rotary valve fitted to the side of the body. This uncovers more and more hole as the degree of turn increases, allowing more fuel to enter the inlet manifold. The same movement also opens the throttle to increase idle/tickover rpm.

The HIF carburettor generally runs rich on cold start and tickover/idle, and can be a problem when it's time for the annual emissions check. It can be very difficult to set the mixture correctly for all running conditions. Consider having a professional with gas-analysing equipment tune your car. That said, most of the symptoms and adjustments discussed in section 15-1 apply to HIF models, although there's a significant difference in accessing the floats on HIF carburettors.

The HIF's integral float chamber makes it necessary to remove the whole carburettor from the car to replace the float and/or needle valve. Turn each unit upside-down and remove four screws from the base - this allows access to the float. The float is removed by undoing the combined screw/pin float pivot from the side of the body. Thereafter needle valve checking and replacement is the same as for earlier SU carbs. Grose Jets are still a good idea for HIFs.

15-3 (Picture 1) Adjustment of a Stromberg carburettor can only be done with a two-piece special adjusting tool, shown here in action! The outer knurled part of the tool serves two purposes: it acts as a centralising guide for the long Allen/hex key, and stops the piston turning.

in carburettor manufacturer to Zenith-Stromberg. Distinguished from the SU by its much 'dumpier' body, the Zenith-Stromberg is erroneously considered inferior to the equivalent SU by many Triumph TR owners. Strombergs were never as easy for the home enthusiast to adjust and tune, possibly deliberately, for they were designed to be pre-set at the factory. However, they should be viewed in the context of providing equal power to the SU with lower harmful emissions.

There are a couple of significant differences between SUs and Strombergs. When adjusting an SU carburettor, the needle stays in place in the piston whilst adjustments to the mixture are made by moving the jet up and down. The reverse is true with the Stomberg carb - the jet is pressed into the body of the carburettor and offers no opportunity for alteration, while the needle is screwed up and down by a special, long Allen/hexagon key. Furthermore, there's no built-in provision to lift the Stromberg piston as in an SU in order to make at least a rudimentary check on the mixture. You can, of course, do so using a small screwdriver and using the

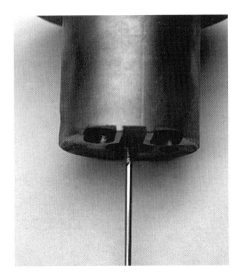

15-2 (Picture 3) The swinging (biased) needle of an HIF carb sitting in its piston...

15-2 (Picture 4) ...and awaiting fitting. The shoulder of the needle used on HS4 carburettors was much plainer.

15-3 STROMBERG CD175-5T SPECIFICS

The SU carburettor was clearly struggling to meet burgeoning international emissions control requirements, so the Triumph company designed an alternative diaphragm-controlled carburettor to help its then current models comply with emissions standards without power loss.

Triumph also introduced a change

15-3 (Picture 2) The general arrangement of Stromberg piston and top cover is straightforward, although you do need to take care when reassembling that the small 'pip' moulded into the diaphragm sits in its recess in the body, and that the top is also correctly repositioned on the body.

reactions detailed in 15-1-8 as your guide but, as with an SU, the most accurate mixture adjustment is achieved when the exhaust emissions are being checked using gas-analysing equipment.

The engine will idle but runs badly at higher speeds

15-3-1 A torn, perforated, stiff or disintegrated Stromberg diaphragm prevents the piston from properly responding to the changing vacuum generated by the engine. Depending upon the degree of diaphragm damage, and

15-3-1 This shows the all-important Stromberg diaphragm as well as the way it is fastened to the piston. Only when fitting a new needle would you use the adjusting tool in this way - but the picture usefully shows where the knurled outer sits when hidden by the main cover of the carburettor. The needle is, of course, screwed up (to enrich) and down (to lean) via the Allen/hex key which goes right to the bottom of the dashpot/damper.

thus vacuum leakage, the engine may idle but will certainly not accelerate and, if the damage is extensive, will perform very poorly indeed. **Caution!** - A torn diaphragm can very easily be brought about by trying to adjust the carburettor without the necessary special tools. Perforation can occur as the consequence of heavy use, while stiffness is the consequence of age and/or lack of use. Diaphragm disintegration can be the consequence of the use of a carburettor cleaner (usually an aerosol).

15-3-2A The O-ring that sits round the shoulder of the needle and prevents the damper from losing oil into the fuel mix. Small but very important. The one cent coin should help our US friends scale the O-ring. Where did I get a cent? It came over in my repatriated TR6!

The car is difficult to start

15-3-2A If the car is difficult to start check the dashpot/damper reservoir. If there's little or no oil present, change the O-ring in the bottom of the piston. This seals round the needle and is intended to prevent loss of damper oil. In due course it will harden, crack or just plain leak. The damper oil then leaks into the float chamber, bringing about the reluctant starting. Replace the O-ring seal as a matter of course if the damper oil is low, but especially if the reluctance to start is accompanied by a 'popping' noise when accelerating. If uncorrected, the damper will stop damping-out needle fluttering and performance will deteriorate.

The seal is held in place by a clip and access from the top (at least for disassembly) is virtually out of the question. A needle adjusting tool is necessary to remove the needle which then allows access through the needle's threaded hole in the bottom of the piston, enabling you to push the O-ring and clip upwards.

15-3-2B The correct operation of the auto choke is another detail to check in cases of difficult starting. The Zenith-Stromberg uses a conventional "choke" or flap, which pivots to restrict airflow through the carburettor's venturi thus increasing the flow of fuel. The degree of choke opening is automatically

controlled by the water temperature - a design feature introduced on the assumption that most owners leave their manual choke "out" unnecessarily long, thus polluting the atmosphere with unburned hydrocarbons. If the auto-choke is failing to fully open when the water temperature reaches normal you may notice that fuel consumption is adversely effected and the car may be difficult to hot start. The movement of the flap is, of course, easily checked with the air cleaner off and if it is not fully opening do check that the water temperature is indeed rising in the pipes leading to and from the choke. Conversely, if the flap is failing to part-close in cooler weather, then the car will be reluctant to start, particularly when the weather is very cold indeed.

The "Cat" (catalytic convertor) is getting very hot

15-3-3 Warning! - Don't delay: straightaway check that the three screws securing the automatic choke assembly to the carburettor are tight. The screws back off over the years which allows the mixture to richen which, in turn, causes the catalytic converter to get very hot - in extreme cases, red-hot. If you fail to spot the loosening screws and the accompanying smell, fuel could drip onto the overheated exhaust system and ignite. If the choke retaining screws are found to be less than tight, it's worth removing them one by one and putting a spot of thread locking fluid (such as "Locktite") on the screws before retightening them.

Engine hesitates, spits and coughs

15-3-4 Assuming the fuel filter is reasonably clean and you're pretty sure the timing is spot-on, the carburettor mixture almost certainly needs adjusting - in this case, probably richening.

Check the mixture using the piston lift technique outlined in section 15-1-8. **Caution!** - Don't be tempted to effect any mixture adjustment without the proper jet adjusting tool: if the mixture is too lean the jet must be raised, so the jet adjusting tool needs turning clockwise. Obviously, when the mixture is too rich the jet requires lowering - achieved by turning the special tool anti-clockwise.

HC reading too high

15-3-5 If the HC reading on a Stromberg is too high, the first step is to replace the needle. The bias spring on a Stromberg needle moves the needle to one side, causing a flat to be worn on one side. Strangely, the (fixed) jet rarely wears (perhaps the material is much harder than the needle?) In any event the required improvement is usually brought about by renewing the needle.

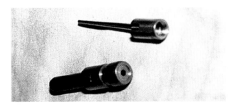

15-3-5 (Picture 1) The needle and, below it, the almost everlasting Stromberg jet which is...

15-3-5 (Picture 2) ...pressed into the body of the carb.

15-4 EMISSIONS CONTROL EQUIPMENT SPECIFICS

There are three aspects to emission controls -
- Crankcase emissions
- Exhaust emissions
- Hydrocarbon emissions

All these emissions pollute the atmosphere and are therefore subject to preventive measures in the form of the anti-pollution equipment that was fitted to the car when it was manufactured. The extent and complication of that equipment depends very much on the year of your car and your geographical location, so the potential combination of problems is considerable. The following paragraphs detail the main symptoms of malfunctioning emission system equipment.

Oil is leaking from oil filler cap/ engine gaskets/crankshaft oil seals

Clearly there is always the probability that gasket or seal leakage is the consequence of straightforward wear and tear. However, if you've already replaced the leaking component and the leak has recurred, particularly if there is also "blow-back" from the oil filler cap, there are two possible causes. Either the crankcase breather arrangements have become blocked and/or your engine's piston rings and bores are worn.

Dealing with the breather system first: MGBs had an ever increasingly sophisticated crankcase breathing system and, consequently, what sounds like a very simple problem with an equally simple solution can, at least with the later cars, become a little more complicated. All systems evacuated the crankcase pressure by expelling air from a breather tube welded into the front tappet chest cover. Crankcase emission control started with a control valve mounted centrally on the inlet manifold with or without (depending upon your location) an oil separator. A PCV (positive crankcase ventilation) valve was then introduced for some markets while, later still, a pair of quite large pipes from each of the twin carburettors were used (via an oil separator where applicable) to remove and burn crankcase fumes.

The most sophisticated and therefore vulnerable arrangement was used from about 1970 for the US market. Instead of just allowing air to exit the engine though the oil filler cap, this system had a supplementary air supply system whereby the air was first drawn through gauze filters and "activated" charcoal in a canister and via a hose to the rocker cover. The PCV valve and hoses that run from the oil separator to the carburettor are particularly vulnerable but clearly any hose or component in the circuit can become blocked, pinched, perished or restricted. This results in reduced evacuation of crankcase pressure, increased pressure within the engine and the sort of oil leaks mentioned at the head of this section.

If remedial attention to the crankcase's breathing does not resolve the oil leak(s), you need to consider engine wear generally and the bore/piston ring wear in particular. It may help if I explain that even in a low mileage engine the piston rings can never form a **perfect** seal - a very small percentage of each "explosion" will escape between the rings

and the cylinder bores and down the small gaps left of necessity in each piston ring.

If the engine is running at 3000rpm it's generating something in the order of 6000 combustions per minute. It's therefore not surprising that engines require a venting system for this pressurised and polluted gas. With a worn engine the build-up of crankcase pressure increases as bores and piston rings degenerate, putting the crankcase emissions control system under increasing load and thus requiring proportionately greater service attention if the car is to run well and cleanly. There will come a time when the frequency of emissions servicing coupled with oil consumption and general poor performance will make it necessary to think about an engine overhaul. However, meanwhile give the emissions system the extra t.l.c. (tender loving care) it needs.

Engine is running rich, with high hydrocarbon emissions and/or fouled sparkplugs

15-4-2 Simultaneously with the introduction of the PCV valve mentioned in the previous section, the carburettor needles were changed to enrich the mixture in order to compensate for the air being introduced into the induction system by the PCV crankcase breather. If the PCV valve, oil separator and/or carbon canister fitted to later systems, or any of the hoses becomes blocked, then there will be a reduced amount of extra air entering the inlet manifold and the engine will run over-rich. Clean the pipework and oil separator, replace the PCV valve and ensure the system is operating as freely as possible.

If this attention fails to resolve the emissions problem consider the condition of your car's carburettor(s) generally and the needles/main jets in particular. They could be worn as described in the earlier sections of this chapter, or the carburettors might even have been swapped for ones with the wrong needles/main jets for your car's emissions system. A set of replacement needles and main jets compatible with the emission system may help on both counts.

High engine oil consumption (but engine not worn)

15-4-3 Almost certainly a faulty PCV valve. Confirm this by warming the engine and then, while it continues to idle/tickover, remove the oil filler cap from the rocker/valve cover and listen for an rpm increase. If revs rise, the PCV valve's rubber diaphragm has probably perforated or stiffened causing the valve to remain open excessively and allowing more evacuation of crankcase gases than intended.

Impossible to obtain a consistent idle/tickover.

15-4-4 For cars fitted with exhaust emission control systems the two most likely reasons are either that the carburettor anti-run-on valves are tired and are opening early, or the ERG valve is leaking.

Dealing with the first point; the anti-run-on valves are mounted in each throttle disc, and can be easily seen with the air cleaners removed. Time and heat cause the springs to weaken and allow the valve to open before it should.

Disconnect the gulp valve and connect a vacuum gauge in its place. Warm the engine and control the throttle mechanism so that the engine is running at about 3000rpm for 10 to 15 seconds, then release the throttle and watch the vac gauge. A reading of less than 20 inches shows a run-on valve is opening and the springs in both need to be replaced. This will entail removing the carburettors from the manifold. If the vac gauge reads over 20 inches, reconnect the gulp valve and turn your attention to the EGR valve.

The EGR (exhaust gas recirculation) valve, as the name suggests, recirculates exhaust gases into the induction system as a method of reducing exhaust emissions - but it is selective in that it should not operate when the engine is at idle or full throttle. It can become choked with carbon and stick open, which will noticeably adversely affect engine idle and reduce top-end power too.

The valve can also leak through its base. To check for leaks, start the engine and set it to idle at about 900rpm. Spray the base of the valve (where most leaks occur) with carburettor cleaner in a similar manner to 15-1-7. If this fails to reveal a fault or if you have not improved idle/tickover after stopping a leak, check that the valve is operating.

Bearing in mind that the valve will be hot, have a helper 'blip' the throttle several times while you feel whether the valve is opening at part-throttle and closing again as the revs drop off. No movement suggests either a faulty (probably in the internal diaphragm) or carbon choked valve: remove it and clean from the base that screws into the exhaust manifold. Replace the valve if the engine fails to idle smoothly once the cleaned valve is back in place.

Engine runs inconsistently/ surges/runs lean

15-4-5 The first checks should be as outlined generally in section 1 of this chapter, procedure 15-1-5 in particular. If, however, you've eliminated the carburettors and induction system as the cause of the problem, there's probably a fault within the emission control systems.

Look for a blockage in the form of carbon build-up, or possibly a pinched rubber hose anywhere in the emission control equipment hoses/pipework, and failing that, check that the charcoal canister is not restricting air flow. You may have to blow through various hoses and the charcoal cannister (if fitted) to check for free-flow.

The engine runs-on ("diesels") when switched off

15-4-6 This uncomfortable occurrence was described in 15-4-4, so please re-read that section generally and the proper operation of the anti-run on valve(s) in particular.

If that doesn't help, and you have the Evaporative-Loss Fuel Control System fitted to your car, I have another suggestion for you. The system has many rubber hoses, any one of which can split or leak from a joint. Furthermore, a canister base can rot, allowing air in. Test your system by closing off the vent at the base of the run-on valve, which should stop the engine after a short delay. If the engine keeps running, there is an air leak, which you'll have to locate and repair.

Chapter 16
Brakes

The original MGB hydraulic braking system was a "single-line" system. This system remained in use in all cars up to

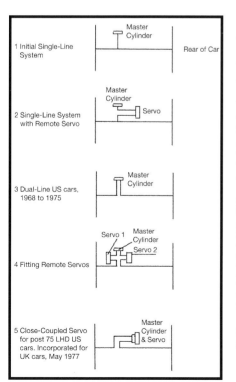

D16 Hydraulic brake circuits.

1968 when cars bound for the USA had "dual-line" brakes fitted (without servo assistance) while UK cars continued with the original single-line braking system. UK and other cars retained the single-line system until 1975 when, simultaneously with the introduction of the rubber-bumper models, all MGBs, regardless of their intended market, had an improved servo-assisted dual-line system fitted.

Diagram D16 may help to explain the diferences between the two types of brake hydraulic system but, in essence, in the MGB dual-line system the front and rear hydraulic circuits are separated to ensure that the failure of, say, the back brakes through fluid loss does not mean total brake failure.

Today, a number of original single-line brake systems have been augmented by a remote brake servo (which is usually located above the passenger footwell). Later B's have dual-circuit brake systems aided by close-coupled servos. Finally, for those with dual-line brakes but no servo, I have shown in diagram D16 how you can incorporate a single-line servo(s) into the brake system.

The symptoms explored in this chapter apply to all system types unless otherwise stated.

Brake squeal (front brakes)
16-1-1 Brake squeal from the front is something that most MGBs suffer from

from time to time. It's not serious and has no detrimental effect on the car's braking performance. In fact, the squealing usually only occurs when you're applying very light pedal pressures and disappears as soon as you become more serious about stopping.

The fundamental cause is a high-frequency vibration set up between the brake discs/rotors and the brake pads. When you put real pressure on the brake pedal you'll eliminate the vibration and thus the squeal. If the squeal persists even under heavy pedal-pressure, you should assume there is something else amiss and read 16-1-2 while examining the front pads with the minimum of delay (**Warning!** - they may be worn out). Some cars are more prone to brake squeal than others and anti-squeal shims used to be available to place between the metal backing of the pad and the caliper's pistons. Modern brake designs and pad materials have reduced the frequency of brake squeal and many modern pads are especially designed to minimise high-frequency vibration (they have a tar-like coating on the rear of the backing to act as a frequency damper). Sadly, few if any of the pads available for MGB's have this anti-squeal backing fitted as standard, but you can buy a packet of four self-adhesive ones from from good auto-parts supliers and apply one to the steel backing on each brake pad.

Alternatively, if your pads are well worn and in need of replacement, pads made from modern materials such as Kevlar are less likely to squeal and, consequently, fitting a set as described in 16-10-2 is another solution. A (poor) third approach is to apply a fairly generous skim of copper-based grease (e.g. "Copper-Ease") to the metal backing of each pad and ensure you replace each pad in its original position within the calipers. The special grease improves the contact between pad and the caliper pistons, thus dampening the vibrations and reducing squeal, at least for a short while. **Warning! - never** use ordinary grease for this purpose, only copper-based grease.

16-1-1 Other manufacturers can supply a very similar product, but this is Mintex's anti-squeal self-adhesive pad backing. It comes in packs of four and you peel the protection off this 1mm thick tar-like strip and apply one piece to the metal backplate of each squealing brake pad.

Grinding noise when braking
16-1-2 This symptom almost certainly signals that new rear shoes or front pads are required - urgently! If you can't tell where the noise comes from you can gently apply the handbrake when the car's in motion: no grinding/grating and it must be the front pads that are worn down to the metal backing while a grating sound when the handbrake is applied means the rear shoes need attention.

"Clanking" noise when brake pedal released
16-2-1 This noise is caused by worn kingpin-related front suspension components. These faults and their remedies are dealt with in chapter 10.

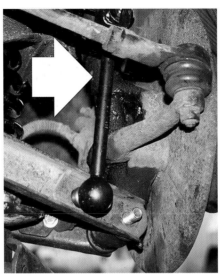

16-2-1 The front suspension consists of numerous moving parts, all of which can wear over the years. However, a clank each time you release the brakes suggests that one or both kingpins shown here, are worn and have excess play (lash).

Steering wheel shakes/brake pedal judders when braking
16-3-1 The steering wheel shakes when braking. About 30% of brake judder problems are, in fact, not connected

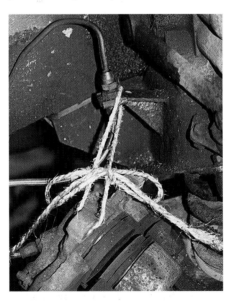

16-3-1 (Picture 1) Undo and tie up the caliper out of harm's way, ensuring you don't strain the flexible hose.

with either the pads or the brake discs. So, before you start stripping brake parts, have the balance of wheels and tyres checked and also ensure that all steering linkages are tight and in good shape.

Check that the pistons are moving smoothly in the brake calipers: any snatching, jerking or sticking can cause brake judder and steering wheel shake.

Distorted brake discs are the most likely cause of steering wheel shake. Note that you can distort the discs if you keep the footbrake applied after a prolonged or very heavy application of the brakes - when the discs are sometimes literally red-hot. **Warning!** - holding the brakes on after stopping in these circumstances encourages the transfer of heat to the brake fluid and, unless the brake fluid has been changed fairly recently, can result in boiling fluid and loss of braking! When you hold the footbrake on with very hot discs the uneven pressure each side of the disc distorts them and they stay distorted as the disc cools down. Result - every time you apply the brakes thereafter you get steering wheel shake.

To check the "run-out" of the brake discs (rotors) use a DTI (dial test indicator) on each disc in turn, preferably one with a magnetic base fixed to a solid part of the suspension. Locate the DTI so that its probe is positioned as near the outside edge of the disc as is practicable without the probe ever going outside the polished, hopefully smooth, part of the disc. Set the DTI's gauge to zero and rotate the hub/

16-3-1 (Picture 2) If the discs (rotors) are distorted there's no practical alternative but to replace both. Get each hub/disc assembly off its stub axle one at a time, put the old disc in a vice (vise) and unbolt the hub.

16-3-1 (Picture 3) Put some protection either side of the new disc (rotor), clamp it in the vice and using new spring washers, bolt the hub up to its new disc.

disc slowly watching for fluctuations in the DTI reading. Run out must not exceed 0.002in (0.05 mm). Too many books and garages think much larger amounts of run-out are satisfactory, but they're not if judder is to be avoided.

The only cure for a distorted disc is to skim it in a lathe if it has sufficient material thickness available to allow this, otherwise

16-3-1 (Picture 4) Put the hub back on the stub axle. The inter-bearing shims should not have altered and if you have looked after them, reassembly should be quite quick.

you'll need to replace **both** discs with new items. In my opinion you're probably better off having the old discs skimmed true than to fit new discs due to the fact that many new discs are too 'green' when machined and, consequently, distort very easily in use.

However, before going in search of a machine shop, if the disc run-out is greater than 0.002in/0.5mm, remove that hub/disc assembly to the bench and identify any one corresponding bolt hole on hub and disc by using typewriter correction fluid. Remove the disc from the hub, clean the mating faces **very** thoroughly, removing all rust, dirt or paint, and reassemble the disc to its hub one bolt hole away from its original position. Refit the hub/disc to the car and test the run-out. If run-out still exceeds 0.002in (0.5mm), remove the hub, take the disc from its hub and if it has sufficient thickness, get it - and its opposite number - skimmed.

Warning! - always replace brake components in axle sets - *i.e.* **both** front discs and if you're fitting new or newly skimmed discs, fit new pads at the same time. This might be the moment to take

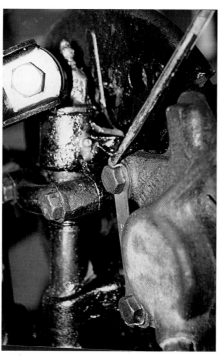

16-3-1 (Picture 5) Be sure to fit a new tabwashers and to turn over the tabs on both caliper retaining bolts so that they're tight against the bolt head sides.

a look at suggestion 16-10-2 about a change of brake pad which might make a virtue out of this necessity!

If you note brake judder shortly after fitting skimmed or new discs, it's probably disc run out caused by the disc being bolted to the hub unevenly (it's best to use a torque wrench) or assembled to the hub without the mating faces being scrupulously clean.

16-3-2 The brake pedal judders under braking. Rear drum irregularities (usually ovality) are usually felt through the brake pedal as soon as the brakes are applied, while front disc distortions are usually felt at the steering wheel. Rear drums can be skimmed to correct ovality, but this is not a great idea as it means the drum radius is a little different from the shoes. New drums are the best answer.

Brakes 'bind' (don't free completely after application)

The brakes may well be stopping the car satisfactorily but if they don't fully release when the brake pedal is released they are "binding". Protracted binding may cause the car to run hotter than you're used to, the fuel consumption may rise and you may feel the car wanting to veer under braking. Does the car seem sluggish? When you de-clutch does it coast to a stop rather quicker than you would expect? You may also find one of the discs/drums is significantly hotter than the others. Occasionally, a disc, in particular, can glow cherry-red. The latter sounds like bad news, but in fact it is very helpful in that you know exactly which wheel's brake is causing the problem.

16-4-1 The first step is to ensure the air bleed vent hole in the screw cap that sits atop the master cylinder is not blocked. You can buy a replacement cheaply enough and for the cost involved

16-4-1 Air moving in and out of the master cylinders must pass through two holes in the cap as indicated by the needles. The top can be separated into two parts using a small screwdriver.

you may prefer that route. The vent holes are tiny but must be able to pass air. The easiest way to check the vent holes is to separate the top from its base and clear both holes with a needle.

Still binding? In which case you need to identify whether it is a front or rear brake that is binding. Obviously, this is more difficult if the binding is short-lived after each application of the brakes. As a rough rule of thumb, if the car pulls to one side while binding, the problem is most likely at the front. If the car's steering is more or less unaffected, chances are you have a rear brake problem. Lets start with the easier rear brake problems and solutions -

16-4-2 Jack up the rear of the car and support it safely. If the binding is fairly constant you can spin both rear wheels and may quickly establish which one is binding. If it is a momentary binding situation, get a partner to apply the footbrake (try the handbrake too) while you test each wheel for freedom of rotation. If there is drag on one wheel,

16-4-2 (Picture 2) Greasing the handbrake cable nipple is easily overlooked: there's no immediate consequence, but it does need regular greasing to keep the internal cable moving freely. The grease is best applied with the handbrake securely "on" – this tightens the outer cables' wound coils and makes the grease run further up and down the inside of the inner cable. This shot suggests I had better practice what I preach very soon as the nipple would appear not to have seen the grease gun recently!

16-4-2 (Picture 4) This is the business end of the rear brake adjuster – you may be able to see the internal flats that give it its "lumpy" feeling when you turn the...

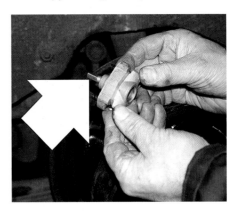

16-4-2 (Picture 5) ...the square-shaped adjuster head that sticks out the rear of the backplate.

16-4-2 (Picture 1) This is the handbrake pivot that usually gets overlooked when it comes to lubrication and, consequently, becomes stiff and only reluctantly "lets-go" when the handbrake is released. This is my GT - and while I would be the first to admit it does not seem to have enjoyed a visit by the oil can recently, I do assure you that this one is not seized (frozen)!

try backing the square brake adjuster off one "notch" (which you'll feel). If that does not resolve the situation or the drag can be felt on both wheels, particularly if the drag only occurs after the use of the handbrake, suspect the handbrake mechanism is partially seized.

The cable pivot on the rear axle is

16-4-2 (Picture 3) The lever that operates the rear shoes when the handbrake is applied is made from two parts that are supposed to pivot freely. Often they seize (freeze) which will reduce the effectiveness of the handbrake and can cause the rear brake to bind.

usually the most vulnerable spot, but poor maintenance of the handbrake's Bowden cable is another favourite! Oil the former, grease the latter, but if they both prove

to be satisfactorily free, or the drag is mainly applicable to one wheel only, then your focus should turn to the handbrake mechanisms in the brake backplates. Two potential problems regularly occur: the pivot on the handbrake cross lever seizes and/or the fore/aft sliding movement of the slave cylinder becomes restricted, even completely seized. Any of these problems will necessitate a strip-down of the rear brakes on that side of the car. The seized lever is usually easily resolved, but take care when you get to the hydraulic cylinder. If it is weeping or in any way suspect, replace it with a new one. Check that the adjuster operates smoothly and take this opportunity to free it off or replace it if in any doubt. Are the rear brake shoes in good order? If you do decide this is a good opportunity to replace them, don't forget that front pads and rear shoes should always be replaced as an axle-set. In other words you'll need to also change the shoes on the other rear wheel before you use the car on the road.

16-4-3 If it's the front brakes that need attention, you start with a slight advantage because you should have an idea from the way the car steers as to which caliper is at fault (it will tend to self-steer to the side on which a caliper is binding after you release the brakes). Nevertheless, keep an open mind and safely jack up the front of the car and spin both wheels in a first effort to find the dragging brake. If you are unable to identify which wheel has a problem, get a pal to apply and release the footbrake while you spin the wheels: this should identify the side with the problem.

What usually happens to cause the drag is that one (possibly both) of the pistons in that caliper become sluggish in action. This can be the consequence of a build-up of brake dust but, frankly, in our MGBs is much more likely to be the result of corrosion in the bores and of the (plated) steel pistons. By all means try the easy route first so, one side of the car at a time, drop the pads out (marking each with its original location) and spray the pistons/bores each side of the caliper with brake cleaner. Get a pal to bring the

pistons out of their bores **very carefully and slowly** by pressing on the brake pedal while you watch that the pistons don't come out too far. You can put a piece of wood (about the thickness of two pad backing plates) between the pistons and disc as insurance since without the pads in place it's possible to pop one or both pistons completely out of their bores.

You should also observe whether one piston is slower than its counterpart in advancing - possibly signalling this is the tight one. Use the brake cleaner, exercise both pistons in and out (you can pull them back into their bores using a G-clamp) until they are both working equally well and maybe help the situation slightly by applying a little red **brake grease** to the periphery of the pistons when they are extended. Put the pads back in their original places and try the brakes to see if there has been an improvement.

16-4-4 If, even after cleaning a caliper's pistons *in situ*, you are still experiencing front brake drag then it's time for more drastic action. Remove the

pads and using the brake pedal, extend both pistons in the offending caliper as far as possible without allowing them to pop out of the calipers.

16-4-4 (Picture 2) For the benefit of those electing to replace the seals, this is the dustshield being removed from its groove - you'll not be able to see it in the picture, but the dust shield has a V-shaped groove in the face that contacts the piston while...

16-4-4 (Picture 3) ...this is the main seal coming out of its inner groove...

16-4-3 This piston is already partly expelled from the caliper and the pins and clips that retain the pads have been removed. If we now remove the pads and very carefully expel the piston a little more, we should be able to clean it up, lightly grease it with red brake grease and eliminate any sluggishness or binding.

16-4-4 (Picture 1) The dust seal on this half-caliper looked good so I wasn't surprised when the piston popped out with very little trouble. However, on examination there are some corrosion marks on the piston and to my mind it needs replacing. Obviously, you're never going to get this far without replacing the outer dust seal (top arrow) and the piston seal itself (bottom arrow) ...but, since you're in need of a new piston, it may be better to reassemble the caliper without changing the seals and trade it in (along with its opposite number) for a pair of reconditioned units.

16-4-4 (Picture 4) ...and this the end result before we thoroughly clean the inside and start reassembly. Ease the piston into the resealed caliper with a little brake fluid or, better yet, a smear of red brake grease.

Clamp the flexible brake hose with a special brake pipe clamp to prevent all the hydraulic fluid in that brakeline escaping and then remove that caliper from the car. Take the caliper to your workbench and ease one piston out of its bore. If it's stubborn you can do so by using an airline or hydraulic fluid pressurised by an "Eezi bleed" system on the caliper's inlet. Clean the piston with brake cleaner, in metholated spirit or clean hydraulic fluid and (felt-tip pen) mark it internally as to which caliper bore it came from. Take a close look at the piston's perimeter - only if it looks in excellent condition should you think about re-using it. Hook both piston seal and dust seal from the bore of the caliper and clean the bore of the caliper including the recess for each seal very thoroughly and seat the new seal and dust seal (which has the internal V-groove) very carefully in that bore.

Repeat the exercise for the other piston. If that's OK too, replace the seals and use new brake fluid or **brake grease** to lubricate the piston before replacing them in their respective bores. However, if any one of the four pistons (two per caliper) is pitted with corrosion and/or the chrome plating is flaking, my advice is do a service exchange deal with your favourite MG parts retailer for **both** calipers. You'll be expected to put the piston(s) back before returning the old calipers, in which case lubricate the internal seal with fresh brake fluid or brake lubricating grease and ease each piston back into its original place as you would with pistons you would re-use.

16-4-5 If the front calipers are definitely not sticking, yet you're still experiencing brake drag and have a single line remote brake servo in the system, then it's possible that the servo unit is faulty and causing the brakes to bind/drag. In my experience it's the caliper nearest the faulty servo that usually binds on, but I've heard of other owners who've had more distant brakes, including rear brakes, bind - so keep an open mind! However, we'll proceed on the basis that it's a front caliper that's binding. If the problem is caused by a faulty servo, the brake will only bind with the engine running (to create the necessary vacuum).

Start by safely jacking both front wheels off the ground, then spin them to ensure both are free of brake binding. Go through the foot brake routine described in 16-4-2. Start the engine but, initially, don't operate the footbrake. Try each wheel for free rotation. All OK? - if so

get a pal to apply and release the footbrake with the engine running while you go through the free-rotation routine. If you establish that the front wheels rotate freely when the engine's not running but that one, or both, calipers drag when the engine is running then it's the servo at fault. To be more exact it's the vacuum control valve or its connection pipe on the servo that is leaking, making the servo

16-4-5 (Picture 1) This is the remote servo's air valve that interfaces with the brake system via a (quite small) piston that is pushed up into the air valve from the arrowed location.

16-4-5 (Picture 2) This is the innards of the all important air valve from a type-6 Lockheed remote servo. The small plunger central to the picture is, basically what controls the drop in vacuum from the far side of the vacuum chamber and thus controls the amount of vacuum assistance this side of the main vacuum chamber adds to the braking effort. If the arrowed pipe becomes porous it allows uncontrolled air to enter the far side of the vacuum chamber which applies the brakes when, in fact, no such application is required.

believe a small amount of braking assistance is needed.

The get-you-home fix is to remove the flexible hose (from the manifold to the front face of the servo) from the servo and close the open end of the flexible hose up. You can use an old bolt, a (repeated) covering of PVC tape, a taped-over polythene bag - in fact, anything that will stop air being drawn into the inlet manifold. The open end at the servo will not matter for a short time. Replacing the (probably perished and leaking) short rubber pipe that connects the body of the servo to the control valve effects a more permanent repair. In about 60% of cases that will fix things. If not, you're faced with a choice of fitting a valve repair kit to your existing servo or replacing the complete servo: I recommend, bearing in mind we are talking brakes, a new servo.

16-4-6 (Picture 1) There are two front brake hoses to degrade and...

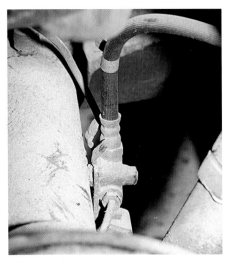

16-4-6 (Picture 2) ...one rear one.

16-4-6 One potential reason for a single front brake or both back brakes tending to bind can be internal degradation of the relevant flexible hose. A flap of internal lining is able to block the flow of fluid in a return direction acting like a one-way valve. Renewal of the flexible hose is the answer, but since all the flexible lines are likely to be about the same age it's prudent to replace the lot at the same time.

16-4-7 Brakes that don't free completely after the pedal has been released are actually more common now that silicone brake fluids are in wider use, particularly where silicon fluid is used with a remote brake servos. These fluids are specifically mentioned by Lockheed, which company warns against using them and points out that the component designs are matched to the characteristics of normal brake fluids and that the characteristics of silicone fluids do not correspond in all respects. One way this shows up is where a type 6 (remote) servo is in use - the air

16-4-7 This is the Lockheed type-6 "remote" servo. There are a couple of small - but important - details to attend to during the installation of a remote servo. They can make all the difference with both the ease of bleeding and the subsequent effectiveness of the system. Point 1 - note that that the arrowed end of the servo is raised in order to give air in the cylinder a chance to escape. In this example you can even see where the supporting bracket has been lengthened to increase the height of the rear of the servo. Point 2 - note that the air-valve has been positioned below the horizontal in order to allow the trapped air to be bled away. This modification requires minor but very worthwhile changes to the servo's main mounting plate which is hidden from view here.

valve is very prone to sticking with silicone fluid and so allows air pressure 'assistance' to remain thus holding the brakes on. A sharp tap of the pedal often releases the pressure.

Brake pedal travel excessive/ feels 'spongey'

If the brake pedal travel reduces and the pedal feels harder when pumped, go straight to 16-5-4.

16-5-1 Assuming this is a situation that has not suddenly occurred, but has slowly worsened over several months, it's probably no more serious than a routine maintenance matter. Start by checking the fluid level in the reservoir - but before you pour loads of hydraulic fluid in to top the reservoir up, check **all** four front brake pads for wear. If they are all more or less evenly worn with only 3mm, or less, of friction material left on them, draw the pistons back (using a G-clamp) and fit replacement pads. The reason why I emphasised you need to check all four pads is that they can wear at slightly different rates depending upon the rubbish that has built up on and around each piston. If you just checked the one pad and found there to be say 5mm of material left, you could decide all was well. However the remaining three pads could

16-5-1 Removing the front brake pads first requires you straighten the flared ends of each retaining pin (seen here) and withdraw both pins. The two clips will then fall to the floor and allow you to lift each pad out with a pair of pliers or Mole grips (vise grips).

already be down to 1mm and not too far away from having no pad material.

Note that significant differences in the wear rate between pads signals a lazy piston that at the very least needs exercising as explained in 16-4-3 before you replace the pads. Move to the rear brakes (16-5-2) if necessary, but if all is now well with the pedal travel, now is the time top up the brake fluid reservoir.

16-5-2 If the brake pedal travel still seems excessive the rear brakes need checking and, possibly, adjusting. Don't forget to get the rear of the car safely up on axle stands (jack stands) and to let the handbrake off before you try and remove a rear brake drum. You may find you actually have to slacken the adjuster off to allow the drum to come off, too. With the drums off, how do the rear brakes look? Any oil or brake fluid in the deposited dust or is it dry and powdery? If there's any evidence of fluid leakage you need to check that the linings are not contaminated with oil and to address any problems you find before doing much else. You should be able to smell the oil resulting from a leaking rear axle oil seal (we explored the remedial work in chapter 12) while, if there's a brake fluid leak, buy a new rear slave cylinder.

16-5-2 I identified the rear brake adjuster in an earlier picture (16-4-2 Picture 5). Because it is very hard to take a picture of the inside of the backplate with the adjuster *in-situ*, I'll have to use this shot as a reminder that it is the TOP feature on the back plate that may, or may not, need your attention. You should not remove the drum to adjust the brakes, though! Note the position of the axle stand (jack stand), securely under the centre of the spring where the axle is fastened.

The main point of the exercise was to resolve your brake pedal travel concerns so, assuming you've found nothing else to concern you, you need to clean the brake shoes, backplates and drums and check the thickness of the lining left above the rivets. These days not all linings are riveted to the shoes but it is equally important to have sufficient friction material on the shoes even when the linings are bonded. The wear rate of rear shoes is normally very slow and I would leave everything alone if there's **at the very least** 1mm of material right around both shoes. The leading shoes (i.e. the shoes positioned nearest the front of the car on an MGB) are particularly important. These provide the greatest braking effect and therefore wear the fastest. Consequently, you need to be particularly sure that the thickness of lining material available on these shoes is adequate. Anything less than 1mm and you need to replace all **four** shoes (i.e. the shoes on both sides of the car).

While you're fitting replacement shoes, make the time to check that the hydraulic cylinder slides on the backplate without binding and replace any stretched springs too. Before refitting the drums, it is important to ensure the friction surface of both drums is free from scoring, grooves or cracks.

With the drums back in place we return to the reason for our interest in the rear brakes: excessive brake pedal travel. The MGB's footbrake system only provides one method of adjustment and that's via the square adjusters on each rear brake backplate. It's worth the sum involved to buy a special adjusting spanner (wrench) to turn these adjusters for, otherwise, you run the risk of rounding-off the square adjusting stubs. The idea is to expand each pair of brake shoes by screwing the respective adjuster in until the shoes are in tight contact with the drums. At this point you should jump into the car and exercise the brakes a few times and then return to see if the rear drums rotate freely. If so, try tightening the adjuster a little more, if not back off each adjuster until each drum does rotate freely. Once the brakes are properly adjusted you should find that not only have you reduced the footbrake pedal travel but probably the handbrake will hold rather earlier in its travel too. It's likely you'll need to re-adjust the rear brakes after something like 100 miles if you fitted new shoes.

16-5-3 Depending upon how sensitive you are you might detect some additional pedal travel if an aged flexible hose (there are three in a B's braking system) starts bulging under pressure. However, it is unlikely that one bulging hose will single-handedly increase the pedal travel sufficiently for it to be noticeable. That said, checking all three flexible hoses while they are under full pedal pressure is no bad thing as part of your search for the causes of excessive brake pedal travel. A bulging hose will be no more than a contributory cause but, even so, it is a problem which should be rectified. I would strongly recommend you change all three hoses simultaneously. The normal hoses are, of course, rubber. Not every reader will appreciate that there are different lengths for the rubber-bumper and chrome-bumper cars and many may not know that you can also buy hoses covered in a stainless steel braid. The quality stainless braided hoses are a shade more expensive but stronger, more resistant to abrasion and give the pedal a more solid feel. I would recommend you use the metal sheaved hoses particularly if you expect to keep the car for some years.

16-5-4 A pedal that is "spongey" looses its solid feeling at the bottom of its travel. This is not quite the same as excessive travel, but since the symptoms could be confused, I have included the problem here. The first things to mention is that new front pads and rear shoes do take a few miles, occasionally a 100 miles,

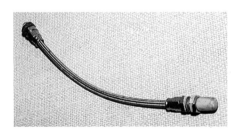

16-5-3 This is an example of a metal braided flexible brake hose - to my mind a superior, if slightly more expensive, to the normal rubber hoses.

to bed in. You may recall I mentioned that the rear brakes might require further adjustment after a short while - in other words, after they've bedded in. You do not have to do anything with the front pads since they are self-adjusting. So, if you have only just fitted new pads or shoes and feel uncomfortable with the feel of the pedal immediately afterwards, take

16-5-4 (Picture 1) The "Eezi bleed" single-handed method of bleeding the brakes. The tyre shown on the left of the picture provides 20psi of air pressure while the bottle/reservoir of fluid saves you getting out from under the car countless times to top up the master cylinder.

a careful look around of course, but the chances are that the new friction surfaces are not yet bedded-in.

If you have not recently fitted new pads or shoes we need to take the matter a great deal more seriously, the master cylinder could be faulty (see16-8).

16-5-4 (Picture 2) The normal rules for brake bleeding still apply, so start at the back left corner (the farthest point from the mastercylinder) and...

However, it's more likely that air is trapped in the hydraulic circuit. The brake hydraulic systems of early cars with a servo are notoriously difficult to bleed, so this might be the cause of the soft pedal.

The solution to air in the hydraulic system is to bleed the system and, if you need to do this on your own, I'd suggest an "Eezi bleed" (or equivalent) aid.

If you have an early car with a single line servo you may need to make two changes to the mounting of the servo before you get stuck in. The servo should be mounted with its outlet angled upward at about 15 degrees - to help air trapped in the system to escape during bleeding. MG adopted this angle at some point during the car's production, so check - yours may already be angled upward and need no attention. For those who find a horizontal servo on their car they need to raise the tail of the servo by fitting a later model's tail support bracket or by fitting a spacer under/extending the existing bracket.

The next point applies to **all** MGBs fitted with the remote brake servo. MG originally bled their brake systems using vacuum and thus air trapped in the system was never a problem for them. However, the control valve was mounted in such a position as to almost guarantee that a small column of air would be trapped under the valve if you had to bleed the brakes by the usual methods. The control valve needs to be turned though about 90 degrees to allow **all** the air to be removed when bleeding the system and if you want to tackle the job you'll find a design for the new main mounting bracket *How to Give Your MGB V8 Power* by the same author and also published by Veloce.

Another tip that you'll find helpful, particularly if you are loath to tackle repositioning the servo, is to run the engine while you bleed the brakes of any servo-equipped MGB.

16-5-4 (Picture 3) ...work progressively to the closest caliper.

Brakes require a lot of pedal pressure

16-6-1 Owners of MGBs without a brake servo should, of course, check every aspect of their brakes first, but may then care to consider fitting a servo as, by modern standards, unassisted MGB brakes do need very firm pedal pressure.

As we discussed a few points ago, new brake pads and shoes do take a short while to bed in and gain their full effectiveness. You'll hardly notice this effect when new rear shoes are fitted, but you could certainly feel a loss of braking performance immediately after a set of new front pads has been installed. You may feel particularly disappointed if you, or your garage, have fitted pads which are of too hard a grade. So, if you have just had new front pads fitted, check everything is in order, let things bed in for, say, 100 miles and if you are still uncomfortable, check what grade of front pad was fitted.

16-6-2 If you've become used to the help a brake servo offers, should it stop functioning properly the brakes will feel as if they're inadequate when you apply normal pressure to the brake pedal. However, provided the hydraulics are intact, the car will normally be safe to drive even with a servo failure.

Be aware that the servo can leak hydraulic fluid **internally**: it collects in the large vacuum chamber, so you see nothing externally but will find you're constantly topping-up the hydraulic reservoir. If this symptom is accompanied by a loss of braking efficiency there is a high likelihood that the servo is in need of a replacement. Unfortunately in one way, but the servo can continue to operate quite effectively even when leaking fluid into the main vacuum chamber. So you should not take an effective servo as any indication as to whether it is leaking or not, but you can check that the servo is operating by running the engine for a couple of minutes (to build up vacuum in the servo) and then switching off. Place your foot on the brake pedal and you should hear a "chuff" noise. Apply the pedal a few more times and note that after about four applications the pedal should go hard and there will be no more chuffing noises. Leave your foot on the pedal and now start the engine - you will feel the pedal depress if the servo is working satisfactorily. No initial "chuff" and/or no secondary depression and you should start to question the servo's effectiveness. However, before you commit to the

16-6-2 A view of the remote servo to focus your attention on the hose that can perish after years of service and consequently detract from the effectiveness of your brake servo. If this hose on your car is in good condition then you have nothing to worry about, if not replace it.

expense of a replacement servo, spend a little money and time on a new vacuum hose. They do start to bleed air inwards after a while and you may be pleasantly surprised by how much difference a new hose can make.

Brakes less effective than usual/pull to one side

16-7-1 If you feel the brakes on your MGB are inadequate for normal driving it's possible that the front pads are contaminated with oil, grease or hydraulic fluid. You're not likely to notice a serious difference in braking power if one or both rear shoes have a little oil/hydraulic fluid contamination. However, you'll certainly detect a loss of braking performance if any oil contaminates the front pads. It's highly unlikely that both front sets of pads will become contaminated at the same time so the car will almost certainly pull to one side if pad contamination is the problem. It will pull towards the unaffected side so if the car swerves left upon braking, check for contamination of the right pads first. If there's oil, grease or hydraulic fluid contamination present you'll need to change the **full** set of front pads for a new set and replace the inner hub seal on the offending front stub-axle or replace the leaking caliper.

16-7-2 If the car pulls to one side under braking and there is no oil or

16-7-1 If there's oil contamination on the front pads do be sure to first check that you do not have a leaking caliper. However, chances are that the hub seal is allowing hub grease to escape. This picture shows the old seal being removed.

16-8-1 (Picture 1) This is the later dual-line brake system with it's close-coupled servo. Note the ease of access to replace the master cylinder.

16-8-1 (Picture 2) Although the system is simpler, the single-line brake system is less easily accessed and you'll probably find it necessary to remove the oblong "blanking plug" from the bulkhead (firewall) in order to get to the rear of the master cylinder...

16-8-1 (Picture 3) ...here. Renewing the clutch master cylinder may necessitate the same access route.

16-9-1 This is one spot (above the rear axle) that deserves a look from time to time for several reasons. Is the pipe-junction weeping? Has an axle-strap broken and are you consequently straining the flexible brake pipe? Is the brake pipe corroding?

hydraulic fluid present on the pads, check the front tyre pressures, particularly if the pull is fairly gentle. If the tyres pressures are correct, take a look at fault 16-5-1 - for it's almost certain a caliper piston is sticking.

Failure of one half of a dual circuit braking system will also reduce braking efficiency and may cause the steering to pull to one side.

Servo failure (if applicable) will appear to reduce braking efficiency because you'll have to press the pedal much harder to obtain full braking performance.

Brake pedal slowly sinks to floor when constant pressure applied

16-8-1 If the brake pedal slowly sinks to the floor when under pressure, replace the master cylinder - quickly! The fault usually, but not exclusively, applies to the dual braking systems of the later cars and suggests the seals within the master cylinder are worn and that fluid is leaking past them. There are repair kits on the market that, on the face of things, will reduce your costs. However, I must tell you that in my experience renewing the seals on a hydraulic cylinder is only

effective in the very short term - so, I suggest with something as important as the brake master cylinder, that a new replacement is the prudent way to resolve the problem. The good news is that you

do not need to change, even remove the servo for either single or dual line systems, the master cylinder can be removed independently.

Brake failure

16-9-1 I've lost my brakes - period. There can be nothing worse than putting your foot on the brake pedal and feeling absolutely helpless for a spit second when there is nothing there - absolutely nothing! It happened to me - once - after I had fitted a part the wrong way round on a "Special" I'd built. A corner of the misplaced part caught and fractured a brakepipe. That was over 40 years ago, before the MGB was born, but I still remember the moment. The first point to make is that, in my case, it was pure inattention that caused my "moment" and when working on or driving your car you do need to pay attention. Does the brake pedal feel a little soft today? Stop and take a look at the fluid level and if it is the slightest bit low, find out why there and then. When servicing or carrying out other work on the car, pay **real** attention to the brake pipe junctions, flex hoses and pipe runs as you carry out your main job. Are they weeping, cracking, rusting, flapping or chaffing? Is that dampness on a caliper or backplate brake fluid? What is that stain on the driveway? This sort of preventative attention could save you from the reading this section in the first place!

16-9-2 There is usually only one reason for a complete brake failure: loss of brake fluid. If the loss is from a fractured pipe a small, sometimes not so small, puddle under the car will tell you where the major problem is. If the leak is not obvious try pumping the brake pedal a few times - you can hardly do any further damage and you should get a clue as to where the leak has occurred. You may find the brakes "pump-up" to a semi-usable level for a few moments - which tells you that you have a master cylinder problem. Alternatively, you'll pump brake fluid onto the road.

The trouble with the chrome-bumper cars is that they have a single line hydraulic brake system, so one holed or

broken pipe is sufficient to rob the whole system of its integrity and you loose **all** braking except the handbrake (parking brake). The post-1975 rubber-bumper cars and post-1968 North American cars have a dual hydraulic system split front/back - which means that a broken pipe on these cars will not result in a complete loss of braking from the footbrake system.

You can also loose the brakes due to a failure of the master cylinder, but if it is a master cylinder failure you probably have only yourself to blame for 99.9% of the time the master cylinder gives you some forewarning: sponginess, a sinking pedal and/or a general loss of effectiveness. If it is the master cylinder at fault I can only make one recommendation: fit a **new** replacement. Don't be tempted to fit a repair kit to your existing cylinder.

Brake failure (temporary)

There are three parts to this issue:

16-10-1 Waterlogged brakes due to very heavy rain or driving through flood water or a ford do have a delay period before they dry out sufficiently to effect any worthwhile braking - and there is nothing to say they will all start to work simultaneously.

The braking delay in heavy rain is usually quite short, although at times it

16-10-1 Waterlogged brakes are caused by a thin film of water covering the disc/rotor and preventing the friction material on the pad making contact with the disc for those split seconds (that seem like eternity!) until the water is driven out of the way. These cross-drilled brake discs (rotors) are primarily intended to stop a boundary layer of gas building up under the pads during extremely heavy braking and reducing pad contact with the disc. However, the holes in the disc also help dissipate water.

may seem like a lifetime before the brakes "bite:" wire-wheeled cars are very prone to this condition since the wheels do little to protect the discs (rotors) from the water. You can sometimes improve the situation by driving a shade slower and/or giving the brakes a dab every few hundred yards to keep them drier. The flooded road or ford is usually difficult to avoid, and offers no long term danger provided you dry the brakes out by driving with the brakes lightly applied as soon as you're clear of the flooded area. Bear in mind that the rear brakes are drum-type which are very slow to dry out after a good soaking so drive cautiously until everything is back to normal.

16-10-2 Another cause of "lost" brakes is a phenomenon that only occurs during, or straight after, very heavy braking has been used - perhaps during an emergency stop or during a long downhill run. This problem is called "brake fade." With brake fade there is usually some braking effect, but the worst cases - where a complete loss brakes is experienced - are usually caused by a combination of brake fade and boiling hydraulic fluid (see 16-10-3).

Pure brake fade is caused when the front pads and discs become so hot - sometimes glowing cherry red from pad friction - that a vapour builds up between pad and disc robbing the pads of their frictional characteristics. You can reduce, but not eliminate, the build-up of this "boundary layer" of gas by fitting cross-drilled brake discs. You'll also help reduce the likelihood of this (fairly rare in MGBs) situation by engaging a suitably low gear when descending a long steep hill in order to reduce the work the brakes have to do and the consequential build-up of frictional heat in the brake components. If you rally or engage in motorsport, then you'll also help minimise brake fade by selecting an appropriate grade of brake pad material. There are four grades of modern Kevlar materials available these days and the correct grade for your intended activities will further help minimise brake fade. "Green stuff" is the usual grade for road use.

16-10-3 Brake fluid absorbs water from the atmosphere and needs to be changed completely every two or three years to ensure the amount of water in the brake fluid is minimal. If you doubt the validity of that policy, reflect upon the rust you will inevitably find inside brake components and consider what the rust is doing to seals and other moving parts

16-9-2 This is the way/place to secure the front corner of the car whether you are working on brakes or any other detail that necessitates elevating it. The wheel can be pulled under the car where is not just out of the way - it is a second-line safety method of ensuring the car cannot completely fall.

within the system. The conventional "dot 4"/"dot 5" brake fluids are hydroscopic and, consequently, absorb water.

Silicon fluids are different - the water remains in suspension as tiny globules. However, over the years the water content builds up.

When you really have to use the brakes unusually hard the temperature of the brake fluid rises dramatically - so much so that it can boil any water it contains. Boiling water will create pockets of compressible steam meaning a loss of brake line pressure and therefore braking power. Result - no pedal, so no brakes, at least until the system has time to cool down and the steam returns to water in suspension.

The way to minimise the likelihood of a recurrence is replace **all** the brake fluid with new fluid straight from the tin and then replace it regularly. Also consider that it is all too easy, once you pedal has returned, to forget about the wisdom of changing your brake fluid - until the next time there's a braking emergency...

It will help to avoid overheating brake fluid if you don't hold the footbrakes on when the car's stationary, particularly when the brakes are very hot. Contact between pads/shoes and a very hot discs/drums transmits heat to the fluid.

Brake warning light illuminates

16-11-1 US cars produced from 1968 up to the introduction of the rubber-bumper cars in 1975, had a dual-circuit braking system but were not fitted with the close-coupled servo that rubber-bumper cars enjoyed. Part of the 1968-75 hydraulic brake circuit was a pressure-differential switch that "tripped" when the front and rear halves of the brake circuit started to operate at different hydraulic pressures - illuminating the dashboard/fascia warning light.

The first thing to check as soon as the light illuminates is the fluid levels in the master cylinder's reservoir. You may find one or other "half" of the reservoir is below the level of the other part - in which case you need to both top-up the fluid and search for a leak, maybe a slight weep or perhaps something altogether more serious. If nothing is obviously wrong with the pipework, check either the calipers and/or rear wheel cylinders, both of which can weep fluid without it being immediately noticeable. If there are definitely no fluid leaks yet the differential pressure switch says stubbornly illuminated you need to consider that the

switch is faulty or that the master cylinder seals have worn unevenly. If the brakes feel absolutely fine then the PDWA (pressure differential warning alarm) switch is the cheapest to tackle first. A very similar switch was fitted to Triumph TR250s and TR6s so, if you can't get a service kit or replacement switch for your MGB, take your PDWA switch body to your local Triumph dealer - for I feel sure British Leyland would have used the same part in both makes of car. However, since you have to break into your hydraulic circuit to replace the PDWA valve, you might be wise to replace the master cylinder simultaneously.

Handbrake (parking brake) performance poor

If you are concerned about the handbrake's effectiveness or the car has failed a roadworthiness test because of inadequate handbrake, first check whether the rear brake shoes are contaminated with oil or hydraulic fluid. If all is well, consider the following -

16-12-1 Are the shoes assembled correctly? The picture may help, but there's a marked reduction in handbrake efficiency if the shoes have been fitted incorrectly (which is very easy to do).

16-12-2 Are either of or both the levers in the backplates seized? There's a picture of the most vulnerable lever at 16-4-2 (picture 3). Also check that the central pivot adjacent to the differential and the clevis pins attaching each cable to the vulnerable levers are all free too.

16-12-1 The brake shoes need to be assembled with the bare area of each shoe leading – *i.e.* nearest the an imaginary mark on the drum as the drum rotates. This is the left side correctly assembled with the direction of drum rotation shown. There will be a mirror-image on the right side of the car.

16-12-2 A reminder of what you saw earlier - these levers can seize solid, but even restricted movement can reduce the effectiveness of the handbrake (parking brake).

If any of these items are restricted in their movement, remove them put them in a vice and move/lubricate them until they move freely again.

16-12-3 Is the handbrake adjusted properly? It should "bite" on the fifth click on the ratchet. If it is coming up to your shoulders your first action should be to ensure the rear shoes are properly adjusted using, I suggest, the correct tool on the square-headed adjuster as per suggestion 16-5-2. Once the rear brakes are properly adjusted, if you still have excessive handbrake lever travel, clamber under the safely supported car and, just behind the gearbox, shorten the handbrake cable using the spring-loaded (it should be a brass) nut.

16-12-3 A properly adjusted handbrake should click-up four notches on the ratchet and then be fully applied: about here - certainly no higher.

Chapter 17
Battery, charging system & fuses

An MGB is, electrically speaking, a fairly simple car. Nevertheless, there are hundreds of combinations of electrical faults that could occur making it impossible to cover every eventuality. I propose to try and provide some information on what I believe are the most common problems and have subdivided these across this and the subsequent two chapters. The battery, generating equipment and fuses are, however, the heart of any car's electrical system and therefore I'll start with these. There are several references to battery connections and electrical terminations in earlier chapters: I plan to avoid duplicating these in this chapter.

Battery performance poor
17-1-1 The battery, or batteries, is/are the heart of any car's electrical system so it seems prudent to start this section by considering these oft forgotten and frequently falsely maligned units. Firstly let me say that all MGBs are at a disadvantage. Not only is the battery almost the length of the car away from the "action" - the starter and generator - but, in the case of chrome-bumper cars, there are two batteries interconnected by yet another long cable.

The connections to the battery are very important in any vehicle, but because of the extra resistance brought about by the remote location of the MGB's battery

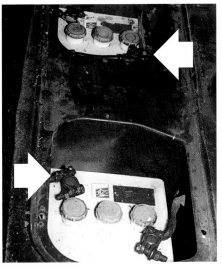

17-1-1 (Picture 1) The standard chrome-bumper cars have a pair of 6 volt batteries tucked away out of sight - and all too often out of mind - behind the seats. They are linked in series by a cable that passes from arrow to arrow which, even in the best installations, adds some electrical resistance and reduces the efficiency of the cars' starting characteristics. Elsewhere we show a single 12 volt installation which does away with this cross connecting cable and is therefore more effective ... and cheaper too!

or batteries the live, earth (ground) and, where applicable, the inter-connections assume even greater importance. All too often these connections are forgotten until the owner has difficulty starting the car, or some other electrical frustration, and then the problem gets laid at the battery's door.

Battery access is undeniably difficult

17-1-1 (Picture 2) Whether your MGB has one 12 volt battery or two 6 volt units, it's imperative that the earth (ground) connection is absolutely clean and secure. You'll note that this terminal post connection looks first class, but the braided lead is kinked and looks as if it might be frayed in the centre forming a constriction to the flow of current. While this may not be a problem just yet, the arrowed chassis connection is definitely corroded and really needs urgent preventive maintenance.

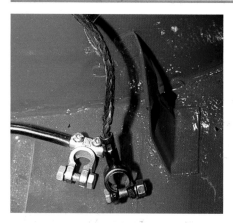

17-1-1 (Picture 3) These are the preferred type of battery terminals - but it is still essential that the inside faces and the terminal posts are clean. Don't over-tighten the clamps.

in an MGB so electrolyte levels tend to get ignored, particularly with today's so-called "maintenance-free" batteries. These sound a good idea for the MGB, but don't take the "maintenance-free" description too literally, they do still need to have the electrolyte topped up with distilled or de-ionised water from time to time, albeit with far less frequency than a normal battery.

The first check when you think the battery performance is poor - particularly when it/they just seem a little tired - is the electrolyte levels.

The second check should be on the clamps connecting cables and the battery posts. All the contact areas of battery terminal posts and terminal clamps must be bright and clean. If they're not, use a piece of fine emery or sandpaper to thoroughly clean the mating faces. The clamps must all clamp up very tightly: if any are loose or the jaw opening is closed or nearly closed, replace them. If the new clamps are still not absolutely tight, slip a couple of 15mm long strips of solder down between clamp and battery posts before you tighten the clamps. Note that if your 'B still has the now obsolete cap-type cable connections they are best discarded in favour of the clamps (I've run both my MGBs with Ford bolt-through clamp- type battery cable connectors for ten years and found them very satisfactory). Whichever battery connectors you use, be sure to smear a good quantity (i.e. much more than the light smear) of petroleum jelly (Vaseline) on all battery posts before you finally tighten the clamps.

Don't forget that there's still one

further battery/body connection on which everything depends, but which is even more out of sight than the others - the bolted connection between the battery earth (ground) cable and the chassis. This is usually behind the left side battery position and to get at it you may need to remove the battery from that side of the car. The ring terminal needs to be clean and the body metal it contacts bright. There needs to be plenty of petroleum jelly between the mating faces, large washers are needed to make the connecting face as big as possible and the through bolt needs to very tight indeed. Then you can forget it again for a few more years!

Finally, the cables that connect with each battery clamp need to be complete and undamaged: I've seen them emancipated through the breakage of individual wire strands, thus reducing the cable's ability to carry current.

If all the foregoing connections are in first class order yet you still have doubts

17-1-1 (Picture 4) This is Terry Tearne's single 12 volt battery solution nicely tucked into the right-side battery compartment of his chrome-bumper Roadster. If you turn the picture clockwise you may be able to read the size-code - "063". Note, too, that the redundant compartment has been put to use, in this case for spares. It also makes an ideal place to hide valuables - although a bit of a pain to access quickly!

about battery health, check to see if over the course of a couple of weeks there is a white powder forming around the base of any or all battery posts. If so, the battery or batteries is/are leaking and probably at the end of their useful life. However, use the following detail to make sure that the battery or batteries are being properly charged before discarding them. Most battery specialists will carry out a test of your battery's capability under load. However if that is impractical, you can get an idea of a battery's condition from observations at home. Test one is to establish the charge condition of the battery(s) using a hydrometer. This works on the basis that the higher the electrolyte's charge, the higher its specific gravity (SG). The hydrometer will measure the SG of each cell - and you should check **every** cell since five good readings and one poor one tells you that you have a problem with that one cell, but that will be enough to create starting problems. The float within the hydrometer is usually colour-coded so you do not need to know how to interpret the actual specific gravity-readings themselves, however for the record these are the SG readings and related state of charge -

    1.12 Battery discharged
    1.24 Battery reasonably
    (about 75%) charged
    1.28 Battery well charged

Any cell reading less than 1.23 really requires that the battery be given a boost charge with a trickle-charger. You can confirm your hydrometer findings by measuring the voltage between the two main terminal posts using a (preferably digital) multi-meter. You cannot do this test in the most telling way at home since nothing really compares to the battery specialist's **under load** test. However, your home test is better than nothing and is at its most accurate if carried out no sooner than 24 hours after the battery was last used (charged or discharged). A fully charged battery will give 12.6 volts on the meter, so this is the ideal you are looking for. With two 6V batteries fitted, this reading is of course across both batteries (as if you were connecting a 12V trickle-charger). A fully discharged battery will still show 11.6 volts so if yours only shows slightly less than 12.6 you would be right to be thinking about topping-up the charge with a trickle-charger to see whether the battery's condition can be improved. If not, and particularly if the hydrometer had indicated that one or more cells are down, a new battery is indicated.

In respect to buying replacement batteries, owners of rubber-bumpered have only to consider which replacement to purchase. However, my own experience with chrome-bumpered cars brings me to suggest that here there are choices. Clearly, you can buy straightforward twin 6 volt replacements, and this will be many reader's choice if only for originality reasons. I suggested in *How to improve your MGB, MGC or MGB V8* (also published by Veloce) that some owners might prefer for cost and availability reasons - to use one single 12 volt battery in the car instead of two 6 volt units. In particular, I made reference to the Ford Escort battery that I have long since used. However, Terry Tearne has refined the idea by using one Type 063 12 volt battery with 44AH capacity. It fits beautifully into the chrome-bumper car's battery slot since it is 7 inches tall, 8.25

17-2-1 (Picture 1) This shot is included for two reasons. Firstly, to remind you to ensure the fanbelt (drivebelt) tension is ok and, secondly, to show owners of early cars with dynamo generating equipment that an alternator (this looks like a 17ACR to me) not only increases the charge rate dramatically but looks good too.

17-1-1 (Picture 5) Whatever the battery or batteries you're using, a specific gravity tester will help you assess the charge within each cell.

inches wide x 6.75 inches front to back (178 x 210 x 172mm).

Battery removal tip: the twin 6 volt batteries fitted chrome-bumper MGBs can be difficult to remove from their cradles, even after you have undone the battery clamps. Once you have got one out, and **before** you fit any new battery, make and fit a (strong) string or nylon carrying cradle. It needs to loop under all sides of the battery and be securely fastened top and bottom - but, in the future, will give you something to get hold of when you want to lift a battery from the car.

Battery not being fully recharged
17-2-1 A dynamo was fitted to cars made during the first five years of the MGB's life while alternators were fitted as standard equipment thereafter.

As soon as there are signs of an inadequate charge rate start your

17-2-1 (Picture 2) Everyone will recognise this as a battery charger, but I wonder if you would know how to connect one to a chrome-bumper car with two 6 volt batteries? You can see the answer here, but first ensure the charger is set to 12 volts (if it is adjustable) and then disconnect the main cable (wire) that runs under the car to the starter motor from the battery. If your car is negative earth (as most will be) couple the positive lead from the charger (usually red) to the battery post you have just "released". If your car is positive earth then you need to connect the negative (usually black) lead from the charger to this post. Step two may surprise some – for you need to connect the remaining lead from the charger to the *other* battery, to the post that has a short connection to the chassis, usually located at the rear/left of the car.

investigation by checking whether the fanbelt (drivebelt) is correctly tensioned (see 6-1). Secondly, ask yourself whether you are using the car for long enough trips to recharge the battery. Numerous short journeys or infrequent use of a much-cherished car may not be keeping the battery fully charged - or it could be that the battery has reached the end of its life. If you think that it is the use that the car is put that is the most likely problem, I suggest you buy a trickle-charger and give the battery an occasional helping hand. Alternatively, an upgrade to the generating system may be the solution. It is not all that difficult to fit an alternator in place of the original dynamo if originality constraints allow, or to upgrade the capacity of your existing alternator. The dynamo to alternator switch brings with it the necessity to change the battery polarity from positive to negative earth (ground), but this is not difficult and adds very little to the cost. To give you the full picture of the other changes involved in positive to negative earth conversions here's an outline check-list -
• The battery connections need to be reversed.
• The coil requires two wires one white, one white/black) reversing - although, in the longer term, it's better to replace the original positive earth (ground) coil with a proper negative earth (ground) one.
• The tachometer's wiring polarity will need to be reversed (see 18-6).
• Reverse the polarity of any in-car entertainment equipment.
• It's prudent to check the direction of rotation of any electric motors/fans fitted to the car - although in the vast majority of cases you'll not find it necessary to reverse the wires leading to the motor.
MGBs were fitted with four models of alternator (ignoring plug combinations): 16AC, 16ACR, 17ACR and 18ACR generating 30, 30, 33 and 40 amps respectively. If you have either of the first three low-capacity units, your local electrical or MG specialist could upgrade your car by fitting the 18ACR alternator from a late MGB. Not only will this pay dividends in terms of generating capacity (which enables you to fit the higher intensity headlamps that are almost a necessity in today's traffic conditions) but, perhaps, more important, provide for greater charging capacity at low rpm.
17-2-2 (Dynamo cars). You think the dynamo has stopped charging. To confirm

that it is the dynamo causing the problems, temporarily fit a bare "jumper" wire between terminals "D" and "F" on the regulator. You'll need a voltmeter to carry out this check, but most multimeters have a DC low voltage scale (e.g. 20 volts DC) which you should select. Assuming the battery is positive earth (ground), clip the negative wire from the multimeter to the centre of this jumper wire and the positive voltmeter wire to the earth (ground) terminal on the dynamo. Check the voltage shown with the engine ticking over at about 800rpm. It should be 15 volts: a reading of about 5 volts will signal a faulty dynamo winding. No reading at all suggests the brushes require replacing, although before you start changing the brushes be aware that you would get the same symptoms if the wire from the dynamo to the regulator was broken, so a continuity check is prudent before you tear into the dynamo.
17-2-3 (Dynamo cars). I can't fit a modern audio system to my positive earthed (ground) car. Modern in-car audio equipment **must** have a negative earth electrical system. Fortunately, there's an easy solution: it is possible to re-polarise the electrical systems of dynamo cars.
Remove both electrical connections from the dynamo, and from the battery: turn the battery (or batteries) around so that the earth (ground) wire can be connected to the negative battery terminal: make the connection, but leave the battery positive wire disconnected for the moment. Temporarily connect a length of 28/0.3 (insulated of course) wire to the smaller (field) terminal on the dynamo and hold the other end against the positive terminal of the battery for five or six seconds. Disconnect the temporary wire, restore the original leads to the terminals of the dynamo (you've now changed the polarity of your dynamo).
Now you've altered the polarity of the system, before reconnecting the battery, give very careful thought to all the other electrical components on the car. The starter should not prove a problem in that it should work with either polarity, as should the lights and the wiper motor. The coil will require an immediate swap around of the two wires powering it and, in the longer term, should be replaced with a proper negative earth 12 volt coil. Early tacho's were cable-driven and will not be affected by a change of polarity, but a positive-earthed electronic one will require attention before you switch on the ignition. We look into this

along with reversing an ammeter's (if fitted) polarity in the next chapter. You are unlikely to have electronic ignition on what was a positive-earthed car, but could now contemplate one of the aftermarket kits once you've changed the polarity of the electrical system. In any event, you should go through the electrical fittings on your particular vehicle with care before connecting the positive wire to the battery. When in doubt ask your local auto-electrical specialist for advice.
17-2-4 (Alternator cars). The alternator seems to have stopped charging. Tests of an alternator's health are rather more complex than those for a dynamo, if only because of the additional complication of an AC (alternating current) generator requiring rectification to provide usable DC (direct current) electrical power via a set of diodes. However, the car contains a simple but very useful built-in checking device in the form of the ignition warning light! Over simplified, but this light signals whether the alternator's output is lower or higher than that of the battery. You'll appreciate that to charge the battery you need your alternator to generate a higher voltage than the battery, in which case the warning light is extinguished. So, if the ignition warning light glows when you are driving along the alternator is clearly failing to charge the battery and you can reasonably conclude that the alternator is failing. However, the ignition light tells you a bit more than that, for if the light gets dimmer as you increase your engine's revs you can be sure there is some sort of problem with the alternator.

17-2-4 This is the contents of an ACR series alternator service kit, the front bearing may not come as a surprise but availability of the brushes (arrowed) may not previously have been appreciated by many readers. You'll note that there are two and that they have slightly different mounting brackets. Which brush goes where will be obvious when you remove the black back cover of the alternator.

On the other hand, if the light gets brighter as you increase the engine revs, you need to get the battery checked out before you lay all the blame on the alternator. A specialist can disconnect the alternator rear plug's main output lead(s) and check for output (using an ammeter) and rectification - so its best to leave the alternator on the car until it has been tested and you're sure it's faulty.

The obvious remedial action is to fit a service exchange replacement unit - and that is certainly the quickest and easiest solution. If you are very keen to save some cash (not that exchange alternators are terribly expensive these days) you could spend an hour, or so, examining the brushes in the existing unit - for nine times out of ten it is worn brushes that bring about an alternator's lack of charge. You'll find it easier to check the brushes with the alternator off the car. The back cover needs to come off and you'll find two small spring-loaded carbon brushes near the centre of the rear of the alternator trying to make contact with the rotor's slip rings. The caps usually slide off leaving the spring and maybe 20mm of brush attached to each cap. If one of the brushes is very worn down then it could well be worth your while buying and fitting a new pair for the small cost involved. You nearest Lucas stockist will have them if your favourite MG specialist cannot help.

If the alternator is really in need of replacement, is this the opportunity to fit a bigger capacity alternator? (See 17-2-1).

Fuse has blown/fuses general
17-3-1 The MGB was designed in the early sixties and, at the time of writing, is basically a forty-year-old design. Certainly by today's standards, with the ever-growing emphasis on electrical equipment and ancillaries, the MGB's fuse system is inadequate. It was upgraded from two to four fuses around 1969 and, subsequently, several line-fuses were also added - but, by the time the car went out of production, it was, fuse-wise, still not as well equipped as more modern contemporary cars. Bear this paucity of fuse capacity in mind when tempted to add an electoral ancillary to your MGB. My earlier book *How to Improve MGB, MGC and MGB V8* (also published by Veloce) went into how you can improve the fusing of the car. This section will not therefore duplicate that information, but is included to make you aware that the fuses in an MGB, particularly a car with two fuses, are highly stressed and need

17-3-1 The four and earlier two fuse holders. The two fuse holders have no installation tricks to worry about, but *behind* the four fuse holder is a small electrical bridge that needs to be positioned in the *top left* corner (as we look at this picture). If you're in doubt, note that the second Lucar connector from the top/left has no electrical connection yet on the (fused) right side there is a side (parking) light connected.

to be scrupulously clean to carry the current required of them. Your first reaction to any fuse problems whatsoever should be to clean the contacts on both ends of the fuse holder with fine emery or very fine sandpaper and also to check that the external surfaces of the fuse(s) are clean too.

The four-fuse system was not as great an advancement as it might seem for basically fuses 1-2 and 3-4 did more or less the same job in both systems - and an outline will be found later in this section. The four fuse block introduced a fuse for each half of the car's side (parking) light system - i.e. one for the left and one for the right side. You may care to consider switching your two fuse block for a four fuse one since, of course, every little helps!

Usually you can visually inspect any fuse that is thought to have "blown" in the expectation that the central wire will have broken. In fact, you may have difficulty seeing inside a blown fuse if the glass tube is covered with black. A continuity test is

by far the best check as to serviceability of any suspect fuse that has not obviously "blown". There is provision for two spare fuses pushed straight into the fuse-holder so a spare fuse should be available if you need it.

As I think every reader will already appreciate, a fuse is intended to protect the wiring in the event of a component failure that causes a "short circuit" to earth (ground). The consequence of such a failure is to draw more current than the wiring can handle and, without a fuse, initially the wire would heat to such a point that the insulation would melt and this would be followed by the wire itself glowing white hot and melting with the attendant danger of fire. So, not only is a fuse very important but the right size fuse is equally important. The MGB uses tubular glass fuses - old fashioned and consequently not so easy to buy at every filling (gas) station. Nevertheless, don't think you can substitute one of the later types of more easily available fuses, you do need to correct replacements and therefore at least the standard two spares.

If you are beside the road and worried about a blown fuse, lets explore the get-you-home options. Firstly, the MGB does not employ a fuse in the ignition circuit so, if your car has stopped due to an ignition problem, it will not be fuse-related. Nor are headlights fused so, again, if you have a roadside headlight problem you do not need to worry about fuses. In fact, it may be helpful to give you an outline of the electrical system and colour codes so you can picture what will stop working when a particular fuse blows -

• The **brown** wiring circuit feeds straight from the battery's positive terminal and is, consequently, unfused and always live as long as the main cable is connected to the battery. Amongst other tasks the brown circuit feeds the ignition switch and also the fuse that connects terminals 7-8 on the fuse block. Terminal 8 of the fuse block provides the **purple** wire circuit with an unswitched but fused power source. The normal fuse rating is 17 amp which should be adequate for interior/courtesy lights although a **slightly** higher rated fuse is often fitted if a cigarette lighter is in frequent use. This fuse will also protect the horn circuit.

• The **white** wire circuit is that part of the loom that becomes live when the ignition switch is "on" but, being an extension of the brown circuit, remains unfused. One part of the white circuit feeds terminals 5-6 on the fuse block. Terminal 6 of the fuse block provides the green circuit with an ignition switch controlled and fused power source. The official fuse rating is 17 amp, but many cars, particularly GT's with heated rear windows, are running with a **slightly** higher rated fuse. This is probably the fuse that feeds the most used electrical features including brake (stop) lights, wipers, tachometer (rev counter), direction indicators, reverse (back-up) lights and the electrical instruments fed via the voltage stabiliser (*e.g.* the fuel gauge).

• The **brown** circuit also feeds the light switch with an unfused power supply. The light switch has two unfused outlets - a red/green wire that leads to terminals 1 and 3 of the fuse block and a blue wire that provides the headlamp dip control switch with its supply when the light switch so directs.

• The **red/green** sidelight (parking light) circuit deserves further explanation. You may have noticed that I mentioned that this one cable feeds two fuse positions (numbers 1-2 and 3-4) in the fuse block. A link or bridge at the back of the four fuse fuse block loops between terminals 1 and 3 to achieve this. Many home enthusiasts fail to notice this link and refit the fuse block upside-down. They then become very puzzled by the consequential anomalies that their electrical system will display since they have erroneously connected the ignition switch controlled green circuit with their always-live purple circuit! Properly installed the red cables that actually run to the left and right side or parking lights are therefore fed by terminals 2 and 4 and are protected by 17 amp rated fuses.

One final point on fuses, if one blows then by all means use a spare fuse of with the same amp rating to replace it: **Caution!** - If you have to use a higher rated fuse, replace it with one of the correct size at the very first opportunity. If the replacement blows soon after fitting you need to investigate and isolate the problem. Once you know which piece

17-3-2 (Picture 1) A line fuse in the overdrive circuit. A line fuse is available from any auto spares shop, you need to cut the wire down to about 3 inches each side of the fuse holder and solder a bullet connector to each end. Unplug the overdrive power supply cable and plug one end (either end) of your new fuse into the resultant open end of the black insulated joint, you'll then need one more insulator to plug the other end of the fuse onto the other original bullet terminal.

of equipment is blowing the fuse you have a choice of get-you-home opportunities. Clearly it is very difficult with something like the windscreen wipers on a rainy day, but wherever possible simply switch off the faulty item (*e.g.* the heater fan). Where the problem is with a piece of equipment over which you have less control (*e.g.* a thermostatically controlled fan) your get-you-home method should be to unplug the faulty item to prevent it from blowing a fuse, though probably taking out several other useful instruments and equipment in the same electrical circuit.

17-3-2 The MGB is basically under fused. This being the case you should fit a "line" fuse (a fuseholder and fuse installed in a single wire) for every piece of addition equipment you fit to the car and, maybe, even protect some of the existing circuits by installing line fuses. In this regard, if your 'B has an overdrive **always** fit a line fuse in the overdrive circuit; without a fuse the consequential damage of a short cicuit can be catastrophic. An appropriate fuseholder and fuse takes ten minutes to fit, but if you're uncertain about doing the job yourself get an inline fuse fitted next time the car is in for service. There's

17-3-2 (Picture 2) This is the meeting place for the front, rear and gearbox harnesses. The numerous wires and the related bullet connectors appear a mess but, nevertheless, this should show you where to look for the junction of your car's overdrive wires and where to insert the overdrive line fuse. Here there are, in fact, three line fuses - and this car is not even fitted with overdrive!

already a bullet-connected junction where the gearbox harness feeds into the main harness at the rear of the engine bay on the right side. The new fuse needs to be plugged into the yellow (white in the very late cars fitted with an inertia switch) wire that carries power to the overdrive solenoid on the gearbox.

The actual current required by an overdrive unit that is engaged is quite low, but the current required to operate the solenoid is higher: a 17amp fuse is probably the best bet.

Chapter 18
Instruments (gauges)

There are five dashpanel gauges on all MGBs: oil pressure, water temperature, fuel level, speedometer and tachometer (rev counter). There was also a clock fitted to cars produced during the last three years, but I do not plan to get involved in horology. Lets look at each gauge individually, bearing in mind that as the cars were in production for twenty eight years and that several variations of manufacturer and style took place.

Gauge or gauges give faulty readings/stop reading

18-1-1 Several gauges. If you find several of the electrically operated gauges are simultaneously behaving strangely (all reading low, all reading high) you almost certainly have a faulty voltage stabiliser

18-1-1 (Picure 1) Small and generally very reliable, but a tired voltage regulator will have a dramatic effect upon the accuracy of electrically powered gauges although...

18-1-1 (Picture 2) ...none of these instruments will be effected.

to replace. However, a faulty stabiliser will not effect the tachometer, speedo, oil pressure or early temperature gauge. There were two types (pre and post-1967) of stabiliser but both types will be found in the same location - screwed to the back of the tachometer.

If none of the electrically operated gauges are working and the heater, direction indictors, wipers and tachometer have also quit, you need to check the "green" fuse.

18-2-1 Oil pressure gauge. Most problems are associated with its pressure feed line. A weep of oil from between the coupling on the end of the line and the rear of the gauge requires you check that a tiny sealing washer (part number 2K4936) is in place - the majority are missing! The oil capillary pipe or line is made from steel and consequently can rust while of course it can also become damaged by vibration or during engine bay work.

18-2-1 (Picure 1 and 2) As described in chapter 7, probably the majority of oil pressure gauge problems lay within the pipework feeding pressure information to the gauge.

18-2-1 (Picture 3) This is the flexible part of the oil pressure line, but note how corroded everything above the footwell gets - just where the flexible line couples into the capillary tube!

18-3-1 Water temperature gauge. This unit received some attention in chapter 13 and you may find it helpful to read what's said there. There are two types of water temperature gauge, the early mechanical type with its expanding alcohol operation and the electrical variety introduced late in 1976. 90% of the former's faults are due to incorrect installation of the capillary tube (see 13-1-10).

The electrically powered version works by the voltage stabiliser providing power to the gauge where it passes though a bi-metal strip and thence to the sender unit located in the engine. As the sender unit warms up it allows more current to pass to earth which in turn increases the current though the bi-metal strip which heats up and alters the position of the needle. 90% of the problems that occur with an electric temperature gauge are not actually at the gauge itself but at the

18-3-1 (Picture 3) The two types of temperature sender used on MGBs. Top of the picture is a (broken) mechanical one, while at bottom is an electrical sender with its spade type electrical terminal.

sensor. If the gauge reads very low or even stays on its "C" stop, you should start by looking for a corroded terminal or a broken wire at the sender. You can check that the gauge and its connecting wiring is functioning by having a partner briefly earth (ground) the terminal onto the engine block while you watch the gauge climb sluggishly to "H." Don't leave the gauge earthed for longer than is necessary. If you then reconnect the terminal to the sender and warm up the engine, the gauge should work normally. If not you have a faulty (open circuit) sender and it needs to be replaced. If the gauge reads "H" when you know the engine's temperature is either cold or at least no more than normal, disconnect the wiring from the sender unit and observe the gauge. It should fall to "C". If it does indeed fall to "C" you have a short circuiting sender unit which should be replaced. If the gauge continues to show "H" then you have a short to earth (ground) in the wiring leading from the sender's terminal to the gauge and you will have to find it by examining all the places where the wire is clamped to or touches the body.

18-3-1 (Picture 1) The early cars had a mechanical temperature gauge - which, properly installed, is pretty reliable. The capillary tube is contained within a protective coil, which should run down the side of the engine and be secured to the lower heater valve screw by clip "1G9529." The *most important* part of the installation, seen here is the *coil* of tube between engine and body. The coil absorbs vibrations and prevents pipe cracking, and is therefore essential. Optional, but good practice, is to give the tube a little extra support by running the lower heater pipe through the middle of the coil.

18-3-1 (Picture 2) All too often the capillary tube is installed incorrectly and, consequently, cracks, releases its contents and the temperature gauge quits. This is one example a poor installation. Here the (arrowed) capillary does at least start down the side of the head but runs straight to the top of the footwell giving nothing to absorb the vibration caused by unavoidable movement between engine and body: it *will* eventually crack.

18-4-1 Fuel gauge. A problem is almost certainly caused by a fault at the sender unit on the side of the fuel tank. The fuel gauge itself is another of the bi-metallic strip type gauges, like the temperature gauge, where the needle position varies with the current passed by its sender unit. However, while the temperature sender is in a hostile vibrating and thermally changing environment, it is nowhere near as unpleasant as the water/salt-corrosive/dirt-blasting home of the fuel

18-4-1 (Picture 1) In the vast majority of cases it will not be the gauge itself that is faulty but...

sender.

There are two terminals on the fuel sender - the main (green/black) feed from the gauge carrying the power and a second smaller earth (ground) black lead. Remove both wire from the terminals, noting the different sizes and thus which will eventually need to go back where. Clean the terminals and connectors - *i.e.* those on both wires and both on

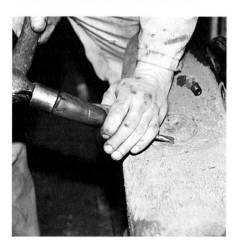

18-4-1 (Picture 2) ...the sender unit hidden under years of mud on the side of the fuel tank. There were two types of sender (as described in chapter 11) but both had two electrical spade terminals – both of which corrode sometimes to the point of disintegrating. You don't need to remove the tank to change the sender unit but you will need to remove the old sender (shown here) with care to avoid damaging the tank's retaining "tangs".

the sender unit itself. A little petroleum jelly (Vaseline) would not be a bad idea and will help to ensure our various tests are based on good connections. Reconnect the wires to the sender and switch-on. If things have not improved we need to check each of the three parts to the circuit (feed to the sender, the sender itself and the earth/ground from the sender). Test one - temporarily, and for no longer than is absolutely necessary, join the green/black feed wire to the black earth (ground) wire and observe the fuel gauge when you switch on the ignition (you don't have to start the engine). If the gauge steadily climbs to "F" you can be fairly sure the gauge and its green/black feed is ok as is the earth (ground) but that you have a faulty sender at the tank. If, on the other hand, the gauge still shows "E" or only goes some way to "F" you have proved very little and need to try another test.

It's not unusual for the black earth (ground) wire to have problems at either end, so to check run a temporary wire from the sender unit's earth tag straight to the negative terminal on the battery. Push the green feed onto its sender terminal. Switch on and see if that solves your fuel gauge problem. If yes, it suggests a faulty earth wire within the harness; if no, it reinforces the notion that it is the sender itself that is faulty, but further checks are required. The earth wire actually connects to the car's body at the boot (trunk) catch, so check that connection. Leave the temporary earth lead in place for a moment, and if necessary, with the ignition switched on, disconnect the green/black lead from the sender unit and temporarily (and as briefly as possible) connect it direct to the temporary earth wire you have running straight to the battery. If the gauge goes to "F" there's nothing wrong with the feed from the gauge but you are left with the possibility that either the sender itself and/or the harness's earth (ground) are the problem. If you have a multimeter you can check the sender's continuity, but by this stage you would be fairly safe to assume that a replacement sender unit is called for.

18-5-1 Speedometer. On an MGB this is a mechanical unit. There were two sizes - a 4 inch (100mm) one for all chrome-bumper cars and an 3.15 inch (80mm) diameter instrument for all rubber-bumper cars. Beyond the two sizes, there are a plethora of variations and part numbers so if the speedo is reading inaccurately you probably have the

incorrect unit for the gearbox. I touched upon the different speedo pinion ratios in chapter 9. Chrome-bumper cars, with and without overdrive, had different speedo calibrations and these varied from 1040 to 1280 cable turns per minute - so if your car reads 18/23% inaccurately it probably has had an incorrect replacement fitted earlier in its life. Rubber-bumper cars had variations too, but at least they were all calibrated for 1000tpm and were of a smaller size, so are not likely to have been fitted to a chrome-bumper car (or vice versa) and should be less of a problem in this context. You can check the calibration of a speedo by reading the very small print on the bottom of its face.

If incorrect calibration is the problem the best thing to do is to get the speedo overhauled and recalibrated at the same time since the cost is modest and you can be sure of an accurate reading at the end of the exercise. Speedy Cables who are based at Abercrave, Swansea SA9 1SQ (tel: 01639 732238) will do an excellent job for much less than the cost of a new unit. However, there is no gain without pain - you will need to give them, or another specialist, some facts to enable them to calibrate the speedo correctly. They'll want to know how many times the speedo cable end of the cable revolves for six full revolutions of the roadwheels - so you'll need to check that detail before you send the speedo to them. They will also need the rolling radius - the distance from the centre to the ground - of your car's rear wheels.

If the speedo needle wavers as you drive the solution is an overhaul as per the previous paragraph. The re-calibration part, and therefore the recalibration information, becomes optional but you may as well get that part of the instrument sorted at the same time.

If the speedo has stopped working

18-5-1 (Picture 1) You may be interested to see the rear of a speedo and how the cable couples to the instrument and...

completely you need to do a couple of checks before deciding exactly were the fault is. You don't need to remove the speedo but will need to reach up behind it to unscrew the knurled ring that fastens the speedo cable to the back of the instrument. Be at little careful not to accidentally disconnect any wires when releasing the cable, but you need to get the end of it low enough to see as you drive the car a few yards. Drive the car forward and check the square end of the speedo cable is revolving - if so you can be fairly sure your speedo needs to be removed and despatched for repair! If the square end of the speedo cable does not revolve then the instrument itself is probably not at fault and we need to investigate its drive more closely. Try pulling the inner speedo cable straight out of its outer sleeve. It should come with minimal resistance and you will either find it comes out with a similar square drive end still in place on the other end or it will come out somewhat foreshortened with a slightly ragged round end. If it's the former (square) end you reveal then suspect that the gearbox drive pinion is faulty, a ragged end and foreshortened cable indicates that the inner drive cable has broken.

Dealing with repairing a broken cable

18-5-1 (Picture 2) ...what the gearbox end of the speedo cable looks like. Handbrake adjustment is top right of the picture.

first, you'll need to do two things. Order a replacement speedo cable and, while that's in transit, get under the car and unscrew the knurled ring from the gearbox end of the speedo cable and remove the other half of the broken piece of inner cable from its outer. Be sure to get the correct replacement for your particular car as there are several different lengths - and it would do no harm to lay the two ends of the original inner on the floor and measure the overall length as insurance. At this point I would reconnect the outer cable to the gearbox, though you have a further choice to make...

You need to decide whether to replace just the inner cable or to do the

18-5-1 (Picture 3) For those that have not seen the right angle drive, the top knurled ring attaches to the gearbox leaving you to screw the cable onto the end facing the camera.

job properly and replace inner and outer. I'd be influenced by whether the speedo had been wavering for many months before the cable broke. If so, then the outer cable is possibly worn and you would be as well to replace the pair although it is a much more frustrating task than merely fitting the new inner into the old outer! If the speedo never wavered until just before the inner cable broke, then the quick solution is to sit in the driver's seat and push the new inner into the old outer. When the square end of the new inner gets to the gearbox you may feel some resistance and need to rotate the inner cable slightly while gently pushing on it until it engages in the gearbox pinion. You'll know the cable's fully home when the brass ferrule on the instrument end of the inner recesses into the outer - at which point you need to refit the cable outer to the rear of the speedo.

If the inner cable that you pulled out

of the outer is in one piece, you may as well push it back inside its outer and replace the outer on the back of the instrument. The problem appears to lay at the gearbox end of the cable - either with the right angle drive in the case of non-overdrive gearboxes or with the speedo drive pinion. There were four pinions used during the MGB's production run. All are of plastic gearwheel type but differ in the number of gear teeth and colour according to whether they are to fit a three-synchro or four-synchro gearbox, whether overdrive was or was not fitted and whether the car had a chrome or rubber-bumper type gearbox.

Added to the variety of pinions, cars with a non-overdrive gearboxes have a right-angle drive that will also need to be checked. So start by removing and testing the right angle drive if it is applicable to your car.

Once you're satisfied that the right angle drive is not the problem, withdraw the pinion housing and take a look at it. The pinion gears are made of plastic and can strip so check right round the periphery: as few as three stripped teeth can stop your speedo. If the pinion has damaged teeth, note its colour and order a replacement. If the gear has stripped, it's worth ensuring that the speedo cable runs freely, or at least without undue stiffness/ binding.

Note that you should not fit a different colour pinion without corresponding changes within the gearbox. If you do, the new pinion will strip straight away and/or upset the Speedo's accuracy. Indeed, if you've recently bought the car and find a stripped pinion, double-check with your MG specialist retailer as he may recommend a different colour pinion to the one you've removed if it was wrong for the car's specification. One final tip, when you remove the pinion housing oil will be lost from the gearbox: minimise the loss by raising the rear of the car before you start and have a clean piece of rag handy to stem the flow of oil. Once you have the pinion out you can reduce the oil flow by temporally replacing the housing.

The only other item within the speedo cable's drive that can be worn is the square section at each end of the inner cable or the corresponding female part in the pinion - which can "round-off". So, if you find that the pinion gear is not stripped, try the end of the speedo cable in the pinion and make sure the drive is positive. If not, you'll need to decide whether it's the cable's male or the pinion's female square (or both) that's at fault and order replacements accordingly.

18-6 Tachometer (rev-counter). Initially these were mechanical units with a drive cable rather like a speedo. This design was superseded when a positive earth (ground) electronic unit was introduced for cars with 5-bearing engines (but still retaining the three-synchromesh gearbox). This tacho was in turn superseded by basically the same unit, but operating with negative earth (ground). Then, about 1973, the tachometer became operated on an "impulse" basis, a system which was retained for the rest of the production run and including all the smaller diameter units used in the rubber bumper models.

If your 'B's tacho is of the very early mechanical variety and is giving cause for concern I'd suggest you follow the same investigatory logic as described for a speedometer.

We'll look at the three types of electronic units chronologically, while simultaneously trying to identify which type you have in your car. Tachometers all have one thing in common, if they should malfunction it will not affect the car's running unless the cables to/from the tachometer have been cut, chaffed, disconnected or damaged. So if your car's ignition is causing problems it is most unlikely that the tachometer holds the solution, in spite of the fact that many of the instruments are closely coupled to the ignition system.

Original 4 inch diameter electronic tachometer, fitted to positive earth (ground) cars. This type of tachometer, along with its negative earth equivalent, necessitated four wires be connected; two white wires, one black and one green. Most had the two white wires looping through a small protrusion from the rear of the case that was in fact a ferrite coil: if you want to check yours without climbing under the dashboard look for the identification letters "RVC" on the instument face. Later versions brought the ferrite coil within the case of the tachometer, although these examples will still require two white cables - but now feeding into the case. A green power feed cable and a black earth/ground lead are also required to make these models work. Positive earthed units carried the part numbers "RVI 2401/01" or "RVI 2401/00B" in very small letters on the bottom of the face. Both positive and negative earth versions work in the same way - by

passing the (white) wire going from the ignition switch to the ignition coil round the ferrite coil, a series of pulses is generated within the ferrite coil that the instrument counts and translates to the analogue needle display. To the best of my knowledge, these positive earth tachometers were only fitted to cars made up to about 1967 and fitted with a dynamo generator. Cars fitted with these tachometers have one white cable going (from the tachometer) to the negative terminal on the coil.

For those needing to switch the polarity of this type of instrument to negative earth (ground), you need to gently bend the tags up around the periphery of the chrome bezel and remove the bezel and glass. On the back of the case there are a couple of slotted screws which, when undone, will allow the internal assembly to be eased carefully forward out of the case. You can leave the green and the black wires trailing through the case if you like since all you need to do to reverse polarity is unsolder each from the PCB (printed circuit board) and re-solder them in the reverse locations. Re-assemble the instrument in its case.

You also need to reverse the polarity of the two white wires, but that can be completed outside the case. Mark one white wire with a pair of adhesive tags and cut the wire between the tags. Cut the other white wire and re-solder (or use proper auto wire connectors and/or a small pair of male/female connection blocks) such that one tagged wire is connected to an untagged wire - thus reversing the flow of current through the ferrite coil. Drawing D18 will remove any doubt as to what has to be done.

4 inch diameter electronic tachometer, fitted to negative earth (ground) cars. These were fitted from October 1967 to about 1973 to cars with an alternator and negative earth (ground) battery polarity and work in the same way as the earlier positive earth units. These tachometers were fitted with the terminal arrangement that you see in the accompanying photograph. Cars fitted with these tachometers have one white cable going from the tachometer to the positive terminal on the coil.

4 inch diameter electronic tachometer, impulse type. The same face size and overall appearance was retained for the penultimate type introduced about 1973 - although the wiring connections were reduced to three. This type of tachometer is called the "impulse" type and can be identified by the fact that cars fitted with them have **two** white/black wires connected to the negative terminal on the coil. One comes from the tachometer and counts the coil's pulses, while the other goes to the distributor's

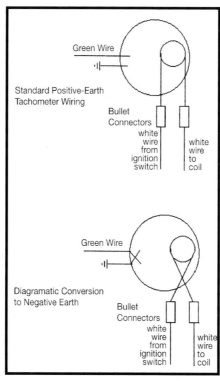

D18 Reversing the polarity of an early tachometer.

18-6-1 (Picture 1) At about the middle of the production run the MGB's tachometer looks like this from the front and...

contact breaker points. The green wire from the voltage stabiliser and the black earth (ground) connection as used in the earlier types of tachometer are retained.

Rubber-bumper car's tachometer. In fact identical to the foregoing type, save for its case being reduced in diameter.

Having described the various types of tachometer, we need to explore some fault-finding details -

18-6-1 Failure of the tachometer to respond when the engine starts, or for it suddenly to jump into life when 3000plus rpm is reached or for you to have to tap it gently is not that unusual and reflects a sticky mechanism. It may be irritating but is no more serious than that and hardly warrants rectification.

18-6-2 If the earlier tachometers, connected via a white wire, are not properly wired to the coil the ignition will not work. Therefore if the ignition is working and the power supply side of these tachometers checked out, one can only conclude the instrument itself is faulty. The final step could be to borrow another tacho in order to check the instrument by substitution. If the original unit proves to be faulty sending it off for repair is the solution.

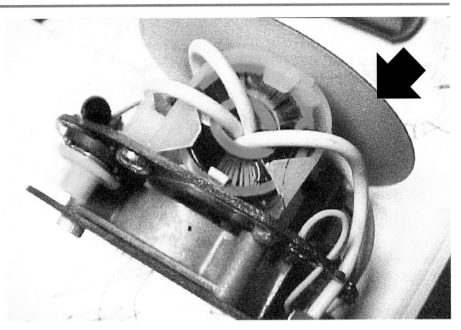

18-6-1 (Picture 2) ...like this from the inside. I have arrowed the dial face and you will be struck by the amount of space required by the coil mentioned in the main text. For the record, this is a negative-earthed chrome-bumper unit with "RVI" in tiny white letters on the face, although all later tachometer designs looked like this even though they were reduced in diameter with the introduction of the rubber-bumper cars.

Chapter 19
Other electrical components

19-1 A general overview as to the methods of checking and indeed maintaining the electrical system seems a very good starting point so, before we get stuck into translating specific symptoms into corrective action, let's first consider the MGB's electrical system.

Many might think that the focal point of an MGB's electrical system is the dashboard/fascia, and while I concede this is a very important area of the electrical wiring system, in my view the main "crossroads" are on the right side inner wing of the car adjacent to the fuse holder. Indeed, this crossroads is where many tests and checks are best carried out. You can use a multimeter or professional voltage sensor, of course, but I actually prefer to make my tests using the two very basic aids shown in picture 19-1 (Picture 3) which you can easily make up at home. One simply provides power to a specific point in the circuit of my choosing while the other checks, by means of a test light, whether power is present at a given point.

You'll note that several of the following problem solving suggestions involve checking, cleaning and reassembling electrical connections throughout the car. At the "cross-roads" these connections are made up of inter harness "bullet" connectors, but this is not the case throughout the car so I thought it helpful to illustrate some of the variety of connectors which will be found - see

picture 19-1 (Picture 4). Every terminal/ connection **must** make good electrical contact with its "mate" if the electrical system is to work, and must keep doing

19-1 (Picture 1) The meeting point of the various electrical subharnesses is an important checking/test-point on an MGB. As a follow-on to my "crossroads" analogy, the "map" looks like the next picture.

so if the electrical system is to be reliable. It's therefore very important that you clean each connection with fine emery paper before you reassemble it and then provide the resistance to corrosion that reliability requires by protecting the cleaned interfaces. This protection comprises no more than a very light smear of petroleum jelly (Vaseline) on the joint before you push the connections together.

Finally, as far as this introduction is concerned, see picture 7. This is included to emphasise how easy it is to buy a selection of modern connectors that I urge you to use when fitting a new electrical part to your MGB. I cannot describe the awful mess a few owners leave after fitting say a fan, a new radio or a tow bar socket. Often the wires do not follow the obvious, if slightly longer, cable route and are therefore left unsecured and unprotected. **Caution!** - The most dangerous malpractice is merely twisting the ends of the wires together. **Always** solder wire joints to bullet and spade type connectors, **always** use proper connectors of the types shown in the associated pictures, **always** insulate the connections.

Whenever you need the ignition switched "on" to investigate or test a circuit for more than a couple of minutes, temporally pull one wire off the coil to take the ignition system out of use. Do not, however, forget to reconnect it when you have resolved the problem!

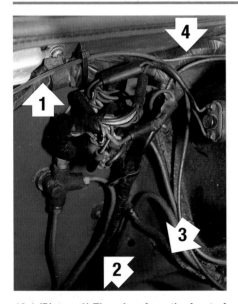

19-1 (Picture 2) The wires from the front of the car (lights, generator, horns and, on some cars, an electric fan) are arrowed "1" while the starter-motor and main power-cables from the battery/batteries (arrowed "2") come up to join the party. The gearbox subharness (overdrive and reversing/back-up lights where applicable) are routed up from the tunnel (arrowed "3") while the instruments, switches and warning lights are connected via the harness that feeds through the bulkhead/firewall ("arrowed 4").

19-1 (Picture 3) These are no more complex than homemade aids to test/check an electrical system. The one on the left is my many times mentioned test light - with a small 12 volt bulb mounted on a crocodile clip. Connect one end to a supposedly live cable and other clip to earth to check whether power is there as it should be. The right-hand test cable is intended to bypass various switches by clamping onto the live battery terminal and supplying power to a specific place in a circuit. Both items are invaluable as part of a get-you-home survival kit!

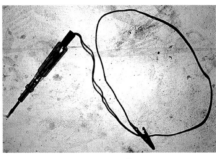

19-1 (Picture 4) One professional version of my test equipment - which you may prefer.

19-1 (Picture 5) The underside of a late MGB dashboard/fascia can seem a little bit of a nightmare to start with – until you realise each male and female multi-plug are unique. However, it is vital that you do a professional job when working under the dashboard. Proper connections (crimped, soldered and insulated) are essential.

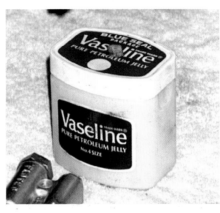

19-1 (Picture 6) A tub of petroleum jelly (Vaseline).

19-1 (Picture 7) Modern connectors are available to anyone fitting new or repairing old electrical parts. They come in single, twin, four-way or eight-way, male and female plugs and, while they may not match the original electrical connections, are extremely efficient and reliable. Use them.

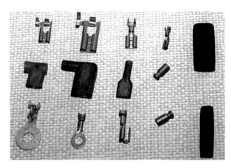

19-1 (Picture 8) A selection of the standard wire connections used by the MGB. The top row are largely female spade terminals. Below them are the plastic insulation covers that are essential: don't forget to slide the correct one over the wire before you crimp then solder the spade connection! To the right there are some examples of male and female "bullet" connections while a couple of "ring" terminals stand out. Did you spot the "piggy-back" spade terminal on the bottom row?

Windscreen (windshield) wiper problems

19-1-1 Windscreen wipers don't work. Start by trying to ensure that the problem is electrical by determining whether the rack and/or the wheelboxes are seized. Try rocking one wiper arm - does it and its opposite number move freely? Does the wiper motor sound as if it is trying to work, but is being restrained? Assuming you are confident that there is an electrical fault, use a test light or voltmeter to establish that power is available on the "green" side of the third fuse (terminal 6) in the main fuse block with the ignition switched on. You can double check the availability of power at this part of the circuit by trying the windscreen washers, heater fan, turn indicators and/or the brake (stop) lights. If all of these are out too, suspect the fuse, the green wires leading from it or a connector within the green circuit in the vacinity of the main fuse block.

Assuming power is leaving the green fuse, you need to check it is reaching the wiper motor. This is easier said than done in view of the motor's location and you'll probably need to remove the wiper motor from its restraining strap. If, sooner or later, you do need to take this route do not allow the body of the motor to "earth" or you will confuse the system and yourself! You will need to now check with meter or test light that the green wire at the wiper motor is getting power when the ignition is "on" - do this with a small probe up the back of the multi-plug and your test light. However, note that from about 1970 the feed wire to the wiper motor started to be route through a line fuse, whereupon it

emerged as a green/pink wire and therefore you'll need to test the green/pink at the wiper motor's socket. Such cars offer the opportunity to first try a shortcut because the green-pink feed also provided power to the washers: try the washers with the ignition on and if they don't work either, the line fuse becomes your primary suspect.

If all is well with the washers, you'll need to drop the wiper motor now and test it. Use a temporary length of wire connected to the battery's positive terminal with a probe at one end to feed power to selected points in the circuit. No need to switch the ignition on, but touch the probe on the R/LG (red/light green) wire up inside the motor's multi socket. The motor should operate for as long as you keep the temporary test wire touching the R/LG terminal. Then move your test lead to the U/LG (blue/light green) terminal. If the motor runs on one but not both circuits, you'll need to repair or replace the motor. See 19-1-4 for repair options. If the motor fails to run on either circuit you need to check the earth (ground) black leads very carefully and even run a extra temporary earth lead from the black terminal. If the motor still fails to run on either circuit you almost certainly need to replace it.

However, if both these tests (R/LG and U/LG) show the motor is operating normally on both circuits, refit the motor and turn your attention to the switch.

The position of the wiper control switch varied during the life of the MGB. To establish whether the wiper switch is faulty, take whatever steps are appropriate to bring the switch forward and allow you access to its back. Make sure you do not disturb the wiring at the rear of the switch. Now, with the ignition switched on and with a test lamp or multimeter, you'll need to test the continuity of the switch at the R/LG and U/LG terminals. Connect one end of your test lamp to earth (ground) and the other to the R/LG terminal on the back of the switch and move the wiper switch from "off" to wipers on slow. You should see the test light/meter register that the circuit has been "made." If the light/meter confirms that the terminal on the switch is operating normally but the motor is still not working, there must be a break in the wire from switch to motor. Check the U/LG circuit in the same way (switch to wipers on fast). If one or both R/LG or U/LG terminals have failed to "make" you should replace the switch.

19-1-2 Windscreen wipers only work at one speed. Obviously not a fault applicable to early single speed wiper cars with the "square" DR3A Lucas wiper

19-1-1 (Picture 1) An early single speed wiper motor and gearbox - note the square case to the motor. Many of the checks detailed apply to this motor too, although we'll devote the majority of the advice is for the slightly more complex twin-speed circular motor.

19-1-1 (Picture 2) The wheelbox on a windscreen wiper mechanism is not a box at all! This is a picture of the rear plate laid back to reveal the "rack" and the driven gearwheel. If one wiper spindle (at the top of the picture) seizes, this can stop *both* wiper arms. Were you to persist in running the wipers without freeing-off the spindle, you can even strip the gearwheel too. Note how the flared ends of the rack tube will be retained by the back cover upon reassembly.

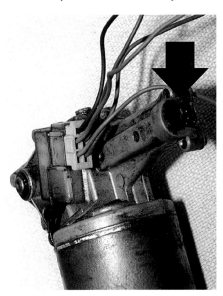

19-1-2 (Picture 1) This is the side of the two-speed "14W" Lucas wiper motor (note the round motor casing) which you will not be able to see until you remove the motor from the car. The all-important (from an electrical fault point of view) plug and socket then becomes much more accessible. The outer rack connecting point is arrowed.

19-1-2 (Picture 2) With the plug disengaged. Note the disposition of the motor socket's five pins. The earth (ground) pin is orientated at 90 degrees to the other four.

motor. However, from GHN4 and GHD4 cars introduced late 1967 the round bodied two-speed motor was fitted along with two speed control. As one speed is operating the power and earth/ground connections can be presumed satisfactory. This being the case and because the wiper switch is easier to get than the wiper motor, I'd suggest you first check the switch's operation with a test light or multimeter as in 19-1-1. If the switch checks out satisfactorily, then you need to get to the back of the wiper motor's socket and test the R/LG and U/LG connections with a temporary power supply lead and probe. Chances are, I am afraid, that the motor will be in need of repair or replacement, for even with the power temporally connected straight to the motor, one circuit will still fail to operate. For motor repairs see 19-1-4.

19-1-3 Windscreen wipers will not automatically park. A few words of explanation as to how the motor should park may help. With the wiper switch moved to the "off" position the wipers should, as you know, continue to operate until they reach their "park" location. In practice, the motor continues to work since it is still being supplied with power via a somewhat convoluted supply that starts with a green (or GK) supply pin on the motor's multi socket. This supply feeds power to one side of a "park" switch. The

other side of the park switch feeds power back to the wiper switch via a N/LG (brown/light green) wire. When the wiper switch is in the "off" position it automatically "makes" between N/LG and R/LG - so power is in fact still being supplied to the motor via the R/LG cable that you will be familiar with if you've read either of the two preceding sections. So the motor keeps going - until the parking cam that is moulded into the drive gear within the motor's gearbox opens the "park" switch. As soon as the switch is opened the power is cut from the N/LG wire and the motor "parks."

If the wiper motor cuts straight out (leaving the blades parked anywhere on

19-1-3 (Picture 1) This is the park switch as it is first seen disengaged from the motor assembly. You do not need to strip the motor to change the park switch. You can see the plunger arrowed. The switch has been slid downwards to disengage the small clip...

19-1-3 (Picture 2) ...seen here (arrowed). The three electrical pins facing the camera have also had the blue, yellow and red wires from the motor brushes unclipped. It's a very good idea to make yourself a little diagram of which goes where before you disconnect the wires!

the windscreen), the parking switch has failed to close its contacts during 90% of every revolution of the drive gear. To check, remove the wiper switch and, making sure it is in its "off" position, touch a temporary power lead connected to the positive terminal on the battery onto the N/LG terminal. If the motor operates for as long as you keep the contact "made" you can be certain that it is the park switch in the gearbox that is the source of the problems. When ordering a replacement park switch, be advised that there are two types and you'll need to have yours to hand in order to describe it accurately when ordering the replacement. If the motor fails to operate then the wiper switch is at fault and should be repaired or replaced.

19-1-4 (Picture 1) To change the brush assembly you do need to strip the motor, and this is the first step - removing the cover and gearwheel by slipping a small circlip off the arrowed end of the gear spindle. You can just see the park switch *in situ,* to the left of the motor's worm.

19-1-4 (Picture 2) Step two is to mark both halves of the casings. I went over the top and used typewriter correction fluid in the interests of this picture! If you forget and put the motor back together out of alignment the motor will run backwards. This is not advised!

19-1-4 Repairing a faulty wiper motor. This is usually a matter of replacing the brushes. The task has been made easier by the availability of a brush holder baseplate assembly complete with brushes which enables you to carry out the task by a straightforward substitution. A workshop manual will explain how to strip and reassemble the motor so I'll confine my advice to two details, leaving most of the amplification to the associated illustrations. If you have to replace the parking switch, there is much to be said for simultaneously fitting new brushes.

Take care when ordering the brush assembly, there are two types and you need the one that matches the parking switch.

19-1-5 Wiper blades travel too far. You can reduce the play in the mechanism by removing both wiper arms, undoing the motor and then pulling the rack out of its retaining tube. Refit the rack after turning it through 180-degrees (to present the other side to the gearwheel) from its original position. Whilst feeding the rack back into its tube but before the rack reaches them, turn both wiper spindles through about 180 degrees (to present a fresh range of gearteeth to the rack).

19-1-4 (Picture 3) We now have the brush assembly off the motor. The brushes proved to be fine. The best check is to look at the third necked brush (arrowed). If the narrow necked section of the brush has been worn away it's time to replace the whole carrier. As you withdraw the motor from the gearbox ensure you do not get grease on the brushes (in case you find they are reusable) and that you do not loose the tiny nylon "pip" off the end of the armature (arrowed). The single-speed square-cased motors are fitted with only two brushes.

19-1-4 (Picture 5) With the armature back in its case, screw the motor case/armature back to the gear case. Double check that you have aligned the markings (arrowed) correctly, check endfloat (lash) and adjust endfloat screw (the tip of which is arrowed) until 0.004-0.008in free movement is achieved. I am using a 0.006in feeler gauge.

19-1-5 It is wear in the wiper mechanism that causes the wiper arms to flop about - specifically wear where the arrows are pointing. The GT's (on the left) and the Roadster's "wheel-box" both wear in the same place - on a segment of the gearwheels that's in plain view and also on the area of rack (not in shot) that drives the gears. Turning the rack over while also presenting a different segment on the same gear wheel gives the system a new lease of life.

Cooling system fan problems
19-2-1 Cooling system fan will not start. There are three potential weaknesses in the MGB's electric fan installation.

First, and foremost, the motor(s) (some cars have two) are right at the front of the car ready to catch all the water spray, salt and dirt that's going, yet they're not warmed by the air passing through the radiator. Furthermore, the 1800cc MGB's radiator really is up to its job and consequently the fan(s) do not get called upon all that often. The sum total is that the 1800cc engine's fan(s) seize and either blow a fuse when they are eventually called upon to cool things down or weld the thermostatic switch closed, or both.

The second weakness, caused by

19-1-4 (Picture 4) The whole motor's operation can be transformed by a drop or two of oil on the rear armature bearing, which necessitates removing the armature from its housing. The pull of the stator magnets makes withdrawing the armature more difficult than you might expect. I think it better to use a plastic knitting needle to run just a little oil into the housing rather than try to get the oil to stay on this bearing when you reassemble armature to motor case. Did you spot the tiny plastic tip to the worm-end of the shaft? Don't loose this small but important component.

19-1-4 (Picture 6) You can test the new brushes and endfloat before finally assembling the gearbox. The black earth wire needs to go to the battery's negative terminal (all cars with this motor were negative-earth/ground) and you can try the R/LG and U/LG wires alternately on the positive terminal to test both high and low speed motor operations. This motor was humming away very happily (in contrast to its noisy grumbling when removed from the car) after a couple of drops of oil and I am disappointed the camera "froze" the armature so successfully!

the same proximity problems, is the plug/socket connection situated behind the grille.

Thirdly, the contacts within the thermostatically-controlled switch mounted on the back of the radiator are strained when the fan(s) start up. This gives the switch a much shorter life than you would reasonably expect. This longevity problem is of course particularly true of cars with two fans, but in truth all cars would benefit from a relay between the thermostatic switch and fan(s). Should you want too follow this non-original recommendation see 19-2-3.

You'll not need the ignition on for the diagnostic work that starts at the back of the thermostatically-controlled switch. Connect a temporary power wire to the positive terminal of the battery, remove the G/K (green/pink) terminal (n.b. some cars may be fitted with black/green wire in place of green/pink) from the switch and briefly touch the temporary feed wire to the G/K wires. Briefly, because if the fan(s) are seized you don't want to cause more problems by prolonged contact. Several things may happen -

a) The fan(s) may run - which tells you that the problem lays with the switch or the power supply to the switch.

b) One of the two fans may run, which tells you that one fan has probably seized and this blew the line fuse in the

19-2-1 (Picture 1) One of the problems that can occur with the MGB's electric fan is that this harness socket and the mating plug on the motor(s) get sufficiently corroded to stop the flow of power to the motor. The connection is at the front of the car, right where water, salt and dirt are flying about.

19-2-1 (Picture 2) Cleaning inside the sockets is difficult but possible with patience and a small rolled-up piece of emery paper. Use a smear of petroleum jelly on the terminals to improve future corrosion resistance while a covering of PVC tape round the outside of the re-united plug and socket may also delay the ingress of water.

G (green) supply cable - hence both fans stopped operating.

c) The motor may run slowly, which tells you that it is in need of some attention. You may need to also attend to the line fuse, but let the motor run for at least five minutes to see if it frees up.

d) The motor(s) may not respond at all, which tells you that you need to investigate the situation behind the front grille. It might be the fan(s), the plugs or the earth (ground) connection.

Having got a clue as to where the problems lay and before starting to carry out any remedial work at the front of the car, first check the power supply and thermostatically-controlled switch are working using your test light or multimeter. Leave the green/pink wire off and remove the green wire from the switch too. Connect your test light/meter across the green wire and to earth and switch the ignition on - the light/meter should indicate power is available. If it doesn't, check the line fuse, then the main fuse block and then the wiring to the fuse block and rectify whatever faults are found until you can turn the ignition on and get power to the green/pink (remember, some cars will be black/green) wire's terminal behind the thermo-switch. Now thoroughly clean the terminals and connectors on the thermo-switch and on the green wire, attach the green wire to the switch (not the green/pink) and attach your test light to the terminal on the switch that will, in due course, carry the G/K wire. You can remove the switch to the kitchen and test

the switch's operation in hot water. However, it is probably just as easy to warm up the engine until either you see the test lamp illuminate (indicating that the switch has operated satisfactorily) or you're sure from the temperature gauge that the thermostatically-controlled fan switch has failed to operate. In the latter case, you need to order a replacement switch.

When you're confident about the power supply and the switch you can re-attach the G and G/K wires to the switch with light protective smears of petroleum jelly (Vaseline) and check the fan(s) themselves. Once the grille is off and the fans become accessible, try spinning the blades - they should revolve with very little resistance. In any event, it would do no harm whatsoever to run a little light oil into the front bearing - although with the fan in place on the spindle that will be more difficult than it sounds unless you remove the fan motor from its cradle. Clean up and smear the contact pins on the plug with petroleum jelly. Time to try the motors again. No need to turn the ignition on, just run your temporary power supply from the live terminal of the battery to the G/K terminal on the thermostatic switch. If all is not well check the earth (ground) black wires and clean every connection, then try again.

19-2-2 Cooling fan will not cut out until ignition off. Almost certainly a case of the contacts welded closed within the

19-2-2 Surprisingly the thermostatic fan switch merely pulls from its rubber surround in the top of the radiator.

thermostatic switch. Remedy - replace the switch. I will just add the caveat that there is the remote possibility that the engine is running very hot indeed and that, consequently, the fan is having to work really hard to avoid meltdown. If, on reflection, you suspect this is the case turn to chapter 13.

19-2-3 Fitting an override switch and/or a relay. While it is not the objective of this book to guide you through upgrading your MGB, there have been several instances where I have felt it essential to point out the advantages of an upgrade, and the cooling fan is one such example. Electric fans are more reliable if it is possible to exercise them periodically. Of course you can run a temporary wire to the GK terminal aback the radiator once a fortnight, but it would be easier to have an override switch in the car that you can flip on from time to time. Since this is not a difficult upgrade I have included a small

19-2-3 If you do elect to fit a relay into the fan circuit, one of these beauties is what you are likely to buy with plenty of electrical capacity for two fans if relevant.

circuit drawing (D19) to help you with both the basic switch and one with a small light to remind you that you're exercising the fan! Such a switch may also be very useful in heavy traffic since you can switch the fan on before the thermostatic switch thinks it is necessary. Furthermore, you can bypass a faulty thermostatic switch too - so, all in all, a really useful upgrade.

A step further in terms of complexity, but one which will extend the thermostatic switch's life is the triggering of the fans via a relay. Diagram D19 also includes a wiring diagram for this.

Lights and horn problems

19-3-1 Lighting defects, especially at the front of the car, are usually due to the bullet-type connections exposed to weather but hidden from sight behind the front grille. These connectors become dirty and/or corroded leading to poor electrical conductivity, but you can overcome these problems by cleaning the bullets with fine emery/sandpaper, using new connectors and a light protective smear of petroleum jelly (Vaseline) when you reassemble each.

Unsatisfactory earth (ground) wires/connections can be a problem as they are often only evident when more than one light circuit is used at the same time (*e.g.* side lights, brake lights and turn signal indicators in simultaneous use). Each system is fine when used or tested on it's own, but the extra demands of two or three circuits can overtax the shared earth path resulting in, for example, the turn signal indicators working the brake lights, all lights going out, dim headlight(s) or erratic indicators! Make sure **all** earth connections are clean, tight and protected with petroleum jelly (Vaseline).

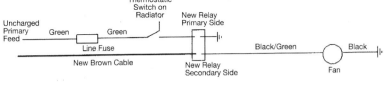

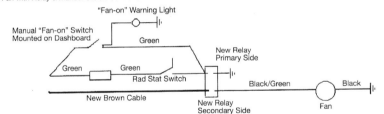

D19 Increasing the reliability of the thermostatic fan switch.

19-4-1 (Picture 1) Although you're not going to remove the engine and gearbox to replace the starter motor, I thought this an excellent picture of a late model starter motor, its close-coupled solenoid and location.

19-4-1 (Picture 2) The starter motor depends on a long chain of electrical connections, the engine earth (ground) strap being one that is easily forgotten. You don't have to use an original earth strap - one such as this example from your local auto-shop will serve perfectly well. Incidentally, you cannot over-earth the engine so feel free to fit a second strap just to be sure!

Starter motor problems

19-4-1 These are covered in the sections prefixed 1-3 in chapter 1.

Direction (turn signal) indicator problems

19-5-1 Direction indicators don't work. The design of the flasher unit built into the B's direction indicator system is rather clever in that the flasher unit stops working if only one 21 watt bulb is working. Thus if your flasher unit stops "clicking" the problem, nine times out of ten, is not the flasher unit itself but one "blown" bulb. You may be vaguely interested to learn that in normal circumstances the front and rear bulbs combine to generate a flow of current through the flasher unit that heats a bi-metal strip until it bends sufficiently to click off. At that point the flow of current stops, the bi-metal strip cools and clicks back to re-make the circuit. You have probably already worked out that with only one bulb operating, the current through the bi-metal strip is insufficient to heat it sufficiently to click off, with the result that the directional indicators quit. Leave them on and take a look front and back - one of the bulbs will be on, one, the faulty one, will be off. Replace the bulb and/or check the electrical connections leading to that bulb. In either case a light protective smear of petroleum jelly will assist longevity.

19-5-2 The flashing rate is slow. UK legislation calls for a flash rate of between 60 and 120 flashes per minute. If the flash rate is very slow you can simply replace the flasher unit and that may do the trick. However if the slow flash rate is the consequence of low voltage (in turn the consequence of poor generating capacity) you will want to address the root cause in any event and an adjustment to

19-5-1 You'll need to remove the lamp glass to gain access to any "blown" bulb, be it side, brake/stop or direction/turn signal indicators.

your control box (dynamo generated cars) or a check/adjustment to the alternator's output may help. As an aside, I feel that the wiring from many an alternator, particularly uprated ones, is frequently inadequate. A second, parallel, brown wire from the other (there are two) **large** termination on the back of the alternator to the starter motor main terminal may assist the car's electrics in several ways - including improving the flasher speed!

There's another reason for a slow flash-rate - resistance in the circuit caused by bad connections and poor earthing (grounding). Go through every connection and clean it, lightly smearing the bullet connectors with petroleum jelly and reassembling using new joining connections.

The column switch can cause problems, but frankly this would be very unusual. If the flasher unit has been changed and you're satisfied with the wiring and bulbs, only then consider changing the column switch - although a modern **electronic** flasher unit will be much less susceptible to voltage drops and should be tried first.

Hazard warning light problems

Fault 19-6-1 The hazard lights are not working. I cannot speak for US residents, but my understanding of the UK situation is that you're not obliged to have hazard warning flashers on cars of the MGB's vintage, but, if they are fitted, they must work - and properly! In the section on directional (turn signal) indicators, I made a point of explaining that these flashers stop working when one bulb is out. This characteristic is **not** carried over into hazard flashers - they are designed to operate with any number of bulbs of any wattage, and will do so at the same flash-rate, regardless. That said, the heating/cooling cycle of a bi-metal strip is still the operating method. A much more substantial internal resistance achieves the different characteristic of the hazard flasher units.

Since the hazard flashers use the same bulbs, indeed mostly the same circuit as the directional indicators, it's unlikely that the wiring/bulbs for a hazard circuit will generate any problems that your flashers will not tolerate - with two exceptions, the switching arrangement and the hazard flasher unit itself. So, in short, if the direction indictors are working well but the hazard lights are a problem, focus on the hazard light switch and hazard flasher unit.

The hazard switch is a double-pole unit that simultaneously cuts off the direction indicator circuits fed from the ignition switch and substitutes an alternative circuit incorporating the more robust hazard flasher unit connected to both sides of the car and fed from the always-live brown power source. So if all the hazard flashers stop working, the first stop must be to establish whether a fuse has been fitted into the brown wire supply to the flasher and/or that the supply to the flasher is live. The hazard warning light circuits work on the basis that power is available all the time but the circuit only operates when the earth (ground) connection to the four bulbs is completed by the switch. So you can use your test light to see that power is on both sides of the line fuse and at the brown cable connected to the hazard flasher. Don't try your test light on the light-green/brown feed that goes to the hazard switch - we'll get to that one later, if needs be!

Assuming all is well with the power supply side, take a few minutes to operate the switch repeatedly before you get any further into the circuit. Any switch that is used infrequently will build up a film of corrosion on the internal (and external) contacts and this can sometimes become so severe as to prevent, or at least inhibit, the circuit "making." You don't need to have anything switched on, just mechanically exercise the switch with, if you think it might help, a squirt or two of "switch-cleaner." I suspect that in 90% of cases, this will fix the problem.

If you still haven't found the fault you can check out the circuits running through the car with a temporary power wire coupled directly to the battery. Leave the hazard switch in its off position, the ignition off and the direction indicator switch in its central (off) position. Briefly, connect the temporary power wire to the green/red output from the hazard switch - the left side hazard bulbs should both illuminate. Try the green/white output from the hazard switch, this time it should be the right side hazard bulbs which both light up. Provided all four hazard bulbs and their respective circuits have proved their operational integrity, you should focus on the switch and the flasher unit.

At this point you have a choice - you can substitute a new flasher unit and thus remove it from the equation leaving just the switch as your potential faulty component if the system is still not yet operating normally, or you can test the flasher unit by bypassing the switch. One side of the car's hazard lights should be enough, so remove the light-green/brown wire from the rear of the hazard switch and touch it on, say, the green/white wire. If the flasher unit is OK two hazard lights will start operating and you will hear the characteristic click-click from the unit. If the flasher's OK order a new switch.

Heated rear window (defogger) problems

19-7-1 The HRW (heated rear window) on a GT can be a significant safety aid, but it's irritating and potentially dangerous when the rear screen fails to clear. This could be caused by one or both of two faults.

The first check is to ensure that power is reaching the screen when the dashboard/fascia switch is on. The test light is the best method of testing, starting at the top of the hatch where you should find two wires emerging from the headlining, passing through a pair of bullet connectors and looping out of sight into the rubber seal that surrounds the glass. Of the two wires that emerge from the headlining, one will be a black earth (ground) wire while the other will be a

white/black wire feeding power from the switch. You're interested initially in the latter one. Pull the bullet connector from its connecting sleeve and connect one wire from your test lamp to it. Connect the other end of the test light wire to earth, switch on the ignition and the HRW switch and the test light should illuminate signalling all is well that far into the circuit. Obviously, if the test light fails to illuminate you need to go back up to the switch end of the wire and test your way back to find and correct why there is an absence of power at the hatch.

You can check the performance of the HRW by boiling a kettle (using a domestic power supply) on the boot (trunk) floor with the hatch open. The rear window will mist up (fog) from the kettle's

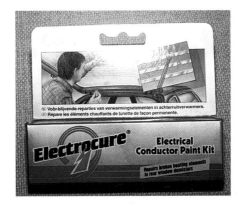

19-7-1 If the HRW has a couple of tiny gaps in the conductive element you can repair it by painting-on this silver based product. However, this pack cost £10 and contains enough product for dozens of repairs. Furthermore, my personal experience was that it was hard to effect a neat repair: I tried it but in the end bought a new HRW!

steam - at which point you remove the kettle and switch on the HRW - is the mist clearing, probably to start with in straight narrow bands that coincide with the cross elements attached to the window?

If the HRW is still not working, then you need to find and clean two electrical connections - each roughly at the centre of and either side of the rear glass. Before you reconnect them try your test light on the same (usually the left) side as where your white/black power feed emerged from the headlining. The test light should illuminate telling you that the power supply is reaching that spot. If the light fails to confirm that power is available,

then you have a breakage in the white/black wire that I would guess is most likely up near the hatch hinge. If the window shows no sign of improvement it is always worth checking out the continuity of the earth (ground) lead. They too can fracture due to fatigue near the hinge.

If all else is in order, it's time to wonder about the thin wiring elements that cross the rear screen. It's unusual for every one to break, but they are vulnerable to mechanical damage when the hatch is closed onto, say, a suitcase: they also become very brittle after years of use. If you look very closely with a magnifying glass you can usually see a small break somewhere along the element and while there are ways one or two can be bridged, you really need to be thinking about a replacement HRW if the number of breaks is extensive.

Engine won't switch off
19-8-1 A wiring fault in 1977 (and a few early 1978) MGBs exported to the USA allows the engine to continue running even when the ignition key is turned to "off." Most cars will only continue to run for about 30 seconds until the fuel runs out - but some will continue to run beautifully even with the ignition key removed!

In a correctly wired car the ignition coil is powered directly from the ignition key/switch and the relay is wired in parallel but independently of the ignition system. The problem with 1977 models is that the ignition relay also controls the ignition system and consequently when the ignition is turned off there is a route whereby a current can flow backwards from the alternator through the ignition light thus holding the ignition relay closed - so the ignition system just keeps going!

There are two solutions: either separate the ignition system from control by the ignition relay or, preferably, fit

19-8-1 This is a diode - which allows electrical current to travel only in the direction indicated by the small triangular marking I have arrowed.

diode "AAU 5034" into the brown/yellow control wire at the alternator. This diode is already in use on post-1976 cars as part of the handbrake-on warning and you will found one under the glovebox of any scrap cars with dual circuit braking systems.

Reversing (back-up) light problems

19-9-1 One reversing light doesn't work. The reversing lights are subject to the occasional accidental knock, particularly those of Roadsters, which can disconnect the tiny plug from its terminals. So if one reversing light is working, I'd start by checking plug is still connected at the rear of the non-working light. If the plug is OK then the problem is most likely solved by a new 21 watt festoon bulb reached by unscrewing the two crossheaded screws from the sides of the lens. There's a consequential problem here for the gasket is likely to be fragile and break when you remove the lens and you really should fit a new one before replacing the lens, otherwise water will enter the light.

19-9-2 Both reversing lights don't work. I recommend you double check that the fused green circuit is OK either by checking the fuse or that other green circuit accessories are working when the ignition is "on." If you find there are other "green-circuit" faults (heater fan, flashing direction indicators, etc) then it's likely the problem is in the area of the fuse block. Check the "green" fuse, check that the fuse holders are clean and that the respective green and white Lucar connections are clean too.

Still not working? Then the problem is more likely to be pinpointed if not actually solved in the engine bay - at the wiring "crossroads." Focus on finding the smallest of the various harnesses, it joins the crossroads from the gearbox. This harness will contain a wire from the overdrive (probably yellow/red) if the car has overdrive fitted. However, it's the two wires to and from the reversing light switch that are of primarily interest. The one taking power to the switch on the gearbox should be green and the other bringing power up from the switch when reverse gear is engaged will be coloured green/brown. I would start by separating, cleaning and lightly petroleum jellying all the bullet connectors of both wires. Take a good look at the two insulated tubular connections and if they look corroded internally, as they almost certainly will,

replace both. Reconnect and try the reverse lights with the ignition "on."

If the problem persists, you need to find out which part of the circuit is at fault. Disconnect the two green/brown wire bullets from their tubular connectors. No ignition power is required if you temporally connect a power feed from the battery to the green/brown cable that returns under the car (to the reversing lights). The reverse lights should illuminate: if they don't you can be pretty sure the problem lays somewhere down the final wiring harness leg that runs under the car to the lights themselves. If they do light up, you've not yet found the fault so reconnect the two green/brown wires and using the same temporary feed straight off the battery (no ignition power needed), connect it to the green wire that runs down to the gearbox. Select reverse gear and hope that the lights illuminate to tell you that you have no gearbox harness/switch problems.

If the lights still stay off then it looks very much as if the problem lies with the gearbox harness and/or the reversing light switch on the side of the gearbox. It could be worth giving the gearlever a few wiggles while still in reverse gear. If that gets the lights to work intermittently then you can be pretty sure that it is the reverse light switch that's at the root of the problem. It's possible that you'll get no intermittent contact - which does not mean that the reverse switch is in order, but could signal that the fault lies with the electrical connections of the switch. Either way you need the car safely up on ramps and to take a look at the switch on the left side at the top of the gearbox.

If you find access very difficult, then you have little choice but to drop the rear crossmember by a few inches. Are the two wire conections sound and in place? Is the switch loose and, if so, what effect does tightening it have on the gear changing (still smooth?) and the reverse lights? If all looks well then the remaining possibility is that the switch itself has failed and needs replacing. In this event make sure you fit the right number of fibre washers to allow the switch to be properly tightened while still allowing reverse gear to be selected without a fight.

Heater fan problems

19-10-1 The heater fan won't work. The heater fan motor is a simple affair and if it stops working it is usually because the supply via the green circuit and fuse has stopped supplying power, or because

the brushes at the front of the motor are worn out. The brushes can also squeal unpleasantly. Although repair is entirely possible, you need to ask yourself whether your time and money would not be better spent fitting an upgraded motor capable of moving rather higher volumes of hot or cold air? These uprated units are available from the trade or MGOC and are almost certainly your best solution.

19-10-1 The heater motor is plain to see and easy to remove via the three crossheaded screws, one of which is highlighted by arrow 1 here. It's very easy to get the motor spinning the wrong way but, fortunately, just as easy to correct this mistake by reversing the two Lucar brush connectors also arrowed.

Windscreen (windshield) washers don't work

19-11-1 There were two types of 'screen washer fitted to MGBs. The chrome-bumper cars were fitted with a manual push-pump arrangement that, it must be said, was inadequate by the time the chrome-bumper cars stopped production. Their performance in today's traffic density is very questionable! Rubber-bumper cars were all fitted with an electric pump 'screen wash - although there were a variety of switches and bottles employed over the years. Regardless of the year of manufacture, MGB GTs have a single central washer jet location (with twin outlets) while the Roadsters have two separate washer jets.

In the case of problems with any of the various combinations of system, manual or electric, single or twin jets, carry out the obvious check of the bottle and plastic pipework before getting too deeply into the system. The pipes harden, crack, kink and get pinched with the passage of time and such restrictions really do make

19-11-1 (Picture 1) This is the early mechanical "push" washer pump. It's a sealed unit as you can see so needs to be replaced if it goes wrong. You won't see the spacer from the driver's seat, but the internally-threaded retaining ring can be seen from the cockpit and needs to be unscrewed to release the old pump. The question is what do you replace it with? There are some ideas in the main text.

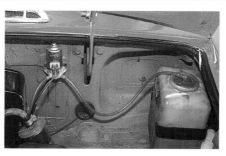

19-11-1 (Picture 2) I did think this washer bottle arrangement on an early MGB worth drawing your attention to for several reasons. Firstly, the washer bottle has been placed on the bulkhead/firewall which helps stop its contents freezing in cold weather, it also reduces the length of tubing required while, finally, it is mounted slightly higher than the original location – which improves the efficiency of the "squirt"!

19-11-1 (Picture 3) This electrical push-switch may also provide food for thought for those with early cars thinking of modernising the 'screen washer arrangement. It can be made to fit in the same central dashboard/fascia location as the "Mark II" cars with very little difficulty.

a difference to the effectiveness of the washers. Further, the tube running down into the washer bottle should have a non-return "foot valve" fitted to its end - it may be there and ineffective, or it may be missing. In either event this allows water in the plastic pipes to run back into the bottle delaying application to the screen. Watch for any tendency to drain back and replace the foot-valve if in doubt.

Focusing on the early manual pump that is a sealed tubular aluminium canister mounted in, or adjacent to, the dashboard/fascia. If this is not working consistently you have two options - replace the manual pump or convert your system to an electric pump one. Originality constraints aside, the latter route is the way to go, in which case you should remove the original hand pump and the washer tube that goes from it to the jet (T-piece in the case of a Roadster). Take a new piece of washer-tube from the jet/T-piece through the bulkhead (firewall) to any 12v electric washer pump you can lay your hands upon. Every auto-shop

will have one, but the original part number was "GWW125" if that is important to you. From the feed side of the electric pump take a second piece of washer tube to the original bottle - not forgetting to fit the pipe's foot valve! The system will work best when the pump is in close attendance to the bottle. The electrical connections are next, starting with a feed wire (green, ideally) running from the fuse block to either a "push" electrical switch of the type shown in the accompanying picture or, if you prefer, a straightforward "toggle" switch mounted within easy reach of the driver. Now you need a second wire (ideally green with a brown tracer) running from the other contact on the back of the switch to one terminal on the pump. Run a black wire from the other pump terminal to a good earth and try it out. Don't forget to clip everything securely in place with

cable ties once you are satisfied with your handiwork. If you want to shortcut the purchasing of components, terminals, etc, I believe you'll find there are several "kits" available, including one from the MGOC.

Getting a malfunctioning electrical system going really involves checking round the electrical circuit with the test light for starters. The best place to start is where the wire (probably green-brown in colour) that comes from the switch to the pump, terminates on the pump. No need to disconnect it from the pump - just make sure the other end of the test lead is properly earthed (grounded). Switch the ignition switch "on" and push the wash switch too. The test light will probably illuminate telling you that the power is reaching the pump and consequently either the pump itself or the earth (ground) connection is faulty. Obviously, check the earth connection out as well as the cleanliness of the wire connections on the pump, but in all probability you'll need to replace the pump.

Chapter 20
Body, paint, chrome & interior trim

The work involved in a full body restoration is well documented elsewhere and outside the scope of this basically "keep 'em running" book. However, a well-maintained body is bound to give better service, appearance and longevity and any car of MGB vintage is bound to require running repairs to parts of the body. Furthermore, maintenance of the car's paint, chrome and trim will also be required from time to time and while short of a full restoration, I trust the following key points will help keep your 'B on the road for that bit longer than might otherwise have been the case. The chapter is sub-divided as follows -

- Rust prevention, maintenance and repair of bodywork: 20-1.
- Body noises, elimination: 20-2
- Paint and chrome maintenance and rechroming: 20-3
- Interior trim panels, seat repairs and carpet replacement: 20-4

RUST PREVENTION, MAINTENANCE AND REPAIR OF BODYWORK

Preventive maintenance

20-1-1 Of all the MGB's components none is more critical than the body when it comes to preventive maintenance. You may think that comment is based on the body being by far the most expensive part of the car to renovate - and you would be

20-1-1 (Picture 1) The sills (rockers) and B-post are prone to rust from the inside – even if the car is stored in wet weather. If you were to dehumidify the air surrounding the car you might stop this attack from within - but better to drill a few holes to apply the rust preventive measures described in the text.

correct, but only partly so. My other consideration is the fact that the body **is** the car in structural terms and, consequently, your safety in the event of a collision will depend upon its integrity. The preventive maintenance described here is important for all MGBs; particularly those subjected to the rigors of salt laden road conditions.

One task that is really not too onerous is to pressure wash the underside of the wings (fenders). The rear wings are fairly straightforward, but it's the front wings that warrant your particular attention because they contain two classic rust traps. These traps need to have the dirt removed from them at least annually for low mileage cars and twice annually for cars in frequent use. Furthermore, once the undersides of the wings are dry, it's definitely worth using an aerosol can of your favourite wax treatment to protect the under wing metalwork. Start with the areas most vulnerable to rust but empty the can's contents across the whole of the under wing area. This work will only take a morning once or twice a year and will definitely pay dividends with years of extra service!

So where are these front wing rust traps? Around the headlamps and the wedge or trumpet-shaped panel located just in front of the top of the splashplate. The latter is both so vulnerable and important that I have devoted a section to it but as part of your pressure washing preventive maintenance you should feel up along the flat top of the wedge to check its integrity. If you find severe corrosion,

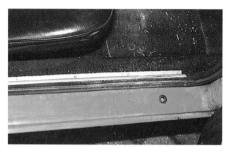

20-1-1 (Picture 2) This is the forward sill (rocker) access hole, you'll also need one about halfway up the A-post. Be generous with the wax applications. Some people even temporally plug-up the drainage slots in the bottom of each sill to prevent the liquid wax from escaping (open them about 24 hours after you have finished injecting the wax).

20-1-1 (Picture 3) The UK market leader in rust-preventive treatments is "Waxoyl" but, while you would not want to deal with a whole car using aerosols, I must tell you that I personally find this fast drying Comma product excellent for small areas and penitrating seams.

perforation or even "give" in the top, ignore the wax treatment for a while and go straight to 20-1-3 for early remedial action.

Though messy and unpleasant to apply, wax based rust preventative treatments are a major factor in body longevity. I've already highlighted the importance of underwing attention, but the best results are obtained with annual overall body treatment. That said, I must confess that I find an application to the whole body too arduous to do in one go and so tend to split the work up and probably cover the whole car every two or three years.

Waxoyl is the leading brand of wax based rust prevention in the UK and I find it excellent for large underside areas such as the floor and each of the four wings (fenders). However, for more intricate parts, particularly those with panel seams, the greater fluidity and speedier drying of Comma's Wax Seal ML gets my vote. You'll need to drill some holes in the car to get access to the insides of some boxed sections. The sills (rockers) are an example, but you may not appreciate how difficult it is to properly cover the inside of the rear chassis rails without a couple of holes in the boot (trunk) area. Nor will you get into the A-posts without a hole drilled in each.

Wing (fender), front, corrosion
20-1-2 The best solution to this problem is to replace the wing or wings. Much of an MGB's bodyshell is of fully welded construction and, consequently, panel replacement is more akin to restoration than maintenance. However, the front wings are retained by bolts and therefore are relatively easy to replace.

Replacement wings are readily available at modest cost. If you're without any bodywork repair experience, I'd suggest you buy genuine "Heritage" (i.e. Rover) replacements although the fit of all aftermarket MGB panelling is good. Replacement wings/fenders are available from numerous retailers. Note that GT wings are different to Roadster's and that there are also differences between rubber and chrome-bumper car's wings.

It's prudent to be prepared for addditional inner wing area work when the outer wings are removed. Corrosion is usually worse than you imagine and you may find you have to have a professional restorer weld some panels to the car in order to give you something sensible to bolt your new wings to!

20-1-2 (Picture 1) More often than not corrosion is worse than you anticipate. This owner had no idea that the top flange of his car's inner wing was not only rusty, but had in fact rusted right though! The corrosion we see on the front valance is less of a problem as this, like the front wing (fender) on an MGB, is bolted to the car. However, it will be a waste of time bolting a new wing to this side without first repairing the top flange - and that's a welding job.

We'll proceed on the basis that the car is in pretty good shape otherwise and that it is just the outer front wings that need replacement. If you own a Roadster the first task is to remove the windscreen (windshield) - which means it makes sense to do both front wings simultaneously. It's not necessary to remove the windscreen of a GT.

Get off the headlights and sidelights (parking lights) and pass the wires through the inner wing so that they are completely out of the way. Although not the main object of the exercise, do take a careful look at the light units, the headlight "bowls" in particular, to be sure they're reusable: order new ones, if required, and consider how much better their condition would have been had underwing plastic shields been fitted.

Get off the easily forgotten bits - the bonnet (hood) buffers and cable clips (for the bonnet release) come to mind. You'll need the front bumper off too.

Tackle the more difficult wing retaining bolts first, starting with the three behind the dashboard (fascia). You may have to remove, or maybe just lower, the wiper motor if you're tackling the right side wing. These three top bolts pass from the cockpit into the top of the wing and are located high up, immediately under the scuttle. Then from inside the car there are three more bolts to remove running vertically down the rear edge of each wing. To get at these you'll certainly need to remove the trim panel on the outside of the relevant footwell.

A further three crosshead screws and their nuts secure the bottom of the wing to the very bottom of the sill, just in front of the door. These are easier to get at, but no easier to remove since they're usually corroded in place. An angle grinder or nut splitter may help. Taking the front grille off is optional - I would, but in any event remove two fastenings securing the wing to the mouth of the air inlet.

The last of the really difficult fixings are situated at the front bottom of the wing

20-1-2 (Picture 2) It is this triangle-shaped top to the "wedge" that usually corrodes and needs a repair panel welding in place whilst you have the wing off the car. However, in this instance the top of the inner wing reinforcer was in pretty good shape but a corrosion hole on the vertical face can be seen. Although unusual, this must be attended to along with the splash guard mountings.

- where three bolts secure the wing to the front valance (apron). If you're replacing both front wings due to corrosion, there's a strong case for also renewing the front valance which is also likely to be corroded too. If the valance is to be renewed you can be rather more brutal when you get to these bolts.

Finally you get to remove the "gutter" bolts using a pair of Mole (vise) grips to ensure the caged nuts under the inner wing do not turn and/or break their cages. As you struggle with these bolts, again consider the protection that an underwing plastic shield would have afforded!

If a sealant was originally used on the wing to body joint, as I hope it was, you may be surprised at how difficult it is to get the wing off. Modern sealants such Sikoflex really do stick and seal, so you may have some hammering and pulling to do - although the wing will finally part company from the car. Clean everything up with a wire brush mounted in an electric drill.

While you have the wing off take time to examine the wedge-shaped (trumpet-shaped might be a better description) panel at the top of the inner wing towards the back. This is an important panel for two reasons - firstly it distribute the stresses within the front of the bodyshell; secondly it provides important weather/water protection for the inner parts of the bonnet cavity particularly, on the right side, the area around the fuse block. If the top has rotted this is the moment to repair it: see 20-1-3.

If all is well, take time to hand paint as much as possible of the inner wings, particularly the mating surfaces, with an anti-corrosive paint such as Hammerite. A couple of coats are well worthwhile, and while you should be generous on the mating surfaces you **must** ensure this paint does not get on any of the outer faces that will, at the end of the job, be resprayed body colour (the paints are unlikely to be compatible). While the protective paint is drying on the inside of the wing over the course of a few days, clean out all screw threads in the wings and on the car with a tap. Before you fit the wings you must paint the area outside the wing just in front of the doors in body colour. The very best job requires you spray paint this area, but it is not all that visible and many a car has had it hand painted in body colour. A few weeks later I would "Waxoyl" the area, which means that afterward you will really have to look closely to see it was initially

20-1-2 (Picture 3) In the event the corrosion was more extensive than first thought (it always is!) and it was decided to replace the whole reinforcer along with the splash guard lips.

hand painted!

It's actually worthwhile buying a fitting-kit of fastenings to aid fitting the new wings. Don't forget plenty of sealant along all the mating faces - this prevents water getting into the joints and causing rust where it can't be seen. The modern sealant most body shops use is "Sikoflex," but a paintable never-setting sealant called "Dumdum" is probably better for home use. You'll need to remove all surplus sealant as soon as you have the wings secured. Where to start? The six bolts inside the cockpit is my advice in order to pull the wing into place as soon as possible. Then I would work forward down the bonnet "gutter" from the windscreen end towards the front.

Before you refit windscreen/windshield (in the case of a Roadster), any chromework and certainly before you apply any wax preservatives, you need to "shape" and paint the new wings: most auto body shops will do the job if you don't feel you can tackle it. The shaping involves several very light skims of body filler, each one of which is then mostly rubbed off - but this process removes the tiny imperfections that will otherwise stand out when the new panel is painted in a glossy top coat. To do a proper and lasting job there will then be several coats of primers and a "guide" coat of gloss, more rubbing down and then several coats of gloss - so painting is no five minute job. You may care to try preparing it and painting the wings yourself on the basis that if it goes wrong you can still resort to the professionals.

Only start to refit windscreen, chrome, lights, etc when all the paint is well hardened - at least two weeks later. Then give the inside wing area a good coating of Waxoyl, not forgetting the area inside the wing just in front of the door.

If you intend replacing both the door and front wing on one side of the car, always fit the door completely before removing and replacing the wing. You can certainly leave painting the outside of the door until it comes time to paint the wing, but the best sequence for aligning these adjacent panels is - door first, wing second.

Front wing (fender), inner, corrosion

20-1-3 Corrosion of the top part of the inner wings and/or the inner wing behind the fuse block is caused by a corroded and perforated "wedge" (at the top of the rear of the inner wing) allowing water ingress in front of the fuse block or a corroded inner wing behind the splash plate. The latter is the worst of these problems and allows water ingress behind the fuse block. To assess the extent of either, or both, problems you'll need to remove the relevant wing (fender): see 19-1-2.

If you can see water around the fuse block or the secondary corrosion described, it signals a serious problem and that early attention is called for: you should make plans to attack the problem no later than the next winter lay up.

Take the front wing off and expect to see something akin to the associated photograph. If you have been vigilant and caught the problem early enough you should find just the top flat part of the wedge is perforated. Any more than that and the repair task, although quite easy for a professional, becomes a restoration project outside the scope of this book. However many MGB owners will want to do the majority of a top flat wedge repair themselves, even if the actual welding is carried out by a mobile specialist or by

20-1-3 Water ingress inside the top of the inner wing (fender) comes from a perforated reinforcer or from corrosion to the next panel as highlighted by these arrows. The only solution is to effect a professionally welded repair as has been done here - although the top lip shown here has yet to be finish welded.

your local MG restorer bringing a single-phase welder to your home. You may, at this point, be reassured to hear that corrosion of the wedge is so frequent that a special top-repair panel is available. I think it may be wise to get hold of your "inner wing reinforcer top" (to give it its full name) before you start hacking lumps of corroded metal off the car. Note that the repair panel comes with its lips turned up (on the inside of the car) and down on the cranked front edge. You, or your welding specialist, will need to seam weld these lips to the original material on the car, so don't remove too much metal or there will be nothing for this repair section to be welded to. There will be a temptation to spot or plug-weld the top in place. It's better than nothing and the seam can subsequently be waterproofed with Sikoflex, but the most professional and long-lasting repair will be achieved by seam welding.

If the corrosion is so extensive that you cannot find sound metal to which the repair top can be welded, you'll have to go to the next stage and fit a full reinforcer

("wedge" to you and I!) panel which is not likely, except in dire cases.

Once the reinforcer top is welded in place do be generous with the paintbrush and your application of several coats of rust-inhibiting paint. Clean up as much of the surrounding panelling as you can and paint that too. Do replace the top splash plate to stop water getting past the top and, of course, the main splash plate itself along with its peripheral seal.

Door, corrosion or impact damage

20-1-4 Most owners will probably think that reskinning a door on an MGB is beyond their experience/ability. Luckily, new doors are available at, what I think is a very modest price - so much so that I think you are better off going for a new door rather than a repaired one every time. This puts sorting a damaged door within the capabilities of a great many owners since it now becomes, more or less, a bolt on job.

The one thing I must stress is that achieving a good fit on a door is a bit of a vicious circle only overcome by a fair bit of adjustment. The weight of an assembled

20-1-4 (Picture 1) Richard Ladds of the MGOC has removed the (arrowed) top capping and is concentrating on the window winder arm. I must say that I like this MGOC's special "Club" door trim panel with its carpeted bottom.

door is surprisingly heavy which tends to make its rear end droop as you fit the internal mechanisms. This means that any initial door gaps you set up will have to be adjusted again - which in turn makes the fit of the leading edge of the quarterlight frame difficult to get parallel with the windscreen (windshield). So don't feel you have done a poor job if you have to make numerous adjustments after the assembly is complete - it's "par for the course."

The first task is to strip the original door - which I think is best done while the door is still attached to the car. I will go through the sequence in some detail since it is not always obvious as to the best order. Furthermore reassembly is the exact reverse sequence, so this detail serves two purposes.

The four screws that secure each capping are obvious, while a central crosshead screw fixes the window winders (and the interior door handles on early cars). The internal door pulls double as armrests in later cars and two screws need to be removed in both cases.

Removing a door panel for the first time deserves a few words - a wide screwdriver between the panel and the door to pop each plastic clip out of the door in turn is probably the best method. Locate the screwdriver as close to each plastic clip as possible - under its lip is ideal because you want to get the clip out of the door and not out of the panel, if possible.

20-1-4 (Picture 2) You can see where the waterproof membrane has been removed and the ends of the two door catch rods. Earlier cars used a similar arrangement, but with a bar instead of a rod. The top rod locks/unlocks the door while the bottom rod opens it from inside the car.

20-1-4 (Picture 3) If you've never done it before, these retaining clips may puzzle you for a few seconds, but they need to be unclipped from their rods to allow each rod to be pulled from the catch.

Don't be concerned if the clips break in the process, they become brittle with age and replacements are readily available. Next you should find a plastic membrane with requires pealing off the inside of the door.

The catch and lock are operated by a pair of rods - these vary from early to late cars in detail but, basically, need to be unclipped at the lock end by levering up the tiny spring tags. Remove the door lock via the three (originally crossheaded) screws in the back face of the door. You may need to twist the lock to detach it from the external key lock and to manoeuvre it out of the door. Unscrew the internal door handle/lock - which you should be able to pull forward and thus remove complete with both rods.

The window glass runs in two independent channels. The front one is an extension of the quarterlight frame and will be the last door component to be removed. However, we need to free the glass by completely removing the rear guide. The top crosshead screw is usually no trouble to find and remove from the inside of the door frame, but the bottom

hex-bolt maybe rusted solid ... You'll almost certainly need to replace both bottom right-angled brackets (they secure the two window channels to the bottom inside of the door), so if either resist, wiggle the right-angle bracket until it breaks or drill out the hex-bolt. You'll eventually need to separate what remains of the right-angle securing bracket from the channel, but this may be best left until the glass has actually been lifted clear of the door.

To remove the glass you need to undo the four short bolts that hold the winder mechanism in place. Note: keep these separate, as they're shorter than most other fastenings and do need to go back in the same place when you're reassembling the door. The door glass is best now held by a partner about halfway up its travel - because you need to slide a pair of "pegs" within the winder mechanism out of a channel that is actually attached to the bottom of the window glass. Once the pegs are separated from the channel the glass can be lifted straight upwards out of the door and you should be able to lift the rear channel out the same way too. You'll find the rear channel comes out easiest by turning it through 90-degrees as the bottom of the channel nears the top of the doorframe and you use the same technique for the front channel too - shortly. First, you have to manoeuvre the window winder/lift mechanism out to leave the door with just its quarterlight assembly attached.

The final step requires you remove the bottom right-angle bracket followed by a pair of plastic bungs from the leading edge of the door frame and, from the resulting holes, a pair of especially deep headed hex-bolts. The quarterlight is also secured to the top of the door by two especially long hex-nuts that are accessed through the two almost triangular access holes in the top/front corner of the door. With these undone, you should be able to lift up, turn through 90-degrees and remove the quarterlight and front glass channel from the door - leaving an empty door shell hanging via its hinges on the A-post.

The eight fastenings fixing the hinges to the A-posts are best left undisturbed - if possible. The six countersunk crossheaded setscrews that you need to remove are not too obvious at first: they're accessed through six holes in the inner panel of the door shell - and most will resist your attempts to remove them. Do try to get them out using whatever it takes. You'll find it necessary to spray lots of penetrating oil in there and to fit a pair of Mole (vise) grips onto the largest crosshead screwdriver you can buy. Some heat may help, as might an impact-driver or a small sharp (metal) chisel. You can drill the heads off any screws that simply will not be moved, but unfortunately that leaves the stubs of the bolts protruding though the hinges which in turn makes it impossible to get the door to slide backwards off its hinges. Consequently, you need to remember that if you are tempted to drill the heads of the screws off, you'll also have to drill down through the (substantial) thickness of the hinge to remove the stubs sufficiently to relase the hinges. You also must try not to open out the diameter of the hinge holes should you be forced to undertake the drilling exercise.

Once you've got the six screws out by one means or another you should be able to slide the door shell backwards

leaving the hinges attached to the A-post as shown in the picture.

It only fair to also tell you that the quarterlight assembly may need some attention. The two mounting studs can shear-off when you are unscrewing the nuts and you can find the spring-loaded pivot has rusted through. In either event it would not be sensible to fit the quarterlight to the new door without first rectifying these details, particularly as all the necessary parts are available. You'll need to remove the quarterlight glass from its frame: this is not as difficult as you might think, provided you take it slowly and work from both **ends**. The glass is nowhere near as fragile as you might expect, so a narrow screwdriver slipped down the end between glass and frame

20-1-4 (Picture 6) Here the quarterlight glass is just going back into its frame with a new glazing seal. The pivot looks remarkably uncorroded and has, I suspect, also been replaced.

will, eventually, enable you to lever the glass from its frame. After that, the repair work will be self-evident. The hardest part of reassembly is to get the new tape seal to stay in place around the glass while you get the glass and seal back into its frame. Provided I've not severely damaged the seal, I leave the original one in place within the frame and refit the glass on a bead of silicone RTV sealer. This is not described as an adhesive, but it sticks so well as to do a superb dual job and makes an otherwise difficult job very easy. I hold the glass in its frame (via a piece of wood) in the vice overnight before marrying it to its quarterlight assembly the next morning.

Here comes the fun ... Start by trial fitting the new door on its hinges via a couple of temporary hinge bolts: check the door gaps front and rear and that there is a parallel alignment with the sill. Offer the quarterlight up and adjust the hole sizes and centres in the top of the door so that the front edge of the quarterlight is parallel to the windscreen. There's a rubber seal to fit between quarterlight and door top so, before you decide all is well, you should try the quarterlight with the rubber seal in place. When that seems satisfactory fit the front pair of securing bolts and tighten everything up.

Once you're confident that the quarterlight will fit the door well and that the door fits the car nicely, strip the door, remove it from the car, apply a self-

20-1-4 (Picture 4) The catch itself *does* come away after you remove three countersunk screws, but you'll need to twist/turn it. The arrow anticipates your next step, removing the glass. This retains the top of the glass channel (guide), which you can just see inside the door to the right of Richard's hand. I have also arrowed the bottom fastening too.

20-1-4 (Picture 5) You may think that the easiest route to removing the doors is to undo the eight (arrowed) screws holding the hinges to the A-post. However, you'd be wrong, for several reasons, but principally because you also have to remove two large nuts from the front side of the A-post. In this instance we can get at the nuts easily since the wing has been removed from the car. However, they are rather more difficult to get to with the wing in place! Best to release the hinges as described in the text.

adhesive sound-deadening panel to the inside door skin and finish paint it inside and out in body colour. I'd generously treat the door with wax treatment before sliding it onto its hinges, but many will leave this to the end of the reassembly process.

Bearing in mind that you're fitting an empty door shell, it may be a good idea to position the door with its trailing edge about 1/8in (3mm) higher than the front. This is to allow for the fact that the rear edge of the door will drop from the extra weight as you fit the door furniture, quarterlights and glass. You 'll almost certainly need new bottom brackets for the window channels and it's advisable to wax treat them before assembly.

Reverse the door stripping sequence, but don't forget to fit a plastic membrane to protect the inside of the door panel. I found my local builders merchant stocked the ideal heavy-duty polythene which I fixed to the door with duct tape (duck tape).

Sill (rocker), outer, corrosion

20-1-5 Repairing small rust holes in an outer sill (rocker) is not, to my mind, a good course of action, since any sill that has corroded sufficiently to perforate really needs to be completely replaced. However, I concede that if you decide to replace the whole outer sill you will almost certainly find that the inner central membrane is rotten too - so the remedial work escalates beyond what many MGB owners can tackle at home. Consequently, I include a few thoughts on patching a sill not so much as a long term solution but

20-1-5 (Picture 1) This sill (rocker) looks reasonable in that it has a couple of small holes low down near the bottom lip and might be seen by many an owner as a candidate for a patch repair to get the car through Britain's annual MoT test. However, the years of experience at MGOC workshop paid-off for this owner since they knew the real story was...

20-1-5 (Picture 2) ...far more serious as revealed when the outer sill was removed. Clearly, there's virtually no structural strength left here and a proper, if much more expensive repair is *essential*.

20-1-5 (Picture 3) This is not a restoration manual and as tempting as it is to use the many sequential and detailed pictures provided by MGOC, I will confine myself to this one to illustrate the safe and correct sill repair that you really should have a professional MGB specialist carry out for you. This picture is doubly interesting since it also shows a second non-standard, but highly desirable, brace/strengthener being fitted just in front of the door pillar. Some restorers fit an additional stiffener nearer to the jacking point.

more in the spirit of getting the car through a mandatory roadworthiness test, such as the British MoT, and keeping it on the road until a full professional sill replacement can be organised.

If you do need to repair a sill panel then the patch must be fully seam welded. To achieve this there must be solid material to weld to right the way around the patch and you must very carefully remove all paint, filler, grease and rust from the edges of the hole. This means you decide the size of the patch after the cleaning up work has been completed and allowing for a 15mm overlap right around the patch. The patch needs to be made from 18swg (1.2mm) thick sheet steel.

20-1-5 (Picture 4) If you feel a compulsive urge to use your welding set - choose the single-skin repair that is clearly required here.

20-1-5 (Picture 5) Patches are acceptable to MoT testing stations in the UK, but I understand this would not pass the German equivalent. Personally, I think there is always a danger that a patch can be welded to a corroded piece of metal and of course, the strongest piece of the new material is only as strong as the part that it's welded to.

Any patch on almost any MGB panel will require a single curvature radius which most will create at home over a pipe or knee. It doesn't matter if the radius is not perfect, although I would prefer a radius that's too large in preference to one that is too tight. I'd tack the two top corners of the patch in place and then stitch weld in about 25mm lengths along to top edge. Hold the patch about 50mm below the top tight against the base and tack it both sides. Do the same again until the patch is tacked right down both sides tight to the base. A final couple of tacks across the bottom are prudent before you start to stitch weld (to minimise heat and thus distortion) round the patch. If I were suspicious about the integrity of the base I might sequence my stitch welds - one per edge until the whole circumference of the patch was welded.

Since this is a relatively short term solution, there seems little point spending too much time on cosmetic finishing, but a splash of red-oxide primer is worthwhile.

Rear hatch leaks (GTs)

20-1-6 Assuming the metal frame on your GT's rear hatch is sound, there are three places that water can leak through the frame and thence into the car. All need to be addressed, the source identified and cured since water sloshing about in a rear hatch will quickly rot out the frame and/or the skin of the hatch. The most usual route for water ingress is the badge which is attached by pushing pins cast into its back into small plastic blind fixing bushes in the door skin. These bushes can get missed out or crack while the holes in the hatch skin that they are pushed into rust or get elongated. Unscrew the internal trim panels inside the hatch and pour a little water over the badges to see if water comes through to the inside. If there is a leak, there are two solutions. Remove the badge -

a) Apply a blob of silicone sealer to each badge pin and press the badge home before the sealer sets.

b) Close the holes in the hatch skin either by welding or with filler, cut the pins off the back of the badge and fix it to the door with the double-sided sticky tape that is available from most auto-shops.

The next most likely spot for water to leak past a rear hatch is the rubber seal that surrounds the glass. Many such seals are 20-30 years old and although they look perfectly sound, they just don't exert the same grip on the glass as was once the case. Furthermore, dirt can get washed into the gap between seal and glass. If it is the seal/glass joint that is suspect and the gaps

are minimal yet you are fairly sure this is the source of your leak, then you can use a special windscreen leak-seeking liquid sealer that is supplied in a tube. You'll need to apply right into the base of the rubber strip's slot via a nozzle, which should come with the tube. However if the gap between rubber seal and the glass is open enough to allow dirt to have gathered, clean out the joint right around the periphery of the seal. You'll be surprised how much grit comes from within the rubber/glass joint, even where it looks fairly tight. A plastic spatula may help to open a slot above the glass to enable you to get most of the rubbish out with a cloth before you move on a few inches and tackle another length of the rubber to glass seal. When you are satisfied that the whole length of the recess is as clean as is practical, run a thick bead of translucent silicone bath sealer as far into the recess within the rubber seal that the glass sits in and right the way around. Push the rubber down such that the excess silicone is forced out and remove the worst excesses straight away. Don't be concerned if the rubber or the glass is smeared with a film of silicone - that will rub off very easily the next morning.

The third potential leak source is between the rubber lip seal and the frame of the hatch. New seals are available, and there is no short cut - you just have replace the leaking seal! You may find it best to remove the hatch via the six crossheaded screws in its hinge and do the job on a large table or even on a bed.

Bearing in mind that the rubber seal is to be replaced anyway and that the chrome trim must not be distorted, it's best to cut the rubber with a craft knife so that the chromium trim 'falls' out.

Windows mist up (fog) frequently

20-1-7 The windows keep misting up. This is a problem that affects both Roadsters and GTs. Many GTs have a significant advantage in that they have a heated rear window (HRW) that certainly should help.

The cars are relatively small, of course, and in conditions where any car will mist up, an MGB will do so more readily. The heater is not the world's best and the airflow that the fan generates leaves a lot to be desired - thus clearing the windscreen (windshield) is a protracted process even though everything is functioning as well as the

20-1-7 There are numerous reasons for windows to mist up (fog). One is a leak from the plenum chamber just above the occupant's knees. Without going into great detail, the vent in front of the windscreen (windshield) allows air into the car and water into the plenum when it rains or you wash the car. The water is intended to escape through this drain tube situated above the gearbox, however, the tube gets blocked with dirt and leaves and traps the water in the plenum, where it either finds a hole or corrodes one and leaks into the passenger compartment. The leaks will dramatically reduce if not stop altogether if you cut the bottom off the drain tube. You will be amazed as to the dirt that you can then tease out of the tube allowing water an easy escape route in future.

design of an MGB allows! As explained in chapter 19, you can upgrade the fan and its impeller and, if windscreen demisting is a problem with your car, this might help you. If it is the rear of the car that is a constant irritation, particularly on days when you would not have expected a severe misting problem, look further for there may be water leakage into the car making it constantly damp. Water ingress might be from the roof, windscreen, hood or rear hatch - or in places that you would never think to look ... A rust perforated plenum chamber, a blocked plenum drain, a weeping heater matrix (losing a little coolant, smell of antifreeze/inhibitor inside car?) a perforated inner front wing or a perforated rear wheel arch will all allow water to seep into the passenger compartment. Then there's the possibility that there is a rubber or plastic bung missing from the floor, thus allowing water to soak the carpet in one spot, possibly under a seat where you'd hardly notice the problem unless you were searching for it.

So exceptional misting problems signal dampness inside the car the cause of which needs to be found and rectified.

BODY NOISES, ELIMINATION
Whistling at high speed

20-2-1 If you have a 1980 MGB and cannot understand where a whistling noise is coming from at highish speeds, the chances are that the headlight chrome trims used at the end of the production run are causing the noise. Earlier style trims will fit and, while not original, will remove this irritation.

20-2-1 This shape of headlight rim will not whistle and is widely available secondhand and new: it was fitted to the vast majority of MGBs.

Buzzing from beneath dashpanel (fascia)

20-2-2 A buzzing noise from under the dashpanel, particularly if it only occurs at a specific engine rpm or road speed, is almost certainly a loose cable, pipe or, less likely, electrical cable vibrating. If you go searching for the offending item, start with the bowden heater control cables and then take a look at the capillary lines that feed the dual oil/water gauge of some models. The latter are designed to be clipped to the bulkhead, but usually a couple of plastic cable ties will stop the vibration.

Tinkling from vicinity of door mirrors

20-2-3 If your 'B has door-mirrors and you're noticing a "tinkling" noise, particularly on rougher roads, this could

be loose mirror glass which is very common. You will need to pull down the top centre of the plastic surround and remove it, catching the glass before it falls of course! You can fit a piece of foam behind the glass before reassembling but since this holds water I prefer four blobs of silicone sealer on the corners of the mirror before refitting the plastic surround.

20-2-3 It never used to be the case, but door mirrors purchased in recent years seems to have a much looser fit of the mirror in its metal frame. The result is an annoying rattle - solved as described in the text.

Rattling from outside car

20-2-4 Annoyed by an external rattle? It's surprising how the rattle from just one loose bolt or metal component "carries," so do a bit of shaking of the likely contenders when you next wash the car. Favourites are loose grilles (particularly the black recessed type), bumpers and overriders, but chrome trim and even door handles have been known to cause rattle.

Once found, tighten the fixings of the offending component.

PAINT AND CHROME MAINTENANCE AND RECHROMING
Paintwork repairs

20-3-1 This section is not included to help you paint large areas like a new door or wing (fender). However, the paintwork on certain areas of an MGB's body is very vulnerable to stone chips. The invisible repair of such damage is quite difficult and even with an exactly matching touch-up paint it is all too easy to rub away an area of originally undamaged paint-work as you try to flat down the touched-in paint. I have rarely achieved a completely

invisible repair by the touch-in route and, consequently, have had to resort to spraying an area far larger than the damaged area - or leave it all alone!

The MGOC have developed a repair kit and methodology that they say is very simple to execute and provides excellent results. Full instructions are provided with each kit but, in outline, you're required to clean the damaged area with white spirit before (and I suggest after) using fine wet-&-dry paper to remove any rust that may have established. Forty different coloured touch-up paints are available and you should use several coats of the appropriate one for your car, allowing each successive layer to dry. The next step is to flat the surface of the newly applied and hardened paint in a circular motion using an abrasive micro pad and holding tool. You're required to lubricate the pad during this operation using soap and water, as one would with wet-&-dry paper. The final step is to gently polish the area using a proprietary cutting-compound such as T-Cut. You can get in touch with the MGOC by calling UK number 01954 231318.

Paintwork protection

20-3-2 After you've spent hours repainting/touching in you will want to prevent the paint chips reoccurring. Positioning an almost invisible clear plastic protective film over the vulnerable areas can do this. On my car I have a low front valance which seems particularly prone to stone chipping, but every owner will find the sills (rockers), particularly just behind the front wheels, peppered with paint chips. The lower rear wing (fender) just behind the rear wheels is another vulnerable spot where this product may be particularly helpful. Called Foliatec, it is self-adhesive and can be bought in 175mm wide strips about 1500mm long. One such strip costs £20, so you do need to plan where you want to cut and apply it to maximum effect. It can be peeled off after use, say, on a rally or drive where you were going over rougher than usual roads, or just left in place. Some readers may be wondering whether they would not protect the sills from stone damage better with a pair of mud-flaps, and this is of course a matter of personal choice. However for my part I have always thought that screws that secure mud-flaps are a perfect route to allow rust to gain a foothold. Consequently this clear film seems a much better, if slightly more expensive, method.

Sources are TR Enterprises (Mansfield, Nottinghamshire. Tel [UK] 01623 793807) and MGOC (Swavesey, Cambridgeshire. Tel [UK] 01954 231318)

Chrome - maintenance and rechroming

20-3-3 On my GT I have a rear bumper that was "plated" (rechromed) and fitted to the car in 1971, and while it has some minor pitting that only I know about, it generally looks superb. However, some owners who go to the trouble of fitting **new** chromed parts find that they rust very quickly - why is that? Chrome plating is porous - period. It lets water through to what is underneath, and if that happens to be steel, then rusting/pitting/pealing can occur with amazing speed. You can alleviate the problem but it is the quality of the plating that is mostly the cause. This is not a book on restoration so a long diatribe on the merits of triple plating (copper followed by nickel followed by the decorative chrome) is out of place here. However, if you, or the preceding owner, have bought a reproduction chrome component or had an original part re-chromed "on-the-cheap," it's likely to have been given no more than a quick flash of chrome without both protective substrates and is, consequently, much more prone to corrosion. While this information may not help your current situation, at least you know why you've got a problem and that, next time, you'll be better off having triple-plated rechromed items. Incidentally, copper being so expensive these days, there's a second-best triple-plating technique that is acceptable which involves a double substrate of nickel.

The chromer will usually repaint the rear of newly rechromed parts, but there's absolutely nothing to stop you painting or repainting the rear with a good rust-preventive paint such as Hammerite from time to time.

So how do you get your car's existing chrome back to the best condition possible? The first step, before applying protection, involves hard work with a proprietary chrome cleaner or metal polish. Solvol Autochrome metal polish will do the initial job provided the rust has not pitted the chrome too deeply. If the chrome proves beyond recall you'll need to get that part rechromed, and my earlier advise about triple-plating needs to be borne in mind. All my plating in the last five years has been done by CES (Central Engineering Services - West Hythe, Kent.

20-3-3 Good chrome on an MGB is a highly desirable feature and therefore needs to be plated well and kept in tip-top order as described in the text.

Tel (UK) 01303 268969), whose whole business is based upon their reputation amongst vintage and classic car and bike restorers.

Protecting chromework

20-3-4 Because chrome is porous, you need to apply a generous layer of wax polish to the chrome work as often as you can. Certainly every time you polish the car's paintwork - more often if you can. There's much to be said for waxing the chromework every time you wash the car. The chrome must be completely dry first, so maybe the wax is best applied the next day. Let the wax dry and then polish it in the normal way. You **cannot** wax polish the chrome too much, and each time you you do you're filling in the tiny (invisible) holes that let the water through to the substrates.

I don't feel it's important to leather-off the whole car every time it is put-away wet. However, it **is** a very good idea to run over the chromework with a leather, particularly the chrome bumpers and particularly if there has been any salt on the roads or you've been visiting the seaside.

I suggest you apply an annual wax-based protective aerosol spray to the rear of the bumpers and overriders. Obviously, if you have half-an-inch of mud stuck to the rear of the bumpers this'll do absolutely no good whatsoever, so pressure wash the rears first, let things dry thoroughly and, a day or two later, apply your protective layer of wax to the rear of both bumpers and overriders. I use a Comma product for this purpose, but of course Waxoyl is very popular and readily available. Similar products will be available in other countries.

By the way, there are certain MGB components that are impossible to wax

polish let alone keep in good order. I am thinking of wheelnuts in particular: if yours are "tatty" then replacements made from stainless-steel are the best solution. While talking wheels, there is a rather attractive chrome wheel embellisher that I have fitted to my car's Rostyle wheels. However, these can get covered in a corrosive combination of brake dust and road grime and while I cannot help with the latter, you can avoid the brake dust by using EBC's Kevlar brake pads. Normal pads are made from materials that carbonise at the temperatures generated when braking even fairly gently. Kevlar does not contain carbonising materials and therefore no dust is created, much to the benefit of your wheel trims.

INTERIOR TRIM PANELS, SEAT REPAIRS AND CARPET REPLACEMENT

Seat has become floppy

20-4-1 Chances are it's the driver's seat for, although not a frequent problem, the frame of the seat are susceptible to the occasional break and the consequential need for a welded repair or replacement. However, you cannot carry out the frame repair work with the seat cover and cushions in place so read 20-4-2 to help you initially strip (and subsequently re-cover) that part of the seat that has broken before you can assess the repair to the frame itself. The early Roadster seats were bolt-adjustable tilt-only, while some GTs had leather covered reclining seat frames. After about 1969 all cars had the reclining seat ratchet mechanism incorporated into the frame. If your frame is causing concern then, in addition to the general integrity of

20-4-1 (Picture 1) Remove the whole seat by undoing the four screws that secure the bottom runners to the floor.

20-4-1 (Picture 2) Find the crack in the frame and strip that part of the seat...

the frame, you need to check out and, as necessary, repair the reclining mechanism. Any squab with provision for a headrest will have the headrest's retaining spring held in place by a piece of tape. The spring is usually broken and consequently will require a replacement which, when the time comes, should also be retained by a piece of sticky tape!

Once the covering is removed you'll need to align the broken pieces of frame and either weld it yourself or get it done professionally. There is an alternative: there are plenty of secondhand frames available and these offer the chance to avoid the welding task completely. This route is not without some difficulties though. As I say, there are plenty of seats available but because virtually everyone wants a driver's side (the right seat in the UK) they are usually only sold in complete pairs - for about £25. The covers of these secondhand seats are always tired and tatty but you need to focus on the integrity of the frame. You could use this as an opportunity to fit recliners to an early car if originality is not a big consideration.

20-4-1 (Picture 3) ...right down to its frame before attempting the welded repair. Shown here is the earlier "diaphragm" support for the base cushion and it looks in need of replacement.

The repair time and work is however minimised if you buy identical seats (ignoring the cover colour) to those fitted in the car and just swap the existing cover from that part of your broken seat to the replacement

Seat material is torn or worn

20-4-2 It's very rare that a torn seat cover can be satisfactorily or economically repaired, so a tear or worn cover will require a new replacement. All MGB seats were supplied with the seat covers made in two "halves" - the base and the back (or "squab" as it's known). Consequently, you don't have to recover both seats nor, for that matter do you need to recover both "halves" of any seat. If it is the driver's seat base that has worn or torn then, provided you buy the matching

20-4-2 (Picture 1) With apologies for the use of an old/tatty seat as my "model", your first step will be to renovate the seat frame. Hopefully that means no more than preparing and painting it, but if welded repairs are necessary then carry these out first. Then you fit the base diaphragm or, in this case, the webbing straps to the renovated frame.

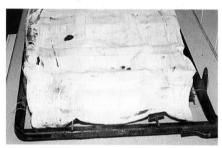

20-4-2 (Picture 2) Lay a (new) piece of hessian over the diaphragm or webbing and...

cover, you need to recover no more than the driver's base. In short, you can recover just as much or as little of your seats as you want, although there will be undoubted cost advantages in buying a set of seat covers and all will match.

There are different types of MGB seat with a wide variety of coverings. Nevertheless, the basic sequence and principles of recovering seats is largely the same for all types. The first order of business is to equip yourself with a good quality cover for each part of the seats you are planning to recover. The seat foams are a conundrum - re-use the originals or replace? If yours are showing any signs of powdering (you'll find the dust under the seats after use) buy new foam cushions for each new cover. **Always**, buy and fit new diaphragms or webbing as appropriate to the seat bases. If your car's seats have headrests fitted, you'll need a bezel for each squab you plan to recover. You'll also need several sharp blades or a Stanley (craft) knife and some suitable adhesives - best also ordered simultaneously with the other recovering materials you need. I also suggest you establish which solvent removes surplus adhesive without damaging car or covers and have some handy, because gluing mistakes are best corrected immediately.

I **very strongly** recommend that you only tackle one seat at a time. By which I mean leave one seat untouched for reference purposes until such time as you are completely satisfied with the refurbished one. Do note that the base foams and seat covers are handed, so make sure you select the correct ones for the seat you propose starting on.

20-4-2 (Picture 3) ...position the foam base cushion on the hessian. Turn the cover inside-out for a few seconds and apply a light coating of adhesive to the *centre* of the seat *cover* (not the cushion) – where it will come into contact with the recessed part of the foam.

20-4-2 (Picture 4) Turn the cover back outside-out. You should find the base cover actually pulls fairly easily over the base foam and is best pulled down all round and adjusted for symmetry before you push the centre of the cover into the centre of the cushion.

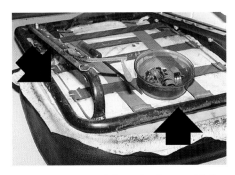

20-4-2 (Picture 5) Turn the "assembly" over and apply a 10mm wide line of contact adhesive around the bottom of the frame where the cover will eventually roll over. A couple of typical places are arrowed.

The seats are fixed to the car via four bolts that pass through the seat runners and carpet into the floorpan. Mark the holes in the runners that the bolts utilise and then undo the back pair (after sliding the seat right forward) and the front pair (after sliding the seat right back). Even if your seats can be separated into base and squab, as surprising as it sounds, it may be best to leave them in one piece - it makes the subsequent pushing and pulling easier as does getting the seat you are working on about waist high on the workbench.

I'd start with the base if you are to recover both base and squab, making a careful note of the locations of various spring clips before removing them carefully (to avoid damaging them). Strip the rest of the seat base, then tackle the squab. You may find the chromed lever on adjustable

seats very hard to remove from its square - persevere. A pair of strong screwdrivers may help you lever it off.

Seats with a headrest can be difficult and surprising, because you sometimes have to leave the headrest in place while you remove the squab cover, undo the tape holding the rear card back and release the spring retaining the headrest! Take notes as you proceed with the stripping. Fix any damage to the frame as described in section 20-4-1 and then repaint the whole frame. If the frame

20-4-2 (Picture 6) I find it easiest to tackle the front first followed by the rear of the cover followed by the two sides. Roll the cover over the frame, ensuring that the sides of the cover are taut enough not to wrinkle, but not so tight as to distort the cushion. If in doubt, peel the cover edge back and start again. Once satisfied with the even tautness of the cover, clip the cover from the inside in the direction of this...

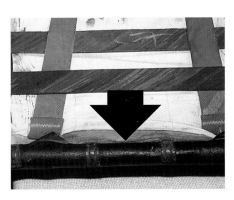

20-4-2 (Picture 7) ...and this arrow. In fact you may just be able to see the edge of two of three clips in this shot.

proves to be rusty, a few extra days delay and the modest cost of sandblasting prior to painting is well worthwhile to ensure your subsequent work is on a sound foundation.

Once the paint is hard fit the new diaphragm/webbing using a looped piece of string round each clip in order to stretch the rubber and allow the clip to enter the frame. Once the diaphragm is in place, glue a piece of sacking to its top face.

Glue the whole of the flat centre part of the new base cover to its foam cushion, making sure not only that the edges of cushion and cover line up, but that the edges of the flat centre are also aligned. Apply a light covering of adhesive to **both** cover and foam and allow it to go tacky (in preference to putting too much glue on the foam alone, allowing the foam to absorb the adhesive and, subsequently, go hard). Apply a bead of adhesive right around front and sides of the frame and position the cushion/cover on the diaphragm. Pull both sides of the cover down over the frame making sure that the piping is aligned with the cushion, and then pull the front/rear of the cover down as far as possible.

Roll the base of the cover around the frame using an occasional clip to ensure it stays in place. You'll need to shape the cover around the supporting legs. You'll also have to push and pull until the tension is about even and the piping flange and edges of the material look comfortable. Once you're satisfied, the rest of the

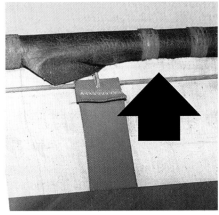

20-4-2 (Picture 8) You can probably see these clips have been pushed on from the same direction as this picture was taken. When you've got all the clips back in place, it's time to start the slightly more difficult squab.

20-4-2 (Picture 9) When it comes to the squab, the rake adjusting handle needs to be removed from relevant seats which, let me tell you, is easier said than done. I had to tap this off with a long blunt screwdriver (under the shoulder) and a hammer (after removing the crosshead securing screw, of course).

20-4-2 (Picture 10) With the seat squab stripped, the first order of buisness is to check that the reclining mechanism (if applicable) is in working order and likely to stay that way. Carry out any frame or mechanism repairs that are required, or find a replacement squab frame.

20-4-2 (Picture 11) The complete frame needs repainting and the arrowed headrest retaining spring (if applicable) taping in place with a few turns of masking tape.

20-4-2 (Picture 12) Masking tape is also required to hold the card back to the squab in place. You should be able to see about six places were I've tapped it to the frame.

securing clips need to be fitted in such a manner that they do not pull the cover out of shape.

Of the two halves, the squab is the more difficult to recover - but with the aid of a tip or two, is perfectly feasible. If applicable, check that the headrest retaining spring is taped in place then tape and screw the card seatback to the rear of the squab's frame. The squab cushion is not handed, so either of those you ordered should be glued to the squab frame. Make sure the lip of the cushion curves around the frame and leave that to thoroughly dry once you are satisfied with the cushion's position on the frame. You may need to remove some seams from the cushion and, where applicable, to trim the top of the cushion back so as to allow about 10mm clearance right around the headrest slide. Some re-covering kits come with a sheet of thin foam that you should glue to the card backing for an added feeling of luxury: **don't** spray glue on the foam, it will absorb the glue and set rock-hard in due course! Spray the glue onto the card, focusing on the edges rather than the centre.

If the seats have headrests, you need to prepare the cover by fitting a new bezel. This is best done on the bench as you need to be able to clinch the tabs really tightly. The bezel comes in two parts,

an inner and an outer: both of which are obvious as to which goes where. I'd measure the position of the bezel in the cover and use the old cover with the original bezel still in place as a guide to where to cut the hole in the cover. Cut the hole tightly rather than generously and then turn the cover inside out to both fit and clinch the bezel.

With the cover still inside out, fit a half round card reinforcer to each bottom outside face of the cover. Look at the old cover for the detail and, if you've not been supplied with the card, note that it should be as thick as possible. You may need to trim the piping flaps to allow the each card to sit flush in its "pocket" but once they fit nicely, glue them in place.

The squab cover is a tight fitting bag that will be very difficult to pull over the foam cushion without some help - from a plastic bag! There are several ways you can use the slipperiness of the plastic bag to your advantage, but it's important that you use one of the following suggestions.

Either lightly tape the top of a 12in (300mm) wide strip of strong polythene (such as you used to line your door trim panels) down each side of the squab cushion and, when the time comes, pull the cover down using the "slip" provided by the polythene. With this method you then pull the polythene strips out from between cover and cushion. The alternative is to use a similar pair of **very thin** polythene strips that you lightly glue to the edges of the cushion and leave in place under the cover. In both cases you need to keep the front centre section of the cushion clear of the plastic. Just prior to your pulling the "bag" down over the squab, lightly apply two 3in wide strips of adhesive down the outside edges of the central flat part of the cushion. These are to ensure the cover follows the contour of the cushion once in place.

Time to pull the "bag" over the back making sure that it is the piping that takes as much of the stress (from the inevitable pushing and pulling) as possible. The rear tail of the cover is generally without seams and therefore is also a good place to grab to pull the cover down over the cushion. As soon as is practicable align the headrest

slot with the housing in the frame. Align the piping carefully and push the front of the cover into the shaped cushion only when you are comfortable with the overall way the cover sits on the squab cushion.

Finally the fix the side flaps to the frame with self-tapping screws. You should be able to find the original holes in the frame using the old cover for guidance

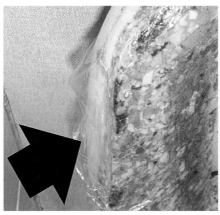

20-4-2 (Picture 14) This picture is important since this next step is the one that "makes or breaks" fitting the squab cover. You can temporally fit thick polythene to the shoulders of the cushion and pull it out when the cover is in place. Altrenatively, very lightly stick a very thin 4in (100mm) wide strip of polythene to the top of the cushion and down about 10 to 12in (250 to 300mm) each side. It's not easy to see, but I've let the end fly a little free of the cushion and arrowed it in order for you to see it. If you are to fit headrests, this is the moment to form the appropriate hole in the cushion and polythene.

20-4-2 (Picture 15) The time has come to make some real progress - pull the cover over the seat foam. Here, I've just got to the end of the easy bit and felt it time to apply a strip of adhesive to the bottom of the card backing.

and by pushing a small needle through the cover. Tap the four corners of the square lightly with a hammer in order to cut a hole in the fabric for the reclining mechanism and then tap the chrome lever back in place with a piece of wood between hammer and chrome. Glue and clip the bottom of the cover to the seat frame and cut off any grossly excessive material.

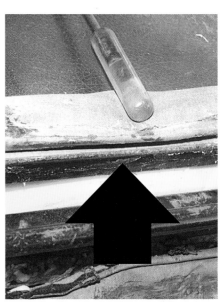

20-4-2 (Picture 16) Pull the back and front of the cover down simultaneously and, when satisfied that the cover is sitting on the cushion, glue the bottom lip of the frame (arrowed) and...

20-4-2 (Picture 17) ...fold the tail up over and back of the lip. Fix the clips in place and turn your attention to the (arrowed) front of the squab cover.

20-4-2 (Picture 13) A 1in (25mm) wide strip of adhesive around the edge of the card is needed to hold the edges of the squab cushion in place. You'll need to make a hole in the foam for the reclining arm (if applicable). Pull the edge of the cushion *over* the card.

20-4-2 (Picture 18) **The front of the cover needs to be pulled down and rolled over the large diameter cross frame arrowed here. Use the four clips to hold it in place. I popped a piece of paper up behind the rear of the cover to emphasise that it is the *front* that wraps round the cross bar, not the rear.**

Carpets damaged or worn

20-4-3 The carpeting is an extremely visible part of your car. Consequently, whether you are buying one individual replacement carpet or a complete set, you would be wise to choose carefully. That way there is a good chance you will only have to buy once! You might think that buying a single replacement carpet would be easier than a complete set. I don't think so because, even with a safe colour like black, the weave, material and even the colour can vary making the new piece look very odd when laying next to the original carpets.

It is impossible to compensate completely for colour fading, but if you're buying less than a full carpet set it's worth getting a sample from the original to enable replacements to be made from the appropriate material (nylon or wool), to have a similar weave and be edge-trimmed, if appropriate.

Even if you are buying a complete carpet set you need to be careful about your choice. The sets with **moulded** transmission tunnel (and in GT sets, moulded rear wheelarches) sit far better than if you try to cut and fit what is basically a flat piece of carpet around these difficult shapes. Furthermore, there are several places (down the full length of the sills [rockers] is one example) where the carpet has to be folded over a right-angle bend, making the closeness of the weave very obvious and important. A cheap broad weave shows up in such places as an apparently threadbare strip

of carpet and thus, to my mind, it's worth paying that bit more for a close-woven material in preference to buying purely on price.

The two floor mats in front of the seats and the sill carpets get the most wear and you'll smarten your car immensely if you fit new replacements for these. Carpets are usually advertised in sets - but if you find a supplier that makes them you'll be able to buy them individually if you ask. Consequently, the cost of bringing your car up to a reasonable standard need not be prohibitive.

The two footwell carpets are very easy to replace so you have absolutely no excuse for driving around with worn ones! They're secured by four carpet clips - special ones that can hardly been seen but are readily available for a very small cost. It's possible that your car's footwell carpets have been stuck in place - which is not a good idea since it prohibits your removing them to dry them out after that inevitable thunderstorm that catches you just when it is impossible to pull over and get the hood up. I recall leaving our Roadster parked, hood down, in France

20-4-3 (Picture 1) **Carpet clips are readily available from any spares stockist and each clip consists of three parts. On the left of this shot are a couple of "bases"- examples of which will probably already be pop-riveted to the floor of your car. It doesn't matter whether you use round or triangular female halves, but in the centre of the picture are a couple of round and one triangular female half clips. These are secured to the underside of the carpet by the thin spiked "tops"- and bottom right you may just be able to see the top and bottom female halves married together. You'll need longer than standard bases to rivet to the floor if you are using sound deadening felt and sticking it to the underside of the carpet.**

20-4-3 (Picture 2) **The wear shown here to the top of this sill (rocker) carpet is almost inevitable on the driver's side of any MGB. The trouble is that as soon as you replace this carpet you'll be starting to wear the replacement in exactly the same spot! Never mind, the cars are there to be used and enjoyed!**

on a blisteringly hot cloudless day. We took a monorail to the "top" of this hilltop town and were sitting drinking a cool beer when we noticed it was starting to cloud over. By the time we were halfway back to the car it was pitch black, by three-quarters of the way back it was raining ... hard. By the time we reached the car the rain was torrential and the interior of the car was absolutely soaked! We got the hood up, sat on several towels and a little later hung the footwell carpets out to dry on the hotel's washing line in order to ensure that the wet carpet to floor contact was too short to encourage rust. It is advantageous to be able to remove the footwell carpets - and particularly helpful if any sound-deadening felt you may have fitted, or plan to fit, comes out too. So stick the felt to the rear of the carpet by all means, but **not** to the floor of the car!

Lay your new carpet in place in the footwell and with an awl or stout needles locate one of the four studs that should be riveted to the floor of the car. If it's missing, rivet a replacement roughly where the corner of the carpet falls - remembering to place a small washer on the end of the pop-rivet before your partner squeezes the rivet pliers. Once you've found the centre of the floor stud with your awl, position the top/ring part of the carpet clip as near the centre of the awl as you can and push the three prongs through the carpet. Turn the carpet back and fit the female clip to the prongs at the rear and then splay the prongs outwards. Finish off that clip by tapping the prongs down tightly. Fit the finished clip to its base and start on another corner of the carpet.

Replacing the sill (rocker) carpets is a shade more difficult and requires you take out the seats, the footwell and underseat carpets and the trim panels (screwed to the outside of each footwell). You'll also need to drill out the pop-rivets that hold the door seal retaining plate in place. While it may sound a bit unnecessary now, a couple of pieces of masking tape stuck to the outer sill or a dimensioned sketch as to where the first and last holes are located may pay dividends when it come time to replace the plate over a new piece of carpet. Temporally masking tape adjacent carpets back out of the way and pull the old sill carpets out. They'll have been stuck in place but it's likely most will come out with minimal difficulty, but will probably leave patches of carpet for you to scrape off with the help of white spirit and/or a wallpaper stripping knife.

Make sure the surfaces of the sills are reasonably smooth before you stick only the top/flat face of the new carpets to the top face of each sill using a contact adhesive applied with a brush. Avoid aerosol adhesives - which can spray everywhere - for this application. Make sure the outer edge of the new carpet pieces are butted up tight to the top lip of the door frame and let the adhesive go tacky before you brush more adhesive on to the vertical sides of each sill and then fix the inner carpet faces. You don't really need to glue the last 25mm of carpet to the floor, bcause that will be covered by the floor carpeting - which you can replace as soon as you are sure all the sill adhesive has flashed-off. Trim any sill carpet excesses that might be seen and reposition the other adjacent carpets. Refitting the two outer footwell panels will probably be the last and most difficult job because, ideally, you really need to get the original screws to back into their original holes. Once you get one in place the rest get a bit easier and you may find that longer replacement screws will make the frustrating task a bit easier. If all else fails, you can always resort to "plan B" and, using the existing holes in the panel as a

guide, drill new 2mm fixing holes in the bodyshell! If you do go down this route remember to drill a hole and fix a screw one at a time.

Door trim panels damaged
20-4-4 Of all the trim panels on an MGB the door panels are probably the most vulnerable as they are attacked from both sides. If your feet are as big as mine you will inevitably, if unintentionally, kick the panels when exiting the car. What may be less obvious, but in fact more damaging, is the water that inevitably attacks the rear of the panels, particularly if any of the drain holes in the bottom of the door get bunged up. The trim panel deterioration is even swifter if the door was not properly lined with a polythene membrane before the trim panel was fitted.

If your car's door trim panels are looking tired, ill-fitting or bulging along the bottom, you can swiftly and for little cost smarten the interior dramatically by replacing them with new ones. The panels are sold in pairs and can be bought from all the popular MGB spares suppliers.

Fitting the new panels can be frustrating, so lets spend a few minutes exploring the basic procedure. Remove the window winder with a crosshead screwdriver. The internal door handle has two (identical) U-shaped plastic trims that have to be pushed upwards (top one) and straight downwards (bottom one). They overlap each other so it hardly matters which one you start with - but it's a question of gently levering say the bottom one down until there is a small gap, whereupon you can lightly tap each with a small screwdriver until it falls out. When you have unscrewed the four screws that secure the top capping and removed it to the side you are ready to start on the door panel. Removal can be done by hand but in my experience the task usually requires a broad bladed screwdriver pushed up close to each of the (numerous) clips that secure the trim panel to the door before you lever each clip out individually from its hole in the door frame. I'd suggest you leave the top front and top left clips until last: they'll hold the panel in place until you are ready to lift it off the door. If there's a strong plastic membrane in place over the door, remove it carefully, if not you will need to visit your nearest builder's merchant/DIY store and buy a sheet of polythene and some duct tape (also called duck tape and elephant tape).

It's important to clear out the bottom well of the door and take the opportunity

to spray liberally a wax-based rust inhibitor into each door's base. Fit the waterproof membrane to the inside of the door and cut the smallest holes practicable for the door handle and window winder shaft.

If you thought you were getting on well - now comes the slow part! Position all the clips in the pre-cut holes in the new panel, offer the panel to its door and concentrate on getting the top two (one at the front, one at the back) clipped into their respective holes in the door frame. Find yourself a pair of long, thin-nosed pliers and a small mirror and progressively work you way round the panel positioning each clip correctly one at a time and pushing it home. Since the most difficult stretch is the front of each door, I would start there and work my way from top/front to top/back corners. You'll probably only need the mirror for the front edge, but will have to lay on your back for the bottom run. It takes but a few minutes to replace the door handle U-trims, the capping and the winder handle ... after which its time to admire the improvement in appearance you've brought about.

20-4-4 The door trim panels are actually quite easy to remove and replace. The winder (just out of shot, top left) is easily removed via its central crosshead screw, but the internal door pull and handle shown here need explanation. The handle first: with a small, blunt screwdriver force the two plastic U-trims apart. The top one will also require lifting outward to allow it to clear the chrome trim line, but you should be able to move the top U-clip up and the bottom one down until they clear the door handle. The early doorpull/ armrest fixing is by the two securing screws which are plain to see. This type of doorpull successfully hides the two crosshead securing screws - but if look up _under_ the armrest, all will become clear!

Chapter 21
Hood (soft top)

The nature of the materials used in the manufacture of soft top hoods (not just the MGB's) result in there being few areas of a hood that can be successfully repaired by the owner. So the secret of a hood's longevity is informed purchase and attention to preventative maintenance.

Maintenance and careful use are by far the most important factors in keeping any hood in good condition. The "Flexglas" windows, in particular, are the part of the hood where the utmost care is needed. Folding and stowing the whole hood properly is **vital** since the most frequent cause of hood damage is incorrect folding. The correct method of folding and stowing the hood is explained in the MGB's handbook but be aware that it should **never** be folded on the windows as this will crease them, the creases will never come out and eventually the window will crack on the crease line. Even washing the windows correctly is important.

Choosing a replacement hood is something that needs to be done with care, so I hope the latter part of this chapter will help you select the best replacement hood for **your** particular needs. Replacement hoods are certainly best purchased on the basis of friends' recommendations or from a supplier with an good reputation to protect. **Never** buy a hood on price alone.

De-icing ragtops. On the basis that prevention is better than cure, a word of advice for those hardy souls who use their ragtops all year - take particular care when defrosting your rear windows. It's better to leave the frost/snow on the "Flexglas" and let it thaw naturally. Never scrape ice/frost off because you'll scratch the window for sure and could even crack the brittle "Flexglas". A little tepid (definitely not hot) water could be considered - but only in the knowledge that hot water on the windows can cause the "Flexglas" to shatter due to the sudden change in temperature. A de-icer spray maybe the safest route if you must clear the back window quickly.

The hood unavoidably moves about when folded causing the minute scratches that inevitably end up making the rear window opaque. There is very little you can do about the movement of the hood, but you can slip an old towel each side of the window as you fold the hood back: this will dramatically reduce the scratching and extend the life of the window.

Bird droppings on hood
21-1-1 How you wash the hood generally, and the windows in particular, can dramatically affect the longevity of both. Washing the hood with **plain water** is very important, but I strongly recommend you wash the windows before anything else and **never** use any abrasive to clean the windows, no matter how fine it is.

21-1-1 Taking care of your hood with lots of tender loving care (TLC) will not only repay you with a prolonged hood life but enhanced appearance too. So wash it *gently*, windows first (before the water gets dirty).

If bird droppings get on the windows they should be soaked off with running water: not rubbed off as they may contain grit, which will scratch the "Flexglas." Birds have varied diets and their droppings can be corrosive and/or abrasive. Seagulls in particular eat shellfish complete with the shells and, consequently, their droppings can be particularly destructive, sometimes containing razor sharp pieces of shell. To emphasise the point: droppings from shellfish eating birds can contain particles hard enough to scratch glass! Prestige Hoods, which has proved very helpful during the preparation of this section, tells me that a visitor to their works was in turn visited by a local seagull. It was a hot day and the droppings became baked on the windscreen (windshield). The visitor tried to clean the windscreen with a tissue and rubbed and rubbed at the offending mess - ending up with big swirl marks deeply etched into the glass. He had to have the screen replaced as the scratches were in the driver's area of vision!

Hood is torn

21-2-1 . Repairs to vinyl hoods are very unlikely to have any lasting benefits. All seams are, or should be, welded, and if one of these splits there is virtually nothing that can be done. It might be possible to glue a patch onto it on both sides. Stitching would be of no use, as the wind pressure will just rip the stitching apart. In any event waterproofing the stitch holes is just about impossible, as they'll open with the wind pressure. So if your hood is torn, move to 21-8-1.

21-2-1 Not much doubt that this rear window has not only been severely scratched, but is also beyond repair. As a matter of fact, if the rest of the hood had been in good shape a new rear window could have been successfully fitted, but the torn hood material dictates a new hood.

Rear windows difficult to see through

21-3-1 A very common problem with "ragtops," but with two solutions depending upon the severity of the problem. If the windows are cracked or yellow with age then it's best to consider a new hood (see 21-8-1) or, at least, a replacement rear window (details follow). However, on the basis that the windows are just difficult to see through try applying Greygate's or alternatively Renovo's plastic window polish - it really does work wonders.

There are three reasons why a window becomes progressively more difficult to see through, and all are unavoidable to some extent. Firstly, the atmospheric grime that hangs around our roads gets on both sides of the perspex. Scratches are the second cause - it is unavoidable that you'll slightly scratch the soft perspex every time you put the hood up or down and, thirdly, the (minute) movements of the hood when folded (caused by vibration) impose microscopic scratches on the plastic too. The dirt

21-3-1 A bottle of rear window polish may be small, but the contents certainly make a dramatic difference to a rear window.

and/or scratches will appear as cloudiness. Erect the hood, shake the bottle of window polish and apply it with a soft cloth - soft enough to be sure it will not scratch the perspex, so man-made fibres are best avoided. Renovo recommend you apply the polish to the cloth on a "little and often basis." You'll find you need to rub the product well in, and I found it necessary to do some areas of the window a couple of times, particularly on the inside. Consequently doing the inside of the window is a bit of a strain, but the result makes it all worthwhile. Don't forget to do both sides of the window.

21-3-2 Replacement rear windows. Take a close look at the rest of the hood because, if it's in reasonable shape, you could at least postpone the purchase of a completely new hood for a while by having a new rear window fitted. This work can be undertaken in the UK by Perfect Rear Vision (Tel [UK] 0181 777 6764) for about half the cost of what you would have to pay for a new vinyl hood. The work can be completed within 24 hours. Whichever company you're thinking of using, check how the replacement window or windows are to be fitted: if they are to be stitched in place water ingress could become a subsequent problem.

Hood leaks

21-4-1 A leaking front seal is a problem most Roadster owners face. Check number one is to ensure the toggle-clamps

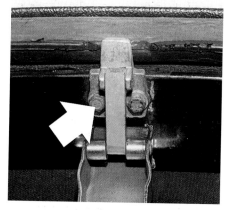

21-4-1 (Picture 1) These toggle clamps are an important element of sealing the header rail to the top of the windscreen (windshield). Adjusting the two screws (highlighted) per clamp may apply a little extra pressure...

are pulling the front of the hood frame (called the "header rail") down tightly onto the top of the windscreen (windshield). You may manage to get an improvement by altering the position of the clamps. More likely however is that the soft rubber seal that cushions/seals the header rail to the top of the 'screen is worn or damaged and needs to be replaced.

21-4-1 (Picture 2) ...but more likely gently pulling the soft seal from its aluminium retaining channel and carefully poking a replacement into place will effect the improvement you seek.

21-4-2 Vinyl materials (as well as mohair and "Stayfast" fabrics) require minimal attention during their lives - although a leaking hood is a problem that most Roadster owners face occasionally. If the hood is chaffed or torn you need to seek the advice of a professional trimmer or to fit a new hood.

Assuming there are no obvious holes or tears, the leaks, which can show-up as condensation within the car each morning as well as the rainwater drips that everyone expects, are probably via a porous seam or two (if your hood is made from vinyl material). If the hood is made from a fabric like material (double-duck or mohair), the leaks could be via a seam, or could be coming straight through the material - although the former is still the most likely.

The solution to porous seams and porous fabric is to reproof the hood, but it must be done with the right product for the particular hood. However, first a word on cleaning the hood material. Reproofing does not have to be a two-stage process, but I'm sure you agree it makes sense to remove traffic grime, bird soiling and, in my case, the inevitable grubby finger-marks from the hood before you reproof. Consequently, the first step for the majority will be to apply the correct pre-cleaner/shampoo for your car's hood. The following will help you select the correct

21-4-2 This is *fabric* soft top cleaner. The aerosol ejects a soft white foam - very similar to seat and trim cleaning products.

cleaner for your hood and all the products listed are available from Renovo -

Vinyl hoods: Vinyl Soft Top Cleaner
Fabric hoods: Soft Top Dry Cleaner
(see picture 21-4-2)

Whatever cleaner you use, follow the instructions on the pack.

21-4-3 Reproofing vinyl hoods. Follow the instructions on the pack and use Renovo's Vinyl Ultra Proofer, or a similar proprietary product. To show how simple the job is, the following will outline what you have to do with the Renovo product once you're satisfied with the cleanliness of the hood and/or tonneau. As with all such products you need to shake the half litre bottle well and pour the contents into a container. Brush the product into the hood, paying particular attention to the seams. In fact, I'd go around all the seams first, and then start going over the whole hood. You should find the hood will dry in under an hour whereupon the hood, but the seams in particular, will be waterproof and you should stay dry. As a bonus, vinyl Ultra Proofer provides protection against stains and UV light

21-4-4 Reproofing a fabric hood. Again use the manufacturer's instructions. For fabric hoods you need Renovo's Fabric Ultra-Proofer or a similar proprietary product. In the case of the

21-4-4 Reproofing of all but the very highest quality fabric hoods is a necessary chore from time to time. It's a fairly quick job with a wide paint brush.

Renovo product, the reproofing involves little more than painting the milk-like proofer onto the hood, although I must say it seems very keen to run off the hood at every opportunity and, consequently, needs to be applied little and often! Clearly it is important to cover the whole hood and to pay particular attention to the seams. Indeed, it is best to work the proofer into the seams first and then go over the whole hood. How you do this is a matter of personal preference, but I used a new, good quality (for nice soft bristles) 20mm paintbrush and attacked each strip between seams in turn. You do need to be a bit careful when you get to the edges of the hood to avoid dribbling proofer over the rest of the car so I had a large rag handy. You can reapply any surplus Ultra-Proofer a day or two later, keep it for a month or reapply it each autumn (fall). The half litre pack will probably do the MG's hood a couple of times.

Hood oil stained

21-5-1 I had occasion to remedy a garage's error after they put an oily component on the mohair hood of my TR! This left a dark stain the size of a dinner plate both outside and inside, which I thought initially had totally ruined the £300 hood. Not so you'll be delighted to hear, thanks to several applications from an aerosol of, wait for it - Carb and

Choke Cleaner! The product is made by Auto Chemicals, who were very helpful when I explained I was seeking something that was virtually 100% Carbon Tetra-Chloride to act as a dry cleaning agent. The Carb cleaner is mostly Toluene, but worked in the same way as Carbon-Tet. I had to rub the surfaces with clean towels to absorb as much of the dirty oil as possible after each application, and I would not recommend this treatment in anything other than a crisis. However, you can imagine what a relief it was to find the solution to an apathetic mechanic's error.

21-5 For emergency use only on fabric hoods - but in the unlikely event of getting oil on the fabric there's a solution.

Hood colour has faded

21-6-1 Applicable only to fabric hood (and tonneau) materials. If your car's hood, hood cover or tonneau is black, blue or brown, and faded, you can brush on a coat of Renovo's soft top reviver to bring the material back to a virtually new appearance. The reviver dries in a couple of hours and the manufacturer recommends you then brush on a second

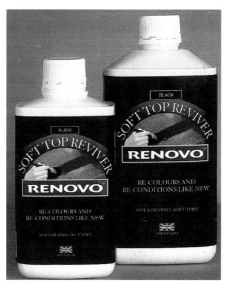

21-6-1 (Picture 1) Available in several colours, the reviver rejuvinates a faded dark blue "double duck" fabric hood of some vintage...

21-6-1 (Picture 2) ...as can be seen from this half-completed hood. If buying a replacement fabric hood, choose one made from colour-fast fabric.

coat for the very best of results.

I'd make sure the hood is clean before applying the reviver. This Renovo product comes in two sizes, but the smaller half litre will be sufficient for an MGB hood.

Other similar proprietary products are available too.

Hood zip stiff

21-7-1 A candle lightly rubbed over a zip in a hood (for the zip-out rear window, in case you were wondering) or tonneau a couple of times each year should ensure they always operate smoothly.

Hood frame stiff

21-7-2 The hood frame pivot points do need the occasional spot of oil, otherwise they can seize and shear. This is more

apparent in cars living near the sea with its associated salty atmosphere or in cars that have enjoyed a long sea journey either as part of their initial delivery or when being repatriated.

Hood worn out or damaged

21-8-1 Obviously if your hood is torn or otherwise damaged then no amount of cleaners or proofing is going to help and you need to buy a new hood.

You have a choice of material and colours, and about the amount of pre-fitting you wish to have carried out for you. Consequently, it should help if I describe the respective advantages of vinyl and fabric materials before we go any further. The problem arises when you come to compare one manufacturer's offering with a competitor's because each basic type of material has sub-grades which makes it important to try and specify your choice of material a little more closely than simply "Vinyl" or "Fabric."

Vinyl or PVC. Vinyl or PVC hoods will top the vast majority of cars, can do sterling service and are probably easier to fit than fabric hoods. Vinyl hoods are easy to clean, light in weight and less bulky, but the cheaper grades can tear easily and are prone to cracking in cold conditions. You need to ensure the outer hood seams are electronically welded to a high standard (possibly warranted) in order to ensure both weatherproofing and seam strength are maximised. Some seam welding can actually weaken the material such that it splits under the inevitable tension that you must employ with a vinyl hood if it is not to flap and flog like a flag in a gale! There are two relevant grades of vinyl - the lowest and cheapest of which tends to be called "heavy duty." For the majority of us living outside the southern parts of the USA or Europe, hoods made from this material will probably give five years reasonable service. However, in my opinion, the extra 20% cost usually incurred by the purchase of an "Original Equipment" superior grade of vinyl hood is worthwhile since such hoods enjoy double the life of the "Heavy Duty" variety.

Fabric. There are some lovely hoods made from what is called "mohair," a fabric material. They are more expensive, attract dirt and need the additional cleaning and proofing described earlier in the chapter. They are also stronger and flexible in all conditions, but heavier and bulkier than vinyl hoods. Mohair fabrics are generally longer lasting than vinyl and

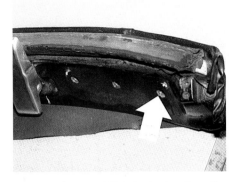

21-8-1 (Picture 1) This is the header rail unfastened from the hood frame via the three screws each side shown here. As you can see the hood material has been roughly cut to fully separate the rail and enable it to be sent away for pre-fitting to the new hood.

offer better insulation too. Some grades are prone to fading which clearly detracts from the appearance of the car. You need to avoid fabric hoods that have stitched top seams - this is not only an obvious potential area for leaks, but the stitching can also become brittle with the passage of time causing the seams to become prone to premature failure. The cheapest fabric material is "Double Duck" but this is particularly prone to fading and may be best passed over in favour of a modern "Mohair" substitute. You are, therefore, probably better off paying a little more for colourfast lightweight mohair, which will also be more pliable in use. There is a heavier "top" grade of mohair that you can choose. I have this material on a TR6 and it is totally weatherproof in the most arduous of conditions and is guaranteed to stay that way for twenty or so years. Its insulation and soundproofing qualities are also excellent. However it is a three-ply material with a middle membrane and an inner light coloured fabric lining and consequently thick, bulky and hard to fold flat.

Plastic window types. Hoods can be made using standard clear plastic for the windows. Clear plastics can be prone to premature UV ageing and you are prudent to specify "Flexglas" for the window material for longevity. Often the main rear window is offered as a "zip-out" option - which sounds like a good idea. However, I must tell you that while I have been through most parts of Europe I've never used the zip-out windows that I have fitted to my TR6 and Triumph Stag:

the hoods are either up or down! The other consideration is that the aesthetics of a welded rear window are, to my eye at least, much better. Welded windows are nicely taught and thus better looking than the seemingly invariably crinkled zip-out rear windows.

Hood frames. There were three different hood frames used during the life of an MGB and you must buy a hood that is compatible to your car's frame. The following fitting suggestions apply to whichever material you have selected for the hood. You can buy hoods pre-fitted with a new header (front) rail - but this certainly increases the cost and is, I feel, a waste of money if your current header rail is in good shape. You can buy the hood without a header rail and fit the hood to your frame/header, and this is certainly the cheapest solution. However, the easiest route (apart from subcontracting the whole job!), and I think the most cost-effective, is to have an experienced hood manufacturer fit one of their new hoods to your header-rail at their factory. There is a small charge for this service and, provided your windscreen frame is properly positioned, the result is easy to fit and based on my experience very satisfactory - although the hood will be very hard to erect for the first few times. More on that shortly ...

Whichever material you choose, it is advisable (especially in cold weather)

to fit the hood in a warm environment. In summer by all means lay the hood out in the sun for half-an-hour, but in winter it is **essential** that you really warm the garage with a space heater for a couple of hours before proceeding with the fitting. Avoid using direct heat on the hood which can easily mark or burn it.

If you wish to fit a new hood to your own frame and header rail, start by removing the rubber front seal, riveted aluminium (careful with this) seal retainer and cleaning up the header rail very thoroughly. Check the header is OK and carefully measure and mark a centre line fully from front to back. Erect the frame and clamp it to the windscreen. Turn the new hood inside out, put the front corners together and mark the centre of the front with a 2in line in crayon or something soft that will be easily seen but will rub off. Reverse the new hood to its normal (outside out) position and fix it to the back of the car, noting that you will have to transpose the rear bar and pop all lift-the-dot fastenings onto their pegs. Bearing in mind that the hood needs to be warm, and that this is particularly true of vinyl - pull the hood forward **hard** and get a pal to run a crayon line around the front edge of the header rail to mark the inside of hood.

Mask to ensure overspray does no damage, then spray the outside/top of the header rail with an aerosol of

21-8-1 (Picture 2) If you go down the pre-fitted header rail route, this is how your hood is returned to you. Note the new and very shiny rear window but, above all, the header rail correctly fitted, the seal strip riveted in place and your front seal refitted. This really makes fitting a new hood very easy indeed.

spray-glue. This is a useful but not very strong adhesive that gives you about five to ten minutes to adjust things. Unclip the front of the frame and ease it back a few inches. Lay the front of the hood on top of the header rail making sure the two centrelines (on header and hood) are aligned and that the line on the hood is about 3/8 to 1/2in (10-12mm) in front of the header rail! Smooth the hood onto the header rail's adhesive and try to re-clip the frame to the windscreen ... yes it will be hard going! However, remember that all hood materials stretch with use and this is particularly true of vinyl. Furthermore, a loose hood flaps, makes a lot of noise and looks unsightly. So try to clip the frame in place but if it just will not come forward far enough you'll just have to peel the hood off the header rail, ease the position backwards a little and try again.

Once you've found the tightest possible place for the hood on the header rail, smooth out all the wrinkles and double check that the hood is still central on the header. Let things dry for half an hour then unclip the frame from the windscreen. Using contact adhesive (spray glue is not strong enough) turn the front of the hood under the header rail and glue hood to header back to a point just

21-8-1 (Picture 3) Park the car in the sun as often as you can for the first couple of weeks after fitting a new hood. It *will* be a struggle to fit, but a new hood is attractive and should stay that way for many years if properly maintained.

rearward of the front seal's rivet holes. As soon as you can, re-rivet the seal's retaining strip, let the contact adhesive set and erect the hood somehow. Give the hood at least twenty four hours to stretch, unclip and fit (I suggest a new)

rubber seal along the front and re-erect the hood. Leave it fully erected for two weeks - if practicable, park the car in the sun - to allow the material to stretch into shape.

Chapter 22
Official roadworthiness tests

These days virtually all cars beyond a certain age in the northern hemisphere are subjected to a check, usually annual, of one type or another. The tests are, of course, intended to ensure the car's roadworthiness and that its emissions are within specified levels.

While the main focus of this chapter is the UK's MoT test, I thought it both interesting and educational to look a little further afield and I am most grateful to my respective international contributors who helped shape the information outlined towards the end of this chapter.

All UK cars over three years old are subject to an annual ("MoT") test that should provide neither a major hurdle nor become the subject of concern since, for the most part, the standards required by the test are lower than most enthusiasts would set for their car.

The main objective of this chapter is preventative in that I have identified the main reasons why MGBs fail their MoTs and described pre-test checks to reveal these potential problems so that they can be rectified before the test.

The average MoT pass rate for all vehicles is 60% and I've found nothing to suggest that the MGB differs from that average. Body corrosion accounts for around half the MGB failures while a further quarter are due to front suspension wear generally and kingpin play (lash) in particular.

Body corrosion

22-1-1 In an effort to understand some of what follows you should know that the MoT standard requires the authorised tester to fail any car with "excessive corrosion" in prescribed locations and generally. The prescribed areas are within 30cm (roughly 12 inches) of any steering, suspension, seatbelt and brake mounting points, while any sharp edges caused by corrosion or damage that renders the car dangerous to other road users, including pedestrians, will also cause failure.

"Excessive corrosion" is defined as weakened metal that given thumb or finger pressure does not feel rigid or crumbles to leave a hole. Each test station has an identical special hammer-like plastic tool that the tester is required to use on any suspect areas. If the tool penetrates or the metal crumbles or disintegrates within a prescribed area, the car will fail.

Perhaps it is no surprise that corrosion brings about more MoT appeals than anything else! I will return to appeals a little later in this chapter.

The test standard required for body fault rectification is lower than most MGB owners would contemplate as acceptable. For example, you're allowed to tape over a hole in a wing (fender) in order to cover sharp edges! If the car does need to repair a panel, then a patch is acceptable though it must be fully welded. This raises the point that would-be owners of MGBs need to approach prospective purchases with a great deal of caution, even those offered with a "full MoT."

Roger Parker of the MGOC tells prospective MGB owners who seek his advice that 85% of their attention has to be directed to the body of any prospective purchase as this is the main problem area. MGB's usual corrosion areas are mostly within 12 inches of a structural, or stress bearing area, and that means a rusty car will fail its test.

Roger, too, thinks that the standard required by the UK's MoT falls well short of what the MGOC regard as the required level of body condition. When a hole is found in one of the single-skinned structural areas, such as the centre body crossmember, then simple plating and decent welding is all that is required to gain a pass. This is fine, as this repair will reinstate the strength in that area for a substantial period of time. However, if the same standard of repair is applied to a hole in the castle section then that simple exterior patch will not address the real problem since a hole on this external panel only appears after the inner structure has actually corroded away. This of course will mean that the structure is significantly weakened, yet the external patch plate will allow an MoT pass. This clearly demonstrates that an MOT certificate is, in the case of the MGB, **not** a confirmation of the cars structure being what Sid Enever (the designer) intended.

Kingpin wear

22-2-1 Kingpin faults and repairs are described in detail in chapter 10. However, since this component causes so many MGB MoT failures, it's worth carrying out your own MoT-style check from time to time, but don't leave it until 24 hours before your car's MoT ...

With the jack placed under the spring pan of a front wishbone, jack up one side of the car until there's about 25mm (1 inch) of daylight under the front wheel. Install some form of secondary safety support like a ramp or axle stand so that the car cannot fall on you if the jack fails, then get a pal to lever the wheel up and down while you observe the kingpin in two respects -

a) Vertical movement between the swivel and housing. This is the principal concern and the tester will be checking to ensure there is an absolute minimum of vertical play. If you find vertical movement, see 10-4-1.

b) Lateral (sideways) movement between swivel and kingpin should not be excessive (i.e. no more than 2mm). The official allowance is surprisingly generous, and I'd carry out remedial action (see 10-5-1) well before the play got to this level.

See the following section then repeat the kingpin checks on the other side of the car.

Front suspension, general

22-3-1 Bottom trunnion. With the car suported as for the kingpin check just described, ensure that the bottom trunnion/wishbone movement is not excessive (i.e. 2mm maximum). Again, it's my opinion that this is too lenient: see 10-4-1 if play is detected.

22-3-2 Bottom wishbone bushes. The often poor exterior appearance of the standard bushes sometimes belies their true internal integrity. The standard bushes are four (per side) rubber cones which, frankly, are not really up to the job - a view in one sense confirmed by MG which fitted one pair (per side) of tubular steel reinforced "Metalastic" bushes to the original MGB GT V8. The standard MGB bushes start to degrade and sections often peel off that part that is visible to the tester resulting in a "fail." While this may appear to be unfair if the internal part of the bush turns out to be sound, it is nevertheless a sensible policy. 10-6-1 describes replacing

or upgrading these bushes.

22-3-3 Top wishbone bushes. The two barrel-shaped top wishbone bushes should have minimal wear and as they are reinforced with a steel tube rarely do give cause for concern. See 10-6-1 if necessary.

22-3-4 Front wheel bearings. Excessive play at the wheel rim can result in a fail. Clearly this is reasonable with genuinely worn front wheel bearings, but the MGB's wheel bearings are rather different to most modern cars and this can result in an erroneous failure.

The problem and remedies are described in section 10-8-2, but be aware that you that you can appeal against a test decision within one month of the test if you feel unfairly treated. Incidentally, that appeal period extends to 3 months if the subject of the appeal is corrosion related.

Other items to check

Now to a brief resume of the other areas that an MoT tester will be looking at so that you can carry out your own pre-MoT checks. Surprisingly, the propshaft (driveshaft) forms no part of the current MoT test, but you will be equally surprised by some requirements that are included in the test.

22-4 Split-pins and other locking devices. These are mandatory wherever they are intended to be installed. Any fastening intended to have a locking device **must** be locked so, for instance, castelated nuts must have a split-pin in place.

22-4-1 For those in doubt as to what a "castelated" nut is - this should resolve the issue. Every one of these *must* be secured by a split-pin if your car is to gain a "pass" in the UK's MoT test.

22-5 Rear axle check strap. A broken check strap attracts a "fail" unless the car is fitted with telescopic rear shock-absorbers.

22-6-1 Flexible brake hoses. A sound but twisted flexible brake hose will fail a car, as will cracks or bulges in these hoses. Check for bulges in all three MGB

flexible hoses while a partner presses the brake pedal hard.

22-6-2 Rigid brake pipes. Testers often site corrosion of rigid brake pipes as a reason for failure. The MoT defines the failure standard as "excessive corrosion" but sites chaffed or damaged pipes as a reason for failure too. The MoT is specific in that it requires the corrosion to not exceed 25% of the wall thickness of the pipe. The difficulty arises when the tester comes to try and measure this. Take my word for the fact that there doesn't need to be much corrosion to cause failure. The tester will visually check, scraping if necessary, any suspect pipes, particularly those that cross the rear axle and which are the most vulnerable.

If you discover corrosion in your car's rigid steel brake pipes, consider fitting "copper" replacement pipes throughout the car, especially across the rear axle.

22-6-3 Handbrake (parking brake). Obviously there are exceptions, but, by and large, the MGB's handbrake is not usually a cause of MoT failure.

22-6-4 Footbrakes. Front brake imbalance brings out the VT30 ("notification of a refusal to issue an MoT test certificate") pad with some frequency. This problem is usually due to a sticking piston within one or both calipers. Cars that are used infrequently are at a major disadvantage in this respect, so daily use for a week prior to your MoT could unstick a lazy piston. Brake imbalance will be evident from the car's reluctance to pull up in a straight line: turn to chapter 16 to resolve the problem before test day.

22-7-1 Excessive exhaust emissions. All vehicles registered before the end of July 1975 will be subject to a visual check for excessive blue or black smoke. However, a car registered after 1st August 1975 has to undergo an exhaust gas test for CO (carbon monoxide) and HC (hydrocarbon) emissions at tickover (idle). The top limits for cars of the MGB era are 4.5% and 1200ppm (parts per million) respectively: ways to reduce emissions are described in chapter 15.

22-8-1 Lights. You really have no excuse if your car fails its MoT due to a faulty external light bulb - for fail it will even if only one bulb is out. Check all the lights are working including full and dipped beam headlights, brakelights (stoplights), direction indicators and, if fitted, hazard warning lights. Lighting defects, especially at the front of the car, are due mainly to the bullet connections exposed to weather but hidden out of sight behind the front grille. Lighting problems are explored in chapter 19.

In the UK the headlight glass should have an "E" cast into it to confirm it meets European standards. The "glass" (including plastic lenses) covering of any light should not be broken, cracked or have pieces missing.

It's difficult to pre-MoT check your car's headlight aim. Be aware that this can gradually vary adversely as the consequence of tired rear leaf springs. You can at least keep a eye on the car's level (the chrome trim strip should be more or less horizontal) and will probably want to correct sagging rear springs for aesthetic and road holding reasons quite apart from the headlight aim issue.

22-9-1 Windscreen wipers and washers. Wipers must clear the windscreen effectively in conjunction with the washers. They must therefore both work and the wiper rubbers must be free of loose or missing edges, nicks, etc. You can run your fingers up both blades feeling for any imperfections and fit new rubbers if either is not 100%.

22-9-2 Windscreen (windshield). A damaged windscreen is a potential failure on three counts. Firstly, if the damage is 10mm, or more, across and situated within the area swept by the wipers and 190mm each side of a vertical line right through the centre of the steering wheel. Secondly, if the damage cannot be contained within a 40mm circle throughout the remaining area swept by the wipers. Thirdly, damage which affects the structural integrity of the screen.

Furthermore dangley-mascots, stickers, internal signs (other than tax discs) and overly deep sunvisors that inhibit forward vision within the sweep of the wipers will also bring about a fail notification, as will anything that impedes the view either side of the drivers seat.

22-10-1 Tyres (tires). There is a minimum tread depth requirement of 1.6mm on every tyre - which frankly is not much when you are dashing along on a wet road. I know my car starts to tell me when the tread is down to about 2.5/3mm by doing some very silly things on a wet road, so what a sports car drives like on 1.6mm tread-depth tyres I hate to think! The 1.6mm minimum depth must be present across the **central** three-quarters of the tyre width. Put another way, you are allowed an area on each side of the tyre where the tread may fall below the minimum stipulation.

Most of us know someone with a little-used car where the tread is still more than adequate, but the tyres are of some age and the walls are crazing/cracking. Somewhat to my surprise the official MoT directive is that unless any perishing, cuts, lumps or bulges exposes the cord, the tyre should pass unless a failure within the structure of the tyre can be noted ... far too lenient for our own good!

Cuts in the tread also have to expose something approaching 25mm of cord to fail the MoT - again, over lenient in my view.

The MoT is understandably very strict about the fact that the arrow on all directional tyres must be pointing forwards. It is not acceptable to tell the tester you only drive the car in reverse!

22-11-1 Seats and seatbelts. The MoT requires that if your seats tilt forward then they must lock in the normal driving position - a detail you can easily pre-test yourself.

Seatbelts are not required on cars registered before 1st January 1965 but, if they are fitted, they must be of the three-point type and must comply with the test that is relevant to the type of belt fitted. Inertia belts fitted to any car are required to take up the slack when someone belts in, although it's OK if they need a little help...

22-12-1 Exhaust system. Two matters require the testers attention, noise and leakage. A car may be failed if the noise level is "clearly unreasonable" or dramatically above that of a standard car of that make fitted with a standard exhaust system.

Any leakage must be a major cause of exhaust gas escape and any corrosion needs to significant (but will include the hangers) to cause a notification of failure. Minor leaks around, say, a properly clipped joint should not attract a fail.

22-13-1 Doors. Both doors must be capable of being opened from the inside and outside.

22-14-1 Rear view mirrors. Cars registered up until 1st August 1978 only require one rear view mirror, which may be positioned on either door or internally. If your car is post 1969, the internal mirror must be mounted on a breakaway stem and have a plastic surround.

22-15-1 Fuel filler cap. The cap on the fuel filler must have a washer which is not torn or deteriorated. There are two reasons for this check - primarily to minimise fuel spillage in the event of an accident but also to guard against

hydrocarbon pollution.

22-16-1 Registration (number) plates. These come under scrutiny for the style and size of letters and spacing. Plates with white (or silver) lettering on a black background may be illegal when fitted to cars manufactured after 31st December 1972 but, surprisingly, are not an MoT failure detail. However, broken, dirty or deformed characters or those in non-standard colours will bring out the "notification of failure" form.

22-17-1 Steering. The steering rack itself is checked for wear but rarely brings about an MoT failure for an MGB. What will bring about an immediate fail is a worn or split rack gaiter (boot). There's one at each end of the rack. The universal joint between column and rack rarely causes a problem, but is checked for excessive play.

The trackrod ends are going to get the car failed if there is wear in them, but you can check this prior to the test by having a partner rock the steering wheel from side to side while you closely observe each joint for rocking or up and down movements.

A split in the gaiter at the base of a balljoint should not bring a failure in itself, but you should replace it as soon as you notice it because water and dirt will otherwise access the balljoint and wear will occur fast.

Steering system remedies will be found in chapter 10.

22-18-1 Shock absorbers (dampers). Oil leaks from the original lever arm dampers can be controversial since MoT failures have been known even though the damper is still fully functional. As there is a design feature allowing the damper to be topped up, a minor damp patch or even a slight weep should make MoT failure for this reason inappropriate. However, there will come a point where the leaks become excessive and the rate of oil loss will be sufficient to warrant failure. Then, in MoT test parlance, the reason for rejection is that the fluid leak is serious enough to indicate that the seal has failed. See chapter 10 for more information.

French testing procedures
22-19-1 With thanks to Philip Chapman. The French equivalent of the MoT is called the "Controle Technique" and has to be carried out by an independent test station run by various bodies such as DEKRA or AUTOSUR. All cars with a normal logbook that are above four years old are tested every two years. 125 points are checked,

and for 68 of them you have an obligation to repair any failure within two months.

Brakes are tested on a rolling road and performance reported as an efficiency percentage front, rear and handbrake.

Front and rear suspension systems are checked with a percentage efficiency of the shock absorbers given.

Lights (side, head, indicators, number plate) could bring about a fail if inoperable, while the dipped beam is also checked but is not a failure item.

Steering and the state of the bodywork are examined. If bodywork faults are not considered dangerous to other people, they'll be noted down to be rectified before the next visit in two years.

Seatbelts will be checked (front and rear) to ensure that they function correctly and are not frayed.

Minor vehicle modifications are allowed but more significant changes have to be validated by *Service des Mines*.

Cars registered before 30/9/1972 are required to have their emissions checked, though if CO is over 4.5% you are not required to have a retest. Cars first registered between 01/10/72 and 30/9/86 are required to have a C0 level of less than 4.5%: if over, you have two months to correct the problem and pass a retest focused on the previous points of failure. Obviously not relevant to MGBs, but cars first registered after 1/10/1986 are required to achieve a CO limit of 3.5%.

If your car passes the test you are given a sticker that is placed in the windscreen for the Police to see. If your cars fails on any points of the test, you have two months to rectify the problem at the garage of your choice and to return to the test station. The first test costs approximately 48 Euro (about £32 or $50) and any subsequent retest costs an extra 8 Euro (£5 or $8).

The French government makes some provision for old/classic cars. You can opt for a "*Collector*" logbook (*Carte Grise*) in place of the normal logbook. However, while a Collector's car may be used at any time, it is geographically limited to a small number of local departments - unless it is travelling to a rally or show, in which case the owner has to pre-inform the scheme's administrators, *Les Service des Mines*. The advantage of a Collector's registration is that you only need to pass the test once.

German testing proceedures
22-20-1 With thanks to Mike Standring. I understand that the vehicle test is carried out by various bodies, the *DEKRA* and

regional *TUV* being the most well known. These bodies run special testing stations as well as providing examiners who go round to your local garage on a weekly basis to provide independent examination of motor vehicles.

There are two examinations which can be compared to the MoT test in the UK: the *Hauptuntersuchung* (Main test) every two years and the *Abgasuntersuchung* (Exhaust test) which is needed every year on cars from the 1970s and 1980s. Passing the *Hauptuntersuchung* results in a round coloured sticker on your rear numberplate, while the *Abgasuntersuchung* results in a hexagonal sticker on your front number plate.

The *Hauptuntersuchung* includes checks on the body condition (damage, corrosion, ageing, wear), the proper mounting of parts (batteries is a favourite) and the appropriate free movement of parts. The correct operation of pedals, controls, levers and switches are checked.

The test also includes ensuring that the configuration of the vehicle is correct (no dodgy spoilers or aftermarket steering wheels thank you...) for only approved parts are permitted.

There are performance tests of brakes, noise level checks, etc, and all requirements must be met.

All the components and systems you would expect are checked well as well as compliance with environmental requirements. Accessory compliance and the identification of the vehicle are also checked.

You are given a report with four results -
- No faults: sticker
- Small faults: sticker (but you are required to promise to sort out the faults immediately).
- Substantial faults: no sticker, you have two months to sort things out and go back for a retest.
- Danger to traffic: no sticker and the vehicle may not be used on the road (it has to be taken away on a trailer).

Making modifications to your vehicle such as aftermarket shockers, fitting a woodrim steering wheel or installing a V8 engine) is quite difficult in Germany. Telling the tester that the MGOC have sold you the kit and that 10,000 other MGBs are running around with it is unlikely to do you any good! They want to see a proper engineer's report in German. Otherwise the type approval of your vehicle is invalid, and your car becomes a danger

to traffic and a definite failure!

The *TUV* and *DEKRA* are willing to test non-original parts for you and, even without an engineer's report, you can have a single approval for your car. It can be an expensive business though.

The German government have introduced a special fixed road tax for vehicles over 30 years old and these vehicles can be recognised by an "H" at the end of the numberplate. Such cars must be largely in original condition and while safety enhancing parts may be added, modifications such as a V8 engine are very doubtful. *DEKRA* and *TUV* do the necessary testing to give your car "H" status.

American testing procedures
22-21-1 With thanks to Kurt Schley. While many European countries have established national standards for classic vehicle equipment inspections and/or emissions checks, the United States has left this task to each of the 50 States. Consequently, each State is free to institute any periodic safety or equipment inspection requirements it feels necessary for the safety of its roadways - or that it feels will add sufficient funds to the State's coffers to make it worthwhile.

Most of the States have not established periodic inspections of any sort. However, in almost all States, the police are authorised to perform a cursory safety inspection if the car has been pulled over for an obvious and blatant equipment problem. Some of these States only allow this inspection if the automobile has already been stopped for some moving violation.

Those few States which have mandated periodic equipment/safety inspections do so either on an annual or bi-annual basis. Authorised agents perform the checks; usually a state licensed independent auto repair shop or service station. In the majority of cases, those States that have instituted vehicle safety inspections apply them to all vehicles, including classics such as MGBs. While some rules and regulations, such as license plates for the vehicles and licensing of the driver are obviously mandatory, most States do not have many other major restrictions pertaining to the vehicle or driver.

All States do require that any driver be covered by insurance or other means of financial responsibility in case of an accident. However, quite a few States do not even require proof of this coverage other than a "ticked" confirmation on the license plate application form.

Emissions testing policies vary from county to county. In most States, emissions testing is mandated by individual counties, rather than by the State itself. This is because the pollution levels are normally into the danger zone only in or adjacent to major cities. In Cleveland, Ohio for example, air emissions testing is only conducted in the county in which the city is situated and those within a roughly 40 mile radius around the city. Further out and there is no emissions testing of any sort.

The need for a county to establish testing stations and regulations is determined by the U.S. Environmental Protection Agency (EPA) The EPA monitors air pollution levels throughout the United States. When the pollution in a particular location is regularly above their established thresholds, the EPA advises the county or counties involved that they should start emissions testing to get the polluting vehicles repaired or off the road.

The EPA cannot actually mandate this action, although it does have the power to cut off various government funds normally available to the county, which is strong incentive for the county to co-operate! The EPA also puts pressure on the State to encourage the county to conform to their recommendation but can come under considerable pressure itself, sometimes in court, to show that the pollution emanates from the county and is not windborne.

In those counties where emissions testing is mandatory there is usually an exemption for some types of older or classic vehicles. The most common exemption is a simple rolling one where any vehicle 25 years old, or older, does not have to undergo testing. Another frequent exemption is for those vehicles that have qualified for State collectors or historical vehicle status. Typically, once a car is included in the State's list it is issued a "collector" license plate and must undergo emissions testing only once. Thereafter there are no restrictions on mileage or the use of the car. These plates must be renewed annually, although there is no additional emissions testing. For "historical" plates, there is no emissions testing required. The vehicle is supposed to be used only for travel to and from automotive events and in club related activities. These plates are issued only once and remain in effect until the vehicle is sold or changes hands.

Not only are the rules different from area to area, but they are also constantly changing. They changed the collectors and historical plates rules three times in twelve months in Ohio. This can be very confusing for the owner of a classic car such as an MGB so the best source of information on safety inspections and emissions testing is the state Bureau of Motor Vehicles. You'd be prudent to also call your county license plate bureau and ask them the same questions and to crosscheck the information received from the two bureaus! Each may interpret the situation differently and another call or two may be required to get the correct information.

Chapter 23
Conclusion, spares kit & clubs

This book is primarily intended to help you get from a symptom to a fault to a fix and, naturally, I hope you feel it helps you do just that, particularly in roadside breakdown situations.

Today we have the communication benefit of mobile (cell) phones and 24-hour parcel delivery services to most corners of the world, so I hope, augmented by these facilities, that I have done something to encourage MG owners to use their cars. When I say use the cars, I do not just mean use them locally and daily, but to use them for holidays, touring and long distance travel.

Prevention is far better than a cure. A high percentage of roadside breakdowns are the result of inadequate servicing. No doubt some of the reasons behind poor servicing is the inconvenience and cost of taking your car to a garage, so the ideal solution is to carry out the servicing yourself - although I would be the first to admit that crawling under (and over) a car on a cold day to service it is not the best part of owning my MGBs. However, servicing the car yourself serves several purposes in addition to ensuring that the work is done thoroughly and at minimal cost. If you have not carried out such work before, ask for help at your local MG club - someone will be pleased to show you how first time round. Your local Technical College probably runs vehicle maintenance courses too.

At the very least I strongly recommend that, **in addition** to the standard service schedule, every 3000 miles, you should change the engine oil and oil filter, lubricate the contact breaker cam and distributor and grease the six front suspension points. Any and every MGB owner ought to be able to learn to do those jobs at home, so the cost will be minimal. If you cannot do the more extensive service work yourself, make sure that at least the sparkplugs, plug (HT) leads, contact breaker points, distributor, distributor cap and fanbelt (drivebelt) are attended to at the prescribed service intervals. In these circumstances, provided you are looking after the basic lubrication yourself, you could consider taking the car to a competent garage every 12,000 miles for a full service. Again, turn to your local MG group for advice as to which garage to use. If those suggestions do not fit in with your lifestyle find another way to get the car properly and regularly serviced.

Get-you-home spares kit
My final point is to reinforce the several references I have made during this book to your carrying a modest number of emergency spares and some test wires with you at all times. Prior to any inter-continental or long distance touring you plan you should approach your favourite club or spares retailer to see what redeemable spares kits they have available. However, the following list represents a minimum get-you-home kit to be carried at all times -

Fanbelt (drivebelt)
Rotor arm
Distributor cap
A distributor baseplate pre-assembled with a new set of points and a condenser

A long HT lead (sparkplug wire)
A sparkplug
Reel of duct (duck, elephant or gaffer's) tape
Spare set of light bulbs
Small tin hydraulic fluid
Empty bottle for water
Emergency tyre inflation kit
Top and bottom radiator hoses
Aerosol silicone spray (e.g. WD40)
Towrope
Basic set of screwdrivers and spanners (three of each)
Torch (flashlight)
Light/reflective coat (to aid your visibility)
A test light
Long piece of heavy-duty electrical wire
Tin of "Radweld"

Clubs
I would consider it a bonus if the book helped younger folk to enjoy the fun and camaraderie of MGB motoring because it's the younger members who hold the key to the future of the marque. Young or mature, all will get more fun from their cars by sharing the experience with others of a like-mind, so join a club - the MG Owners Club or MG Car Club are international and cater not only for UK but overseas members too. There is of course the North American MGB Register in the USA and other clubs in other countries throughout the world.

By joining a club not only will you get pleasure from the mutual interest and use of the cars, but technical advice and help to locate spares come as part of most clubs services too!

Index

Related titles from Veloce Publishing -

How to Improve MGB, MGC & MGB V8
Roger Williams

Covers all aspects of improving these cars for today's conditions and for higher performance generally. How to improve power, braking, appearance and comfort. Checked and approved by the MG Owners Club.

How to Give Your MGB V8 Power
Roger Williams

All the information you need to build a V8-powered MGB roadster or GT. No matter whether you intend to convert an existing four-cylinder car or build a car based on a new bodyshell, this book contains all the advice you need to build the car of your dreams at the smallest possible cost.

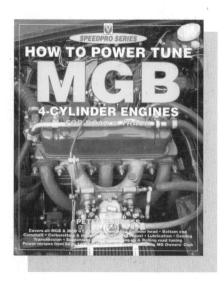

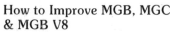

How to Power Tune MGB 4-Cylinder Engines
Peter Burgess

All you need to know about getting the maximum performance for road or track from the MGB's four-cylinder B-series engine. A book packed with easily understood and down to earth advice based on the author's many years of hands-on experience.

MGA
John Price-Williams

The definitive history of the MGA, the first British sports car to sell more than 100,000 units and be capable of topping 100mph. Included Le Mans prototypes, the Coupe, Twin Cam, 1600 and 1600 MkII models; competition history; "secret MGAs"; the USA success story; restoration notes, and much more.